The Morning Chronicle's

LABOUR AND THE POOR

VOLUME IX

BIRMINGHAM

The Morning Chronicle's

LABOUR AND THE POOR

VOLUME IX

BIRMINGHAM

CHARLES MACKAY

Edited By
Rebecca Watts & Kevin Booth

Ditto Books
www.dittobooks.co.uk

First Published by Ditto Books 2020

© Ditto Books 2020

A catalogue record for this book is available
from the British Library

ISBN 978-1-913515-09-6 (hardback)
ISBN 978-1-913515-19-5 (paperback)

Cover Image:
Birmingham from the South
Engraved by W. Harvey
Image courtesy of The Birmingham Museums Trust

"We place our feet in winter upon a Birmingham fender, and stir a Birmingham grate with a Birmingham poker. We ring for our servants with a Birmingham bell, and we write our letters of business and affection with Birmingham steel pens. Birmingham supplies our tables with spoons and forks, though not with knives, and our bed and window curtains with rods, rings, and ornaments. We cannot dress or undress, whether we be men or women, without being beholden to the aid afforded us by Birmingham."

Contents

List of Illustrations

Preface

This work attempts to be a faithful reproduction of the "Labour and the Poor" letters as printed in *The Morning Chronicle*. Only obvious typographical errors and omissions have been corrected. Variations in the spelling and hyphenation of words have largely been retained. We hope any such inconsistencies prove to be of some historical interest to the reader.

As much as possible we have tried to recreate the original layout and styling of the text and all factual tables have been reproduced as closely to the originals as possible with only minimal alterations made where necessary to improve readability.

Not all letters were titled. Where missing we have added titles to the Table of Contents to assist navigation and explanation of content. The letters themselves are as per the originals.

A handful of illustrations have been added to each volume. These did not appear in the original text but hopefully provide added interest.

R. W.
K. B.

Introduction

In 1849 a leading London-based newspaper, *The Morning Chronicle*, undertook an investigation into the working and living conditions of the poor throughout England and Wales in the hope that their findings might lead to much needed change.

The reputed catalyst for their "Labour and the Poor" series was an article written by Henry Mayhew recording a journey into Bermondsey, one of the most deprived districts of London, which was printed in September 1849. Following this it was proposed that an in-depth investigation be carried out and "Special Correspondents", the investigators, were selected and distributed around the country. The first article or "Letter" appeared on the 18th of October 1849 and the series would run for almost 2 years and 222 letters.

The well-known and respected writers and journalists recruited for the task included Henry Mayhew who was assigned to the Metropolitan districts, Angus Bethune Reach to the Manufacturing districts, Alexander Mackay and Shirley Brooks to the Rural districts and Charles Mackay to investigate the cities of Birmingham and Liverpool. The author of the letters from Wales is as yet unknown.

The "Labour and the Poor" letters were extremely popular at the time, being widely read throughout the nation and even abroad. The revelations in them caused quite a stir amongst the middle and upper classes of Victorian society. *Letters to the Editor* poured in with donations for specific cases of distress that appeared in the letters and also for the general alleviation of the suffering of the poor. A special fund was set up by *The Morning Chronicle* to collect and distribute these donations.

These *Letters to the Editor* have been included in this series, predominantly in the Metropolitan district volumes whose letters elicited the majority of responses. They provide a unique window into the thoughts and sentiments of the Victorian readership as they react to the incredible accounts of misery and desperation being unveiled.

The Morning Chronicle's extraordinary and unsurpassed "Labour and the Poor" investigation provides an unparalleled insight into the people of the period, their living and working conditions, their feelings, their language, their sufferings and their struggles for survival amidst the poverty and destitution of 19th century Britain. An investigation of such magnitude had never before been attempted and the undertaking was truly of epic proportions. Its impact at the time was profound. Its historical importance today is without question.

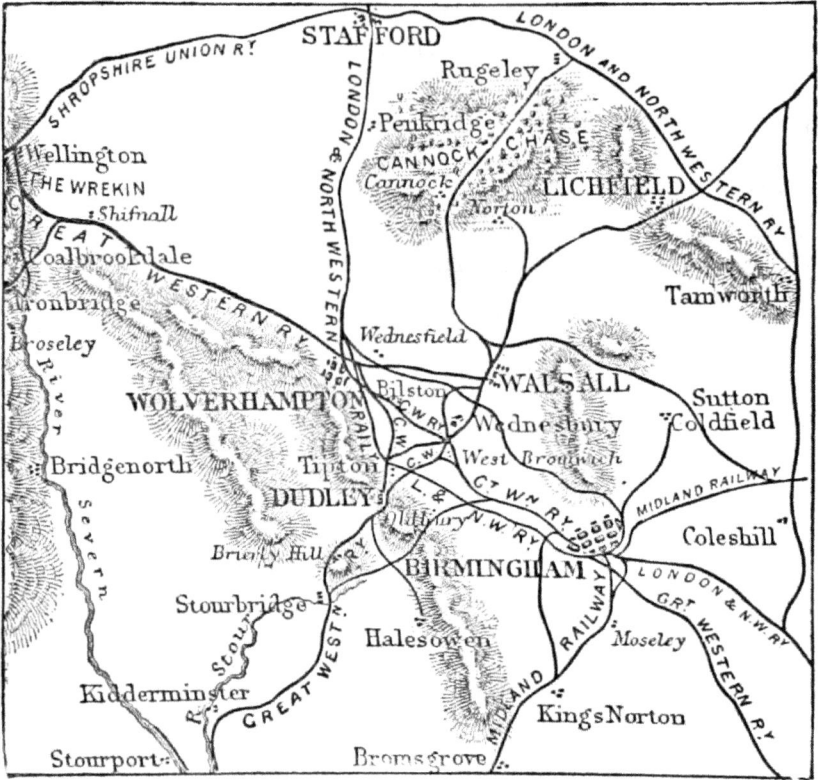

Map of Birmingham and the Surrounding District

LABOUR AND THE POOR.

———

BIRMINGHAM.

[FROM OUR SPECIAL CORRESPONDENT.]

PAROCHIAL AND MORAL STATISTICS.

LETTER I.

Birmingham was called by Burke, more than half a century ago, the "toy-shop of the world." By this phrase the orator intended to express both the flimsiness and elegance of the various manufactures of the town, and the extensiveness of the markets which it supplied. It is not easily ascertainable whether among the men of Birmingham at this time the word "toy" had the meaning which it now conveys; but if the stranger at Birmingham inquires at the present day whether it manufactures "toys," and what description of toys it most excels in, he will be furnished with a list of articles which will somewhat surprise him, if he attach to the word its usual meaning. The "toys" of Birmingham are divisible into three great classes—heavy steel toys, light steel toys, and toys in general. The first includes articles by no means intended to be played with, such as the tools used in the trades of the carpenter, the cabinet-maker, the upholsterer, the machinist, the farrier, the shoemaker, and scores of other trades. Hammers, pincers, adzes, compasses, choppers, awls, nut-cracks, toasting-forks, turn-screws, saws, spades, and edge-tools of every description, form but a fraction of the immense variety of articles that are classed under this head by Birmingham manufacturers. The light steel toys include clasps, buckles, brooches, tassels, beads, chatelaines and a whole host of articles made of steel, for the adornment of the house or the person; while the general toy manufacture includes metal, pearl, horn, glass, and florentine buttons in all their countless varieties, and a perfect maze of knick-knacks and gilt or plated trifles, which it would take a whole advertising sheet to make a catalogue of. Birmingham, in this sense, still remains the toy-shop, or rather the work-shop, of the world; and supplies Europe, Asia, Africa, America, Polynesia, and Australia, not alone with trifles, but with an immense variety of

1

necessary articles. There is scarcely a house in Europe or America that is not indebted for some portion of its luxury or its comfort to the enterprise and ingenuity of the men of Birmingham. We place our feet in winter upon a Birmingham fender, and stir a Birmingham grate with a Birmingham poker. We ring for our servants with a Birmingham bell, and we write our letters of business and affection with Birmingham steel pens. Birmingham supplies our tables with spoons and forks, though not with knives, and our bed and window curtains with rods, rings, and ornaments. We cannot dress or undress, whether we be men or women, without being beholden to the aid afforded us by Birmingham. It is that town which supplies half the globe with buttons for male costume, and with hooks and eyes for the costume of ladies. Pins and needles and thimbles principally come from Birmingham; and we never sit upon a chair or table, or lie upon a bed, or tread upon a floor without deriving advantage from the industry of the metal-workers of that town and neighbourhood; for Birmingham supplies England, Scotland, and Ireland, and many parts of the European and American continents with nails, tacks, and screws. Not only in life, but in death, we have recourse to Birmingham. There is scarcely a coffin that is laid in the lap of earth within the limits of Great Britain that is not held together by the nails, and ornamented with the plates and handles and other funereal gewgaws of Birmingham. The Australian ploughs his fields with a Birmingham ploughshare, shoes his horses with Birmingham shoes, and hangs a Birmingham bell around the necks of his cattle, that they may not stray too far from home on the hills or the rich pasture lands of that country. The savage in Africa exchanges his gold dust, his ivory, and his spices for Birmingham muskets. The boor of the Cape shoots elephants with a gun expressly made for his purpose by the Birmingham manufacturers. The army, the navy, and the East India Company's service draw from Birmingham their principal supplies of the weapons of destruction—the sword, the pistol, and the musket. The rifleman of the backwoods of Canada and the Hudson's Bay territories would be deprived for awhile of the means of trade or sport, if Birmingham should cease its fabrication of gun barrels and locks; and all the tribe of sportsmen, whether they frequent the jungle, the moor, the mountain or the lake, carry on their recreation by the aid of Birmingham. Even the far distant men of California are obliged, in default of policemen, to defend their treasures by Birmingham guns, dirks, and daggers. The negroes of the West Indies, and the slaves of Cuba, cut down the sugar cane with Birmingham matchetts; and grass is mowed, and corn is reaped, in England and the Antipodes, by scythes and sickles of its manufacture. In large and small articles it is equally industrious and equally successful; it turns into the world millions of buttons, and millions of pins, pens, nails, screws, hooks and eyes per day, and even per hour—and administers to a greater extent than any other town in the world, to the comforts, the conveniences, the necessities, and the luxuries of civilized life. The town is *par excellence* the town of metal, and fully nine-tenths of its population depend for their subsistence on the various manufactures which it carries on in iron, steel, zinc, brass, copper, gold, silver, electro-plate, and the substantial as well as the showy goods which it daily turns out in all these materials.

But, before entering into any account of these manufactures, and their countless and minute divisions and subdivisions—and before describing the social and moral aspect of a place which is one of the most peculiar and remarkable in England, a few words of introduction, devoted to the consideration of its past and present state as a parish and a borough, will be necessary.

The first view of this remarkable town, especially if seen from the place where the tickets are collected on the railway, is not prepossessing. To the casual glance from that distance it appears to be built upon a plain—to be composed of mean, dingy, dirty brick houses—and to be enveloped in dense clouds of smoke, which are poured forth from no less than four hundred tall chimneys. Neither domes, spires, nor towers are to be seen amid the mass of building—nothing but red brick houses, and perpendicular columns polluting the atmosphere with smoke. But Birmingham improves on a closer inspection. When the eye has once become accustomed to its climate, and the feet have made acquaintance with its streets, it is found to be built not upon a plain, but on a number of hills and hollows, and to possess some wide and handsome streets, and two or three fine public buildings and churches. It stands on an elevated site, in a dry and healthy part of Warwickshire, and occupies as nearly as possible the centre of England.

It has been said that the damp atmosphere of Lancashire is highly advantageous to its peculiar industry—the spinning of cotton—and that the dry atmosphere of Warwickshire is equally favourable to the profitable production of iron, steel, and plated goods. Birmingham is considered a healthy town; and it is remarkable that in the great years of the cholera, 1832 and 1849, when other parts of the country suffered so severely, Birmingham was almost, if not wholly, exempt from the visitation.

The name of Birmingham is probably derived from Broomwich, or Bromwich, with the addition of the Saxon word "ham" or home. A great number of places in the immediate neighbourhood derive their names from a similar source, among others Castle Bromwich, Little Bromwich, West Bromwich, Bromsgrove, Bromley, Broomhill, &c. The common pronunciation of *Brummagem*, which the "schoolmaster" has in vain endeavoured to supersede, would seem to prove that tradition is more correct than learned authority in this and other instances; and the great "schoolmaster" himself obstinately persists in giving the word the popular and vulgar, but possibly correct, pronunciation. "Brummagem ware" was long the designation of all goods that were showy but not substantial, and has been applied to every description of article that Mr. Carlyle would more emphatically pronounce to be a "sham." A showy but inferior actor has been called a "Brummagem Garrick"—and an over-rated dramatist a "Brummagem Shakspere." The character of Birmingham in this respect has improved of late years, and its manufactures now compete not alone in cheapness and in outward appearance, but in intrinsic excellence, with those of all possible rivals, either at home or abroad.

Mr. Hutton, the only historian that Birmingham ever produced, and an exceedingly bad specimen of the article, claims for the town and its industry an antiquity nearly two thousand years prior to the Christian era. He appears to think that if the ancient Britons drove chariots, and carried shields and breastplates, and were skilful in the use of the scythe, the spear, and the javelin, Birmingham must have forged the iron and steel for them. The first authentic information connected with the manufactories of Birmingham occurs in the pages of Leland, who describes it as it existed in the reign of Henry VIII. He says: "I came through as pretty a street as ever I entered into Birmingham town. This street, I remember, is called 'Dirtey' (meaning Deritend). There be many smiths in the town that use to make knives and all manner of cutting tools, and many lorimers that make bittes, and a great many naylors." It is not known when the button manufacture, now carried on to so large an extent, was introduced into the town, and Birmingham was not greatly celebrated, even for another of its great staple articles—guns—till the commencement of the eighteenth century; but its antiquity as the great mart for edge tools, or heavy steel toys, is in all probability such as to justify the historian in considering it the oldest manufacturing town in Great Britain.

The borough of Birmingham includes the ancient town and parish, and the adjoining parishes of Edgbaston and Aston; the last mentioned including the hamlets or townships of Deritend and Bordesley, and Duddeston-cum-Nechells. Its total area is 8,780 acres. Its extreme length is five and three-quarter miles, its average breadth three miles, and its circumference nearly twenty-one miles. It is estimated to contain about 100 miles of streets and 40 miles of suburban road. The town of Birmingham, properly so called, scarcely occupies more than a third of this superficies. The population of the town was found by the census of 1841 to be 138,210, and of the borough, 182,922. Of this number 4,673 were stated to be Irish.

The growth of this town has been rapid, though not to be compared to the growth of Liverpool, Manchester, or Glasgow, for it was a noted town before either of these three was ever heard of. In the days of Henry VIII., when Leland first mentioned it, no account of the number of its inhabitants has been preserved. About a century after this time (A.D. 1650), if we are to believe the guesses of Hutton, the population of Birmingham was 5,471. Fifty years afterwards, according to the same authority, its population had nearly trebled itself, amounting in 1700 to 15,032. In 1741 its population was 26,660; in the next forty years it nearly doubled itself, amounting, in 1781, to 50,295. In 1791 its population was 73,653; and in 1818 it amounted to upwards of 90,000. The present population of the town is not accurately known, but it is estimated on sufficient authority to be about 190,000 for the town, and 230,000 for the borough. Of these numbers at least 50,000 are supposed to be of the poorest class, inhabiting about 2,000 close, ill-built, ill-drained, and unwholesome courts, for which Birmingham is as notorious even as Liverpool.

The borough is divided into 13 wards, including 10 wards in the parish and town of Birmingham proper; and although incorporated by Royal Charter under the provisions of the Municipal Reform Act in October, 1838, it has the great disadvantage, for all sanitary and general purposes, of being governed by various independent and sometimes conflicting boards. The number of these jurisdictions appears to be eight. There are first the Birmingham Commissioners, acting under the 9th George IV., cap. 94, for paving, lighting, watching, cleansing, and otherwise improving the town, and for regulating the police and markets; second, the Deritend and Bordesley Commissioners; third, the Duddeston and Nechells Commissioners, performing similar duties in those two townships, which now form part of the borough; fourth, the Poor-law Guardians; fifth, the Municipal Corporation; and sixth, seventh, and eighth, the Surveyors of Highways for Deritend, Bordesley, and Edgbaston.

The borough of Birmingham possesses no property, and has no funds for general or sanitary purposes, except such as it can borrow on the security of the rates. As I shall have occasion to enter upon this subject in another letter, in connection with the sanitary state of the town, I shall confine myself in the present letter to Birmingham as a parish. In this respect it is governed by a local act, and appears to be less afflicted with the plague of pauperism than any town in England or Scotland of similar wealth and magnitude. Irish paupers, that are so constant a source of expense and annoyance elsewhere, do not trouble Birmingham to any great extent. There is no demand within its boundaries, as there is in the Liverpool Docks, and in the agricultural districts, for unskilled labour, and for the services of men who only require health and a pair of hands to become useful. In Birmingham a labourer must be skilled to have the slightest chance of obtaining a livelihood. Accordingly it is the mechanic, not the mere labouring man, that is in request, and the horde of Irish vagrants keep aloof. The few Irish who reside in the town are chiefly "navvies," bricklayers' labourers, and dealers in cat and rabbit skins. Even in the dreadful times of 1846 and 1847, when upwards of 600,000 Irish paupers landed in Liverpool, very few made their way to Birmingham; and it appears from a return made by the assistant overseer, charged with removals, that for a period of nine months, from June, 1847, to March, 1848, when the Irish immigration pressed with its most intolerable weight upon the sea-board towns, Birmingham was only put to the expense of about £205 for the removal of Irish paupers. Their numbers were 85 men, 98 women, and 92 children; in all 275 persons. This, of itself, is a remarkable fact, and would seem to show that the immigrating Irish upon that occasion were not without a knowledge of the places upon which it was most advisable for them to fasten themselves. The total pauperism of Birmingham in the melancholy year 1847, cannot be stated with any precision, in consequence of the confusion in the parish books, caused by various changes of system, both in pauper management and in the mode of keeping the accounts;

but subsequently, from the half-year ending Lady-day, 1848, the statistics of pauperism can be more accurately dated. They exhibit a very remarkable decrease in the numbers of the in-door and out-door poor, a result attributable to two causes simultaneously in operation. First, the general revival of trade and manufactures in all their principal branches; and secondly, the application of a stricter test of destitution by the new guardians, who came into office on Lady-day, 1849. A return presented to the House of Commons, to its order, dated the 25th of July last, showed a general decrease of in-door and out-door pauperism throughout most of the counties of England and Wales. There was a slight increase upon some of the agricultural, and a great decrease in nearly all the manufacturing counties. The three counties in which the greatest decrease took place were, the West Riding of York—Leicester—and Warwick. In the West Riding the decrease was 17.3 per cent., compared with the previous year; in Leicester, 17.5 per cent.; and in Warwickshire, 35.8 per cent. These returns included both the aged and impotent and the able-bodied poor. A second return, confined to the adult able-bodied poor, exclusive of vagrants, yielded a similar result generally for England, and particularly for the three counties above cited. The decrease for the West Riding, in this class of pauperism on the year, was 31.5 per cent.; of Leicester, 34.4; and of Warwickshire, 66.8. This decrease in Warwickshire is almost, if not entirely, attributable to the increased activity of trade in the town of Birmingham, and the districts more immediately connected with its peculiar manufactures. The gradual decrease is shown in the following statement of the in-door pauperism of the parish, furnished for this inquiry by the parochial authorities:—

Total in-door pauperism for the half-year ending
Lady-day, 1848 16,222
Ditto, Michaelmas, 1848 11,741
Ditto, Lady-day, 1849 12,743
Ditto, Michaelmas, 1849 9,226
Ditto, Lady-day, 1850 2,990

The out-door pauperism experienced a similar diminution. Prior to Lady-day, 1850, there were six relief stations in various parts of the town, where the relieving officers attended to receive applications and grant relief. The consequence was, that some of the paupers having been relieved at one station, immediately made application at a second or even third, and were again relieved with money or food. The new board of guardians devised a remedy for this abuse by appointing a pay clerk with a central station, at the workhouse, and this officer alone administered relief to the various applicants recommended by the relieving officers. By this means, double and treble allowances, dishonestly obtained, became impossible. In the last week of the old system, the number of out-door paupers was 5,453, and the cost of relieving them was £369 5s. 5½d. The first week of the new system showed a diminution of upwards of 400 claimants, the numbers being 5,041, and the cost £342 7s. 5¾d. Before the expiration of the parochial half-year the numbers had decreased to 4,238, and the cost to £288 12s. 8¾d. Amongst this number there was not a single able-bodied male pauper. The great majority were helpless old men and women; many above seventy years of age, with a few able-bodied women, mostly young widows with large families. Among other reforms introduced by the new board of guardians, which led to a diminution in the number of claimants for relief, was the abolition of the out-door labour test. Prior to the month of January, 1850, as many as 280 able-bodied male paupers were employed by the parish in grinding corn at the parish mill, for which labour, pursued every day, they received weekly the sum of 2s. 6d. in money, and loaves according to the number of their families. Another batch of able-bodied male paupers was employed in stone-breaking upon Birmingham-heath, receiving wages in money, and loaves, not according to their work, but according to their real or supposed necessities. It was resolved to put an end to this system, and to grant no relief to able-bodied paupers, unless they consented to enter the workhouse. The result was a diminution of three-fourths of their numbers within the first week. Within three months the whole of them ceased to become burdensome to the parish, and were lost sight of altogether, with the exception of a few who were known to have found profitable employment in the manufactures of the town.

Like most other parishes, Birmingham has a vagrant shed or office, where tramps and houseless persons are relieved with a night's lodging. Prior to the present year, the tramps were relieved, not alone with a lodging, but with a supper of bread and soup, and a breakfast of bread and milk. The nightly allowance for a man was six ounces of bread and a pint of soup, and for his breakfast six ounces of bread and a pint of milk. For a woman, the supper and breakfast were five ounces of bread at each meal, and the same allowance of soup and milk as a man. Children received half the quantity delivered to a man. While this system lasted the vagrant shed was never short of visitors. The following return for the years 1847, 1848, and 1849 shows the numbers that received this hospitable treatment at the hands of the parochial authorities:—

TRAMPS AND VAGRANTS RELIEVED BY THE PARISH
OF BIRMINGHAM WITH FOOD AND LODGING.

	Men.	Women.	Children.	Total.	Irish.
1847 ...	13,703	3,750	3,806	21,259	7,051
1848 ...	13,674	3,116	1,801	18,591	4,416
1849 ...	8,730	1,975	1,626	12,331	5,002

The gradual diminution in the numbers during these three years was due to the increasing prosperity of trade, and not to any change of system introduced by the parochial authorities. The tramps were occasionally violent, and used profane and obscene language, and sang indecent songs. Sometimes, also, money was found concealed about the Irish paupers. A new system with regard to tramps was introduced on the 1st of January, 1850, by which lodging alone was given, and food was only administered in extreme cases, where it was obvious that the applicants were really sick or destitute. The following is the result from the 1st of January to the 7th of September inclusive:—

TRAMPS RELIEVED WITH LODGING BY THE PARISH
OF BIRMINGHAM, 1850.

Men.	Women.	Children.	Total.	Irish.
1,459	500	426	2,425	902

The average poor-rate of the parish of Birmingham is about 5s. in the pound, but this includes the borough rate for the support of the police, the county and borough prisons, and other civic charges. The total rental of the borough upon which assessment was made in the year 1849, amounted to £615,212, of which £462,025 was for the town and parish of Birmingham, and the remainder for the parishes of Edgbaston and Aston.

The number of infant paupers in the Asylum of the Birmingham workhouse appears to average less than 300. Some years ago they were employed by the guardians in pin-heading, by contract, for the pin-manufacturers of the town; but this system has been discontinued, and the infant paupers receive an industrial training in the trades of the carpenter, the tailor, and the shoemaker. The number of lunatic paupers at the commencement of the present year was 109, of whom

57 were males, and 52 females. At the commencement of the succeeding half-year, the first week in July, the number of lunatics was 140,
of whom 74 were males and 66 females.

The statistics of crime in Birmingham for the last ten years have
just been published by Mr. Stephens, the superintendent of police
for the Borough. The following return shows the number of persons
taken into custody, for all kinds of offences, from the formation of the
police force on the 20th of November, 1839, to the 31st of December,
1849. It will be seen that in every year, considerably more than one-
half of the whole number were discharged by the magistrates, and that
only about one-eighth, upon an average, and sometimes not above
one-tenth, were committed for trial.

	Taken into Custody.	Dis- charged by the Magis- trates.	Sum- marily Convicted or held to Bail.	Com- mitted for Trial.
1839 from Nov. 20 to Dec. 31 ...	783	465	230	88
1840	5,986	3,740	1,627	619
1841	5,556	3,521	1,441	594
1842	4,938	3,331	1,020	587
1843	3,363	2,258	852	553
1844	3,259	1,735	1,040	484
1845	4,165	2,658	1,015	492
1846	4,315	2,947	901	467
1847	4,027	2,694	753	580
1848	3,557	2,126	853	578
1849	3,405	2,109	893	403

A first glance at this table would seem to prove great and undue
officiousness on the part of the police, and an arrest of persons for very
trivial offences. The returns for the year 1849, in which the various
offences are duly set forth, will throw some further light upon the
matter, and exonerate the police from an excess of zeal. In that year
it will be seen that the returns are lower than they have been in any
year since the establishment of the police force, with the exception of
the years 1843 and 1844. In this number of 3,405 persons arrested are
the following large items:—

Assaults	263
Assaults on the police in the execution of their duty	184
Wilful damage	157
Disorderly characters	220
Drunkards	812
Riot and breach of the peace	21
Total	1,657

Thus it appears that 1,657 persons out of 3,405, or about 48½ per cent., were taken into custody either for drunkenness or the violence which springs from drunkenness; for it may fairly be presumed that riot, breach of the peace, assaults on the police in the execution of their duty, and offences of this class, are for the most part, if not wholly, committed by persons under the influence of intoxicating liquors. Other large items in the return are:—

Vagrants	127
Offences under the Street Act and by-laws of the corporation	86
Suspicious characters	52
Gambling	36
	301

Deducting these two, there remains the number of 1,447 persons to be accounted for under the heads of more serious offences against life and property. But even here it appears that the greatest number of offences is included under the head of simple larceny, and that the more heinous classes of offences are exceedingly rare. The following are the principal items:—

Simple Larceny	485
Larceny in a dwelling-house, to the extent of 5*l.* and upwards	4
Ditto, under 5*l.*	76
Ditto, from the person	180
Ditto, by servants	70
Misdemeanours, with intent to steal	188
Embezzlement	35
Fraud	46
Uttering, or having in possession, counterfeit coin	52
Receiving stolen goods	27
Attempt to murder	1
Shooting at and stabbing	12
Manslaughter	9
Burglary	10
Housebreaking	18
Forgery on the Bank of England	2
	1,205

After all these deductions, there remain 232 prisoners, whose offences are ranged under the following heads:—

Rape, assault with intent, and other offences against public decency	26
Child dropping	2
Bigamy	2
Attempts to break into shops, &c.	37
Cattle and horse stealing	4
Attempts to defraud	11
Offences against the currency	18
Absconding from bail	2
Runaway apprentices	6
Attempted suicide	10
Cruelty to animals	4
Deserters from the army	27
Desertion of families	37
Hawking without license	6
Illicit distillation	5
Keeping disorderly houses	2
Perjury	1
Prison breaking	2
Reputed thieves	3
Illegally pawning	1
Rescue and refusing to aid peace-officers	26
	232

The educational statistics among these 3,405 persons, the drunk and disorderlies included, show what statistics have proved in every other town and district in which they have been collected, that the great mass of offenders against the laws, both of sobriety and morality, are either totally unable to read and write, or can read a little without being able to write, or can read and write imperfectly. Of these persons 2,730 were males, and 675 females. The following figures will show the amount of their knowledge, or rather of their ignorance:—

	Males.	Females.	Total.
Neither able to read nor write ..	1,100 ...	391 ...	1,491
Able to read without writing, or able to read and write imperfectly	1,453 ...	274 ...	1,727
Able to read and write well, but without other education ...	150 ...	10 ...	160
Having a superior education ...	27 ...	— ...	27
	2,730 ...	675 ...	3,405

Of these 27 persons of superior education, 2 were convicted of assaults on the police in the execution of their duty, 2 were fined for being drunk and incapable of taking care of themselves, 1 was committed for larceny, 1 for fraud, 1 for an attempt to defraud, and 1 for a breach of the peace. The remainder were discharged by the magistrates.

The statistics of drunkenness in Birmingham thus appear to be very high—and in this respect figures do not belie, but confirm the character which large classes of its working mechanics have unfortunately acquired. The workers in metal are proverbially thirsty; and many of the trades which consider their employments unwholesome—such as the gun-barrel grinders, the pearl button turners, and others—are said to drink with the idea that it is necessary to their health and strength. For their supply there are in Birmingham 564 public-houses and houses of entertainment, including hotels, inns, and taverns, in which wine, beer, and spirits are sold. Of these not above 50 or 60 are *bonâ fide* places for the accommodation of travellers. There are known to be 661 retail beer-shops, 54 wine and spirit merchants, 14 ale and porter stores; or in all, 1,293 establishments, large and small, for the supply of intoxicating liquors. The total number of houses in the borough is about 43,000; so that in every 33 houses one is a wine, beer, or spirit shop, of a higher or lower degree.

If we suppose that each of these 1,293 establishments maintains four persons, either as part of their families or as servants—and the supposition is moderate rather than extravagant—it will follow that 5,172 persons live in this industrious town by the sale of intoxicating drinks—or 1 in every 45 of the whole population. This is a larger number than is employed in some of the staple trades of the town. According to the census of 1841 there were but 3,000 button-makers, 1,000 pearl-workers, and 2,400 gun-makers in Birmingham; and as many, if not all of these, included women and children, it is but too probable that very few branches of industry, in the most industrious town in Europe, employ so many persons, young and old, as the sale of intoxicating liquors. It may furthermore be mentioned that the number of shops for the sale of beer and spirits exceeds those for the sale of bread, including hucksters and chandlers' shops, by no less than 422—the number of bakers and hucksters being 871 only.

One principal cause of the intemperance which appears to prevail to so great an extent in Birmingham is said by some employers to be the number of beer shops in the town, which are frequented by young boys. The apprenticeship system is gradually dropping into disuse throughout England. In no part of the country are so many children and young lads employed in manufactures as in Birmingham. The great majority of these boys, from 11 or 12 years of age upwards, work for their own wages, and own no allegiance to their masters or employers after they have left the workshop. The old licensed victuallers or public-house keepers would not allow young lads to frequent their houses. Their customers objected if youths under 21 were permitted to smoke and drink in their tap-rooms or parlours, but the beer-shop keepers have no such scruples, and it is no unusual sight to see precocious men of fifteen or sixteen years of age, drinking and smoking, and playing at games of chance in these places, utterly uncontrolled by parental or any other authority, and taking liberties of behaviour in which full-grown men would be ashamed to indulge. It is impossible to walk the streets of Birmingham after seven or eight o'clock at night without being painfully impressed with the fact, that the youthful workpeople of the male sex are prematurely depraved; and have all the vices, without the common sense of adults. Perhaps, too, the elder workmen of no town in England more obstinately observe "Saint Monday" than the working men of Birmingham; and it is a common complaint among employers that when trade is good and wages high, they not only keep "Saint Monday," or "shackling day," as some call it, for drinking and pleasure making, but add a Tuesday, and even a Wednesday, to the idle days of the week. "From various causes," says the Rev. T. Bowring, in his annual address to the subscribers to the Domestic Mission, "Birmingham is a very drinking town. Some drink because the work is hard, and others because they have no work to do; some because they are flush of money, and some to keep up their spirits when the purse is low. There are some who lose no work, and yet find time for tippling, and others who sot all the day long." The great number of clubs among the working classes of Birmingham are a cause, though by no means a necessary one, of the enormous evil of intemperance. In walking through the streets, and looking at the bills in the public-house and beer-shop windows, it will be found that scarcely a beer or spirit shop in twenty is without one or more clubs, which meet periodically within it. Many of them are provident and friendly societies, and sick and burial clubs, both of men and women; and those who know any thing of the habits of the working classes of England, may be sure that the members of no club are allowed to meet in such places without being obliged to spend money in drink. But as the clubs of the working men of Birmingham form a very peculiar feature in the town, and are believed to be organized to a greater extent, and for a greater variety of purposes, than in any other town in England, I propose to devote a letter of this series to the consideration of that subject alone, and merely allude in the present instance to the great number of them which meet in public-houses, as one of the great predisposing causes of the intemperance for which the town is noted. Guinea clubs and five-pound clubs are among the most common and the most mischievous of these associations. They are chiefly got up by the landlords of beer-shops. The following is a copy of a printed bill, of which any one who will take the trouble may count scores in a walk of half an hour through the streets of Birmingham:—

"A guinea club is held here every Monday evening. Whoever joins the same, or brings a member, will confer a favour on his obedient servant."—(Signed by the landlord.)

Each member of these clubs puts in threepence, sixpence, or a shilling, according to numbers or previous arrangement, and the guinea produced is put up for public competition, and purchased by the highest bidder, who not unfrequently pays as much as five shillings out of the twenty-one for the "accommodation." The loan is repaid by weekly instalments, and in three cases out of four is only sought for drinking purposes. The public-house interest in Birmingham is very strong, and boasts of being able, not only to influence parochial and borough affairs, but to return one of the two members to Parliament. But notwithstanding the intemperance which may be alleged against the working classes, it appears from the police returns that the state of crime in Birmingham is not formidable, and that the town bears a worse character for drunkenness than for any other more serious breach of the laws. The principal cause of this absence of gross offences against property is doubtless to be found in the generally prosperous condition of the town, and in the fact, for which Birmingham is noted, of the great numbers of its small master manufacturers—men holding a middle rank between the great manufacturers of other towns and the journeymen operatives who work for wages. It has been said of Birmingham, that its manufacturers leave off business with an amount of capital which the Manchester manufacturer considers barely sufficient to begin the world with. It is generally estimated that there are from 1,900 to 2,000 of these small masters in the town, who live generally in a state of comparative comfort, who husband their originally small resources, live within their means, run no commercial risks, and increase by slow but sure degrees. The journeymen they employ are for the most part in the receipt of good wages. The poorest of these masters are sometimes called "garret masters," and either have their little workshops attached to their own dwellings, or hire steam power in the numerous mills that partition off corners of their premises for this purpose. These form a singular and peculiar class in Birmingham, and will be described in connection with the various trades in the future letters of this series.

LABOUR AND THE POOR.

—◆—

BIRMINGHAM.

[FROM OUR SPECIAL CORRESPONDENT.]

SANITARY CONDITION.

LETTER II.

The many conflicting jurisdictions in the old parish and new borough of Birmingham, combined with the fact already stated, that the borough possesses no funds except those which it can borrow on the security of the rates, have prevented Birmingham from taking many necessary measures for improving the beauty and amenity of the town, and for providing in various ways for the necessities of the public health. Many attempts have been made, but hitherto in vain, to consolidate the eight boards which govern in various ways the several districts of the borough; and large sums of money have been expended in procuring or opposing private and public bills in Parliament. A small river, a tributary of the Thame, called the Rea, runs through the lower portion of the town. One set of commissioners expend the public money in keeping the sewerage out of this river, and another set, with equal powers, expend money in directing it in. The medical sanitary inspector of the borough, in the appendix to an official report to the Board of Health, affirms the stream to be "a great nuisance to the town through its whole extent. I have seen the stream," he adds, "when it has been as black as a strong solution of Indian ink." "There is," says Mr. R. Rawlinson, civil engineer, in his report to the Board of Health, "no general plan of the district; and though nature has combined the whole so as to render one set of sewers imperative, there is no power to levy a common rate, although the benefits must be general. However willing all may be to act in concert for the common good, their present acts imperatively forbid, or lack the necessary powers to sanction, such a measure. The Commissioners of Birmingham have made sewers, but have no power to construct private drains, or to compel parties to construct them, although large sums of money have to be expended to remove and cleanse accumulations of foul, dangerous, and highly offensive matters, which might more cheaply be passed into their sewers."

A committee of physicians and surgeons represented these and other facts to their fellow-citizens in the year 1841, and in 1848 the Ratepayers Protection Society drew public attention to the manifold deficiencies of the existing system, or want of system, and its injurious effects upon the public health. "The three boards in Deritend and Bordesley," said they, "have no powers for promoting the comfort and the health of the inhabitants. Where filth accumulates there it must remain. The surveyors of Deritend, the surveyors of Bordesley, and the Commissioners of Deritend and Bordesley, make, levy, and collect rates. One board professes to repair and mend the footpaths, and another the horse-roads, neither allowing the other to encroach upon its prescribed jurisdiction by even the removal of a stone. The external appearance of the hamlets has not been in the least improved during the last century. The stagnant filth, and the putrid accumulations, which are allowed year after year to exist in the several parts of Deritend, without any attempts at their removal, or any efforts being made on the part of the authorities to relieve the industrious poor from the baneful effects of inhaling the atmospheric impurities they engender, are a disgrace to civilization."

The commissioners for the ancient town and parish of Birmingham are a body that still exists; although their powers ought most indubitably to have merged in those of the officers of the new corporation, established under the provisions of the Municipal Incorporation Act. The commissioners were originally appointed in the year 1769, by an act of the 9th of George III., "for laying open and widening certain ways and passages within the town of Birmingham, and for cleaning and lighting the streets, lanes, ways and passages there, and for removing and preventing nuisances and obstructions therein." Subsequent acts extended their powers, and authorized them to levy rates on the inhabitants; and an act of the 9th of George IV. (1828) authorized them to purchase the fairs and markets of the town, to erect a market and a town-hall. The last-mentioned edifice is the pride and ornament of the town, and one of the most beautiful buildings in England. From 1828 to 1849, as stated by Mr. Haines, their clerk, the commissioners raised by way of rate upon the inhabitants of Birmingham proper the sum of £255,949 for highway rates, £207,447 for lighting, paving, draining, and general improvement; and for the building of the town-hall £47,825, or a total of £511,221—without burdening to the smallest extent the outlying parishes or hamlets of Edgbaston, Deritend, Duddeston-cum-Nechells, and Aston.

The mistake made was at the incorporation of the borough, when the powers possessed by these commissioners should have been extended from Birmingham proper to all the outlying hamlets, and vested in the new officers. The want of Birmingham at the present day is a competent central authority, which shall absorb all minor jurisdictions, and take the whole question of the public health under its cognizance and care. In default of such an authority, armed with sufficient powers, Birmingham at present suffers from the existence of about two thousand narrow, and for the most part unwholesome and undrained, courts, many of which are the perpetual seats of typhus, and from the want of an adequate supply of water. It has no sanitary staff with power to compel the removal of nuisances throughout the whole borough, and has no power whatever to prevent the overcrowding of small tenements; and last, but certainly not least, it has no means of compelling a sufficient drainage. Those who consider public parks a necessity to every great town, will regret that, besides all the deficiencies above named, Birmingham does not possess a single acre of green grass where the people and their children can walk or amuse themselves.

An account of a visit to a large number of courts and districts inhabited by the poor will show the deficiency of the water supply, and the poisonous impurity of the water that is provided; as well as the general filth and insalubrity of the dwellings of the poor. To the account of this visit I shall append a short narrative of the steps that have been taken towards the erection of baths and washhouses and the purchase of a public park. The reader will thus have a tolerably accurate idea of the sanitary operations of this great and prosperous borough, and be enabled to decide whether they are sufficient.

Birmingham possesses every natural advantage, and is said to be, notwithstanding the powerlessness of its authorities, one of the healthiest towns in England. The rain fall is estimated, after careful observation, to be one-third less than that of Manchester, Liverpool, Bolton, or Lancashire generally. The undulating surface of the new red sandstone formation upon which the town is built, gives a general slope and inclination to the streets, which carries off the rain. Many theories have been broached to account for the healthiness of Birmingham amid the operation of causes which render other equally populous places unwholesome; but medical testimony seems to unite in the verdict that Birmingham owes this advantage to its gravelly soil, its elevated situation, and its undulating surface, and that not even the errors, or the omissions, of its governing bodies can wholly neutralize the good effect of these fortunate accidents.

The courts of Birmingham are chiefly situated in the main streets in the old town and the outlying hamlets. They are built on the model of those at Liverpool, and are generally so narrow at the entrance that two persons cannot enter or issue from them abreast. They are not so greatly overcrowded as at Liverpool, except in one or two districts inhabited by the Irish; but are estimated to contain a population of not less than 50,000 persons. Cellar occupation is almost, if not entirely, unknown. The new courts that have been constructed within the last ten or twelve years, for the occupation of the labouring classes, are so far an improvement upon those of the old model, as to have about double or treble the width of entrance from the street, and to be in all respects more spacious; but even the best of them are narrow and confined. Many of the old courts are unpaved, and in addition to the puddles of rain water and other worse moisture that stagnate in the holes of the soft and broken surface, they are encumbered with ashes, decaying vegetables, and nameless filth. There is often but one privy to a dozen of houses, and very few of the courts are supplied with water, except from a pump in the middle. In one place, called the Club-buildings, and so named, it appears, more than a century ago, from its having been erected by a club of working men for their own accommodation, the discomfort, filth, and squalor were extreme. The houses or cottages are built on the sides of an open space of sixty or seventy feet square. The under part of each house contains an ashpit, a privy, and a *brew*-house, the latter being the name given in Birmingham to a washhouse. Above this, entered by a ladder from the outside, is the dwelling, consisting of one room. On passing up the ladder the inhabitant not only smells, but sees the contents of the ashpit and the privy. Some of these cottages are used as workshops during the day. I entered one in company with the Inspector of Nuisances, who was obliging enough to escort me to some of the worst places to which his duty called him, and found it inhabited by an English woman and her husband, both out of work. The husband was a glass-blower. The room had not, to all appearances, been whitewashed for years, and there was a large hole in the roof. There was one pump in the middle of this court, and all the water used by the inhabitants, either for domestic or culinary purposes, had to be carried up the outer ladders in pitchers or other utensils. It was painful to witness little girls of eight or nine years of age struggling along the court, and up ladders, with loads of water far too heavy for them to bear. In another place, called Myrtle-row, Green's Village, containing houses or cottages of three rooms, built back to back, there was but one pump for fifty-three dwellings. The pump was at one extremity of the row. There had been a second pump at the other end, but it had rotted away, and the property of these fifty-three dwellings being divided between three owners, who could not agree among themselves, the pump had not been repaired. Two of the owners were willing to contribute to the expense; but the third was obstinate in refusing—and so nothing was done. I could not ascertain the number of people in these fifty-three houses; but the inspector estimated that it could not have been less than from three to four hundred. There were eight women round the pump at the time, waiting for their turn to get water. One of them asked me to smell the water, for "she was sure," she said, "that I would not taste it." I looked into her pitcher, and found the water of a greenish colour, and smelling as strongly of gas as if a gas-pipe had burst, and were emitting a stream through it. My hand, after immersion in it, smelt strongly of gas. The woman said that there was not enough even of that "filthy stuff" to wash the house with; and that she was obliged to buy water at a halfpenny a can for drinking purposes. More than a score of women soon gathered round the inspector and myself—all vociferous in their complaints of the "gas water." One woman said that the very floor of her room stank of gas for hours after she had washed it, and that there was a continual smell of gas about her hands and clothes. Another said it had cost her ninepence during the week for water purchased at a halfpenny a can from the water-carriers. This is a trade of which I shall have to speak in a subsequent portion of this Letter, and which has been called into existence by the inadequate supply from the pumps in the courts inhabited by the poor. This court, in addition to the evil of this offensive gas water, was rendered disgusting by garbage of almost every kind, and by accumulations of filth caused by the want of convenience for common decency and health. In one court of eight houses, in London 'Prentice-street, all fully occupied, and teeming with dirty and ragged children, there was not a drop of water of any kind for the inhabitants. There was a pump which had been out of repair for six months, and the landlord had refused to mend it. In another court branching off from the same street there was not even a pump, and until two years ago there was not a privy, but on the complaint of the Inspector of Nuisances the landlord had been compelled to erect one. In some of the narrow lanes, even more wretched than the courts, known by the name of the "Gullets," and of which there are several in the town, the deficiency of water is even more deplorable, and the deficiency of privies still more disgusting. To one house which we entered a small yard was attached; a ragged and very dirty counterpane was nailed across the corner of it—which being lifted displayed a sort of ash-heap—the only place for the men, women, and children of this wretched hovel to retire to for the purposes of nature. When and how, if ever it was cleaned, I could not ascertain, but made my escape from the place as fast as I could. In another house in the same "gullet" a venerable old man and his wife were at work; the man was engaged in planing a deal board, and the wife, at the other side of the room, was making boys' caps of the cheapest kind, at sixpence a dozen. The man complained that often he could not stand to his work, on account of the smells from the neighbouring tenements, and showed the inspector where the fœtid moisture from an adjoining cesspool percolated into the room. He said they had no water but such as they bought from the street carriers at a halfpenny a canful. The rent of the place was 2s. 6d. a week. In a similar place in Digbeth, in a congeries of courts swarming with pigs, children, hens, and lean dogs, where the water from the pump was not impregnated with gas, the supply was quite inadequate even for the culinary wants of the inhabitants, and was too precious to be "wasted" for house-washing, or the necessities of personal cleanliness. The many evil consequences of the impurity of the water supply are too obvious to need recapitulation; but among the equally numerous ill effects of a deficiency, which are not quite so obvious, though very deplorable, are the quarrels and fights that arise among the women while waiting for their turns at the pump. It is trying to the temper of the hard-working poor to be obliged to undergo the extra labour of carrying their supplies of water into their houses, and quarrels that begin under these circumstances are sometimes of the bitterest. These quarrels give the magistrates of Birmingham considerable trouble, and occupy no mean portion of their time to adjudicate upon; and many of the cases of riot and breaches of the peace that swell the annual figures in the elaborate returns of the superintendent of police are traceable to this cause. Lest the middle and upper classes of Birmingham—unaware of the filth, misery, and discomfort of the poor, of which they have never perhaps seen the proofs—should imagine that a stranger "taking notes" among them has exaggerated, even unintentionally, the sanitary deficiencies of the town, I append to my own statement, derived from careful observation, the following extracts from a document, bearing the name of "Joseph Hodgson, surgeon, F.R.S., medical sanitary inspector for the corporation of Birmingham," which appears in the appendix to the report of Mr. Rawlinson, presented to the Board of Health in June, 1849. Since that period no effectual steps have been taken to remove any of the evils which are therein described:—

"Many of the courts," says Mr. Hodgson, "are not only undrained, but have no proper privy accommodation, the cesspools and the middens are in contact with the houses, and the material percolates through the houses, and creates bad smells in the adjoining premises, which is a great and constant nuisance to the people. In the course of my visits as sanitary inspector, I have very frequently found courts in which the pumps were so situated that the water was rendered impure by the percolation from the privies, and from other impurities going into them. I think one of the greatest evils among the lower classes in this town is the condition of the privies, the mixens, and the surface of the courts. The common practice in this town is, that the manure should mix up with the ashes and rubbish of the mixen, and there it lies till the place is full. There is very frequently a dispute as to who is to remove it, and at whose cost it is to be done, till it overruns the seats, runs into the court, and gives rise to obnoxious exhalations, which, in my opinion, are injurious to health as well as to decency, to say nothing of the injurious results which often arise from the percolation of the more fluid parts of the contents of the privies into the neighbouring buildings. ... Not only is the condition of the privies very bad among the lower classes, but also among the better classes they are extremely bad, and the public gutters or ditches of the town, in many situations, are made to answer the purposes of cesspools. I would particularly mention as one place, the Hagley-road, where this has happened, the water-closets of some of the houses absolutely discharging themselves into the road. There is also another evil which I beg to mention—the drainage of privies in all parts of the town runs into gutters, brooks, or ditches. That is brooks (call them rivulets, if you please) running into the river. These in time become sewers. Now it frequently happens that privies are built and the contents are discharged into a dry brook, where they accumulate, and means have not been taken to cover over all these places. The medical inspectors have, however, been the means of covering over some of them. There are also nuisances belonging to the public authorities themselves, viz.:—Depôts of manure by the sides of the canal; there is one in Fazeley-street, one at Walmer-lane-bridge, and three opposite to the hospital in Bath-street. In the summer time swarms of flies, millions upon millions of flies, infest the houses in the neighbourhood. ...

"Further, a very large portion of this town is totally without drainage; as an illustration, I would instance the Workhouse-field, a large portion of the neighbourhood of St. George's Church, and particularly the suburban parts. In many parts of the town the old drainage is not of sufficient depth to drain the cellars, and it is further of very imperfect construction, in many places, I believe, having a flat bottom. The new sewage is most beautifully executed; it is impossible to conceive finer specimens of masonry than they exhibit; the flushing apparatus in them appears to be most perfect. I am sorry to say, however, that the inhabitants do not make much use of them for house-drainage, and that on account of the expense attending it; for they will not do it until some compulsory powers are given to the authorities to cause them to do so."

1. John Wesley's Chapel—2. Entrance to No. 5 Court, John Street.—3. No. 1 Court, Steel House Lane.—4. A Court, John Street.—5. No. 2 Court, John Street

Dr. Russell, the other medical sanitary inspector for the Corporation of Birmingham, is quite as emphatic as his colleague:—

"A very large proportion of the courts of this town, more particularly in the older parts, are closely built, and are narrow and ill-ventilated. They are generally paved with pebbles; some are not paved at all. There is often no attention paid to their level, and where that has originally been well laid down, it has become, by neglect, broken up, so that there are large spaces in which the wet lodges and vegetable refuse matter accumulates. The above observation as to imperfect state of repair is not confined to the courts, but may be extended to the interior of the dwellings. The drainage of these courts is very imperfect; often the drains are choked up at their outlet, so as to be rendered useless. In some courts may be observed perfectly good drains, but the level of the court is so bad that the drains are useless. There is a want of good privy accommodation in these courts, and in some instances there is none at all. The mixen and ash-pit form always one arrangement, the consequence of which is that in a short time the pit becomes full and choked with filth, and being open to the weather, it soon becomes filled with liquid stercoraceous filth, which decomposes the mortar and penetrates through the walls, and either flows into the adjoining house or shop or is seen running down the surface of the yard in streams, emitting a foul and disgusting odour into the atmosphere of the court. These are evils alike injurious to the health and morals of the people who reside in the courts. ... The powers of the commissioners do not extend into these courts, and the occupiers are left to the mercy of the proprietors, who are sometimes too poor or too mercenary to remedy the evil, or are often shamefully indifferent to the comforts of their humble tenants. ... A power is wanted to level and drain these courts, and also to compel proprietors to keep them in proper repair when once levelled and drained, for without this latter power the other provision will obviously be of no avail. The whole of the mixens and privies require to be reconstructed, and suitable plans to be devised for the removal of the filth and excrementitious matter. Many of the better class of workmen are in the habit of keeping pigs in these courts. The pig is a kind of investment of capital, and the produce of the sale of it is often appropriated to the payment of some debt, probably arrear for rent. These habits of frugality ought not to be lightly interfered with, but the exhalations from the sties, and from the barrels of putrid and putrefying meat on which the pigs feed, tend to render the atmosphere of the courts very unwholesome. At present there are no places appropriated as depôts for the refuse of the town, and it is deposited in large heaps in exposed situations, often in the middle of a dense population. There are three or four of these collections near the town, and the stench from them is very bad."

Although these descriptions will not apply to all the courts of Birmingham, they but too faithfully portray the state of the habitations of large sections of the people. Few cottages even of the better class are constructed with a proper regard to the health and comfort of a civilized community. One group of cottages, in Deritend, to which I was led by the Inspector of Nuisances, might serve as a model to the authorities, or to the friends of the working classes, in constructing the new dwellings, which, sooner or later, Birmingham will be compelled to erect in self-defence against contagion, and against the demoralization and pauperism which are the certain results of physical discomfort, dirt, and foul air. This group is called "Crowley's cottages." It is entered by a narrow passage from the street. The first glance impresses the visitor in its favour, and more careful examination shows it to be a superior place. The group forms the two sides of a triangle, the third being faced by the River Rea. The yard is paved with large red tiles, fitting as neatly and as closely as the squares of a chess-board. The houses, each consisting of three rooms, are oil-painted white, with green verandahs and venetian blinds. I looked into one of them that was unoccupied, and found it fitted up with every convenience. The walls were handsomely painted in oil, not whitewashed, and the fixtures included very superior grates, brass door-handles and window-knobs, and other luxuries not usually found except in houses that let at three or four times the rental. The rent of them is from 2s. 6d. to 3s. per week. There is proper privy accommodation, an abundant supply of water, a common drying ground, on a small green plot fronting the river, which is fitted up with poles and lines for the use of all the tenants. The cottages were built by a gentleman of the name of Crowley, who lives in one of them himself, somewhat larger than the rest. His object was to build a superior kind of dwelling for the working classes, and he is represented as being extremely particular in his choice of tenants. I was sorry to be informed that he was not satisfied with the result as a commercial speculation. He has certainly done much to improve the tastes and habits of his tenantry, and has accustomed them not only to convenience, but also to architectural luxury. The whole place is as scrupulously clean as an old maid's parlour, and every convenient corner is adorned with a statue. The tenants all spoke in the highest terms of him, and considered it a privilege to be admitted into the court.

This gentleman has possibly expended too much upon the court, and it is not to be expected that his example in this respect will be followed. Still the new courts, generally, although they do not so grossly offend either the eyes, the noses, or the lungs of their inhabitants, or of chance visitors who stray into them, as the courts of an older period, are far from being as clean and wholesome as they might be. Though for the most part well paved, they are generally too confined for proper ventilation, and the drainage is incomplete. Were there no other fault to be found with them, the existence of a pump in the middle, as the sole source of the water supply, might be justly considered a serious evil. The ordinary work of the poor is hard enough without the additional labour of pumping water and carrying it into their houses; and it is scarcely to be expected that the mother of a poor family will, under such circumstances, expend as much water in keeping clean her house, her clothes, her person, and those of her children, as she would do if water were properly laid on from the main. Water should be always available without the hard labour of the poor, if it is expected that the poor should make proper use of it. The want of water is, in fact, the great evil in Birmingham. There are so many pumps and wells, private as well as public, that the attention of those in better circumstances has not been sufficiently directed to the necessities of those less fortunate; and only one water company, which does not supply more than a third part of the town, has been established. This company was incorporated by act of Parliament, the 7th George IV., cap. 109. Its original capital was £120,000, which was raised in shares of £25 each, with power to raise £30,000 additional. The act provided that £116,925, the estimated expense of constructing the works, should be subscribed before the company commenced operations. The subscription was not completed till 1830, upwards of four years after the act had been obtained—a fact which is of itself sufficient to show either that the projectors were not very active or the public not very favourable. The first supplies of water from the main—the first, in fact, ever procured in the town from any other source than the public and private pumps and wells, or the rain water from the roofs, collected in tubs, was introduced in March, 1831. The company derive their water from the river Thame, and a brook near Salford Bridge, in the parish of Aston. They have two reservoirs, one on the Lichfield-road, about two miles from Birmingham, and the other at Edgbaston, at an elevation level with the top of the town-hall, and, consequently, far higher than the upper stories of the highest houses in Birmingham. The company are obliged to supply water to every inhabitant making a written application; but although the rates are low, and the advantages great, the houses of the wealthier citizens of the upper and middle ranks alone appear to be supplied. Comparatively few proprietors of the houses or cottages in the courts or poorer streets have made application. Whether any prejudice still exists against the company, I cannot state; but I find in a continuation of Hutton's "History of Birmingham," published in 1835, that a prejudice originally existed. "Considering," says the writer, "the great convenience, the purity of the water, and the low rates at which it is supplied, the company have not met with that encouragement that was reasonably to be expected, but the prejudice against the establishment is fast declining, and it may ere long be as extensively useful as its most sanguine projectors desired." That time, however, has not arrived—if we may judge from the facts already stated, that not above a third of the inhabited houses in this borough have, in the fifteen years that have since elapsed, made application to be supplied with the water of the company.

It does not even appear that the general supply of water in the better districts, although possibly sufficient for all the culinary and domestic purposes of the inhabitants, is sufficient for such public wants of the town as the flushing of the sewers and the extinction of fires. One reason given for the non-supply of the dwellings of the poor, is the unwillingness of the owners to incur any expense. It is alleged on behalf of this class of houses, that they have very great difficulty in procuring their rents; that they are compelled to let their property to weekly tenants, or run the risk of receiving no rental at all if they let them for a longer period; and that in the few instances where application has been made to the water company, and the pipes have been laid on, the tenants have cut away and removed the lead and cocks, and sold the fragments as old metal. It would be unjust, however, to condemn all the poorer classes for the misdeeds of a few, and it is likely that the cupidity and ignorance of the proprietors of these houses—many of them small shopkeepers and others, or mechanics, who have saved a little money—are more to blame for this state of things than the poor people who are compelled to inhabit their filthy hovels at a high rental.

The deficient water supply has called into existence a class of water-carriers who procure their subsistence by travelling round

the town and vending water at the rate of a halfpenny per can of
three-and-a-half or four gallons. These persons, who have each a
horse and cart, fill their barrels at the public wells, of which there
are many, all derived from one spring or bed of water, having several
outlets. The chief of these is known as the "Lady Well." Hutton, in
his history of Birmingham, says that this well is sufficiently copious
to supply with water a city as large as London; but in this respect he
was mistaken, as this and all the other wells often fail in the summer.
I found it a frequent complaint among the poor in the various courts,
that the pumps did not always yield enough even of bad, or gas water
for the scanty purposes of house-washing. "Many of the wells now
in existence in Birmingham, when first made," says Mr. Rawlinson,
"yielded comparatively pure water, and it was used for drinking and
all other purposes, but at present this water can only be used for
washing and scouring; the supply for cooking and drinking has to be
drawn from some other source, namely, the public pump, or water
cart. The public pump yields identically the same water as the private
pumps, only it may be drawn from a lower depth, and the 'quick
draft' of a more constant pumping does not allow it to stagnate in the
well, and this gives it the appearance of greater purity, although in
reality the same water." One of these public pumps is situated at the
east end of the wall surrounding the original parish, or "old," church
of St. Martin's. Of the churchyard adjoining, and at the edge of
which the pump is situated, Hutton says:—"It is so extremely small
that the ancient dead must have been continually disturbed to make
way for the modern, that little spot having been their only receptacle
for 900 years. A son not only succeeded his father in the possession
of his property and habitation, but also in the grave, where he could
scarcely enter without expelling half-a-dozen of his ancestors. The
antiquity of this churchyard," he adds, "will appear by surveying the
adjacent ground. From the eminence on which St. Martin's stands
proceeds a steep and regular descent, broken only by the churchyard,
which, through a long course of interment for ages, is augmented
into a considerable hill, chiefly composed of the refuse of life. We
may, therefore, safely remark in this place, that 'the dead are raised
up.' Nor shall we be surprised at the rapid growth of the hill when
we consider that this little point of land was alone that hungry grave
which devoured the whole of the inhabitants during long ages, till the
year 1715, when a new graveyard, that of Mr. Philips', was opened."
Around the pump which stands at the outer wall of this teeming

churchyard, filled up with the dead of twenty or thirty generations, which Hutton has thus described, I counted eighteen men, women, and children, with cans and pitchers, waiting their turns. I asked one man if he thought the water was good for drink? He replied that he thought it was excellent. These poor people required the water, impregnated with the gases of a graveyard, for their private use, and not for sale. The wells where the professional water-carriers fill their carts are situated at a short distance down the hill spoken of by Hutton. At the first of these the water is pumped into the carts by an engine, and each water-carrier pays a tax of two shillings per week for permission to use the well, and for the convenience of the engine. Thirty-four carriers regularly draw their supplies from this place. An old man, stationed at a little box inside the gateway, keeps watch and ward, and sees that no carrier enjoys the privilege who has not paid his money, and been duly entered on his list. Each of these carriers makes upon an average from ten to twelve visits to the well every day, and vends the water in certain districts of the town, where he has established a connection. In an open space behind this spot are three other pumps, where the water-carriers have not the advantage of the engine to save them the labour of filling their carts. Seventeen carriers are entered on the lists of the watchkeeper, or clerk, at this place. They each pay 1s. 3d. per week for permission to fill their carts as often as they please. On asking one of these men what sort of a business he had, he replied, "It is rather bad just now; the water-works have cut up the trade. In dry weather, when the water fails in the pumps in the town, we can manage to make a good living." "What do you call a good living?" "I call a good living, such as a man ought to have at this work, three shillings or three and sixpence a day after he has paid for the feed of his horse." "Do you often make as much as that?" "We can't make anything like that all the year round; very often we cannot make two shillings a day."

I could not ascertain that any steps were in contemplation to introduce a more plentiful supply of water, generally, or to persuade or compel the proprietors of the two thousand courts, inhabited by 50,000 men, women, and children, to lay on the water for their tenantry. But until something is done, this large population will neither be so healthy nor so moral as it might be; the richer classes will not be free from the danger of typhus or other contagious disease; and the ratepayers in general will be burdened with an extra poor-rate, to pay for the support of wives left widows, and children fatherless, or of fathers and husbands disabled from active industry by the ill-health which never fails to fasten upon the frame of him who has not a sufficiency of pure water for his daily ablutions, and for the ordinary purposes of his household.

But if Birmingham has not yet taken the proper steps in this important matter, its attention has been directed from time to time to the necessity of imitating the example set by Liverpool, London, Manchester, and other large towns, and providing public baths and washhouses. On the 19th of November, 1844, a public meeting was convened by Mr. Thomas Phillips, then mayor of the borough, and held in the town hall, at which Lord Lyttelton, the owner of considerable property in the neighbourhood, the borough and county members, the Rev. J. P. Lee, the head-master of the grammar school, and now Bishop of Manchester, and several gentlemen of local influence, attended, "for the purpose of considering the propriety of establishing public baths and places of recreation for the inhabitants." Resolutions approving the project generally, and suggesting the erection by public subscription of four sets of baths and washhouses in four different quarters of the town, were agreed to, and a committee was appointed to carry them into effect. Considerable sums were subscribed at the meeting, and in ten days the advertised amount was within a fraction of £4,000, or £3,994 4s. The subscriptions flagged considerably after this time. Nearly all those who intended or were able to subscribe gave their names or money at the commencement, and, although every exertion was made by the committee, the subscription never amounted to more than £6,000. As this sum was quite inadequate even for the construction of one out of the four sets of public baths and washhouses which had been proposed, to say nothing of the parks and gardens, which were meant by the term "places of recreation" embodied in the resolutions of the public meeting, the committee, after due deliberation, and after being fully convinced that no more subscriptions could by possibility be obtained, determined to return the money to the benevolent donors. This was accordingly done. The question, however, in spite of this inauspicious commencement, was not allowed to rest. It was brought forward from time to time in the town council, and it was ultimately resolved to erect one set of baths and washhouses as an experiment, and to levy the necessary amount by a rate on the inhabitants. A site was chosen in Kent-street; a design sent in by Mr. D. R. Hill, a local architect, was adopted, and the buildings are now in course of erection. The estimated cost, including the land, is £10,000. The building is of the Elizabethan style, and will be, when completed, an ornament to the town. The plan includes fifty-three small baths, warm and cold, in the male and female departments, first and second class; two tepid plunge baths, one for males and one for females; and one large swimming bath. The washhouse will be fitted up with twenty-five separate washing troughs, and the drying closets, one for the washhouse and one for the laundry, will contain all the usual conveniences and the modern improvements which the experience of other places has proved to be desirable. The rates of admission, both to the baths and washhouses, will be on the same scale as those adopted at similar establishments in London and Liverpool. Should the experiment prove a successful one, and pay its expenses, it is proposed to erect in succession three other similar establishments at convenient distances and in the most thickly-peopled parts of the town.

Nothing effectual has yet been done to provide a public park or place of recreation, and Birmingham at present does not possess a single open spot where her hard-working inhabitants can indulge themselves with a gulp of fresh air, or a run upon the greensward. There can be no doubt that the people of all classes would highly prize and keenly enjoy the privilege. Fourteen or fifteen years ago there was a broad walk around St. Philip's Churchyard, which stands on the highest ground in the town. This walk was planted with large trees, and although possibly not very salubrious, on account of the encumbered condition of the graveyard, was, in default of a better place, the favourite resort of the people on the summer evenings, and of nursery maids and children during the day. But this broad and fa-vourite walk could not be spared. The ground was too valuable as a burial place; the greater part of the fine large trees were cut down— the grand walk was dug up; and the whole strip around the enclosure was added to the overflowing burial ground. The destruction of this promenade excited much ill-feeling in the town; the workmen em-ployed were obstructed and assaulted at their work, and constant riots and disturbances took place. Ultimately several persons were arrested and sent to prison; and the ill-feeling engendered by the circumstance, though now almost forgotten, continued for a considerable time after the walk had been finally covered with graves and tomb stones.

It should be mentioned, in connection with this great want of the people of Birmingham, that the proprietors of the Botanical Gardens at Edgbaston throw open their grounds every Monday to all comers, at the charge of one penny; and that considerable numbers of the people avail themselves of the opportunity. But this accommodation, although kindly meant, does not supply the public want, and has the disadvantage of being in some respects injurious. In the first place, the public require a park, where they may stroll without payment—not only upon Monday, but on every other day of the week. The Botanical Garden is not equal as a promenade to St. James's Park in London, which may be considered both a botanical and an ornithological garden, for the recreation and instruction of all classes at all times. The London park is free, but at Birmingham the far inferior gardens cannot be entered without the penny fee; and, what is equally to be regretted, they are not like the parks of London, and every other civilized town and city, open on Sundays. It was proposed by some parties to open the Birmingham Botanical Gardens on Sundays, but the idea was considered irreligious, and subversive of all morality and decency. It was in vain to argue the point, and its friends speedily ceased to press it. Two evil consequences result. Either the working-men of Birmingham and their families take longer and more expensive journeys in search of the fresh air and the green grass, the enjoyment of which is so essential to their morals as well as their physical health, or they pass the Sunday in the town in amusements that are by no means so innocent or so healthful, or pass their time in suburban tea-gardens amid gin and beer and tobacco-smoke, to the odour of which no female can be habitually subjected without the loss of self-respect and womanly feeling. In addition to these evils, the opening of the gardens to the public on that particular day of the week and not on any other, encourages the working classes in the bad habit of keeping "Saint Monday," or "Shackling Day." They are already well enough disposed to do so, and to waste a day that should be devoted to honest labour. They need no further inducement of this or any other kind.

It must not be supposed, however, that the project of a park has not engaged the anxious attention of many philanthropic men in public and private life. The great difficulty to be encountered is the high value of land in the immediate vicinity of such a thriving and increasing town. The borough, although but eleven or twelve years old, is considerably in debt. Nevertheless the question has been brought forward in the town council, and a fine estate conveniently situated being at present in the market, it has assumed a tangible shape for the approval or rejection of the governing body. At a meeting of the town council in August last the mayor stated that he had received an

offer from the proprietors of the Aston-park estate (the representatives of the family of the illustrious James Watt) for the disposal of
that property to the council as a place of recreation for the people
of Birmingham. This estate comprises 375 acres of good land at the
north end of the town. The price asked was stated by the mayor to be
above £100,000 and less than £200,000, and was afterwards conjec-
tured by Mr. Muntz to be £350 an acre, or £131,250—a price which
he affirmed to be three times more than its value. It was finally agreed
that the communication, made officially to the mayor, should be received by the council, and that a committee should be appointed and
authorized to open a communication with the proprietors of the estate, with the view of obtaining the option of a refusal of the purchase
until the end of the ensuing session of Parliament. The pecuniary
position of the borough, according to the published accounts of its
assets and liabilities to the 31st of March last, does not at present
seem very favourable for the realization of this project. It has already
borrowed £120,000 upon the security of the rates for building the borough gaol, the lunatic asylum, and the public baths and washhouses.
The magnificent town-hall is, moreover, unpaid for. It is, therefore,
probable, unless the inhabitants come forward and support the town
council by declaring their willingness to bear an additional rate for so
necessary a purpose, that the project of a park for the people of Birmingham will not meet with immediate success. Perhaps, however, if
the authorities and inhabitants of Birmingham have ever heard of
the admirable method by which a few public-spirited individuals in
Birkenhead have contrived to present the fortunate dwellers in that
town with a public park, free for ever, they will be induced to consider whether the example might not be imitated, and whether, by
judiciously purchasing an eligible piece of ground of 200 or 300 acres,
they might not lay out a belt around it in plots for ornamental villas
for the rich inhabitants, and so make a third part of the park pay the
expenses of the whole, as the people of Birkenhead have done. The
question is well worth their consideration and that of all other large
and increasing towns, which have no open spaces within their limits
for the health and innocent amusement of the multitude of toiling
men, without whose presence and exertions no town can be either
great or prosperous, and for whose moral and physical health it is the
bounden duty as well as the interest of the governing classes, and the
men of leisure and refinement, to provide.

LABOUR AND THE POOR.

—◆—

BIRMINGHAM.

[FROM OUR SPECIAL CORRESPONDENT.]

THE METAL, FLORENTINE, AND HORN BUTTON MANUFACTURE.

LETTER III.

Among the great staple manufactures of Birmingham, that of buttons holds the foremost rank. A few metal and pearl buttons are made in London, Sheffield, and Dublin; but all these places together do not manufacture 1 per cent. of the whole number manufactured in Birmingham, which is the great button-shop of the world, and produces the article in countless millions in every variety of material. The date of the introduction of this trade into Birmingham is not precisely known; and the most extensive manufacturers in the town are not aware how long it has been in existence. The oldest firm now in the business dates only from the middle of the last century; but as buttons appear to have been worn in the Saxon period, there must have been a considerable manufacture, either in Great Britain or on the Continent, many centuries ago. In Chaucer's time the English of button was "*knopp*," equivalent to the modern word "knob," derived from the ancient Saxon "*knopf.*" Chaucer uses the same word to express both a button and a bud. In the "Romaunt of the Rose," he describes "Richesse" as wearing a robe of purple, "with *knoppes* fine of gold." In the same poem he speaks of the rose—

> " Aboute the red roses springing
> The stalke ywas as rishe right,
> And thereon stood the *knopp* upright."

When the old Saxon word gave place to a word of Norman derivation does not appear. Allusions to the button are frequent in English and Continental literature at the end of the sixteenth and the commencement of the seventeenth century. The word button is of French derivation, and signifies a "bud," a "pimple," or any "round excrescence."

"*Bouton de la rose*" signifies a rosebud, and in this sense the word is used by Shakspeare, in *Hamlet*, act 1, scene 3—

> "The canker galls the infants of the spring,
> Too oft before their *buttons* be disclosed."

In another scene, he makes the saucy *Rosalind* say, that among the signs of a lover are his having "his hose ungartered and his sleeve unbuttoned." Queen Elizabeth's famous proclamation for regulating the dress of the London apprentices makes no mention of buttons, but orders, among other matters, that they "shall wear no other than a plain upper coat of cloth or leather, without pinking, edging, stitching, or silk about it." Leather buttons were at one time worn, but whether upon the leather doublets of the apprentices is not mentioned either in the history or the tradition of the town. In the time of Shakspeare, "silk" buttons were known, as we learn from a passage in *Romeo and Juliet*, in which *Mercutio*, speaking of the thrusts of a duellist, says, "One, two, and the third in your bosom: the very butcher of a *silk* button." In the Chandos portrait, the garment of Shakspeare is ornamented with buttons; and a well-known contemporary portrait of Sir Walter Raleigh is plentifully studded with them. In the time of Charles II., gold, silver, and steel buttons were common among the upper classes; and at this time an attempt appears to have been made to "protect" the English button manufacture by totally prohibiting the importation of buttons from Germany, and France, and every other foreign country. This act was not repealed until the year 1824. Pepys, in his minute and interesting Diary, lets posterity into the secrets, both of his vanity and his costume. He notes down that he purchased "a camlet cloak with gold buttons," and that his brother brought him a "jackanape's coat with silver buttons." He states, among his expenses, that in one month he spent £55 or thereabouts in clothes for himself, and only £12 "about" for his wife. Among the items of the expenditure on himself was one for a "new shag gown trimmed with gold buttons and twist," and about eight months afterwards he records that he put on "his new coloured silk suit and coat, trimmed with gold buttons." In 1688, a lad of 15 years of age is advertised as having left his friends. He is described as wearing a coat of "a sad colour, with black buttons." An advertisement in a newspaper of the year 1680 states that a gentleman left in a coach "a light-coloured cloth coat, lined with blue serge, with gold and silver buttons," and directed it to be returned to the office of the Master of the Rolls, in Chancery-lane. In 1699, the fashionable coat was of Spanish drugget, lined with Persian silk, the buttons being of silver and the buttonholes being silver frosted. In the reigns of William and Mary, Queen Anne, and the two first Georges, the gentlemen appear to have been guilty of as great extravagance in buttons as honest Pepys. In the reign of George I., the button interest, which had been strong enough, fifty years previously, to procure an act prohibiting the importation of foreign buttons of every kind into England, procured a still more remarkable intervention of the legislature in its behalf. By the act 4 Geo. I., cap. 7, it was enacted that no person should make, sell, or set upon any clothes or wearing garments whatever, any buttons made of cloth, serge, drugget, frieze, camlet, or any other stuff of which clothes or wearing garments were made, or any buttons made of wood only, or turned in imitation of other buttons, on pain of forfeiting 40s. for every dozen of such buttons. By the 22d section of the same act it was enacted that no person should wear or use any such clothes under a similar penalty. At the commencement of the reign of George III., it is recorded by a "pleasant collector and describer of antiquities," who writes in "Hone's Year-Book," that in his youth, and the youth of George III., the usual dress of the little independent country squire, "a character now worn out and gone," was a "plain drab or plush coat, with large silver buttons." It was not, however, until metal buttons began to be made of a less expensive material that large numbers of people were employed in their manufacture. The cheaper kind of buttons at this time appear to have been made of bone, wood, or horn; but as soon as iron, brass, steel, plated, and other metal buttons came into fashion, the men of Birmingham began to devote themselves largely to the manufacture. Hutton states that the "toy" trades first made their appearance in the town in the reign of Charles II., probably before the passing of the act already alluded to, which prohibited the importation of foreign buttons. First in pre-eminence among the "toys" he places the button. Writing upon the subject in the year 1780 he speaks of remembering the long coats of the grandfathers of his generation "covered with half a gross of high tops (a kind of button), and the cloaks of the grandmothers ornamented with a horn button nearly the size of a crown piece." In the time of Hutton, and for half a century previous, buttons were made in Birmingham of glass, horn, bone, pearl, iron, brass, and hard white metal. At the present day all these materials, and many others, are used. The button manufacture employs, as nearly as I can judge, after minute and careful inquiries, from 5,000 to 6,000 people, of whom fully one-half, if not more, are women and young children. The pearl button trade alone employs about 1,200 men and 800 women and girls; the horn button trade about 300, principally women and children; the metal button trade, including trowser buttons, vest buttons, livery and crest buttons, and the few plated and gilt buttons that are still worn, about 500, principally adults; and bone and glass buttons, from 300 to 400. All the rest may be considered as engaged in the manufacture of the Florentine, or covered button, in all its countless varieties. This button, which is more extensively worn than any other, is almost wholly manufactured by young women, assisted by female children from the age of eight or nine upwards. Before entering, however, into the present state of the manufacture, and of the operatives, a short history of the changes of fashion in this article will not only be interesting in itself, but necessary to the due understanding of the subject, and of the manner in which great changes of manufacture operate upon the social and moral condition of the working classes.

A partner in the oldest button manufactory in Birmingham, to whom I applied for information on the subject, stated, that to the best of his belief there was no considerable business done in buttons in Birmingham prior to the middle of the 18th century. The oldest kind of button of which he had any knowledge was called the "hard white," a plain flat button without ornament, composed of a mixture of brass and spelter, or zinc. This button, of the vest size, was sold a hundred years ago at the price of 4s. 6d. a gross, and is still manufactured, but not to any great extent, and sold at sixteen or eighteen pence the gross. The next that came into fashion was very large, of the size of half-a-crown. It was called a white metal button, and was ornamented with a pattern of "prince's plumes." This was an expensive button, and the best kinds were sold as high as a guinea a gross. But little variety of manufacture was introduced till the end of the century, but horn, bone, and hard white buttons were used by the poorer classes. The tailor was in those days a considerable button manufacturer, and made buttons by covering a bone or wooden mould with pieces of the cloth used for the garment. This practice is not yet entirely superseded, although the superior beauty, cheapness, and convenience of the Florentine button is fast confining it to village tailors in poor and remote districts. Steel buttons were also made at this time, but not in very large quantities. It was the introduction of the gilt and plated button between 1797 and 1800 which gave the greatest impetus to the button-manufacture of Birmingham. This button became almost immediately fashionable. Good workmen were scarce, and the best journeymen earned often as much as five guineas a week. Children were introduced in large numbers into the manufactories, and in the course of a few years the trade employed as many as 5,000 people. The plain gilt button, worn on a blue coat, was the great favourite for many years, and was sold at from 21s. to 25s. the gross. Shortly after the introduction of the plain gilt button the "fancy gilt" button engaged the attention of the manufacturers, and called into the trade a new supply of artisans. These beautiful buttons, which are still worn by a very few persons, and occasionally do service on wedding coats, were made in every imaginable variety of pattern, and the ingenuity of the manufacturer was constantly taxed to invent novelties. The fashion lasted for about five-and-twenty years, when the Florentine or covered button was first successfully introduced. This novelty, after a preliminary struggle to force itself into use, made its way, and ultimately ruined the trade in gilt buttons, creating much distress and suffering among the large numbers of workpeople. The following statement, derived from a gentleman in the town, who began life as a working man, and was a button-burnisher nearly half a century ago, details more fully than the narrative of the manufacture just quoted, the rise, progress, and decay of the gilt button, and the consequences to the working population:—

"In the year 1799," said he, "being then in my seventh year, I began to work at the hard white metal button trade, along with my father and mother, who both worked for one large manufacturer in the town. I continued to assist them daily for ten or eleven hours a day, until I was twelve years of age. They received wages for me, but how much my labour earned I cannot say. I had no education, and no chance of obtaining any. At twelve years of age I began to get wages for myself. The trade was very prosperous at that time. My earnings at turning the white metal buttons at the lathe were 3s. a week. At fourteen I received 4s. a week. My father was a button turner, and my mother a button rubber, or polisher, and also a driller. She drilled the holes in trowser buttons. My father got from 21s. to 24s. a week, and my mother from 7s. to 8s. or 9s., according to her industry. My wages continued to rise at the rate of a shilling a week per annum—so that when I was sixteen I earned 6s. a week. Owing to the intemperate habits of my father we were always in poverty. The button-makers at that time were all greatly addicted to drinking, and my father was not worse than the rest. Drunkenness was the curse of his class at that time, as at the present. The hard white metal button trade was one of the best in Birmingham for the journeymen, and a most excellent trade in my young days. It was, however, superseded to a certain extent by the introduction of a new and very superior button—the gilt and plated—and considerable distress ensued, as the workmen were not skilful enough to adapt themselves all at once to the new manufacture. I, being a favourite apprentice, was turned over, as a great privilege, to the new trade in the same manufactory; and I may state that I never worked for any other all the time that I was employed in the button trade. Before I was out of my time I could earn 20s. a week, and a year afterwards I made from £2 to £3 a week. In 1813 and 1814 my average earnings all the year round were 35s. a week. By this time I had managed to pick up some instruction in my leisure hours, and could read and write. I began to improve myself with books. The state of prosperity in the gilt and plated button trade lasted until 1825, which may be considered the last good year it has known. The principal departments of the trade were—First, the *cutters out*. These were mostly women, who passed the sheet of metal under the press, and cut out the round blanks. They earned from 8s. to 10s. a week, according to the amount of work, being paid by the piece. The second were the *solderers*, also women, who earned upon an average about 7s. a week. The shank makers were then, as now, a separate trade. The third were the *stampers*, principally men, who stamped the patterns on the upper, and the maker's name on the lower, surface of the button, and earned from 20s. to 25s. a week. The highest and best paid class of operatives were the gilders and burnishers. The gilding was considered prejudicial to health, as it salivated the work people very much, and also formed an excuse for drinking. The gilders were paid by the piece. Some slight gilding was done as low as 6d. a gross, and other processes were paid as high as 25s., according to the quality. We had a union of the trade; no trade was more active. We had a sick and burial club, our only legal hold in those days, but our principal object was to keep up wages. There was generally a good understanding between the employers and the employed. In 1826 the Florentine, a covered button, was introduced, and our trade gradually declined. In 1829 it was looked upon as nearly annihilated. The gilt and plated button trade employed men principally at good wages. The Florentine button, wrought by machinery, employed women and children only, and a few tool makers. Vast numbers of persons were thrown out of work, including the cutters-out of the blanks, the shankers, the turners, the burnishers and finishers of the metal buttons, as well as the die-sinkers and various other businesses. Many thousands of people were deprived of bread by the rapid popularity of the covered button. A meeting of the trade was held in 1830, and it was decided that a deputation of working men should proceed to London, with specimens of the buttons, and wait upon the King, the Duke of Clarence, and the principal nobility, to solicit their patronage to turn the tide of fashion into its old channel."

My informant was a member of this deputation, and from the newspapers of the day preserved by him, I gathered the following particulars of the result:—On the 12th of February, 1830, the following document, signed by 32 working button-makers, was produced before a county magistrate, and its truth verified on oath:—

"We, the undersigned, on behalf of ourselves and the other operative manufacturers of *gilt* and *plated* buttons in Birmingham, beg to represent our deplorable situation from the want of employment occasioned by the variation of fashion, in so extensive a degree as to cause a great abandonment of the use of those articles. As benefit is generally derived from good example, we are confident that our distress would be much reduced if gentlemen in your high and influential station would only condescend at the present period to appear with those articles upon your dress, instead of covered buttons, now so frequently introduced.

"Being most deeply impressed with the conviction of others immediately imitating your example, our masters, upon our application, have most kindly consented to give us a few sets of buttons—one of which, of the best quality, we humbly beg now to present to you, with our request of your acceptance, hoping you will so far sympathize in our sufferings as to confer upon us the favour of promoting and wearing them, which is the only object of our intrusion."

Armed with this document, and with specimens of their choicest manufacture, supported with money by their employers, and followed by the good wishes of the whole town, except the Florentine buttonmakers, the deputation prepared to go to London; but not before their friends had endeavoured to create a public feeling in their favour by various articles in the local papers, and by hand-bills, placards, and other modes of publicity. The following, among many other pleas in behalf of the gilt buttons, will cause a smile at its reasoning, and the *naïf* determination of the writer to make out a strong case for his favourite article:—

"The superiority of the gilt button over one that is covered with cloth," said the writer, "must strike every one at the first glance; the latter, being of the same colour and kind as the coat, is in no way distinguished from it, and is altogether lost in one general shade, which presents to the eye one dull uniformity of ground without the slightest relief. The gilt button, on the contrary, is really a beautiful object. *Its quality suggests wealth.* It is richness itself; and in contrast with the coat on which it is placed, *its brightness must afford unmixed pleasure to the beholder—while the wearer himself must feel gratified at the respectability of his appearance!* If a new cloth button be necessary upon a coat which has been worn, it shows at once the worn and shabby state of the coat, by contrasting new with old cloth; but if a rich gilt or plated button be placed upon a coat the worse for wear, it refreshes it, and gives it the impression of newness. Instead of making the coat look worse, it really makes it look better, and enables the wearer to use it much longer; so that the saving in the coat, which lasts much longer and looks much better, is considerable.

"As appearance and cheapness constitute excellence, I hope I have succeeded in furnishing reasons for serving this destitute class of mechanics, many of whom are starving with their families, *by a perverted taste and mistaken economy of the public.*"

It was stated at this time that the button trade of Birmingham employed, directly and indirectly, about 17,000 people—a far greater number than it employs at present; and that more than two-thirds of the number were interested in the prosperity of the gilt and plated button. There was a notion very generally prevalent that the act of George I. could be enforced, and that not only the manufacturers of Florentine buttons, but the tailor who used and the man who wore them on his coat could be punished. It was not long before the metal button makers discovered that this notion was founded upon an error—and that they could not, as they were well disposed to do, compel a free people to conform themselves to the standard of "Brummagem"—or consign the wearer of covered buttons to the tender mercies of the magistracy. Counsel's opinion was taken upon the subject—and it was found that the wording of the act was too loose to apply to such a button as the Florentine button. The best authorities were clearly of opinion that it was not a covered button within the meaning of the act, inasmuch as it was not made of "cloth, serge, drugget, frieze, camlet, or any other stuff of which clothes or wearing garments were made." Perhaps it was also deemed that even if this obsolete act did apply to such buttons, the attempt to enforce it would certainly lead to its immediate repeal. However that may be, all thought of reliance upon it, to prop up the manufacture of metal buttons, was soon abandoned. The deputation went to London early in February, 1830. It was well received by the press and the public, and as soon as its object was made known, it was equally well received by the principal nobility and leading people of London. George IV., the Duke of Clarence, several of the Cabinet ministers and of the nobility; the Lord Mayor and Sheriffs of London, all accepted sets of the buttons, and promised to wear them. Sir Richard Birnie, the Bow-street magistrate, when informed that these buttons were made principally by heads of families, and that the rival button was made by women and children of tender years, declared from the bench "that he would wear the gilt buttons for this reason, if for no other." The deputation, on its return to Birmingham, received the thanks of the trade assembled in public meeting, and orders began to pour in for gilt and plated buttons. The fashion revived, and the manufacturers and workmen went on pretty well, and without much reason of complaint, till 1836—when, unluckily for all parties, and for the character of the town (which severely suffered in consequence), some manufacturer, over-hasty to get rich, introduced a cheap mixture for gilding the buttons. It was called French gilding in the trade, and by the workmen was designated "slap-dash." The composition of the mixture was kept secret. It produced, by a rapid process and at a very cheap rate, an apparently very fine gilding, which had but one disadvantage—that, however, was a fatal one—it did not wear. The buttons tarnished after a short exposure to the weather—and even in the shops of the retail dealers before the grosses were unpacked. A dull rim, gradually extending over the whole surface of the button, invariably formed upon it; and a new coat, ornamented with such buttons, looked shabby before it had been a fortnight out of the hands of the tailor. Such "Brummagem ware" threw discredit upon gilt buttons generally, even of a better and honester manufacture. Orders speedily began to diminish, under the effect of the "slap-dash," and by the year 1840 the trade was in as deplorable a condition as ever. The old expedient, which had succeeded so well in 1830, was again tried. The deputation waited upon Prince Albert, and upon other distinguished and influential personages; all the machinery of agitation was put in motion in the usual way; but although much sympathy was expressed, the fashion was not to be turned in that direction any more. The "slap-dash" had done its work, and at the present time it may be said that the gilt button trade is all but extinct. A few are made with crests for livery suits, and the army and navy require a certain number, but the public taste is decidedly against both gilt and plated buttons, and in favour of the Florentine. A set of burnisher's tools, that cost £150, are not worth above £5 at the present time, and the gilt and plated button-makers, after suffering severe privation for want of work, have either found their way to the workhouse, or have been absorbed by the other branches of the button trade, or in the general business of the town.

The *Florentine* button business next claims attention. It was first introduced into Birmingham, in the year 1820, by a person of the name of Moreton, and is so called from the material with which it is covered—*Florentine* cloth—of the same fabric that is used for ladies' boots. The name is now generally applied to all buttons that are covered with cloth, silk, or velvet. For six years the manufacture did not make any great progress. Like all new things, it had to work its way through a period of difficulty, but after 1826, as appears from the foregoing statements, it began to supersede all other coat and vest buttons. The fashion of male attire had been gradually growing more sober, and the gilt button was too gay for the taste of the generation. The tailor had done his best, in default of the manufacturer and in spite of the law, to compose a button by the simple process of sewing a circular piece of cloth upon a mould. The result was not very handsome, and its clumsiness possibly suggested to the original inventor of the Florentine button the desirability of an improvement. The Florentine button manufacture, as at present carried on, employs, in all probability, upwards of 4,000 women and female children in Birmingham. There are several manufactories of this article, some of which employ from 500 to 600 people, of whom not above one in forty is of the male sex.

But before describing the effect upon the public morals of the employment of such large numbers of female children at so early an age, some account of the process of manufacture will be necessary. If the reader will take a Florentine button, and dissect it, he will be the better enabled to understand the details. He will find it no easy matter to take such a button to pieces. On the contrary, he will find it extremely difficult to separate from each other the parts of which it is composed, and will have to employ both strength and skill for the purpose. He may with a penknife remove the Florentine covering with the exception of the edge, which turns into the under side. He will then discover a circling of iron or zinc. By the aid of a screwdriver or other convenient tool he may separate this circle or disc from the wide ring of similar metal varnished, which forms the under surface of the button. Having done this, the whole of the internal mechanism of this simple and ingenious article will be displayed. It will be seen to be composed of five separate pieces—*first*, the cover of Florentine or silk; *second*, a disc of metal, which gives the shape to the button; *third*, a somewhat smaller disc of brown pasteboard or wadding; *fourth*, a disc of coarse black linen or calico; and *fifth*, a disc of metal, from which an inner circle has been punched out, so that the cloth or calico above may slightly protrude, and form the shank of the button. To cut out these parts and put them firmly together, so as to produce a good, elegant, and cheap article, was the task reserved for the inventor of the Florentine button. A description of one out of many similar manufactories will show how and by whom it is at present accomplished, and by what means Birmingham is enabled to supply the constant demand for Florentine buttons that comes to it from every part of the world—a demand which one such manufactory could easily, and very often does, supply to the extent of a million of buttons per diem.

The manufacturers do not open their doors to all comers. They do not choose that rivals in trade should know the novelties of patterns that they may be engaged in producing, and they are somewhat jealous of foreigners. The consequence is that every manufacturer scrupulously preserves his workshop from the intrusion of strangers, and it is by no means uncommon to see a notification, in large and very legible letters, on the doors of a warehouse, directed, not against ordinary, but extraordinary visitors, stating that "*No foreigner can be allowed to visit this workshop.*" But if the manufacturer be once convinced that a visitor is not connected with the trade, and has no piratical designs upon his patterns or his modes of manufacture, he is quite as urbane and accommodating as can be desired. The scene that presents itself to the privileged stranger on entering one of these great button factories is novel and interesting. Ranged in rows on either side of a long room he will see from fifty to a hundred girls and young women from the age of fourteen or fifteen to four or five and twenty, all busily engaged, either at hand or at steam presses, in punching out the metal circles, slightly larger than the size of the button which is to be produced. Before each press the workwoman is seated, holding in her hand a sheet of zinc or iron, about two feet long and four inches broad. This she passes rapidly under the press if worked by hand, and still more rapidly if worked by steam, punching or cutting from the sheet of metal from fifty to sixty discs in a minute. As they are cut they fall into a receptacle prepared to receive them, and the sheet of metal, thus perforated, is cast aside, and a new one taken in hand, which rapidly undergoes the same process. The perforated sheets are removed, tied up into bundles, and sold to the founder to be again melted up and produced in the form of sheets of metal. In other rooms a similar process is performed upon strips of Florentine cloth, of pasteboard, and of linen and calico, the workpeople being somewhat younger. One girl can cut out 400 gross, or 57,600 of them in a day; and a young woman, at the slightly harder operation of punching out the metal discs, can get through 200 gross, or 28,800 in a day. The circles intended for the upper and under sides of the button undergo another process. The upper discs pass into the hands of a new set of girls seated at presses, worked either by hand or steam, like the foregoing, where each receives in rapid succession a blow, which makes it the identical size of the button required, and turns down an edge around it. The lower disc undergoes a double process, one of punching, in order to make an orifice for the linen or cotton protrusion which answers the purpose of a shank—and another of stamping, to impress it with the manufacturer's name or trade mark. These last are afterwards removed to another part of the factory, where they are coated with black or white varnish, according to the colour of the intended button. The five pieces are now ready for being permanently joined together, and they pass into the department of a woman who employs a number of children of from seven to ten years of age, to assist in the process. The business of these little creatures is, to place all the five pieces, one after the other, in regular order, into a small machine constructed to hold them, and then to pass this machine, which gives a spectator the idea of a dice-box, under the final touch of the press, which, without stitch or seam, or adhesive matter, is to fasten the five component parts of the button into one beautiful whole. This is done with great rapidity, the edges of the upper and lower surfaces enfolding within each other, in the firmest manner, the outer covering and inner portions of the button, without the slightest roughness, or the least chance of their ever coming asunder. Each room or workshop is under the superintendence of a man whose business it is to keep the presses and machines in order, and who is called the "tool-maker." This class of artisans are said to receive high wages, often as much as £3 a week. The younger children, or "putters in," earn from 1s. to 1s. 6d. a week; the girls, from twelve to fifteen or sixteen years of age, earn from 4s. to 5s., 6s., and 7s., according to their industry and attention; and the women average from 9s. to 10s. The very young children are not directly employed by the manufacturer. They are not under his control or care, although they work upon his premises, but are engaged and paid by women, who themselves work by the piece, and who are alone responsible for them and for the work they do. In one workshop which I visited I found a young married woman, of about three and twenty years of age, busily engaged at this process— working herself—and superintending at the same time the work of thirty-two little girls, of whom the youngest was eight, and the eldest eleven. The young woman had engaged to perform the work at a certain sum per gross. She was very pale, thin, and slatternly; and the children, who almost filled the little room in which the work was carried on, were for the most part dirty and ragged. They were divided into two classes, the younger class to put the pieces together, and an elder class to press them in the machine. Their fingers plied their task with marvellous rapidity. On asking the mistress how she managed to keep so many young children regularly to their work, she replied that it was very troublesome to do so. They wanted to play rather than to work, and she was obliged to look very strictly after them to save herself from loss by employing them. Being permitted by the master of the manufactory to put any question I pleased to the children, I selected one without taking her from her work or letting the rest know what was being said. She replied, in answer to my inquiries, "that she was nine years old, that she gained eighteenpence a week, and knew her letters. She could not write, and was not taught, as she only went to a Sunday-school. She went to bed soon after she left off work, and did not learn anything at home. She was too tired." I then selected another intelligent looking child, and put the same series of questions. The answers were very similar, and the only chance of education the child had was at the Sunday-school, which she did not always attend, as she liked to walk out into the country when the weather was fine. She could not write, and did not know what the multiplication table meant. Out of eight children, taken at random among the thirty-two, only one could write, and she had been to a day-school before she was put to the button trade.

Upon stating the result of my inquiries to the manufacturer, and asking his candid opinion upon the employment of such young children, he replied, unreservedly, that he would be exceedingly glad if the Legislature would interfere to prevent it. No individual in the business, however strongly he might feel upon the subject, could, he said, dispense with the services of these infants. To do so, while his neighbours did not, would only lead him to bankruptcy without effecting any good. The children had no chance of education, and such reading as they acquired at the Sunday school, even if they attended, which many did not, was of very little use to them without writing and arithmetic. A girl who could write and who knew something of figures was very difficult to find. He could always employ such girls in the warehouse, in packing up the buttons in grosses, and keeping an account of them: but he could not get a sufficient number for his purpose. The wages of such a girl would be at least a shilling a week more than the wages of a girl of the same age employed in button-making. "No man," he said, "would be more delighted than he would be, if it were forbidden to employ children under twelve years of age, either in button or any other factories. The price of buttons would rise accordingly, and it would, he thought, make little or no difference to the public. The difference of price betwixt adult and infant labour did not go into the pockets of the consumer, but into those of the retail dealer. A vest, or shirt, or coat, would not be charged more to the public if the buttons cost two or three farthings additional; and those farthings would make all the difference between the labour of men and that of young children. The profits made by the retailer of buttons were immense—often as high as four or five hundred per cent. upon the wholesale price. Florentine coat buttons, which originally sold at 5s. the gross, are now selling at 1s. the gross, or twelve for a penny; so that the buttons upon a dress coat, seldom amounting to more than twelve, actually cost but a penny in the first instance. If they were raised to double that sum by the employment of adult labour, there would be no hardship to the public, and many a man would be enabled to educate his child instead of sending it out to labour at such an early age, and thereby preventing it from being educated at all." Another large manufacturer expressed similar views as to the desirability of preventing the employment of infants, either in the manufacture of buttons, or of pens, pins, nails, screws, and other art-

icles, which are supposed to keep from 20,000 to 30,000 children in
Birmingham from every school but the Sunday school. He also dwelt
upon the fact, that these girls, when they arrive at womanhood, are
utterly unfit to fulfil the domestic duties of wives. They know nothing but the manufacture in which they are engaged. They can neither
read nor write; and while from their ignorance in these respects they
cannot form the fit companions of instructed and intelligent mechanics, they are equally unfitted for being useful in a household. They
cannot cook for their husbands, nor even mend their own clothes. It
is impossible to estimate the number of women that grow up annually
in this condition in Birmingham; but all who know anything about
the town and the habits of the working classes admit it to be a very
great and serious evil.

The *Patent Linen Sewn Through Buttons* is another kind of manufacture, which is carried on by a very similar process, and entirely
by the labour of young women and children, superintended by a tool-
maker. This neat and useful button was introduced about five years
ago, and has almost entirely superseded the old wire-thread button
used for under garments. There are only three establishments in Birmingham (or in the world) where this button is made; and the largest
exclusively devoted to it employs about seventy women and girls. The
button is composed of four pieces, two of metal and two of linen. The
metal pieces are rings of zinc, which are cut or punched in the manner already described in the account of the Florentine button, and the
edges of which enclose and keep together the pieces of linen that form
the upper and under surfaces of the button. As its name indicates, it
is sewn through, when used on the garment, in the same manner as
the old wire-thread button, and requires no shank. The wages are
about the same as in the Florentine business, and the condition of
the women and children precisely the same.

The manufacture of *Horn Buttons* is one that is interesting from
its antiquity, and from the modern improvements that have been introduced into it. Long before metal buttons were made for general
wear, and while gold and silver and richly-plated buttons were used
by the rich, the horn shared with the bone button the patronage of
the poor. At present the horn button is used principally for shooting
coats and vests, and for shoes and boots. It is an ingenious and interesting, but simple manufacture, and produces beauty from a very
unpromising, if not offensive, material. The horn button is not made
from horn, as the name indicates, but from the hoofs of horned cattle.

The hoofs of horses are not suitable for the purpose. Birmingham procures its principal supplies of the article from London. Prior to the year 1826, the manufacturers did not exhibit much taste in the production of this button. In 1826 to 1836 the manufacture improved, and from 1836 to the present time a constant succession of novelties has been brought out, and the horn button has rivalled in beauty of design the choicest specimens turned out by the manufacturers of metal buttons. On applying at the workshops of one person in the town, who was represented as doing a considerable trade in the article, and as employing a large number of young children, I was closely questioned as to my object in wishing to see the process. I answered the inquiries of the manufacturer without reservation, and met with the first and only refusal that I ever received in the town, couched in language which neither bespoke the man of politeness nor of education. On referring to the report of the Government inspector on the employment of women and children in factories, published in 1841, I found the workshop of this manufacturer unfavourably spoken of, for its unwholesomeness and for the ragged and dirty appearance of the children employed. Upon making application to another and more extensive manufacturer, and explaining my object, I was received with the utmost courtesy, and was conducted over every part of the establishment. The smell of the hoofs in the first stage of the manufacture is certainly disagreeable to a stranger; but it was represented as not unwholesome, and as never having been complained of by the workpeople, either young or old. When the hoofs arrive, they are thrown into a large cauldron, and boiled until they are soft. They are then cut into halves, and the sections transferred to the workshop. Here they undergo the same process as the sheets of metal in the Florentine button manufacture, the "blanks" being pierced or punched out by young women seated at hand-presses. The blanks, which are of a whitish colour, are then placed in vats in a strong dye, either of black, red, or green, the only colours which the hoof will take, where they remain till they are thoroughly dyed. Black is the most common colour used. The next operation is to fix the shank, which is done while the blank is soft and hot. This is a rapid process, and, like most of the other operations, is performed by children. In this establishment the shanks are manufactured by a beautiful machine, wrought by steam power, and requiring only the superintendence of one toolmaker. The machine feeds itself from a coil of brass or iron wire, suspended from the roof, and cuts and twists it into shanks by one process, at the rate of 360 per minute, 21,600 per hour, and 237,600 per working day of eleven hours, or nearly 75,000,000 per annum. The horn button, after being shanked, remains but a plain piece of rounded hoof, not even flattened or smooth on its surface. The next operation is to place it in a mould, having an orifice for the shank to fit in. This mould merely contains the maker's name or trade mark, and is for the under surface of the button. A dozen moulds are generally included in one iron box, or rather the mould contains a dozen repetitions of the same pattern. When the buttons are ranged in this receptacle they are heated over an oven, till they are almost as soft as wax, when an upper mould, containing the pattern which is to be impressed upon them, and which fits closely upon the other, is placed over it. The two are then subjected to the press, and the buttons are taken out round and complete, with the exception of an occasional roughness round the edge, resulting from the overflow of the molten substance. This is afterwards pared off. The buttons are then fixed by their shanks upon a plate of metal, and subjected to the operation of a brush, or a series of brushes, moved by steam power, which gives them the last touch, and produces a beautiful polish. They are now ready for carding and packing. The only operation that requires the superintendence of adults is that of stamping or pressing, and the workmen in this department, and not the owner of the manufactory, employ children to assist them in placing the buttons in their proper position in the moulds, and transferring them to the brushing machines. The manufacturer, as in the Florentine button trade, has merely a nominal control over a large proportion of the persons who work in his establishment. He neither engages them, pays them, nor dismisses them. They are the servants of his servants; and although he may exercise a general supervision, they do not stand towards him in the intimate relation of employed towards employer.

There yet remain several branches of this manufacture to be noticed, the most important of which are the pearl, the glass, the stone, the agate, the ebony, and other fancy buttons, and the stud manufacture—all of which, the pearl button more especially, give employment to large numbers of people. These will form the subject of a subsequent letter.

LABOUR AND THE POOR.

—◆—

BIRMINGHAM.

[FROM OUR SPECIAL CORRESPONDENT.]

THE PEARL AND FANCY BUTTON AND STUD MANUFACTURE.

LETTER IV.

The pearl button manufacture, as stated in the preceding letter of this series, gives employment to about 2,000 people in Birmingham. Of these 1,150 are male adults, and members of the Pearl Button Makers' Union, or Friendly Society. The remainder is estimated to be composed of fifty or sixty men who have not joined the union, and of the boys, women, and girls, who are employed in the operations of filing, polishing, drilling, sorting, and carding the buttons. Pearl buttons include the large buttons worn on shooting coats, and the smaller buttons, either drilled or scolloped, which are worn on vests, besides fancy pearl for ladies' dresses, boot-buttons, shirt-buttons, and studs. The pearl workers sometimes combine with the button manufacture that of various fancy articles made of or veneered with mother-of-pearl—such as counters for cards, reels for work-boxes, card-cases, knife-handles, leaf-cutters, &c. The beautiful shell from which these articles are made is commonly called the mother of pearl oyster, and is known to naturalists as the *Concha Margaretifera*.

"The pearl oyster," says Mr. McCulloch, in his 'Commercial Dictionary,' "is fished in various parts of the world, particularly on the west coast of Ceylon; at Tuticoreen, in the province of Tinnevelley, on the coast of Coromandel; at the Bahrein Islands, in the Gulf of Persia; at the Sooloo Islands; off the coast of Algiers, off St. Margarita, or Pearl Islands, in the West Indies, and other places on the coast of Colombia; and in the bay of Panama, in the South Sea. Pearls have sometimes been found on the Scotch coast, and in various other places.

"The most extensive pearl fisheries are those on the several banks not far distant from the island of Bahrein, on the west side of the Persian Gulf, in lat. 26° 50′ N., long. 51° 10′ E.; but pearl oysters are found along the whole of the Arabian coast, and round almost all the islands of the gulf. Such as are fished in the sea near the islands of Karrak and Corgo, contain pearls said to be of a superior colour and description. They are formed of eight layers or folds, whilst others have only five, but the water is too deep to make fishing for them either very profitable or easy.

"The fishing season is divided into two portions, the one called the short and cold, the other the long and hot. In the cooler weather of the month of June, diving is practised along the coast in shallow water; but it is not until the intensely hot months of July, August, and September, that the Bahrein banks are much frequented. The water on them is about seven fathoms deep, and the divers are much inconvenienced when it is cold; indeed, they can do little when it is not as warm as the air, and it frequently becomes even more so in the hottest months of the summer. When they dive, they compress the nostrils tightly with a small piece of horn, which keeps the water out, and stuff their ears with bees' wax for the same purpose. They attach a net to their waists, to contain the oysters; and aid their descent by means of a stone, which they hold by a rope attached to a boat, and shake it when they wish to be drawn up. From what I could learn, two minutes may be considered as rather above the average time of their remaining under water. Although severe labour, and very exhausting at the time, diving is not considered particularly injurious to the constitution; even old men practise it. A person usually dives from twelve to fifteen times a day in favourable weather; but when otherwise, three or four times only. The work is performed on an empty stomach. When the diver becomes fatigued, he goes to sleep, and does not eat until he has slept some time.

"At Bahrein alone, the annual amount produced by the pearl fishery may be reckoned at from 200,000*l.* to 240,000*l.* If to this, the purchases made by the Bahrein merchants or agents at Aboottabee Sharga, Ras-ul Khymack, &c., be added, which may amount to half as much more, there will be a total of about 300,000*l.* or 360,000*l.*; but this is calculated to include the whole pearl trade of the gulf; for it is believed that all the principal merchants of India, Arabia, and Persia, who deal in pearls, make their purchases, through agents, at Bahrein.

"The Bahrein pearl fishery boats are reckoned to amount to about 1,500, and the trade is in the hands of merchants, some of whom possess considerable capital. They bear hard on the producers or fishers, and even those who make the greatest exertions in diving hardly have food to eat. The merchant advances some money to the fishermen at cent. per cent., and a portion of dates, rice, and other necessary articles, all at the supplier's own price; he also lets a boat to them, for which he gets one share of the gross profits of all that is fished; and, finally, he purchases the pearls nearly at his own price, for the unhappy fishermen are generally in his debt, and therefore at his mercy.—(Manuscript Notes communicated by Major D. Wilson, late Political Resident at Bushire.)

"Pearl Shells, commonly called Mother-of-pearl shells, are imported from various parts of the east, and consist principally of the shells of the pearl oyster from the Gulf of Persia and other places, particularly the Sooloo Islands, situate between Borneo and the Philippines, the shores of which afford the largest and finest shells hitherto discovered. On the inside, the shell is beautifully polished, and of the whiteness and water of pearl itself; it has the same lustre on the outside, after the external laminæ have been removed. Mother-of-pearl shells are extensively used in the arts, particularly in inlaid work, and in the manufacture of handles for knives, buttons, toys, snuff-boxes, &c. The Chinese manufacture them into beads, fish, counters, spoons, &c.; giving them a finish to which European artists have not been able to attain."

Mr. McCulloch will, perhaps, in the next edition of his valuable work, see reason to expunge the concluding paragraph, and to own, after examination of the beautiful articles in mother-of-pearl shell which Birmingham will send to the great Exhibition of 1851, that European artists can not only equal, but excel those of China, in the finish and elegance of their work.

Five kinds of pearl shell are employed in the button manufacture of Birmingham and in the manufacture of mother-of-pearl toys. The first is called the Buffalo Shell; so named from its coming to this country packed up in buffalo skins. It is the smallest and commonest shell used in the manufacture, and is imported principally from Panama, and sold to the trade at about £15 a ton. The second is called the Black Shell, or Black Scotch. It comes principally from the Sandwich Islands, whence it is sent to Valparaiso and shipped for England. It sometimes reaches this country by way of Sydney. It fetches a price of from £15 to £30 per ton, according to the quality and size. A very small portion of the interior of this shell is white; the large outer rim being of a blackish tint. This outer rim was formerly considered worthless. Large quantities have been buried under the streets of Birmingham, forming, with broken tiles, bricks, and "rubble," the substratum of many of the new streets of the town. Within the last few years it has become a valuable article of commerce, and is made into a very beautiful button for shooting and other sporting jackets. There is a constant demand for buttons of this kind, which alone gives employment to many hundreds of men. A church originally established by the Irvingites on New Hall-hill, is built over a place where the button-makers of twenty or thirty years ago used to cast the refuse of the black Scotch shell, and it is estimated that under its foundations lie several hundreds of tons of this material, worth at the very lowest calculation from £15 to £20 per ton. So changeful has fashion been, that the blackness of the shell, formerly considered a defect, is now looked upon as a beauty; and the upper surface of the button, instead of being turned, as formerly, of the interior of the shell, is turned of the exterior, as being of a more variegated black. The origin of the term Scotch, as applied to these shells, is not very clearly known. In a note to Beckman's History of Inventions, relating to pearls, it is stated that "irregular pearls are called *baroques*, or Scotch Pearls, because abundance of such were once found at Perth, in Scotland; and that some years ago, artificial pearls of an unnatural size, called Scotch pearls, were for a little time in fashion." It is possible that the name of Scotch applied to the pearl may have been extended to the mother-of-pearl shell for some similarity of colour or appearance. The third description of shell is called the Bombay, or White Scotch—a shell of a purer and more uniform whiteness than the last-mentioned. It varies in price from £20 to £50 per ton, according to the size, soundness, and quality. The fourth is the mother-of-pearl shell, from Singapore; a thick, large, and beautiful shell, white to the very edge, and worth from £80 to £90 a ton. The fifth is the mother-of-pearl shell from Manila; as large, beautiful, and valuable as that from Singapore, and only differing from it in having a slight border of yellow around the outer edge. It also commands a price varying from £80 to £90 a ton. Occasionally these shells, which are not unfrequently of the size of an ordinary dinner plate, have been sold at as high a price as £120 a ton.

The first operation in the pearl button manufacture is called *piecing*, or cutting. The workman holds the shell firmly in his left hand, and by means of the lathe and a hollow revolving tube of the diameter of the proposed button, pieces, or cuts out, the blank, of the entire thickness of the shell. If the blanks are for shirt studs, or other small buttons, they are afterwards slit into the requisite thinness. The second operation is performed by boys, usually employed by the workmen, and not by the master manufacturer. It is called *filing* or *flattening*, and merely consists in flattening the shell on both sides with a common file. If the button is intended for a coat or vest, the third operation is that of *bottoming*, or turning the upper surface at the lathe, so as to give it the required convexity. The fourth operation is that of *shanking*, and the fifth that of *edging*, or smoothing the edges, both of which are performed by boys and girls. The last operation is that of *polishing*, which is principally performed by women. They stand at the tread-wheel and give the button its beautiful brilliancy by first of all coating it in a mixture of oil and pounded rotten-stone, and then rubbing it against the smooth revolving stone, set in motion by the foot. The button is now complete, and being gathered in quantities, they are conveyed to a shop where they are carefully sorted, according to their colour—the whitest commanding the highest price, and the yellow and discoloured ones being thrown aside. This part of the business, and the subsequent operation of carding, are performed by girls.

Shirt buttons and shirt studs, and also the fancy pearl buttons, undergo only a portion of these processes. The ordinary shirt buttons have to be drilled with two or four holes, according to the pattern—a process which is performed at the lathe, by young girls, with very great rapidity. Another process which the more expensive kinds undergo is that of *topping*. Here also the services of women and girls are brought into operation—and the scollopping, dotting, marking, cutting, and beading are almost entirely performed by them. All the workpeople—men, women, and children—are paid by the piece or gross, upon a scale agreed to by the trade, and enforced by the union. The average wages of the men are, according to their ability and industry, from 20s. to 25s. a week; of the women, from 7s. to 9s.; of the boys, from 3s. to 4s. 6d.; and of the girls and young women, from 3s. to 5s. 6d. A price sometimes paid for drilling four holes in pearl shirt buttons is ½d. per gross, at which rate a girl would have, before she could earn 5s. 6d., to drill holes in no less than 132 gross, or 19,008 buttons, containing 76,032 holes, or 12,672 holes per day. The price paid for sorting and carding averages 10d. for a score of gross—so that, to earn the same wages of 5s. 6d., a girl would have to sort and card the very same number of 132 gross. The sorting and carding is much more easy and pleasant work than drilling the holes—and girls who can read and write are generally selected for this stage of the business. The piecing, filing, and drilling are considered to be unwholesome work. The pearl dust, which generally fills the airiest workshops, affects the lungs of the workpeople, and the nature of the business is considered to be so injurious to health as to exclude the pearl workers from the ordinary Friendly Societies.

The pearl button trade is in a prosperous state at the present time—so prosperous that there is a general complaint of a want of hands to execute the orders that pour into the town. I am informed that there are only three pearl button manufacturers in Great Britain besides those in Birmingham; they have their establishments at Sheffield, and do not employ more than from twelve to twenty men. I am not certain of the correctness of the statement, but it is made on the authority of persons who ought to have the means of knowing. There is also one small pearl button manufacturer in Dublin. Some of the pearl button manufactories in Birmingham are on a large scale, and employ from 100 to 150 people. One establishment employs upwards of twenty girls in the single operation of carding and sorting. In one establishment of the kind, the men, without solicitation from any parties, but solely from reading in the newspapers what was doing elsewhere, organized a committee of their own members, and procured subscriptions for the proposed monument in Birmingham to the memory of Sir Robert Peel. The sum subscribed was £11. This circumstance, while it corroborates the statement that trade is good among them at the present time, is highly creditable to their intelligence and public spirit as a body. There are, besides these large manufacturers, many small masters who work at their own houses, either by contract for some of the general and Florentine button manufacturers who execute orders for pearl work, or on their own account, buying the shell and selling the buttons at the end of every week to the factors or dealers. These independent operatives are called "garret masters," a name given to the small masters in various other trades in the town. The larger manufacturers and the operatives combine in accusing that portion of them who do not work by contract at the prices of the trade-list, but on chance sale among the factors, of having severely injured the trade by forcing sales at unremunerative rates. I subjoin a statement made upon the subject by a manufacturer, and another statement made by a deputation of operatives—both tending to show the evils which the working classes sometimes bring upon themselves and upon their trade by attempting to carry on business without sufficient capital to enable them to wait for the sale of the article which they produce. The manufacturer said—"There is at present a union of the pearl-workers, which has been established by the mutual consent of masters and men, and which appears to give satisfaction to both. The number of small masters in the trade, men without either capital or credit, was formerly very considerable. There is no great mystery in pearl button making, and a man if he chooses can set up in the business for a few shillings. If a man were of irregular and dissipated habits, and did not like to conform to the rules of a shop, or if he had any dispute with his employer, he would occasionally become 'saucy,' and set up for himself. He could hire the necessary tools for 4s. a week, and could purchase from the shell dealers as small a quantity as 14 lbs. of shell, for a few shillings more. Of course, in the shell trade, as in every other, the poor man pays the highest price, and a 'garret master,' buying 14 lbs. or 28 lbs. of shell, would pay at a rate almost, if not quite, double that which would be paid by the large manufacturer, who bought several tons at a time, and had his choice of the market, and his discount for ready money. Provided with this shell, the garret master sets to work, and, by the aid perhaps of his wife and children, produces by the end of the week a certain quantity of buttons. Saturday night brings its wants and liabilities, and it becomes imperative for these masters, or for nine out of ten of them, to convert the buttons into money. They cannot wait until an order comes for them, and the quantity thus produced is too small in most cases to be worth an order, and consequently they are obliged to make the round of the factors or dealers, and offer them for sale. If it is early in the day they will not sell under a fair price; but the factor, not probably wanting the article at all—or, if he does want it, knowing full well that he can get it at a greatly reduced rate as the hour for closing business draws nigh—refuses to purchase at the fair market price. The garret master has no other resource, and is pretty sure to return before night, and sell his goods for any sum that the factor is pleased to give him. These factors are designated 'Slaughtermen.' They are generally dealers in shell, so that they manage to make a double profit out of the garret master;—in the first place by charging enormously for the shell, and in the second by underpaying him for the buttons produced out of it. The small masters at the present time are for the most part men who are not 'in society,' and one inducement for some of them to set up for themselves in this way is the liberty it enables them to take of playing at cards in beer-shops; and of drinking and smoking away the Monday and Tuesday, which they cannot have in a regular shop. A good many men have tried this system for a while, but few have been able to carry on above a

month or two. The practice, however, at one time, brought down
the price of buttons, and was productive of great injury to the trade.
The manufacturer not uncommonly endeavoured to protect himself
against such a ruinous competition by reducing, wherever he could
do so, the rate of wages. There has been considerable agitation in the
town upon the subject, and a general strike of the trade took place in
1849. The trade, however, has lately been placed on a better footing,
and the union seems to be firmly established. The scale of prices
which has been agreed upon gives satisfaction both to masters and
men."

The statement of the operatives was to the following effect:—"In
1825 the pearl button trade was in a very flourishing condition. The
wages of a man were from 18s. to 30s. a week, according to his work
and ability. But from 1826, or thereabouts, wages gradually decreased.
Buttons began to grow cheaper in the market, and the factors or merchants undersold the manufacturers. Many of the masters, therefore,
resolved to cut down the wages of the operatives. In 1839 a man's
wages were several shillings a week lower than they were in 1826.
There were at least a hundred garret masters at work in the town—
men who had no money—and who employed their wives and young
children to assist them; and journeymen who, for bad character or bad
workmanship, could not get employment in the regular shops. These
small masters bought four or five shillingsworth of shell at a time, and
hired tools to work it, and when the buttons were made, sold them
below the usual prices of the large manufacturer. They were prices at
which they could neither live themselves, nor allow any one else to
live. Several meetings and consultations between the masters and the
men were held, and the masters proposed a reduction of the rate of
wages to the extent of two or three shillings a week—which they considered, under all the circumstances of the trade, a fair remuneration
for the men's labour, and an ultimate settlement of all disputes. There
was no union among the workmen, and they were obliged to submit.
Some of the men, however, resisted, and resolved to set up in business
for themselves and try what they could make of it. This increased the
evil, because they had not the means either to buy shell at a fair rate,
or to wait over the Saturday night for a sale for their buttons. A gross
of buttons was often sold at thirty, or even forty, per cent. under the
fair price. They wanted money for their Sunday's food, and also to
buy a new supply of shell to begin again on Monday. They could not
wait over the last day of the week. The resistance of the men to the

reduced wages thus made matters worse, and lowered prices still further. The public gained nothing by the reduced prices, for the whole benefit went into the pockets of the slaughtermen, and the trade was ruined, both for the respectable master-manufacturers, who had sufficient capital and knew how to conduct the business properly, and for the hard-working operatives whom they were willing to pay a 'fair day's wages for a fair day's work.' Early in 1844 further reductions were made by some of the masters, but a few of the largest manufacturers continued to pay the price agreed upon in 1839. Things were getting so ruinous, going on daily from bad to worse, that the pearl-workers resolved to call a general meeting to prevent further reductions, to organize the trade into a regular union, and to establish a fund for a burial club. The trade came forward very generally. The chief employers looked favourably on the movement, and some of them signed a paper pledging themselves to support the union. In about six months upwards of 400 men joined the society, and paid 2d. a week towards the fund. Still the trade did not improve so rapidly as was expected. The prices of 1839, proposed by the masters themselves, were agreed to by the union—but there was a good deal of disunion as well as union, and things were not thoroughly brought right until 1849. At that time not above twenty masters were giving the wages agreed upon as a fair compromise in 1839, and accepted by the union in 1844, and the merchants and factors who gave out orders were paying considerably less. It was then resolved by the union that forty men, working for the factors at the low rates, should be called upon to strike, the union undertaking to support them while they remained out of work. The forty men selected struck work accordingly. The factors then had a meeting, at which they determined to throw all their men out of work. They did so, and 450 men were discharged, the factors hoping by this means to break up the union by throwing the support of this large number of men upon its funds. These 450 men and the other 40 all made common cause with the union, and agreed to stay out if the union would pay 5s. a week to every married, and 4s. a week to every single man out of work. When these men were thrown out of work it is likely that from 150 to 200 women and children were thrown out of work with them; but no accurate statement of their numbers was kept. The men were all determined. Several meetings were held, and the public sympathy was so much roused in favour of the operatives that £500 and upwards were subscribed in aid of the strike. It cost the union at last about £200 a week to keep up the strike. It lasted from the middle of August to the 1st of December, and cost altogether about £1,500, of which £1,000 was paid out of the funds of the Pearl Button-makers' Society or union. The factors were not so united as the men. They had orders on hand which they were obliged to execute, and they gave in, one by one, to the terms of the trade; so that, before the month of October was out, the expenses of the strike began to be reduced, by the men being taken on at the equalised prices of 1839. On the 1st of December the equalised price list was agreed to by the whole trade, including the factors or merchants, and things have since gone on more satisfactorily. The union numbers 1,150 men. It does not meet at a public-house, and never has since its commencement."

So far the statements of masters and men, as to the effects of the union; but it may fairly be questioned whether the journeymen are correct in attributing the present comparatively satisfactory state of the trade to the organisation which they have established. The pearl button has become fashionable, and home and foreign orders pour into Birmingham faster than they can be executed. One order alone within the last few months was for 60,000 gross, or nearly nine millions of buttons. Every available hand is said to be employed; and such are the demands for some kinds of pearl buttons, that over production is for the present impossible. The "garret master," at such a period, has his choice of the market; for if one factor will not give him a fair price for his work, another will. Of course, should the trade be ever again depressed by the cessation of orders, the garret masters will have it in their power, as they did before, to increase the depression. If they will continue to manufacture when there is no demand, and insist upon a sale of their produce at any price, rather than not sell at all, it will be utterly beyond the power of any trade union to keep up the price, either of buttons or of labour. Production without orders, by men who cannot wait until the trade revives, invites the factor to make cheap bargains, and to lay up a stock. No buyer could, under such circumstances, give the usual price, as his only chance of repayment is at a future, and probably a remote time. The true remedy for the evil in such cases is the cessation of production, and the expenditure of the workman's skill and energy upon some other branch of manufacture for which there is sufficient demand to remunerate him. As long as small manufacturers and operatives are needy, and are not sufficiently provident to lay by a store to help them over periods of depression in their trade, as the larger manufacturer is compelled to do—so long will the "slaughterman" speculate upon their necessities, and so long will they increase the evils of underpayment, and of ruinous competition among one another.

The manufacture of shirt-studs employs many hundreds of people. Besides the pearl studs, plain or ornamented, which are chiefly made by young women, there are infinite varieties of studs produced in Birmingham, of almost as many fabrics as buttons themselves. Gold, silver, steel, glass, ebony, agate, cornelian, enamel, pearl, ivory, and bone, employ in various ways the invention of the manufacturer, and the taste and skill of the workmen who produce these articles. Gold and silver studs, whether plain or set with precious stones, employ the jeweller rather than the button manufacturer; but studs of all the materials above mentioned, and of many others, are manufactured both in pearl button factories and by the general button manufacturers and small masters. Birmingham has long been celebrated for the length to which its "toy" manufacturers will make an ounce of gold go in the production of cheap jewellery. It used to be a saying, "Give a Brummagem manufacturer a copper kettle and a sovereign, and he will produce a hundred pounds worth of cheap finery." The manufacturers who devote themselves to the stud business keep up in this respect the ancient fame of their town, and produce gilt, burnished, and enamelled studs of great beauty and durability at prices so low that they would seem to leave no margin for profit. A beautiful shirt stud, burnished and enamelled, and of countless varieties of pattern and colour, has been sold wholesale at the rate of about 30s. per gross of sets, or less than a penny per stud.

Glass buttons, chiefly used for children's dresses, and for exportation to the African market, employ a number of young girls. Glass studs, to imitate precious stones, are also manufactured by girls. There are two principal varieties of glass buttons—the one plain, the other knob-shaped, and made in a mould, and worn for gentlemen's vests. The sheet-glass, stained of red, blue, green, or yellow, having first of all received a coating of lead, to give it strength, is cut by hand into small squares. The squares are then rounded, by having their corners roughly cut off with scissors. The edges are then ground on a wheel, and the button is made perfectly circular and smooth at the rim. The next operation is to fasten the shank, which is joined to a round piece of zinc, the size of the button, and soldered to the lead on the under surface of the glass. This is a very expeditious process, and the buttons produced are among the cheapest manufactured in Birmingham.

The vest button is made in a mould. A long rod of glass, of the colour required, is melted at the end in a furnace, as if it were a piece of sealing wax. The end is then clasped in a mould, in which the shank has been previously adjusted, and the button is produced, and only requires the smoothing of the edges to be ready for carding.

The manufacture of glass studs, and of polished black glass buttons for coat links, is more laborious. Both are produced at the lathe by women and young girls. Agate, cornelian, and stone buttons, at present so fashionable for vests, are imported from Bohemia, and shanked and finished in Birmingham.

Among other buttons not yet enumerated are the four-hole iron and brass buttons used for trowsers, the steel button for ladies' dresses, the wooden button for over-coats, and the bone buttons for underclothing. The four-hole iron and brass buttons are manufactured in very large quantities, and employ both sexes and all ages. The blanks are first cut out by hand or a steam-press; in some factories by men, and in others by women and girls. They are rendered concave at another press, under the descending punch of which they are placed, one by one by the finger of the operator, with great dexterity, and jerked out by the machine. The holes are pierced or punched out, and afterwards countersunk by the application of a hand-steel piercer to each hole separately, so as to render it smooth at the edges and prevent it from cutting the thread. The brass buttons are then placed in a solution of aquafortis to be thoroughly cleaned, and are thence transferred to an earthen pan, containing a preparation for giving them a white coating resembling silver. The preparation is composed of common salt, cream of tartar, and silver; and the buttons, being stirred in it with the hand or a brush for a few minutes, receive a permanent white coating. The steel button—at one time the most fashionable button worn, and still, in some of its varieties, worn upon court suits—is chiefly manufactured at Birmingham for ladies' and children's dresses. There appears to be no factory at which it is exclusively produced—those who manufacture it making other kinds of buttons, as well as brooches, buckles, chatelaines, and other light steel toys. In the steel button and brooch factories, the operation of polishing the buttons and other articles is performed both by men and women. They work for the most part together in one room, and it is a striking, but by no means pleasant, sight to see them, men and women, sitting before large wheels, which perform their rapid revolutions by steam power. Men and women are alike covered with dust and dirt. The work is by no means agreeable or light.

The wood button is an easier manufacture, and is produced by wood turners. The bone buttons for under clothing, drilled with four holes, are chiefly manufactured by the horn button makers. It is considered an unwholesome occupation, from the quantity of bone dust which fills the workshops. The processes are similar to those employed in the production of the pearl button, and employ many women and children.

It might be thought that the button manufacturer, especially if he manufactured upon a large scale, would produce the shank as well as the button; but this is not often the case. One or two of the principal manufacturers use on their premises an admirable machine for making button-shanks, similar to that described in the previous letter in the account of horn buttons—but generally it is found more economical to purchase the shanks of those who make it their sole business to manufacture them. The "Directory" contains the names of six shank manufacturers; and it was computed more than seven years ago that three of these produced every year the enormous quantity of 600,000,000 shanks. The present annual production may be estimated at 1,000,000,000, or upwards of 3,000,000 per working day.

In all branches of the button trade—with the exception of the patent linen sewn-through button, the bone button, and the buttons for under clothing—there is a constant demand for novelty of design and pattern. One firm, in the general button trade, that has been in existence but little more than fifteen months, has produced in that time 740 different patterns of coat buttons, 249 of crest and livery buttons, and 1,135 of vest buttons. Another firm has produced in three years upwards of 5,000 new patterns of Florentine buttons. The novelty consists of constant variations of size, shape, texture, material, colour, and pattern. One of the oldest firms in the trade has kept no record of the number of its patterns, but within the last thirty years has four times commenced numbering them at 1, and has each time reached the cumbrous mark of six figures, or 100,000. As an instance of the saving effected by extensive tailors, if not by the public, in consequence of the cheapness of the Florentine over the ancient gilt and plated button, it may be related that a celebrated firm in London, which less than twenty years ago paid as much as £1,000 per annum for its button account, now pays less than £150, although it uses double or even treble the quantity. Birmingham not only supplies the immense home demand for buttons, but exports large quantities to almost every part of the world. The Florentine button of Birmingham is far superior to anything of the same kind made in France or Germany, and is equally cheap, if not cheaper. An attempt recently made to introduce continental buttons proved a failure, for the reasons just stated. The men of Birmingham, though quite willing to allow foreigners to see what they do, and rather unwilling to let them see in all respects how they do it, do not actually fear foreign competition in their own or in any of the markets of the world. In some markets Birmingham, on account both of the excellence and cheapness of its buttons, may be said to possess a practical, though not a theoretical, monopoly. Two kinds—the round gilt and plated button, such to be employed for pages' and children's dresses, and the plated and gilt sugar-loaf button, used for the same purpose—although somewhat out of fashion at home, continue to be manufactured by millions. Many ton loads of them annually leave Birmingham for the coasts of Africa, where they find a ready market among the negresses, who wear strings of them as ornaments for their legs and arms, and exchange for them gold-dust, ivory, and spices.

Upon the whole, the condition of the adults employed in the button manufacture of Birmingham may be considered to be favourable. They receive a fair rate of wages for work that is not exhaustive, nor, with a few exceptions already noticed, unwholesome. The hours of labour are nominally twelve hours a day, but out of these two are allowed for meals—thus reducing the actual day's work to ten hours. Though liable to the distress caused by sudden changes of fashion, which throw out of work the hands that may have been engaged for a lifetime in one particular branch of a manufacture—and of which the case of the plated and gilt button manufacturers ruined by the invention of the Florentine button was the most striking—it must be remembered that such cases are rare, and that only one has occurred within the memory of a generation. In this respect, therefore, the button makers have not had much to complain of. With regard to the employment of such large numbers of children in the manufacture of the Florentine, the horn, the glass, and the pearl button—a very serious and important question suggests itself, which is, whether society does not pay too dearly for the cheapness which renders necessary the employment of these infants? The master manufacturers themselves, as will have been observed from the statements made in this and the preceding letter, do not directly employ many young children under thirteen years of age. Infants from seven upwards are employed by the adults to assist them, and the manufacturers have little or no control over them, and neither know their names, their age, nor the amount of remuneration which they receive for their labour. The "cobbers," who are mostly boys of seven or eight years of age, are employed by the metal button stampers to arrange the buttons in a row, in readiness for the stamp, and must work as long as the adults whom they assist. If the adult has been keeping holiday, or Saint Monday, and is desirous of making up for lost time by working over-hours towards the end of the week, the child must be over-worked, and towards night it is no rare occurrence to see children nodding over their labour. A witness examined by the Government Commissioner, in 1840, stated that when there was extra work of this kind, the boys got sleepy and tired, and had to be shaken, or otherwise intimidated, to be kept awake. The boys sometimes object to the over-work, and would not, if left to their own free-will, submit to it—especially in those cases where the extra amount they earn is not given to them but to their parents. Many parents in Birmingham not only partially live upon the labour of their infants, but are known to borrow money, to be repaid by the future labour of their offspring. Another witness, examined on the same inquiry, stated "that he had often seen boys of 7, 8, or 9 years old severely beaten and knocked about for not being able to work fast enough for the men when the latter were anxious to make up for lost time." Parents often employ their own children to assist them as "cobbers," or "cobs." The "putters-in," or young girls who assist in the Florentine business, are, in the same way as the "cobbers" or "cobs," removed from the control and superintendence of the manufacturer, being hired and paid by older girls working on their own account. It is the opinion of many that if all these children, both male and female, were employed directly by the manufacturer, they would be better treated than they are at present; but it is argued on the other side, that the ordinary stimulus of self-interest is not sufficient in the case of such infants to keep them to their work, and that the necessary amount of labour could not be extracted from them by any other than the present system, when they work under the eye of the individual whose own earnings depend to a large extent upon the effective assistance which they render. It is quite clear, whether the system be or be not remediable, that, so far as the future interests of their children are concerned, it is highly injurious. Confined as they are for ten hours every day at the very least—and often, in cases of extra hours being taken by the adult whom they serve, confined for two or three hours in addition—they are too weary and sleepy, and in every way unfit, to attend an evening school with advantage. They are not only trained to one particular branch of a manufacture, such as cobbing, or putting-in, by which they learn nothing likely to be of service to them in their future life, but they are completely shut out from the chance of education on week days. On the Sunday their physical health requires fresh air and exercise; and they must forego this advantage to a great extent if their parents send them to a Sunday-school. It may be questioned whether the education they receive at a Sunday-school is calculated to be of much service to them. Doubtless, it is better than no education at all; but, as the greater portion of the Sunday-schools object to teach writing, arithmetic, modern geography, physiology, or any of those branches which fit the young mind for the active life of the world, it is clear, however good in itself such education may be, that it is not sufficient. But, as this point is of great importance, and as the evil of the employment of such infants in the various sub-divisions of manufacture is not confined to the button trade, but extends to the pin, the nail and screw, the pen, and many other branches of industry, I propose to make it the subject of a separate investigation, without reference to the particular manufacture in which the children may happen to be engaged. I shall merely say, in addition to the statement with regard to the button trade, that although the adults and young women of fifteen or sixteen upwards appeared, as far as I have seen, to be generally well paid and well clad, the young children were almost without exception ragged and dirty in the extreme. Many of the cobbers stood to their work without a sufficiency of clothes to cover them;—their knees peering through holes in their trowsers, and their shoulders through their shirts or jackets. They had for the most part a sickly and unwholesome look. The female children, or "putters in," were equally squalid and pale, and prematurely serious, if not melancholy, in the expression of their countenances. The women employed in the manufacture—even in that hardest, most disagreeable, and most inferior branch of it, the grinding and polishing of steel—expressed their satisfaction with their earnings, as being far superior to what a woman could earn at any description of needle-work. Eighteen-pence or two shillings a day were the common wages of a woman who chose to work with regularity, and many were able to earn as much as 14s. or 15s. a week. Very few complained of the hardness or unwholesomeness of their work.

LABOUR AND THE POOR.

BIRMINGHAM.

[FROM OUR SPECIAL CORRESPONDENT.]

THE MANUFACTURE OF FIRE-ARMS.

LETTER V.

According to the census of 1841, the number of persons employed in Birmingham in the various subdivisions of trade required in the manufacture of a gun, in its three great parts—of barrel, lock, and stock—was 2,400. This number, however, cannot be held to have expressed with anything like accuracy the total number of persons who procured their subsistence by the gun trade of Birmingham. Beyond the limits of the town and borough, in the outlying districts, and in the towns of Wolverhampton, Bilston, Darlaston, Wednesbury, West Bromwich, and Walsall, reside large numbers of gun-barrel filers, gun-lock filers, gun-lock makers, gun-lock forgers, and countless other trades, all dependent for their orders upon the gun-makers of Birmingham and London. A gun gives employment to almost as great a variety of trades as the mechanism of a watch. Of this latter it was stated before a committee of the House of Commons that there were a hundred and two distinct branches of the art, to each of which a boy might be put apprentice.

It is probable that at the time of the last census the 2,400 persons mentioned in connection with the gun manufacture of Birmingham only included the gun-barrel makers, the gun stockers, and the gun finishers—and that if the calculation had included the numerous trades beyond the limits of the town, employed in lock-making in all its complicated processes and sub-divisions of labour, the number would have been from 5,000 to 6,000. At the present time it is estimated that about 1,000 persons are employed in Birmingham in the manufacture of gun-barrels alone; and that if this number were multiplied by six, the product would represent as nearly as possible the

total number of persons in the town and neighbourhood who are employed in the manufacture of fire-arms. Birmingham principally supplies the British army and navy and the East India Company's service
with muskets, and executes orders for some of the locks, and nearly
all of the barrels, used by the various persons who reside in London
and other parts of the country, and call themselves gunmakers—but
whose principal business is to put together and otherwise finish the
materials which Birmingham produces. Besides military guns it supplies fowling-pieces and sporting guns of every variety for the home
and colonial trade. It also manufactures large numbers of inferior
guns for traffic with the Africans. There is a constant demand for
guns for Africa. "There is," said a manufacturer, "no end of the quantity of guns made here for that market. I do not know whether they are
wanted for purposes of war among the tribes, or for sporting, but probably for both. I should imagine that the battles among the countless
tribes, whose very names we are ignorant of, create the greatest portion of the demand. The Kings of Ashantee and Dahomey are both
said to be good customers. We do not know in Birmingham to whom
they go, as the manufacturers here merely execute the orders which
they receive from the merchants of London and Liverpool. The larger
portion are taken by the Liverpool merchants. They are bartered generally for gold dust, elephants' tusks, palm oil, spices, &c. I should
say that the wars among the blacks constantly keep a couple of thousand men at work in Birmingham." The trade with the United States
is not so extensive, as the Americans prefer to manufacture their own
gun-barrels. Birmingham, however, and the districts around, supply
the United States with large quantities of locks, which are produced
better in quality and cheaper in price than in America. But before
describing the present state of the trade, a short account of its rise
and progress in England will be necessary.

Though small arms were introduced at a comparatively recent
period, there is some doubt as to the derivation of the word "gun."
The article was produced in Germany before it was known in England, but we did not borrow the word from the Germans. Guns, or
small arms, before the adaptation of the flint and steel to that purpose, were provided with a matchlock, and were called *büchsen* or
boxes, *donner-büchsen*, or thunder-boxes, and sometimes *hakenbüch-
sen* or "hook-boxes." From the word *hakenbüchse* is derived the French
arquebuse; and from *donner-büchse*, by an odd corruption, comes the
English word "blunderbuss." After the use of the flint and steel be-

came common, the Germans called the gun a "*flinte.*" The word "cannon," derived from the Latin, *canna*, a tube, was probably the root of the word gun. At least, if that be not the derivation, no other more probable can be suggested.

"The first portable fire-arms were discharged" (says Beckmann, in his 'History of Inventions'), "by means of a match, which, in the course of time, was fastened to a cock for the greater security of the hand while shooting. Afterwards a firestone was screwed into the cock, and a steel plate or small wheel, which could be cocked or wound up by a particular kind of key, was applied to the barrel." At Dresden there is preserved an old *büchse*, on which, instead of a lock, there is a cock with a flint stone placed opposite to the touchhole, and this flint was rubbed with a file till it emitted a spark. This firestone was not at first of a siliceous nature, like that used afterwards, but a compact pyrites or marcasite. But as an instrument of this kind often missed fire, a match, till a late period, was retained along with the wheel. It appears that these fire-arms were invented and used in Germany at the beginning of the sixteenth century. *Muskets*, of which the name was derived from the Latin *muschetus*, a male sparrowhawk, were invented in Spain, and are said to have been first used at the battle of Pavia. They were introduced into the Netherlands by the Duke of Alva in 1567. The lock was invented in the city of Nuremberg in 1517. Pistols were known about the same time. The name is supposed by some to be derived from the town of Pistoia in Tuscany, where they were originally manufactured; and by others, from the Italian *pistola*, an abbreviation of epistola, a letter or missive. The first muskets—those used in the sixteenth and seventeenth centuries—were very heavy, and could not be used without a "rest," and, as already stated, were provided with matchlocks. On their march the soldiers carried only the "rest" and ammunition, and had boys who carried their muskets after them. It was a slow process to load them, not only on account of the unwieldiness of the pieces and because the powder and ball were carried separately, but from the time it took to adjust and prepare the match. These muskets were used in England as late as the civil wars in the time of Charles I. A lighter musket of the same form was then introduced, which was fired without a rest, and these continued to be used till the fourth year of the reign of William III., when the introduction of the flint superseded the old matchlock.

There does not appear to have been any considerable manufacture of fire-arms in England in the sixteenth century. The old matchlocks were imported from Holland and Germany, and it was not until the reign of Charles I. that the English began to make small arms for themselves. The first authentic notice of the English gun-trade is in the year 1638, when the master, wardens, and Society of Gunmakers of the city of London were incorporated by charter of King Charles I. Hutton, in his "History of Birmingham," unaware of the existence of the London corporation of gunmakers, relates a tradition that King William III. was the means of introducing the gun manufacture into Birmingham, and into England at the same time. He says: "King William was once lamenting that guns were not manufactured in his dominions, but that he was obliged to procure them from Holland at a great expense, and with greater difficulty. Sir Richard Newdigate, one of the county members, being present, told the King that genius resided in Warwickshire, and that he thought his constituents would answer his Majesty's wants. The King was pleased with the remark, and the member posted to Birmingham. Upon application to a person in Digbeth, whose name I have forgotten, the pattern was executed with precision, and when presented to the Royal Board gave entire satisfaction. Orders were immediately issued for large numbers, which have been so frequently repeated that they never lost the road." This is all the information given by Hutton on the subject; but it is evident, from the charter granted to the London gunmakers, that guns must have been produced in England more than half a century before this time. There was, however, a greatly increased demand for military guns in the time of King William. "At this period," says the writer of a scarce pamphlet on the manufacture of fire-arms, published in 1829, "the old pattern musquet with the match-lock was superseded by the invention of the flint-lock of the form now in use; and as this was so much superior to the old pattern, it was immediately and universally adopted by all the European nations. Europe at this time being engaged in a general war, the manufacturers of fire-arms, both in London and on the Continent, were unable to supply with sufficient promptitude the demands made upon them for arms of the new pattern. William III., anxious no doubt to be supplied with arms, and finding the manufacturers employed in this branch of trade unable to supply his wants—Birmingham, then rising into importance as a manufacturing town, caught his attention, and, as Hutton states, a pattern of the arms was executed by a Birmingham artist, and being approved of, orders for them would of course follow."

From this period the gun trade in Birmingham very rapidly increased. At the peace of 1714, when the orders given by the Government ceased, the attention of the manufacturers, who had organized large establishments for gun-barrel making and other branches of the trade, was naturally directed to the peace demand which was likely to arise. Fowling-pieces and pistols for home consumption, and trading guns for exportation and barter with the natives of Africa, North and South America, and the islands, gave steady employment to a considerable number of people.

Before the abolition of the slave trade, the Birmingham manufacturers were largely employed by the merchants of London, Liverpool, and Bristol, in producing guns, which were called "slave guns," and sometimes "Guinea guns." They were produced at a very cheap rate— sometimes as low as 5s. 6d. each. These fire-arms neither underwent, nor were intended to undergo, any proof whatever. Immense numbers of them were made with the certainty that if ever they were fired off, they would burst in the discharge. They were called "sham muskets," and "Dutch guns," and were exchanged for slaves on the coast of Africa—a gun for a man.

But, although a considerable trade was carried on in these wretched guns, for this abominable purpose, and there was a population in the town wholly dependent on the gun and pistol manufacture in its various branches, the manufacturers of Birmingham and the neighbourhood were not in a condition to execute the orders that poured in upon them in consequence of the war with France, which broke out in 1793. There were no establishments large enough to take the contracts of the Government, and the Board of Ordnance despatched Lieutenant-Colonel Millar, an artillery officer, to Germany, to purchase muskets. In this service he was engaged for nearly two years, and purchased nearly a quarter of a million of small arms. It was at this time, and for some years subsequently, the practice of the Ordnance department, when the Government needed a supply of arms, to engage with one or more individuals for the number required. These contractors again contracted with the trade, the Board of Ordnance sending down "viewers," or inspectors, from the Tower of London, to inspect them when ready for delivery. The barrels of these arms were either sent up to the Tower, to be proved, or they were proved in the private proof-houses of the manufacturers in Birmingham, under the superintendence of the inspector. About the year 1798, the Ordnance department purchased some land in Birmingham, and erected a proof-house and view rooms, for the purpose of proving the barrels and inspecting the arms after their completion. At the same time the Ordnance department began to make its engagements directly with the individuals employed in the manufacture of the barrels and the locks, and with the gunmaker to set them up complete. From 1793 to 1798 the Irish Ordnance department made large demands upon Birmingham for fire-arms, to arm the militia, fencibles, yeomanry, &c. required for the suppression of the rebellion. During the same period the volunteers in England and Scotland, who purchased their own fire-arms, gave orders which increased to a considerable extent the activity of the manufacture, both in Birmingham and London. But notwithstanding the quantity of guns which were supplied during these years, the Government, in 1803, when war was again declared, found itself without a sufficiency. For an army of 177,000 men, it had but 150,000 firelocks. It was therefore obliged once more to have recourse to Germany, and purchased 293,000 firelocks for about £700,000. "The state of destitution," says the writer of the pamphlet already quoted from, "in which the arsenals of our country were at the period of the war in 1793, and afterwards in 1803, appears to show a remissness on the part of the Board of Ordnance in not having an adequate supply of small arms, and more particularly at the latter of these periods. For, notwithstanding the bareness of our magazines at the peace of Amiens, the Board of Ordnance then ceased giving out orders for any further supply of small arms. Had it still kept the manufacturers employed during the interval of peace, they could have made the number of arms which the Government was compelled to purchase on the Continent, of a superior quality and uniform pattern, and at about one half of the price." Notwithstanding the wants of the Government, the Board of Ordnance did not give any extensive orders in Birmingham until March, 1804, and these orders were at first executed with considerable difficulty, in consequence of the scarcity of hands. The manufacturers, at the peace, discharged a large number of their workmen, who became absorbed by the other trades of the town; but by degrees the greater portion of them, allured by the high wages to be obtained, returned to their old trade, and from 1804 to 1815, the gun manufacture flourished in Birmingham to an extent never before or afterwards attained. From March, 1804, to December 31, 1809, there were made at Birmingham for the Government, independently of fowling-pieces, and guns for the home, colonial, and foreign trade, 1,066,443 barrels, and 857,518 locks. During the 13 years of war there were fabricated in private establishments in Birmingham and London, and at a small manufactory set up by the Government at Lewisham, 2,673,366 stand of arms. Of this number there remained in store, or in use in the army and navy, after the pacification of Waterloo, 939,256—leaving 1,634,110 lost by the chances of war, or remaining in the hands of the allies. From 1803 to 1815 inclusive, Great Britain furnished to her allies and to her own army, navy, militia, and volunteers, upwards of three millions and a quarter of small arms of various kinds, as appears from the following table:—

Arms furnished to the allies (including
   muskets, carbines, pistols, &c.) 2,143,643
Ditto to the regular troops 349,882
Ditto to the regular militia 59,405
Ditto to the local militia 151,969
Ditto to the volunteers 307,583
Ditto to the navy 215,233

       Total 3,227,715

Birmingham produced more than two-thirds of these guns in their complete state, and nearly the whole of the gun barrels. The following table shows the number of barrels for every description of fire-arms, produced in each year at Birmingham from 1804 to 1815 inclusive:—

Years.	Muskets.	Rifles.	Carbines.	Pistols.	Total in each year.
1804	80,123	62	...	...	80,185
1805	110,833	2,938	3,120	1,158	118,049
1806	112,222	15,106	4,418	2,276	134,022
1807	155,839	1,873	6,536	8,942	173,190
1808	229,355	6,334	15,245	21,402	272,336
1809	265,049	1,433	5,571	16,608	288,661
1810	299,382	133	313	6,405	306,233
1811	316,760	1,886	178	3,611	322,435
1812	409,961	2,260	7,694	16,347	436,262
1813	413,918	466	24,878	51,576	490,838
1814	282,215	91	6,566	23,313	312,185
1815	98,689	...	442	4,117	103,248
Total ...	2,774,346	32,582	74,961	155,755	3,087,644

The following is the number of locks it produced within the same time:—

Years.	Muskets.	Rifles.	Carbines.	Pistols.	Total.
1804	81,021	20	...	...	81,041
1805	91,148	4,721	4,006	...	99,875
1806	102,047	11,980	...	...	114,027
1807	119,389	8,047	1,420	6,071	134,927
1808	175,589	5,947	1,899	9,440	192,875
1809	223,345	2,412	205	8,811	234,773
1810	290,539	1,288	24	10,080	301,931
1811	333,142	2,690	179	9,643	345,654
1812	412,234	134	9,585	24,291	446,244
1813	371,694	99	23,805	62,018	457,616
1814	347,396	...	3,601	20,191	371,188
1815	98,684	...	368	...	99,052
Total ...	2,646,228	37,338	45,092	150,545	2,879,203

The next table shows the total number of complete arms manufactured and set up in Birmingham yearly during the war:—

Years.	Muskets.	Rifles.	Carbines.	Pistols.	Total.
1804	36,606	85	...	...	36,691
1805	50,789	839	...	200	51,828
1806	60,756	1,597	...	1,800	62,353
1807	58,323	1,788	...	1,800	61,911
1808	87,336	3,296	...	2,759	93,391
1809	148,600	557	...	2,217	151,374
1810	182,596	1,139	...	3,060	186,795
1811	219,873	1,924	...	5,074	226,871
1812	274,026	1,525	4,123	9,067	288,741
1813	279,681	497	17,934	22,531	320,643
1814	168,049	721	8,595	6,784	184,149
1815	68,800	727	8,126	982	78,635
Total ...	1,682,610	14,695	38,778	54,474	1,743,382

To these large numbers of fire-arms made for the Board of Ordnance must be added those made during the same period for the East India Company, the locks and barrels of which were manufactured in Birmingham, and sent to London to be made up into finished arms, and also the fowling-pieces and trade guns. The former have been roughly computed at from 800,000 to 1,000,000, and the latter at about 500,000.

The following statement, made by an intelligent working man, supposed to be the oldest member of the gun trade in Birmingham, will show what was the condition of the working men at this period. It will be seen that wages were very high, and that the operatives in this trade and their employers had reason to thank the Emperor Napoleon for sending them such profitable employment. He said, in answer to my inquiries:—

"I was apprenticed to a gun-stocker in Birmingham in the year 1804. The trade was very active at that time on account of the war, and the gun-stocking was considered one of the best businesses going. The gun-barrel forging and the lock making were equally brisk. I never heard how many men were employed in the manufacture of fire-arms in this town at that time, but there must, one way or the other, have been many thousands. There were fourteen contractors for the Government. My employer was not a contractor, but worked for a contractor, and we turned out of our establishment as many as 800 guns in a week. It was calculated that Birmingham at that time produced at the rate of a gun a minute all the year round, night and day, Saturday and Sunday. This would be 10,080 per week, or 524,545 per annum. I do not know whether the statement was correct; but it was the general belief of people in the trade during my apprenticeship. I cannot state the wages received by the gun-barrel forgers or grinders, or by the lock-makers; but those of the stockers were very high. In the year 1808, in the fourth year of my apprenticeship, I earned as much as £3 a week, of which £2 were my master's 'stint,' and £1 was for myself. The price of provisions was very high. I paid 10d. a pound for meat, and often as much as 7s. for a peck of flour. I was out of my time in 1811, and could then earn from £3 to £4 a week single-handed. The trade was so good that I was obliged to engage boys to help me. I took three apprentices. Between us four, I being just then turned of 21 years of age, we earned about £8 a week, and after I had paid the apprentices, I had upwards of £5 for myself. The boys trimmed the stocks out and let the barrels in, and also the locks. The workmen were paid by the piece, and some, being quicker and more expert than the rest, made more money. I knew one very clever workman who could stock ten guns a day single-handed. The price at that time was from 1s. 8d. to 2s. for stocking a gun; and if he chose to work hard six days in the week, he could have made from £5 to £6 as his wages. He did not, however, stick so close as that, and preferred a Monday's drinking now and then. There was a union of the gun-stockers, but they never held together well, nor did any good. The trade struck once when I was an apprentice. The price for stocking a gun was then 2s., and the men wanted 2s. 6d. The masters refused to make the advance, and the men, after being out a fortnight, were obliged to give in without getting a rise. 'Bounty money' was very common in our trade during the war. It was the practice for a workman to hire himself for a year to a master, and agree to stock, within that period, a certain number of guns every week, upon condition of receiving the bounty. The bounty was paid down at the time of agreement, and was at the rate of a pound per annum for each gun produced per week. That is to say, if a man bound himself to finish fifty guns per week for a year, he received a bounty of £50 over and above the price of his work. The common bounty was £50, as fifty guns a week were about as many as a man could undertake with safety, but sometimes men took the bounty of £100, and were able to complete the bargain. They were of course obliged to obtain assistance, and take on apprentices. I have heard of instances, but not often, of men receiving the bounty, and afterwards running away. The employer had the power of bringing up a workman before the magistrates if he received his bounty and would not do the work. The penalty for breach of the contract was imprisonment, besides restitution of the bounty money. Our trade went on well until the Battle of Waterloo, and for some time afterwards. The Government at the peace gave the contractors three years' work in infantry and other guns, and paid a very high price for stocking. It was as much as 3s. a musket. This was soon reduced, however, to 2s. This work kept us going until 1818, and after the contracts were out many of the gun-stockers, or all who could not obtain employment in fowling pieces and African guns, were obliged to distribute themselves in other trades. They turned their hands to carpentering, or anything. Very few of them had saved money. They thought the war would always last, and that they would always be able to earn high wages. I was like the rest. I had saved nothing; and being unable to procure employment at my old trade, I would have been glad to have been employed as a porter to carry coals. Indeed, I would have accepted any kind of work; and, after being quite out of employment for a considerable time, I was obliged to accept a place at an oil-cloth factory, at 14s. a week."

I shall return to the story of this working man in a subsequent portion of this letter. The history of the trade will be more intelligible if I break off his narrative here, and relate other circumstances which did not fall within his experience.

In the year 1804, the Government, with the view, as alleged, of checking the large prices demanded by the Birmingham gun manufacturers, and of increasing the supply, resolved to establish a gun manufactory of its own. The subject was not brought under the notice of Parliament until 1806, when the sum of £15,000 was voted for the erection of suitable buildings for the fabrication of locks and barrels at Lewisham, near Blackheath. The further sum of £7,000 was granted in the following year. Operations were not actually commenced until 1808. It was both predicted and wished by the Birmingham people, that the Government would fail in its experiment; and they loudly complained of the unfairness of the competition. They alleged that the Government enticed away their best workmen, and they asserted that instead of manufacturing at a cheaper rate, it would ultimately be found that private traders could have supplied with sufficient promptitude all the arms required, and at a cost considerably under what the nation would have to pay in turning gunmaker for itself. The result verified the prediction. Up to the 1st of July, 1810, the Lewisham gun factory had cost upwards of £66,000, and the Government was only in a position to turn out 25,000 barrels and 18,000 locks in a year; while Birmingham, at a much cheaper rate, was turning out upwards of 300,000 barrels, 300,000 locks, and 186,000 stand of arms in a year. The Government had also an establishment in the Tower; but its operations were confined to the rough stocking and setting up of arms, with the materials supplied from Birmingham and Lewisham, and by different private manufacturers under contract with the Board of Ordnance. In consequence of the complaints of the Birmingham and London gunmakers, a commission of military inquiry was instituted to investigate the working of both these establishments. The commission, after a long inquiry, decided in favour of the works pursued at the Tower, and against those of Lewisham. The commission recommended that the Ordnance Department should confine itself to the setting up of guns, and that it should cease manufacturing both locks and barrels. The Board of Ordnance, however, resolved, notwithstanding the report of the commission, to continue its experiment; and, in 1813, obtained the authority of Parliament for the erection of a second gun barrel and lock factory at Enfield, in Middlesex. This new manufactory was not completed until 1815, when the war was at an end. It cost upwards of £70,000 in building and machinery. "Both of these establishments," says the author of the pamphlet from which a portion of these particulars have been taken, "were perfectly useless; and this continued till the year 1819, when the manufactory at Lewisham was dismantled, and the building and machinery sold by auction. At the manufactory at Enfield, as if for an excuse for keeping up the establishment, a few workmen were employed in repairing old arms; and by a peculiar system of economy a number of old waste gun-barrels were cut up, and worked into nails and other iron-mongery for the Woolwich department—a most singular process of transmuting metals, as the cost of such manufacture must have been in about the same ratio as that of exchanging silver for iron. It may be added, that in addition to this branch of manufacture, the workmen were employed for some months in making fencing masks for serjeants of infantry, to protect their faces while learning the broad-sword exercise. The cost of these to the country was equally extravagant." No returns of the annual charge upon this manufactory, or of the number of articles fabricated, was ever published; but the loss to the country was estimated by the Birmingham gun manufacturers, in 1828, to have then exceeded £500,000. They also stated that the Board of Ordnance, by sending its agents through the country and bidding against the private manufacturers of arms, raised the price of walnut timber used for the stocks of fire-arms from 2s. 6d. a foot to 7s., 8s., and even 12s.—thus inflicting a serious injury upon every one who held a Government contract.

In the year 1816, the gun and lock makers, and other inhabitants of Birmingham, signed a requisition to the high bailiff; and on the 21st of May, a public meeting was held, and very numerously attended, at which the injury inflicted upon the private manufacturer, and upon the tax-payers generally, by the wasteful competition of the Government, was pointed out. The folly of attempts to manufacture gun-barrels—of which the principal items of expense were coal and iron—at such places as Enfield and Lewisham, removed at least a hundred miles from the coal and iron districts, was also dwelt upon by the principal speakers. It was resolved that a petition to the House of Commons should be presented, and that a deputation, composed, with two exceptions, of persons unconnected with the gun trade, should proceed to London. They were instructed, before having the petition presented, to seek interviews with the Lords of the Treasury and with the Board of Ordnance. In pursuance of these instructions, they sought and obtained audience of both, and urged upon the Government the policy and necessity of relinquishing entirely the fabrication of fire-arms—of applying the establishments of Lewisham and

Enfield to some other purpose—and of leaving the future supply of arms and materials entirely to the enterprise of private individuals. The Government did not accede to the propositions, and the deputation, therefore, resolved to present their petition and bring the subject under the notice of Parliament. It was placed for that purpose in the hands of the members for Warwickshire; but in the forenoon of the day on which it was proposed to present it, the Board of Ordnance made an offer to the deputation, which, though it did not entirely meet the demands of the Birmingham manufacturers, the deputation deemed it expedient to accept. In a letter of the 6th of June, 1816, the Secretary to the Board of Ordnance informed the deputation, "that the Master-General and the Board, having taken into consideration the representation submitted to them, and adverting to the extensive and ample store of arms in the several Ordnance depôts, had come to the determination of not employing the Ordnance small arms manufactory for any other object than that of the repair of arms." He added "that, should a demand arise for the supply of new arms, the Board would receive from the trade the same proportion of such supply as was furnished in the time of the war, provided the manufacturers were able and willing to supply as good articles and at as low prices as the Board could provide them by their own manufactory, or obtain them elsewhere." Upon this the deputation returned to Birmingham, and the petition was not presented.

In the year 1813 a proof-house for guns, in addition to the proof-house of the Ordnance department, was established in Birmingham. Before that time every manufacturer proved his own gun-barrels on his own premises—or, as in the case of the slave guns, dispensed with the process altogether. In the course of the year 1812 several meetings of the gun barrel and gun makers of Birmingham were held, "to take into consideration the imperfect manner in which gun-barrels were proved, and to devise a remedy." It was ultimately resolved that application should be made in the next session of Parliament for leave to introduce a bill, making it compulsory for all barrel makers to have their barrels proved, either at the proof-house to be erected in Birmingham or at the proof-house of the Gunmakers' Company in London. This act received the Royal assent on the 10th of July, 1813, and a proof-house was erected accordingly. This building and the process of proving will be described in a subsequent Letter, along with the other processes to which a gun is subjected in its three great divisions, of barrel, lock, and stock. At present the proof-house is introduced in connection with the statistics of the trade. There are now two proof-houses in Birmingham—one belonging to the Board of Ordnance, where not only the gun barrels but the locks are proved and viewed; and the other belonging to the Gunmakers' Company, where gun barrels for private orders undergo the proof. The following is an account of the guns and pistols proved at the latter establishment, from its first opening to the end of the year 1828. It does not include muskets for the Government—but only fowling-pieces and trade guns of every description:—

Years.	Gun Barrels.	Pairs of Pistols.	Total.
1813 to 1814	14,861	6,664	21,525
1815	77,991	13,143	91,134
1816	116,686	10,745	127,431
1817	87,217	9,456½	96,673½
1818	129,935	14,843½	144,778½
1819	102,499	18,118	120,617
1820	66,099	18,469	85,568
1821	63,754	10,825	74,579
1822	56,419	9,535	65,954
1823	97,926	10,521	108,447
1824	104,713	8,611½	113,324½
1825	159,740	11,555	171,295
1826	125,745	14,425	137,170
1827	73,306	8,649	81,955
1828	68,615	8,362	76,977

I regret that I am not able to append a statement of the guns proved every year, from 1828 to 1850 inclusive. Though several attempts have been made to procure it for me, there seems to be some obstacle in the way. Whatever it is, I have been unable to surmount it. Why the information should be withheld, I am at a loss to imagine.

A continuation of the statement made by the aged gun-stocker, whose experience of the trade during the war has been already detailed, will afford an idea of the state of the gun manufacture during the last few years, and of the causes which operate to elevate or depress the condition of the operatives:—

"After working at an oil-cloth factory for three years, I went to London and tried to get employment at my old trade. I was after a time successful, and remained nine years in London. I worked at gun stocking for a contractor to the East India Company, and received from 30s. to 2l. a week. The wages were not regular. The barrels and locks of these guns were principally made in Birmingham and the neighbourhood, and were sent to London to be set up. I returned to Birmingham in 1830, and got permanent employment at an average of about 27s. a week. I remained on Government work for ten or twelve years, when my eyes began to fail, and I could not see to do the fine work with the care required. In 1842, I was obliged to take work on the common guns, such as are made for the African trade. They are the commonest guns produced in Birmingham, and there is always a fair demand for them from the London and Liverpool merchants. I prepared the beech stocks from the rough, and got from 18s. to 20s. a week. The Government guns have walnut stocks. Walnut is a harder and better wood, and requires a superior finish. The wages of gun-stockers became very low, and the trade from 1842 to the commencement of 1848 was not in a good state. There was, however, a great stir in the gun manufacture in 1848. The French Revolution cut out plenty of work for us. There was such a demand for guns from the continent, that we could not supply them fast enough. Wages were for a time as high as they were during my apprenticeship. As much as 3s. was paid for stocking a single-barrelled or store gun. This stir lasted for about seven months, I think. There was not a man in the trade that could not get plenty of work at high wages. The manufacturers were obliged to take on men and boys to learn the business. A good stocker could earn from £3 to £4. I do not know what the forgers, grinders, borers, and lockmakers could make; but I suppose, if the stockers were so well paid, that any man who knew his business, and chose to work in any department of it, could have made money at that time. There was so much work, that the stockers grew saucy and would not work at bad or very hard stocks which required extra labour. They would pick and choose. Sometimes the men, after working hard for the week, and gaining £3 or £4, would play for the week after. Very often they would not work above three days in the week. The men in our trade drink a good deal, when they have high wages; but I don't know that they are worse than the men in other trades. I should think they are not. Wages are very low in the gun trade now. The demand caused by the French Revolution has long since died away, and I know of instances in which the same men do not get above 1s. 2d. for stocking a double barrelled gun, who would have got 2s. 6d. or 3s. for stocking the same article in 1848."

Upon application to a master manufacturer for information on some points to which the attention of the working-man had not been directed, I learned that prior to the year 1836 there was a considerable trade in guns and pistols with America. Since that time the Americans have begun to manufacture the barrels for themselves, and they have also got supplies of an inferior kind of gun from Liege, in Belgium. Double-barrelled guns that sold to the Americans in 1834, 1835, and 1836, for £3, have been reduced as low as 30s., in consequence of Belgian competition. The Belgians supply a gun for the American market as low as 21s. or 22s., but the locks are not equal to the English locks. The principal American gun barrel manufactory is at Hartford, in Connecticut. From April, 1848, to the end of the year, the price of military guns for the continental market was nearly doubled. The demand came principally from Sardinia, Sicily, and Denmark, and my informant said that he had the greatest difficulty in executing orders for want of hands. He could at that time have sold more than ten times the number of gun barrels which he was able to produce. The continental demand has now wholly ceased, and many of the manufacturers have large quantities on hand which were executed in the expectation of its continuance.

The principal varieties of fire-arms manufactured in Birmingham, besides the military musket and the African gun, are the fowling-piece, the blunderbuss, the rifle, the fusil, the carbine, and the pistol. To non-professional readers a short statement of the characteristics which distinguish each may be interesting:—

The *Musket* is the commonest description of gun, and is used for military purposes alone, except in Africa, the kings and chiefs of which, as already stated, make large demands on Birmingham for the article. In Europe and America, the musket is never manufactured for sportsmen. Muskets are commonly brass-mounted. They have a large and heavy barrel with a wide bore of three-quarters of an inch. They are generally stocked up to near the end of the barrel. The stock reaches within a few inches of the muzzle. The African gun is stocked with beechwood, dyed, and is produced at a wholesale price of from 7s. 9d. to 8s. 6d. The military guns are percussioned, but the African guns are made with the old flint-lock.

The *Fowling piece* is a much lighter gun altogether. It is lighter both in the stock and barrel. The bore is not uniformly three-quarters of an inch, as in the musket, but is usually smaller. Fowling pieces for duck shooting are usually of the same bore as the musket, and very long in the barrel. The fowling piece is altogether a superior article, and is mounted with steel instead of brass.

The *Blunderbuss* has a short barrel of from 12 to 18 inches, and a wide bore, with a bell nose or muzzle, which gives it a very formidable appearance. This was the article in favour with the highwaymen of the olden time.

The *Fusil* only differs from the military musket in being smaller in the bore and lighter altogether.

The *Carbine* is the same as the *fusil*, except in length. It is considerably shorter, and is solely intended to be used on horseback.

The *Rifle* derives its name from the spiral groove inside the barrel, which causes the ball to spin round or rotate on its axis while passing through the barrel, and thus to acquire a more direct course on its progress towards its mark. The number of evolutions made by the ball in passing through the grooves varies in different rifles; but one complete evolution in three feet of rifling is considered about the average. The number of turns in the spiral, and the depth of the grooves, vary according to the practical result aimed at by the manufacturer.

The price of a gun varies according to quality and mounting—from the common African gun at 7s. 9d., to the double-barrelled rifle at thirty or forty guineas.

As this Letter has already extended to a considerable length, and a number of interesting details have yet to be given of the multitude of trades engaged in the manufacture of one gun—from the gun-barrel forger and the gun-lock maker, to the setter up, or finisher of the complete instrument—I must postpone the conclusion of the subject, and the examination of the present social state of the operatives, to a future communication.

LABOUR AND THE POOR.

—◆—

BIRMINGHAM.

[FROM OUR SPECIAL CORRESPONDENT.]

THE MANUFACTURE OF FIRE-ARMS.

LETTER VI.

It will afford an idea of the great number of trades, for the most part quite distinct from each other, which are employed in the manufacture of a gun, if I select from the "Birmingham Directory" a list of the master manufacturers of the town and neighbourhood employed in the production of lock, stock, and barrel. There are, according to this authority, 114 who call themselves gun makers, 44 gun-barrel makers and forgers, 1 gun-barrel borer, 4 gun-barrel browners, 15 gun-barrel filers, 6 gun-barrel riflers, 3 gun-barrel welders, 2 gun-breech forgers, 1 gun break-off fitter, 3 gun-case makers, 6 gun engravers, 31 gun finishers, 20 gun furniture makers, 33 gun implement makers, 65 gun-lock filers (of whom only 7 reside in Birmingham, and the remainder at Bilston, Wednesbury, Walsall, and West Bromwich), 36 gun-lock makers, 22 gun-lock forgers, 2 gun-nipple manufacturers, 4 gun percussioners, 8 percussion-cap makers, 14 gun polishers, 22 gun stockers, 3 gun-stock varnishers, 3 gun-wadding makers, 1 gun hair-trigger maker, and 7 gun-smiths. Some names appear in two or more of these departments, so that a combination of some of these various trades in one person is not unusual; but, generally speaking, the three great departments of lock, stock, and barrel are so completely distinct, that there is but one establishment in the town where the whole of the parts are manufactured and set up. The operative gun-barrel forger knows nothing of the business in the other parts of a gun, nor even of the other departments of handicraft required in the progress and completion of the very barrel which he makes. The trades employed in making the lock know but little of each other, and nothing of the barrel or of the processes of manufacture which it undergoes, while the stocker is ignorant of every part of the manufacture but his own. The list, ample as it is, does not include the whole of the trades in either of the three great divisions of the manufacture of fire-arms, as will be seen from the following sketch of the various processes to which each of the parts is subjected before they are finally joined together to form the complete gun.

As the most important part of the gun is the barrel, I shall commence my description with an account of a visit to one of the principal establishments in the town, where I received most valuable and interesting information upon the subject of the manufacture generally, as well as on the social condition and earnings of the workmen. On entering the spacious premises I was conducted to a shed, to see in its first stage the raw material of the future gun-barrels. A large heap of loose steel lay upon the ground. Around it were gathered a number of boys and men, engaged in sorting the material into smaller heaps, preparatory to its being consigned to the furnace. A process, the reverse of turning the sword into the ploughshare, was here going on. Among the peaceful articles about to be converted into murderous implements, and forming a very heterogeneous mass of articles, lay innumerable sheets of waste steel from the button and pen manufactories, from which the blanks for buttons and pens had been pierced or punched out; fragments of steel chains, dog-collars, old knives and forks, steel fenders, hammer-heads, locks, keys, horse-shoes, coach-springs, hinges, iron spoons, steel tubing, fragments of rods from iron bedsteads, and countless other articles in steel and wrought-iron. If any cast-iron is found among the mass, it is carefully excluded as unfit for the purpose of being manufactured into gun-barrels. The next step in the process is the making of the iron. Here a picturesque scene presents itself. The odds and ends of iron and steel, having been bound together, are thrown into the furnaces, which glow with a white heat as the iron doors are opened to receive them. Half a score of men, naked to the waist, their breasts, arms, and faces shining in the red light, and trickling with perspiration, wield large and heavy pointed rods of iron, with which they stir the metal in the furnace, every now and then taking out their rods to dip them in an iron tank full of water which stands close by. The object of this is to prevent the rods from being fused or smelted along with the metal which they are employed in stirring; and ever as they are dipped in the water it bubbles up and boils. When the metal is sufficiently heated, it is taken out of the forge with long iron pincers by the half-naked smiths, and dragged along the iron pavement, leaving a brilliant trail of sparks behind it. The next operation is to hoist the mass upon a stupendous anvil, upon which a still more stupendous hammer, weighing no less than three tons, moved by steam power, descends with equable but gigantic force, and gives it a blow which compresses it into about half its previous bulk, and sends the sparks out on every side in a glittering shower. A turn of the enormous pincers, which still hold it upon the anvil, presents another side to the hammer before it again descends, and two or three blows convert the shapeless mass into a thick bar of iron.

This process, however, is but preparatory. In another part of the premises sheets of cold iron, already manufactured, and which have undergone this and the additional process of rolling at another part of the establishment, are subjected by lads to the jaws of a Titanic pair of shears, moved by the same steam power that sets the hammer in motion. These shears—of which the under jaw is stationary, and the upper one, a ton in weight, moves with a slow and quiet motion—cut the iron sheet, which is held to it by a lad. The sheet is from three-quarters of an inch to an inch thick, but is snipped through with as much ease as if it were a piece of writing-paper. At every descent of the quiet but powerful shear, a new length is severed in the same way. These lengths of cold iron are destined to be made into gun-barrels. Taking one of these lengths, let us trace its progress. After being cut it is cast into the forge, and heated to a white heat. It is taken out of the furnace by a workman called a *roller*, who, seizes it with his pincers, passes it between two rollers, revolving upon each other, and moved by steam power—the one concave, and the other convex. Issuing from the side opposite to that which it entered, it is seized by the pincers of another workman, also called a roller, and is found to have curled round in the form of a tube. It is now passed in the same way through a smaller pair of rollers of the same construction, under the pressure of which its edges are brought a little closer than by the first operation. This having been done, a *mandril*, or long bar of iron, is passed through it, and it is once more consigned to the furnace. When of a red heat, it is taken out to undergo the next process, which is that of *welding*. The business of the *welder* is to hammer it round and round on the mandril, so as to make the edges cohere, and to make the mould a perfect tube, without trace of seam or jointure, so that the most practised eye would fail to discover its points of cohesion. In this state the mould is not above 18 inches long, and is much too short and thick for a gun barrel. The next process is to draw it out to the requisite length, a few inches greater than that of the proposed gun barrel. Once more it is consigned to the fire, whence issuing red hot, the mandril is inserted through it, and it is subjected to the operation of a pair of rollers, which in less than half a minute squeeze it out to about double its former length. While still red hot, it is passed back by the workman through a smaller pair of rollers, and receives a few inches of additional length. On an average each mould is subjected seven times to this process, at the end of which it is to all outward appearance a gun barrel, but very rude and rough, and requiring much additional labour of a very different kind to complete it. In this manner are formed the barrels of all the common and cheaper kind of guns, such as are used for the export trade to Africa; and also contract guns of a superior kind for the military service. The barrels of fowling-pieces, called the twisted barrels, which are mostly of Damascus iron, undergo a different process. The following is the manner in which Damascus iron is manufactured, by a description of which the reader who supposes that the city of Damascus has anything to do with the matter will be undeceived.

Three bars of iron and three bars of steel, each three inches wide and half an inch thick, are placed alternately upon each other, so as to form a 3-inch pile, that is, a pile of iron and steel three inches wide and three inches thick. Especial care is taken that the iron and steel are placed alternately. The pile, after being heated red-hot (or, more properly, raised to a welding heat) in the furnace, is rolled or reduced into a bar three inches wide and three-quarters of an inch thick. This process of course increases the length by diminishing the thickness of the bar. It is next cut into pieces of equal length by means of the steam shears, or other cutting instruments—which pieces are piled again, four high, making the pile once more three inches thick, care being taken to have the iron and steel bars so placed as not to have two iron, or two steel sides together. These piles are then put in the furnace, heated to welding heat, and rolled into square rods half an inch thick. These rods are again cut into lengths of about three feet, again heated, and, being fixed into a machine, are twisted into the shape of a screw from end to end. Two of these twisted rods (one forming a right-hand screw and the other a left, with an equal number of twists or screws in each) are then welded together, and afterwards passed through the rolls, coming out in strings about a quarter of an inch thick and three-quarters of an inch wide. The strings of this thickness are for the fore-end or thinnest part of gun-barrels. Two other (right and left) twisted rods are also welded together, and rolled into strings of the same width, but about three-eighths of an inch thick, and these are used for the back part or breech-end of gun barrels.

The Damascus iron, when polished and rubbed with an acid, displays a beautifully mottled appearance, or "figure," which is much admired. At one time horse-shoe stubs were greatly sought after for the purpose of mixing with the steel, as they were of the best iron, and were thought to aid in the production of the "figure." People made it a business to collect these stubs, which often sold as high as 10d. or 1s. per lb. to the gun-barrel makers. They are no longer in the same demand. The Damascus iron having been made, the end of the rod is then grasped by the twisting machine, and held fast by a revolving vice moved by steam power, and twisted while in a cold state, around a mandril, with as much ease as if it were a piece of thread wound round a lady's finger. This is the first stage of the twisted gun-barrel. It is next consigned to the furnace, till it is of a proper heat, when the edges of the spiral are welded together by repeated blows from the hammers of the welders.

The gun-barrel, whether of the common steel or of the twisted Damascus, is now ready for the next operation, which is that of boring. The business of the gun-barrel borer is to clean and polish the interior of the tube, and at the same time to work it to the size or bore required, and to give it a perfectly smooth and even interior surface. This operation is performed by steam power, and is superintended both by men and women. These workpeople are begrimed with dirt, and their hands and faces are black with a thick and pulpy oil, which assumes its colour and consistency from the steel grindings and filings which are wrought out of the gun-barrels. The women have no trace of the sex in their countenances, and are as black, dirty, coarse, and masculine in their appearance as the men among whom they labour. The process of boring is performed by an angular rod of the hardest steel, which is made to revolve in the barrel by steam power, and which scrapes the inner surface as it turns. It is necessary that this rod should not be heated, as the friction would in a short time wear down the angularity and render the rod useless. A constant dripping of cold water is therefore directed upon it, and by this means the boring of an ordinary barrel may be completed in about forty-five minutes. For fine boring the superior barrels of Damascus steel, oil instead of water is used. The barrels are bored with a succession of rods, and the process generally occupies from two hours and a half to three hours, at the end of which time the inner surface of the tube becomes as beautifully smooth and polished as a mirror.

The interior of the barrel being thus completed, it is passed into the hands of a workman whose business it is to bring its outer surface into a more proper and sightly condition, for as yet it is but rough and coarse as it passed from the hammers of the welders. This is the most picturesque part of the manufacture of a gun. Entering a large and gloomy shed, into which a kind of twilight is all the light that penetrates, the visitor sees a number of immense grindstones revolving with dizzy velocity. The steam power which sets in motion all the other machinery of the "mill" moves these ponderous blocks of sandstone, of which the smallest measures, when new, from five to six feet in diameter, and is two feet wide in the rim. The weight averages three tons; and such is the velocity at which they turn, that when it has been wished to stop them for any purpose, without stopping the whole machinery of the establishment, they have been known to continue their revolutions for more than ten minutes after the connecting bands have been displaced. Let the reader picture to his imagination no less than twelve or thirteen of these ponderous stones whirling around at this fearful rate, under a dark and gloomy shed—let him further picture a constant dripping of water upon them from a tank on the roof, and conjure before his mind's eye a workman seated before each of them astride upon a wooden block called a "horse," and holding with both hands a gun-barrel to the fast-revolving rim—let him fancy the loud sharp noise of the grinding, the monotonous whiz of the machinery, the semi-darkness of the place—and picture to himself a stream, or rather torrent, of sparks rushing upwards to the roof, from the iron tube which each workman holds, as if the very substance of the metal were being converted by his grindstone into flashes and sparks, and as if that conversion were the whole object of the process—and he will have a faint and imperfect idea of the scene presented in the grinding shed of a large gun-barrel foundry. Should the hand of the workman come into contact with the grindstone, the flesh would be ground or torn from the bones; or should the barrel itself, as presented to the grindstone, revolve in the naked hands, the agony would be too great for endurance. The right hand of the workman is therefore protected with a thick piece of leather, fitting on the thumb and palm, while the left grasps a mandril, which is inserted through the bore of the barrel. It is curious to note that each workman is the colour of the stone at which he works. Clothes, hair, face, and hands, are covered with the mingled dust of the grindstone and the steel. Some of them are formed of red sandstone blocks, and the workman, from top to toe, is of a dingy red. Others are of a lighter-coloured stone, and the workman is of a dirty yellow; and others are as gray as granite—workmen and stone alike. It is not usual for women to be employed at grinding gun-barrels at the grindstones, but they are often employed at the lighter work of grinding ramrods. The gun-barrel grinding is considered the most unwholesome as well as the most dangerous part of the gun manufacture. The steel dust is thought to affect the lungs and shorten the lives of the workmen; and there is also a danger that these immense stones, whirling with such great velocity, may be unsound or flawed, and that they may fly to pieces, and maim or kill the workmen. I entered into a conversation with a grinder upon these and other points connected with his occupation. His grindstone was at rest, and he was engaged in indenting the surface of the rim with a pick, to give it additional roughness. His hair, eyebrows, and eyelashes were filled with a red dust; his hands, his face, his cap, his clothes, his shoes, were all red, but of a somewhat darker tinge than his red grindstone, from being intermingled with steel and iron dust. He was a man of about thirty years of age, and looked strong and healthy. He said—

"My grindstone weighed, when it was new, about three tons, and was exactly six feet six inches in diameter. The natural grit is not sufficiently hard to grind the barrels, and we are obliged to roughen it. The diameter of this stone is now only four feet. It has been ground down to this size, and will be ground down to about two feet before I have done with it. A grindstone does not last very long. It might take about four months' work to grind it down from six feet and a half to two feet. Some stones are harder than others, and therefore last longer. I sometimes grind a stone down ten inches in a month, and take nearly a ton weight off it. The stones sometimes fly. A stone may be very safe for a month or two, and then a man may grind down to a flaw, and the stone may fly and break his skull, or blind him, or otherwise injure him. No accident ever happened to me, though I have often had a stone fly when I have been at work. I know every day that an accident may happen either to me or my neighbours, but I am not afraid. Constant habit inures us to it, and strangers who hear of these things are a great deal more frightened than we are. There was an accident about four months ago at one of the gun-barrel shops in this town, and a man was hurt very badly, but not killed. Pieces of stone weighing a ton or more have been known to fly through the roof of the shop. Sometimes a stone splits right in halves. We receive good wages in this business. The steel dust affects our eyes and our lungs, and we risk our lives besides. We therefore expect good wages. A grinder ought to get £3 10s. a week when in full work. We generally do when trade is good, but we don't often get full work. In 1848, when guns were wanted for the revolution, we were capitally well off. Those were good times for us, and I wish they'd come again. We have not full work now, not above three days in a week. Barrel-grinding is hard as well as dangerous work, and we are obliged to eat and drink well. I have meat three times a day—at breakfast, dinner, and supper—and I drink a good deal of beer. A pot of porter does not go far with me. I require good feeding. If a man was to 'clam' himself down he would soon be killed at this business. There are a good many small masters in our trade. They hire steam-power, and work for the gun-makers, and do nothing else but the grinding. They require few tools but the grindstones, which are rather expensive on account of the cost of carriage of such large blocks. The best come from Bilston, and may cost £5 or £6."

After the barrel is bored and ground it becomes necessary to have it proved. For this purpose, and before any greater expenditure of labour or money takes place, a "pin," or "nut," is screwed to the breech end, and the barrel is conveyed to the Proving House. This establishment, as stated in the previous letter, was founded in 1813, at the instance of the Birmingham Gunmakers' Company, who obtained an act of Parliament for the purpose. The business of the proof house is under the control and direction of three wardens, who are annually chosen from the general body of guardians and trustees of the company. In addition to the members of the corporation of gunmakers, the lords-lieutenant of the counties of Warwick, Worcester, and Stafford, the members serving in Parliament for these counties, and the magistrates acting in and within seven miles of the town of Birmingham, are *ex officio* guardians of the company. The act was obtained to ensure the proper and careful manufacture of fire-arms in England. Under its provisions, "every person who shall use, or cause or procure to be used, or to be begun to be used, either by ribbing, break-off fitting, or other process, in any progressive state of manufacture, in the making, manufacturing, or finishing of any gun, fowling piece, blunderbuss, pistol, or other description of fire-arms, usually called small arms; or who shall offer for sale, or sell, or cause or procure to be sold, or who shall take, or receive, or cause or procure to be taken or received, or permit or suffer to be received on his behalf, any barrel which shall not first have been duly proved, and marked as proved, at the proof house, established at Birmingham, under the provisions of the act, or some other proof house established by law, shall forfeit and pay for every offence twenty pounds, such penalties to be recovered in a summary way, before two justices of the peace, the one-half to go to the informer, and the other half to the poor of the parish where the offence shall be committed." As many gun-barrels burst in the severe proof to which they are subjected, they are put to the test before they are mounted. Boys may be seen at all hours of the day in the streets of Birmingham carrying the barrels on their shoulders to this establishment, where they are duly received and entered, and proved with all convenient rapidity.

The buildings connected with the proof house form three of the four sides of an interior court; at one extremity of which, and detached, is a small powder magazine. The proof-house itself is a detached building. All the interior of this room is lined with plates of cast-iron, from three quarters of an inch to an inch in thickness; the door and window-shutters of the apartment are also of cast-iron. The barrels are set in two iron stocks; the upper surface of one has a small gutter, to contain the train of powder; on this train the barrels rest, with their touchholes downwards, and in the rear of the breeches of the barrels is a mass of sand. A second mass of sand is formed before the muzzles of the pieces under proof, to receive the balls. When the train of powder is laid, and the gun or pistol barrels placed on the stocks, the window shutters are closed up, and fire is set to the train from without, by the insertion of a bar of red-hot iron through an orifice in the wall. A deafening explosion succeeds. After a short delay, lest any of the barrels should have hung fire, the window-shutters are opened, the smoke dissipates, and the attendants remove the barrels.

The scale of proof is the same as that used by the Board of Ordnance, and by the London Gunmakers' Company, and is at the rate of from three to five times the quantity of powder that would be used for the piece in actual service. It is regulated according to the number of balls to a pound. For a ball of one pound, eleven ounces of powder are used; for two balls to a pound, five ounces and five drachms—and so by a gradually descending scale to balls of from 45 to 50 in the pound, when the weight of powder for proof is five drachms and a half. The fee for proving varies from 2½d. to 1s. per barrel. For any common barrel not above the calibre of 13-16ths of an inch, the fee is 6d.; for every pair of common pistols, 6d.; for every twisted barrel, 9d.; for every pair of twisted pistols, 9d.; and for every barrel above the calibre of 13-16ths of an inch, 1s. It is curious to observe the fantastic shapes into which the barrels that burst under the severe trial of their strength are contorted, twisted, and rent. What is called "spilly" iron, or iron with which sand or other foreign material has been wrought in the process of melting, invariably bursts under the proof. Sometimes the barrel splits into ribbons of iron—at others, it presents an appearance like a stag's antlers; sometimes the end is separated like the prongs of a trident, and sometimes one large gash, or rip, is disclosed from end to end; sometimes the twisted barrels are partially untwisted, and present an appearance not unlike corkscrews. The barrels that appear to have undergone the proof satisfactorily, and that have not burst, are taken out and put aside to undergo a further test, while those which have burst are condemned as old iron. After twenty-four hours the barrels are again examined, and if no discoloration from the saltpetre appears on the exterior, which is a certain sign of a flaw in the iron, they are considered to be fit for service. Should there be any suspicion of a crack or flaw, however slight, which the saltpetre has failed to disclose by discoloration, the gun-barrel is filled with water, and a ball larger than the bore is hammered down into it, and compresses the water so violently, that if there be the slightest crack, it oozes through and betrays the unsoundness. Should the barrels have undergone satisfactorily all these tests, they are marked with two separate marks—one for viewing, and one for proving. The marks made are very light, and are imprinted by a type, or seal, slightly touched by a hammer. The object of the slightness of the mark is to prevent the practice of "sweating" the gun—that is, filing down the barrel after it is proved, to diminish its weight—a practice attended with considerable danger, and occasionally resorted to to meet the demand for light and handsome guns. Some German and Belgian gun-makers are accused of forging the London and Birmingham marks. Such an accusation shows the estimation in which the compulsory proving of British guns is held on the Continent. The marks are very simple and easy of imitation—the one for proof consisting of two sceptres crossed with a crown in the upper angle, and the letters B and C in the left and right, and the letter P in the lower angle. The mark for viewing only differs from the first in substituting the letter V, for the letter P, underneath the crown; and in omitting the right and left letters. In the brisk times of war and revolution, one gun-barrel factory produced for proving as many as 1,000 barrels per week.

Accidents are of rare occurrence at the proving-house; but it happened about three days after my visit to the establishment, that a fatal accident occurred to two very intelligent workmen, who had gone over it with me, and explained the processes. The guns were charged with powder in a separate room, a copper ramrod being employed for safety instead of an iron one. Suddenly, when these two men were conveying from this room a large quantity of gun-barrels which had been charged, and before they had reached the door on their way to the proving shed, the whole of the barrels carried by one of them exploded. One of them received several balls in the groin and other parts of his body. He was immediately conveyed to the hospital, where he expired shortly afterwards. The other received several severe wounds; but happily they were not fatal. The walls and roof of the charging room were blown down by the force of the explosion; and some of the gun-barrels were driven through the air over the adjoining canal. The cause of the accident has never been precisely ascertained.

To return, after this melancholy digression, to the progress of the gun-barrel. Having been proved, it passes into the hands of a workman, called the *Jiggerer*, who makes and fastens the tail pin, or pin that is screwed to the breech end. After this, no further progress can be made in the manufacture of the gun until the second of the three great component parts of barrel, lock, and stock, is prepared. The lock manufacture is a separate business, and is carried on to a large extent in Birmingham, as well as in the towns and villages around, particularly at Wolverhampton, Darlaston, and Wednesbury. The number of pieces in a lock is very considerable, and each piece employs workpeople who produce no other part of the lock. The two great divisions of the gun-lock trade are the *forgers* and the *filers;* the forgers being those who manufacture the various pieces in the rough, and the filers those who file them, polish them, and fit them together. The following is a complete list of the pieces in a percussion lock, amounting in all to fifteen:—the plate, the cock, the tumbler, the tumbler-pin, the bridle, the bridle-pin, the scear, the scearspring-pin, the mainspring, the mainspring-pin, the swivel, and the swivel-pin. In the common flint lock, still used in African and export guns, there are eight pieces, in addition to those in the percussion lock. They are—the cock-pin, the jaw, which holds the flint, the hammer, the hammer-spring, the hammer-spring-pin, the roller, and the roller-pin. In Darlaston alone there are from 300 to 320 gun-lock filers. The average earnings of a single hand are about 15s. per week; a man, and a boy to help him, will earn 23s. a week, working a full week, at 14 hours per day. There are from 50 to 60 gun-lock forgers in the same town. A man and a boy will earn, at this branch of the manufacture, about 26s. per week, also working a full week at 14 hours per day. There are, alto-gether, about 20 women employed in these two trades at Darlaston, whose earnings are from 10s. to 12s. a week. Besides these, there are several cock-stampers, whose earnings are about 20s. per week; and pin-forgers, for the interior work of the locks, whose earnings are about 18s. per week. In these four trades in Darlaston, there are about 250 boys employed, from eight to seventeen years of age, whose wages vary from 3s. to 8s. per week. Fourteen hours to the day is the average of the time they work. Darlaston is the principal place for musket locks. Wednesbury manufactures locks for fowling-pieces, and sporting guns generally. In Birmingham, as well as in the neighbouring towns, large numbers of boys are employed in the two great branches of the gun-lock. These boys are not employed directly by the master manufacturers, but they work on their own account for the foreman of the shop, or other workman who requires assistance. They are rarely, if ever, apprenticed, and their employers, persons of their own class, have no control over them after working hours. They are their own masters, except when they live under the parental roof; but, like the rest of the juvenile population in the receipt of wages for piece work, they are said to assume very early the bad habits of manhood, without having the sense or judgment to acquire the good ones.

About ten years ago a patent was taken out for an improvement in the manufacture of gun-locks, which has diminished the number of hands employed. Formerly every piece of the gun-lock was forged by hand on the anvil. By the new process, the parts are stamped in a die, by which means considerable labour and expense are saved. The gun-lock forgers resisted the improvement, and left their work; and the gun-lock filers assisted them in their opposition, by refusing to polish, file, fit, or set up any locks that were not made by hand, on the old principle. They established a society for resisting the stamped locks, and for buying off the new men whom the manufacturers introduced into the business. When the gun trade languished, as it did for some years prior to the revolutions of 1848, they found they could not carry on their opposition, and were glad to accept of work as it offered. But when the revolutionary demand for guns was made from Sardinia, Denmark, and Sicily, in April, 1848, and Birmingham found itself unable to manufacture either barrels or locks with sufficient rapidity, they renewed their opposition, and struck work. The strike did not last long, for the men, finding that machinery was too strong for them, gave in, one by one. The feeling against the stamped locks continues the same; but the men generally appear to be aware of the uselessness of further resistance. There is at the present time no want of hands for all the work required. One of the principal gun-lock factories in Birmingham turns out above 700 complete locks in a week. This trade is generally brisker than that in gun-barrels, as quantities of locks, without the barrels, are exported to the United States and elsewhere.

Barrel and stock being now ready to be united, the two pass into the hands of the *Stocker*, who has provided himself with the third component part of the gun—the stock. The stocker grooves and indents the stock, which is received in Birmingham in a rough state from many places in the neighbourhood, which grow and shape the wood for the purpose. Beech is used for the stocks of the cheap guns, and is grown in large quantities near Stroud in Gloucestershire. Walnut timber is used for the better class of guns. The stocker cuts out chambers in the stock to receive the lock, fits in the lock and barrel, grooves the under part of the stock to receive the ramrod, and puts the implement generally into shape. The wages of the stockers at the present time are from 15s. to 18s. a week; and it is considered that, one year with another, they are without work for eight or ten weeks. There has been a considerable reduction in their wages within the last few years. The low prices at which the Government contracts have been taken since April in the present year have been the means of still further reducing them. When the stocker has done with the gun it passes into the hands of another operative, who is called the "*Screwer-together*" or "*Putter-up.*" As the name implies, his business is to screw on the various parts of the gun. He screws on the heel-plate, made of brass for the butt end of the military, and of steel for the sporting guns; he also screws on the guard that protects the trigger, puts in the trigger-plate, lets in the pipes to hold the ramrod, puts on the nose or nozzle-cap to prevent the nozzle end of the stock from splitting, and screws in the side pieces, and all the other mountings whatever they may be. The wages of the *screwers-together* average 25s. per week, and, like the stockers, they consider themselves fortunate if they can procure nine or ten months' employment in the year.

A new series of adventures now befalls the barrel, lock, and stock, with their mountings. They have all been joined together at considerable expense, but they have been united only to be dissevered. Another workman, called the *Finisher*, deliberately takes the gun to pieces, and unscrews and unfits everything—lock, barrel, and mountings. Assisted by boys, he files and smoothes the mountings, and afterwards sends them to another shop or mill to be polished by women. The lock, having undergone all the necessary filing, is sent to the engraver. If the gun be for the African market it has an elephant and the word "warranted" upon it—and if for the military service at home or abroad, it has the figure of a crown with the words "Tower-proof." The stock in the meantime is sent to the "*Maker-off*," who makes it elegant in all its proportions—doing, in fact, a sort of fine cabinet work, preparatory to its being turned over to the *Cleanser*. The business of the cleanser is to smoothe its surface from end to end with glass or sand paper, and to stain and polish the wood. The cheap beech stocks are stained with logwood and other dyes, each master having his own peculiar stain or preparation, for which he makes to himself a character, and the ingredients of which he keeps as secret as he can, lest his rivals in the business should take away any portion of his custom. The superior gun-stocks, being made of walnut wood, only require polishing, and not staining. While these processes have been going on with the lock and stock, the barrel has also been undergoing a variety of operations. One manufacturer prefers to have his barrels polished at a lathe—another has them filed, smoothed, and burnished by women—a third, especially if they be intended for the African trade, has them merely *browned*, to prevent them from rusting—and a fourth has them painted in imitation of Damascus steel. The real Damascus barrel, for sporting guns of the more expensive kinds, after being polished, goes to the "browner," who, when he has received it, puts a wooden plug into each end, and then, with a fine piece of rag or sponge, covers the barrel with lime and water, or whiting and water, to clear off any particle of grease which may be remaining. It is then put aside to dry. When dry it is brushed all over with a clean hard brush to take the whiting off again, and then the following mixture is wiped over the barrel with a clean sponge or rag:—Tincture of steel, nitric acid, blue stone, sweet nitre, and sublimate of mercury. These ingredients are put into a bottle, and diluted with water, according to the strength required. This mixture, thus diluted, being applied two or three times, the barrel is left to dry. The moment the mixture is applied, the beautiful "figure" begins to show itself. When the liquid is dry upon the barrel it is seen that it has thrown up a rust upon the barrel. This rust is then scratched off the barrel with a fine steel-wire scratch brush, which, at the same time that it takes off the rust, puts on the barrel a high polish. This process is repeated at intervals for three or four days, until the figure is well brought up, and the barrel attains a high polish, as well as a beautiful brown colour. It is then scalded all over five or six times with boiling water, being scratched all over each time with the scratch brush to produce as high a polish as possible. It is afterwards well rubbed up with a soft rag, and then, the barrel being oiled all over, the process of browning is complete. The boiling water is used to scald or "kill" the rust, as, if the barrel is well scalded, the rust will never rise again; if not, the rust will very quickly make its appearance on the surface of the barrel, and eat off all the polish and the beautiful brown colour. With respect to the mode of producing the imitation Damascus—that being a secret in the possession of only one, or at most two persons in Birmingham— it is not possible to give much information. It is quite certain that the mixture applied to the barrel is applied in the same way as stencilling is done to the inside walls of houses—namely, a thin plate of metal has all the beautiful marks of the real Damascus iron cut out upon it. This plate is then placed round the barrel, and the mixture laid on the barrel through the holes or pattern in the plate. This mixture being of a very adhesive and hard nature, when dry, will not easily rub off the barrel. There are at present very few imitation Damascus barrels made.

Lock, stock, and barrel, being thus prepared, are brought back by their several workmen to the *finisher*, who puts them finally together. The *finisher* is, in fact, the gun-maker, and performs for the gun what the ordinary watch-maker performs for the watch. The article under-goes no further process, and is now ready for market.

This description applies principally to the common flint guns, which form a steady trade in Birmingham. The military guns and fowling-pieces have, after leaving the premises of the "*screwer-together*," to pass into the hands of the *Percussioner*, who, having employed the nipple-maker and the cock-maker to produce these two articles for him, screws the nipple into the breech-end of the barrel in a position to receive the blow of the cock, files and fixes the cock, and drills the hole of communication to the inside of the barrel where the charge lies. The percussion lock was invented by a Scottish clergyman, the Rev. Mr. Fordyce, of Aberdeenshire; but since his time it has received great improvements, especially that of the copper cap. The introduction of this superior lock into the military service was long resisted by the British Government and the Board of Ordnance—probably not for the sole reason of the customary dislike of innovation which is chargeable against all Governments, but on account of the great expense of the change. The flint lock is now entirely superseded in the military gun, both in Great Britain and on the Continent, and is only manufactured for the African and colonial trade. The flints for these guns are supplied from London.

On inquiring into the general condition of the men, women, and children engaged in all the various departments of the gun trade, I found that they suffer from fluctuations in demand, with the exception of the lock forgers and filers, who are in this respect in a somewhat better state than the barrel-forgers, stockers, finishers, or others engaged generally in the production of the complete gun. The foreign demand for locks provides them with pretty regular employment; whereas the members of the other branches of the trade are dependent principally upon the demand for sporting guns, the African exports, and the irregular orders of the British and foreign Governments. "Wars and rumours of wars" are good for this trade, and the near approach of the sporting season always produces an increased demand, and a consequent improvement in trade.

An extensive manufacturer represented to me that, generally speaking, of the whole of the workmen employed by him in the various branches of the gun trade, those who were engaged in the gun-barrel forging, grinding, and boring, who all worked by the aid of steam power, were far more regular at their work than the lock forgers and filers, and others who worked at vices and presses. The men seemed, he said, to acquire regular habits from the regularity of the machine on which they were dependent, and to feel aggrieved at any waste of the power occasioned by neglect. The lock forgers and filers, not being dependent on steam, frequently idled away the Monday and Tuesday of every week. The same manufacturer kept for a twelvemonth an account against all his men of their hours of attendance, and stated that he did not find that they wasted the Monday and Tuesday more frequently when trade was good than when it was bad. I was particular in my inquiries upon this point, as some manufacturers complained greatly of their workmen, that, when orders poured in upon them and the men could earn as much in three days as they formerly earned in six, they were contented with the three days' work, and passed the other three in drinking and card-playing. I could find no reason for the belief that such a waste of time and opportunity was general, although in some instances it did undoubtedly occur, and caused a serious loss to the manufacturer as well as to his workmen. The prices at which guns are now manufactured for the Board of Ordnance, as already observed, have had the effect of reducing wages. A few years ago a contractor's recognised profit per gun was 3s.; it is now only 9d. The engraving, which was formerly charged 3d., is now done for 1½d.; the percussioners receive 7d., instead of 9d.; the polisher 5d., instead of 8d.; and the browner 5d. instead of 7d. In the cheaper guns for Africa, there is also a considerable competition against Birmingham from the Belgian manufacturers of Liege; and the Americans have lately been endeavouring to be independent of Birmingham in all the departments of the gun business except that of the lock, which they are not able to produce of similar excellence even at more than double the price at which Birmingham can supply them. A few weeks ago eleven men were engaged in the town to go out to Baltimore, in the United States, as stockers and finishers, and to receive six dollars a week wages, besides house rent and two acres of land. For the best sporting guns Birmingham and London have acquired a character for such cheapness, elegance, durability, and excellence in every way, as to cause the manufacturers to believe that they will be able to defy all the competition in the world. They have no fear of being undersold either by Belgium, France, or the United States, in the superior class of fire-arms.

LABOUR AND THE POOR.

———◆———

BIRMINGHAM.

[FROM OUR SPECIAL CORRESPONDENT.]

THE CONDITION OF FACTORY WOMEN AND THEIR FAMILIES.

Letter VII.

The metal manufactures of Birmingham employ large numbers of women and young girls, as well as children. It is doubtful on which of the two sexes the manufacturers are most dependent for labour. There is scarcely a branch of the numerous trades, and sub-divisions of trade, in the town, in which women and children do not find occupation, with the exceptions of glass-blowing and the smelting and forging of iron, steel, and brass. From the tender age of seven to sixty and upwards, females may be found in the larger or smaller workshops and factories, engaged at work which is not always consistent with the notions elsewhere entertained of womanly strength, or even of decency and propriety. In Birmingham women work among men at grinding and boring gun and pistol barrels—at polishing ramrods and bayonets—at making and polishing iron tips for boots and shoes—at door-hinge, wood, screw, and nail making—at pin making—at steel pen making—at horn, bone, pearl, metal, and glass button making— at lackering—at varnishing—at drop and spangle making for lustres and chandeliers—at the papier maché trade—at japanning—at the manufacture of jewellery—at coffin furniture and ornaments—at the Britannia metal trade, and at a score of others; besides being largely employed in wrapping and packing the finer descriptions of brass, steel, tin, and plated goods, and in carding, sorting, and otherwise pre-paring for the retail dealer every description of smaller article which the town produces. In some of these branches of manufactures the wages of women are comparatively small, but, taking one with an-other, the average amount paid for a full week's work at ten hours a day seems to be from 8s. to 10s. At the screw and nail making, and also in the pin, the hook-and-eye, the bone and horn button, and some other trades, wages are seldom above 6s. or 7s. a week; but in the superior department of the steel pen manufacture they are often as high as 14s. for the best and most industrious workwomen. 14s. a week may be considered the maximum of a woman's earnings. It is not easy to estimate the total number of women employed in the town. In some of the Florentine button, steel pen, and screw manufactories, there are from 150 to 600 women and female children employed, while in the smaller workshops there is scarcely one that is not more or less dependent on female labour, or in which women and men do not work together. Including those in the large factories and in the smaller workshops, as well as the women who work in their own homes, it is probable that between 20,000 and 30,000 women and girls are employed in the manufactures of Birmingham.

The physical, moral, and intellectual condition of these women— their education as children—their capability when married to perform the duties of wives and mothers—and the influence of their occupation upon themselves and their children and their homes, as well as upon the general character of the town, are highly important points in the social history of Birmingham. The early age at which they are sent into the workshops deprives them but too commonly of all chances of education, except such as are afforded at evening and Sunday schools. At evening schools they do not very generally attend, and if they do they are too much fatigued with the day's labour to derive much advantage. At most of the Sunday schools the Bible is the only spelling book, and as writing, arithmetic, and all secular instruction are rigorously excluded, they cannot (having no other day from which they can be spared from their labour) make much, if any, progress in secular knowledge. The Factory Act does not apply to the manufactures of this town. By the Act of the 7th of Victoria, cap. 15, sec. 73, factories are defined to be, all buildings, &c., in which steam, water, or any other mechanical power is used to work any machinery employed in preparing, manufacturing, or finishing, or in any process incident to the preparation or manufacture of cotton, wool, hair, silk, flax, hemp, jute, or tow, either separately or mixed together, or mixed with any other material. There is no factory of this kind in Birmingham; but, whether the women and children employed in the metal are not as worthy of the attention of the Legislature as those engaged in the textile manufactures of the country, or whether society does not greatly suffer from the ignorance and degradation in which so many females are compelled to labour from childhood to old age, will perhaps appear more clearly after the perusal of the following statements. In pursuance of my investigations into the general condition of the working population of this town, I felt that there was none of more importance than this, not only because employers, in many instances, exact too great a quantity of labour from young children, but because, in cases which are unfortunately but too notorious, dissolute and worthless parents live in comparative idleness upon the labour of their offspring.

The educational part of the subject will necessarily apply to the male as well as to the female children of the town, and I shall therefore reserve it for a separate detail, and confine myself in the present letter to the social and moral state of women and female children. It is impossible to be long in Birmingham without hearing a very generally expressed opinion among all classes—the clergy, the magistrates, the great manufacturers, and the more intelligent working men—that the labour of women in factories, mills, and workshops is prejudicial to themselves, to their husbands, to their offspring, and to society. Their want of education unfits them for the proper discharge of their social, moral, and religious duties, and their almost total ignorance of domestic economy renders them no helpmates for the working men whom they marry. Their association with men in workshops and factories either leads to early immorality, or to marriage before they have attained the proper age, or have acquired any means for the establishment or maintenance of a household. Among other evils, which must not be forgotten in the catalogue, is the neglect of their children. This is a necessary consequence of their absence from their homes for the whole or greater part of the day. The children are left under the care of improper persons; and frequent accidents, and an undue mortality among the infant population of the town are the results. The girl who works in the metal trades of Birmingham is too commonly ignorant of everything she ought to know. She may have learned to read a little at the Sunday-school, but most commonly she can neither write, reckon, sew, nor cook. She knows nothing but the small branch or subdivision of manufacture in which she may be employed. She can worm a screw and nothing more. She can polish a ramrod at a wheel, or drill a hole in a button; she may be able to lacquer a brass ornament, or to black or varnish a coffin plate or handle; but she knows nothing of the management of her house or family, and often wastes by her ignorance as much of her own scanty earnings, or the earnings of her husband, as in the hands of a clever and better instructed woman would have provided herself and family with many of the necessaries which they are obliged to forego, or even with the humble luxuries which she has perhaps never heard of.

As a general rule, the workshops of Birmingham are the property of small manufacturers, and are constructed without reference to the health or comfort of those who are employed in them. Of late years many men of larger capital have appeared in the town, and have erected works properly ventilated, and with every convenience for decency and good order as well as for health. The steel-pen factory of Mr. Gillott, for instance, is a model of its kind; and the brass foundry establishment of Mr. Winfield is equally deserving of the favourable mention of all who take an interest in the sanitary as well as moral questions which affect the working classes. But such large and extensive concerns are rare; and in the smaller workshops and factories, men and women but too commonly work together in small, ill-ventilated rooms and attics, and girls and women are subjected to a physical, as well as a moral contamination which is greatly to be deplored. While men and women work in the same room or shop, as they must necessarily do in many branches of business, there is no effectual remedy for the moral contamination which they may receive from the improper or ribald conversation of their male associates, except the better education of both sexes. It is in the power of the manufacturer, however, to effect much good even in this respect, by selecting educated, well-behaved, and moral men, as foremen and tool-makers. In another important particular a great evil might be prevented if the manufacturer would enforce upon his workpeople the decency which it is to be supposed he practises himself, and if he would erect separate necessaries and water-closets for the men and women. No female can retain her purity of mind and conduct, or be in a condition to profit by the lessons of morality and religion, if she be daily and hourly subjected to the notice and remarks of men, in passing to or from such places. This evil, so prevalent in Birmingham, was pointed out, in 1841, by the commissioners appointed by the Government to inquire into the employment of women and children in factories; but little or nothing has been done, in the interval, except by some of the larger manufacturers. The small workshops remain in this respect in a state which is disgraceful to a civilized country, and which cannot but inflict much moral injury upon the mothers and children of the poor. These, however, serious as they are, form but a portion of the many evils to which women are subjected by being sent to labour at an early age. With these preliminary remarks I proceed to detail the evidence which I collected upon the subject generally, from clergymen, from medical men, from workmen, and from the women themselves, whom I visited at their own houses. The first statement which I shall present was made by a gentleman who has raised himself by his good conduct and industry to a highly respectable position in the town:—

"I was an operative button maker for fifty years of my life. I was born and bred among the working classes, and know their virtues and their vices. My own history and experience will throw some light upon the condition of women who work in factories. The early association of the sexes, and the control exercised over women by tool makers and others who have the management of workshops, and give out work to them, very often leads to improper intercourse, or to early marriage to hide or atone for past evil. Young men and women think that by clubbing their earnings, they will be in a condition to keep house and support a family, and they contract marriages long before they are justified in doing so. The case of my father and mother is but one of thousands which are still more common at the present day than when I was a child. My father was a metal button turner. My mother was in the same business in the same shop. My father was of age when he married, and that was all. He had no money to buy furniture. His wages were about a pound a week, and my mother's about 8s. or 9s. at the very utmost. They procured furniture on credit, and never got rid of their furniture debt as long as they lived. That debt hung like a millstone around their necks, and may have been one of many causes which drove my father to the gin-shop. My mother had eleven children, of whom I was the eldest. She was employed in the button manufacture all that time. My father had no comfortable home. He could not have, while my mother was obliged to work in a shop all the day. My mother worked at her trade till the last. Often till the day before her confinement she was at the lathe, and often returned to her work within three weeks. It was my business, as the eldest child, to nurse the younger ones. I was a nurse at five years old, and had sometimes to mind the children at home that they did not set their pinafores on fire, and sometimes I had to go to the factory to attend to the infant. My mother was allowed to take it with her, and it used to lie in a tub of sawdust, and sleep or roll about till it wanted the breast. I was obliged to watch over it and amuse it. I was put to work at the buttons at seven years of age, and I thought myself very fortunate in being relieved from the disagreeable labour of nursing the baby. We had a wretched place to live in. My mother ran home daily at one o'clock to get a hasty dinner for my father. She had no time for cooking anything. Bread and treacle, or bread and butter, was our usual fare, except on Sundays, when we got a joint of meat, and had it cooked at the public oven. My mother was a perfect slave. She could not read or write. She was naturally a clever woman. My father could read and write, but he took no pains to let his children have the same advantages. He never sent any of us to school, but sent us all to work as soon as it was possible that we could earn even as little as 6d. a week. He was always in debt, and fond of drink, and became latterly quite reckless. He spent his earnings in liquor, and trusted to my mother to feed the children somehow or other—he did not care how. Often and often, when only seven or eight years old, I have been sent to the huckster's to beg and pray for a loaf on credit to save us from starvation. I earned my food at that time, but did not always get it. The price of bread and other articles always went up when we were in debt; and our landlord, not being able to get his rent, allowed our house to fall into a miserable condition. He would not whitewash or repair it; and we were in constant dread of being turned out into the streets. My mother did double work—in the shop and at home. I have known her to sit up till three or four o'clock in the morning, after a hard day's work, washing and mending our wretched clothes. When four of her children were ill at one time of the small pox, she had to go to the shop to work, or we should have starved. She paid a neighbour 1s. 6d. a week to look after them. During her long years of misery she several times tried to do without the shop, and make the labour of her husband and children support us all. My father's earnings were so small, and his drinking habits so inveterate, that very little found its way into my mother's possession. Her attempts to stay at home were in vain. She had always to go back to the shop. We have often been without fire and food in the winter, and exposed to distress and suffering of the most deplorable kind. When I was apprenticed I could not write my name. My sister, who was also sent to the button trade as soon as she could earn a penny a day, was never taught to read, nor to write, nor to use the needle, nor to cook, nor to wash. The whole of us were equally ignorant. It would be of no use to detail my own experience at that time, were it not, unhappily, the experience of thousands of people at the present day. The same causes are still at work. I constantly hear of, and see, cases quite as bad as mine was. Young girls prefer the work of shops to that of domestic

servants. Though confined during the day, they are their own mis-
tresses at night, or have every evening and the whole of every Sunday
to themselves, which they could not have in service. Such work as
'lacquering' is a favourite with them. It is tolerably well paid, and easily acquired, and it gives them freedom instead of thraldom. When
they marry, they are quite unfit to be the companions and helpmates
of intelligent and thrifty men. They make but miserable homes, and
miserable homes send men to the alehouse and the ginshop. I believe
that the employment of women in factories is one great cause of the
intemperance of the working classes. When a man knows, if he returns to his home as soon as his labour is over, on a winter night, that
his wife has no fire alight for him, and no comfortable place even to
sit down in, he strolls into the warm ginshop, and soon learns to like
the place and the society. He goes from bad to worse, and his wife
speedily learns to imitate his example. A drunken husband makes a
drunken wife, and then the whole family goes to ruin. The children
receive no education, and are sent to work as soon as they can stand.
The more the children earn, the more is left to the parents for the
ginshop. Such was the case in our family, except that my mother
did not drink, and such is the case with scores and scores of families
in the town at the present day. My father worked at the lathe till
within a week of his death. He had been drinking every day for a
week previously. He died of a complication of diseases, brought on
by intemperance. When I went to see him, being then married and
having a family of my own, I found him in a wretched room, without
a bit of bread in the house, and not a farthing of money. I had to
bury him. My mother died in childbed of her eleventh child, a few
years before my father. Sorrow, privation, and hard work ruined her
constitution. If she had had a sober husband, his wages might have
supported us all. I could name many such men as my father, now at
work in the town, some as bad, and a good many worse—drunken
and lazy fellows who never work at all, but depend entirely on their
wives and infants to support them. In justice to my father I must say
that he never did this. He always was willing to work when he was
sober, and during his life he worked very hard. But many men that I
know will not work at all. Others who do work think that the whole
amount gained by their wives is so much drinking money gained for
themselves."

The next person who gave me the history of her life in connection
with this question was a woman apparently of about sixty years of age,

whose countenance retained the traces of considerable beauty. She resided in a narrow dirty court, but her little room was clean, and her personal appearance very tidy and respectable. Though uneducated, she spoke with great feeling and propriety. She said, in answer to my inquiries:—

"I began to work in a button factory when I was seven years old, or thereabouts. I could not have been more; but I never knew my exact age, not to a year or two. I must be more than 60. I am a great grandmother. My father was a screw-filer, and did not get very good wages. He was very poor. I was his only child. He put me to work when I was too little to do it. I had to stand at a vice, and file spectacle frames. I was not tall enough to reach the vice without standing upon a stage. I went to work at seven in the morning, and left off at seven in the evening. I earned 6d. a week. My father hired me out for three years to learn the business, but took me away before the time was up, because my wages were not paid regularly. I then went to service to nurse a child. I suppose I was under ten years of age. I had never been to any school. I did not know my letters. I stayed in service for about two years, and was then put by my father to learn the button wiping, which is to wipe the gilt and plated buttons dry after they leave the burnisher, and to card them. I got 2s. 6d. a week for this, and worked at it for about three years. I did not go to school all this time. I had no instruction. I never went to any church or chapel, but rested myself all the Sunday. I married before I was seventeen; I think that was about my age, though, as I said before, I can't tell to a year how old I was. I should think I must have been under seventeen. I went to the New Meeting Sunday school for a little while before I was married, and learned to read. I have never learned to write at all. I can't say that I can read now without spelling. It is hard work for me to read, and I seldom do it. My husband was a gun-lock filer, and was about five-and-twenty. It was during the war when we married, and he got tidy wages in his business. For two years his wages were sufficient to support him and me, and I had no occasion to go to the shop to work. I minded the house, and learned how to cook and wash. I also taught myself how to make shirts at this time, by taking an old one of my husband's to pieces, and cutting out by that pattern. After the peace the gun business was ruined in Birmingham. My husband could not get half enough work, and wages fell very low. We were in such distress that I was obliged to go out to work. I got employment at a skin factory. I had to turn a large wheel. I walked round and round, exactly as horses do when they are employed in turning wheels. My work was a horse's work, and I almost worked myself into the grave at it. I had two children at this time. I earned 6s. a week, and had to pay 1s. 6d. out of it to have them taken care of, at a kind of school in the court. From eight in the morning to four in the afternoon were my hours of work, and very hard work it was. I remained at it for eight or nine months, when I was obliged to give it up, as my strength was failing me. My husband tried all kinds of odd jobs at this time. I never knew what he earned. He would never tell me. Even when in full work, at his trade of gun-lock filing, I never knew his earnings. He began to drink when he fell into distress after the peace. Whatever he may have earned at odd jobs, he gave me very little of it. I never got 10s. in a week from him; no, nor 10s. in two weeks. He used to keep me very bare, and come home drunk. I often vowed that when he came home he should find the cupboard empty, but I never had heart to serve him so. Whenever I could earn a shilling I spent it on him and the children. When I left off turning the big wheel I went back to the button wiping, and I have been at it ever since. I work at it still. I never in my life earned above 8s. in a week by the hardest work I ever made. About 7s. a week are the usual wages, but more may be earned by over hours when trade is brisk. I sent the two children to the Old Meeting Sunday-school, and they have both learned to read and write. My husband has never gone back to the gun-lock filing, but has been more or less at the brace-bit making. We have never been out of debt since we were married. We have always been behind with the rent. I have always kept out of debt with the hucksters. If I have not had money to buy tea and bread and other things, I have gone without them. When I worked at the big wheel I often lived upon bread and tea. Two ounces of tea-dust that cost 2d. served us all four for a week. I had not half enough food to support me. The button-making is not near such hard work, and it is better paid; but I cannot earn enough to live comfortably and pay my rent. I scarcely ever have any other dinner now than bread and butter and tea. On Sundays we manage to get a bit of meat, but not on other days. I often earn no more than 5s. in the week; and in the winter, which is a very expensive time for coals and candles, I earn less than in the summer. The trade is not so good in the winter, and I cannot get full work. I try to gain a few pence extra by sewing watch-bags. They are made of leather, and I can sew a gross of them in a week by sitting up late. I can clear about 7d. a gross after buying the thread and candle.

I sometimes work at the watch-bags till my head becomes dizzy and my eyes begin to swim. Often and often I work till I can scarcely see what I am doing, and I am obliged to give it up. The most dreadful life in this world is the life of a poor woman with a drunken husband. I don't call it living at all. It is worse than death. My husband is very quarrelsome when he drinks, and fights a good deal. He never fights me—I must say this for him—he never struck me in all his life."

I have given the story of this worthy old lady in her own words, without any other alteration than in the sequence of the story. The Old Meeting Sunday-school to which she alluded is supported by the Unitarian body, and is one of the few Sunday-schools in the town which allow writing and arithmetic to be taught on Sundays. A young woman who married her son happened to drop in as she was answering my enquiries; and was curious to know what object I had in asking these questions, and noting down the answers in a book. Having told her that I was desirous to ascertain exactly what kind of life was led by women who were employed to work in factories and workshops, she said that she would be glad to answer any questions I might put. She said:—

"I went to work when I was only six years of age, at the whip-cord making. I worked at it till I was fourteen. I got sixpence a week at first, and then a shilling. I often went the whole day without bite or sup—so hungry and so tired that I had like to have dropped at my work. When I was about seven, I went for a few weeks to a Sunday-school and learnt my letters. I went, after I was fourteen, into a button factory. I was a cutter out of metal buttons, and had to work at the press. It is rather hard work for a man, and very hard for a woman. I earned about 8s. a week. I worked at this till I was twenty-four, when I got married. My husband is a whip-cord maker, and did not earn much. It is a bad business now—and wages are low. I went to work again the week after I was married, and continued working for fifteen months, till I had my first child. I think I was at work in a fortnight after my confinement. I worked for four days and caught a violent cold in the breasts. I suppose it was by working at the press. I felt the cold handle of the press strike a cold right up my arm. It seemed to trickle up to my elbow and shoulder. I got bad breasts, and was obliged to leave off work and send for the doctor. They were very bad indeed. This was thirteen years ago, and they have been bad ever since. My husband said at the time that he would never allow me to work in a shop any more as long as he could do a job of work to support me. He said it was not fit for a woman to do such work as I had done. He is a very sober, hard-working man, and I believe he brings home every penny of his earnings. We have suffered a great deal of distress, and I have often been tempted to go back to work to earn a little to help to keep house, but my husband will not hear of it. We manage to jog on somehow or other. I think I am a good manager. I make every penny go as far as I can. My husband works for himself a little, and makes whips and does jobs for carmen. He has walked to Walsall to-day—I think it is about eight miles off—to try and sell some whips, and he will walk back again. The worst time for our business is the winter. The railways have done it a deal of harm, and not near so many whips are wanted as there used to be. I have had children, and have had bad breasts each time. Three of the children are dead. I know a great many women who work in shops, some older and some younger than I am. They all think it a cruel thing to be obliged to work when they have families. A woman with a family has quite enough to do to look after her home and children and keep things tidy; and I am sure the money they earn is no gain. They must waste more than they earn by neglecting their families. I have heard many women say they would as soon die as live, if they were always to go to the shops to work. I have suffered a good deal, even with a good husband; but I don't know how some poor women manage at all."

A third woman, very careworn in appearance, and prematurely aged, partly in answer to inquiries, and partly of her own accord stated as follows:—

"I have been married for twenty years, and have worked all that time at the screw business. For a full week's work I get 7s., but I seldom have a full week. It is many a long month since I have earned as much as that. There are 'discounts' in our trade, and we get twenty-five per cent. less than the book prices. If I really earn 10s., I only get 7s. 6d.; and if I earn 5s., I only get 3s. 9d. The discount is sometimes more than that. My husband is also in the screw business. There are the same discounts for him as for me. When he earns a pound he only gets 15s. Discounts are common in the screw business, and in several other trades in Birmingham; and I wish to heaven they were all done away with. My husband gets about 15s. or 16s. a week. I 'worm' the screws, and am paid by the gross, according to the length and weight of the screw. The shortest are a 1¼d. a gross for worming, and so on according to the size up to 4d. or 4½d. a gross. I have had twelve children. Six of them are dead. I have always been obliged to go out to work and to pay somebody to mind the children for me. I have paid from 1s. 6d. to 2s. 6d. a week. The eldest now alive is a girl of eighteen, who works at the same shop with me. The next is a boy about ten years old. The rest are quite little things. One is an infant, and I sometimes get leave to run for a few minutes from the shop and give it the breast. It only gets the breast before I go to work, and when I come home at dinner time, and again at night. It is fed with pap, and I think many of my children have died from improper food when I have been away. The nurses give children stuff to quiet them, and also feed them too full with windy things that make them bad in the stomach. I am sure mine have been served so. I often think I should not have lost so many beautiful babies if I could have stayed at home myself to take care of them. When I have come home at night I have found them cold and wet and miserable, poor things; quite wretched for want of proper care; and yet I have paid for the best care I could get. My eldest boy fell down into a deep cellar when he was two years and a half old, and broke his collar-bone. It was all through the inattention of a girl that had charge of him. He was a fine child before that; but he is now a poor weak thing. He seems dull in his mind; and I often think he will grow up not quite right. He is very strange and wild in his ways, and does not seem to understand what is said to him. My mother was left with a large family. I had to go to work long before I was seven years old. I cannot read or write. I do not know any of the letters. I have never been to any school, except once or twice to a Sunday School. I know nothing but hard work. When I come home at night I feel as if I should like to lie down and go to sleep; but I cannot do so. I must look after the children, and mend their things for them, and 'fettle' the house a bit. Saturdays and Sundays are my hardest days. I sit up late on Saturday night mending and washing; and on Sunday I work like a slave from morning to night. Sunday is very fatiguing. It is the hardest day of all the week to me. I get up early to clean the house. My daughter helps me. After the house is cleaned, I have to wash all the children, and get them ready for the school. It is first one thing and then another. I have to look to my own clothes when I have done with theirs, or I should have to go in worse rags than I have got. I have to cook the dinner and see to everything, and keep the children from crying and quarrelling. I have to do a whole week's work on the Sunday. Often, when it is a fine day, and I hear the bells ringing for church, I feel

quite melancholy and miserable. I should like to go out like other
people. I should like to go to church. I used to go when I was first
married, but I can't now with my young family. I cannot see them sit
in dirt and rags, so there's no church for me, and no holiday, and no
pleasure. My daughter goes out, poor thing, her age requires it, but I
cannot. We have been for years without having anything warm and
comfortable for dinner except on a Sunday; not even a warm potato,
as we have no time for cooking on a week day. My eldest daughter
could do the cooking, but she is obliged to go out to work as I do. We
work in the same shop. My husband was a teetotaller for six months,
and I am sure we never led in all our lives such a happy six months
as that. He could not keep to it. I am sure if he had, that either me
or my eldest girl might have been kept from the shop; but it's no use
complaining, as I dare say I'm not worse off than other people."

The daughter of this woman, a pale and dirty but fine-featured
girl, who in the course of the day had seriously injured two fingers of
her hand by getting them accidentally squeezed by the tools, said:—

"I have worked in the screw-mill with mother for about ten years.
I am near eighteen. I had only four days' work last week, and received
2s. One week with another I can earn 3s. 6d. or 4s. I can never earn
more than 4s., however hard I may work. I have to turn the heads
of the screws at the lathe. I get a shilling for turning 50 gross. I
don't know how many hundreds or thousands that would make. I
could not do so many in a day; but I could do 40 gross. There is a
discount off what I earn, the same as off mother's wages. Besides the
discount, all the girls and women have to pay 2½d. a week each for
sweeping the shop. I would rather sweep and clean my part of the
shop, and save the 2½d.; but we are not allowed. Every one must
pay. I had to pay 2½d. out of my 2s., last week for the sweeping, and
should have had to pay all the same if I had only earned 1s. There
are about 170 women and girls in our shop. They all pay alike. I
can read a little. I learned reading at the Sunday school, but I have
never read any books all through. I seldom read. I am obliged to spell
some of the words. I cannot write. I can count a little. I don't know
what multiplication or subtraction means." [The mother of this girl
corroborated the statement as to the shop sweeping. It will follow,
if the statement be correct, that the proprietor receives the weekly
sum of £1 15s. 5d. from his workpeople for the cleaning out of his
workshop. It is evident that a great deal of cleaning may be done for
such a sum.]

The statement of another woman will suffice. She was a very sub-dued and sorrowful-looking person, and seemed as if suffering from want of sleep. She said:—

"I work in the screw business. I earn about four shillings, but could earn more if I had full work. I have not been to work for a month, but have stayed at home to nurse my little girl, who is ill of the small pox. She is seven months old. The doctor gave her up yesterday, and says she cannot live. If the child dies, I shall return to my work. Her illness has caused us great distress, but I could not go to work and leave her. I have six children. The eldest is going on twelve. I went to work when I was about thirteen, and married when I was going on twenty. My earnings when I was married were about 7s. a week. My husband is a white-smith, and makes fire-irons. His wages are only 14s. a week. He is a sober man. I did not leave off working in the shop when I married, and have never kept away except in sickness and confinements. I am obliged to work up to the last minute before confinements, and have often been afraid that I should be taken with 'the pains' in the shop. I return to work as soon as I can. We want all the money we can earn. My eldest boy went to work before he was ten. He works at a press. He can read a little, but he can't write. He learned at a Sunday-school. The eldest but one can read a little better than the eldest; but he can't write. He often reads to me and his father in the evening. He reads the Bible; and I am very fond of hearing the stories in it. My husband cannot read or write; neither can I. I wish I could. I never had a chance. I went to a Sunday-school when I was a girl, and learned my letters, but I was never taught anything else. It was only children teaching each other like. When me and my husband married we had no furniture; and we went to live with his sister. We managed to get a few things together by degrees. You may call it furniture, but it is very poor. My husband has been laid up for 14 weeks at a time, but he is considered rather a healthy man. He belongs to no sick club or society. When out of work he applies to the parish, and he's had jobs at stone-breaking. He is in work now at his trade. We seldom have meat except on Sundays. We buy half-a-pound or a pound of 'bits' or 'scraps' from the butchers, and mix it up with 'taturs.' We cannot get more out of our wages, with eight persons to feed. We get a little tea now and then, and I find it a great comfort. Besides the work of the shop, I have all the work of the house to do—all the cleaning, and washing, and mending. When the day's work is done, the house work begins, and I almost drop asleep over it sometimes, I am so tired. I mostly cook the dinner overnight by boiling the 'taturs.' They get cold, and are ready to be fried up warm the next day with a little lard. We have no time for much cooking. There is only an hour for dinner—from one to two—and we have to go home, eat our dinner, and be back at the shop by two. If we are not in by a quarter after two we are fined a penny. My husband and me never go to church nor to chapel. We have not things fit to go in; or else we should like well enough to go. The children all go to the Sunday-school that are old enough. We do not live all in one room; we have two sleeping rooms and a kitchen. All my children have been healthy enough, except the two youngest. My last child has always been very sickly; and I have been very weak myself for the last three years—partly, I think, because I am half starved. I scarcely ever know what it is to have enough to eat."

I append to the statement of these hard-working women the following remarks by a reverend gentleman employed on a mission to the homes of the poor. He said—"My duties necessarily lead me to see the poor at their own houses. I see both the husbands and the wives. It is the complaint of some husbands that their wives are out all day at work, and that they can't in consequence have comfortable homes. But I am convinced that in the great majority of cases where women go out to work, their husbands might support them if they chose to be sober. The great and monster evil of Birmingham is the drunkenness of mechanics. It is this that forces women to work, and to neglect their families, and that creates a whole host of evils. Often in my visits to the poor I find numbers of infants entrusted to the care of some old woman, who is past work, or of some girl of ten or eleven years of age, quite unfit to be entrusted with them. The week before last I was called upon to visit and console a family in which a child of five years of age had been left under the care of its elder brother, only nine years old, and had been burned to death in the absence of its mother. Such cases are not rare. I have known of several since I have been in Birmingham; and from what I daily see, my wonder is that they are not much more frequent. I find that women who work in shops or factories know little or nothing of domestic duties or economy. Their houses are almost always in a dirty and unhealthy state. I sometimes find a large pan in their sitting rooms or kitchens filled with water, in which their clothes and persons have been repeatedly washed, until it is quite offensive. They do not throw the water away after once washing in it, but use it again and again, or allow it to stand in the room—partly, I suppose, on account of the labour of pumping it and carrying it into their houses. Wretched homes of this kind weaken the moral feeling. If the husband takes to drinking—either from the wretchedness of his home, or any other cause—the wife in time learns to imitate him, and seeks comfort from the same source. There are many exceptions, no doubt; and the heroism of some women who are afflicted with drunken husbands is really most admirable. But it is not every one who can resist evil temptation and the pressure of misery. One woman in a workshop very often corrupts another, and they soon learn to expend a portion of their earnings in gin and 'fourpenny.' It is a very common practice for women to cheapen articles at market, in order to screw the 'gin penny' out of the price. In addition to this evil, I remark that the natural innocence and modesty of young women are injured by the associations of the workshop. Young women earning their wages in this manner have too much liberty; and before marriage they very often seek amusement in the evenings at singing taverns, amid men who drink and smoke. But when they marry their hardships begin, and most of them marry far too early. The more intelligent and steady mechanics like to marry servants, rather than factory girls. A domestic servant is generally clean and tidy, and knows the management of a house, how to cook and to sew, while very few girls who work in shops know the use of the needle, even to mend their own clothes."

A committee of physicians and surgeons of Birmingham, in a sanitary report on the condition of the town, published in 1840, drew attention to some of the evils of which the continued existence at the present day is proved by the above statements. This report, which bears the signatures of Drs. Blakeston, Corrie, and Palmer, and of Messrs. Baynham, Hodgson, Russell, Ryland, and Wickenden, notices the improvidence too common among mechanics and their wives, and adds "that drunkenness, with all its attendant miseries, prevails to a great extent, though it is by no means to be regarded as a characteristic feature of the mechanics of Birmingham in particular." "It most generally prevails," they state, "among that class of workmen who obtain the highest wages, but who are often found in the most deplorable and abject condition. The improvidence of which we are speaking is to be traced in very many instances to extreme ignorance on the part of the wives of these people. The females are bred up from their youth in the workshops, as the earnings of the younger members contribute towards the support of the family. The minds and morals of the girls become debased, and they marry totally ignorant of those habits of domestic economy which tend to render a husband's home comfortable and happy. This is very often the cause of the man being driven to the alehouse, to seek that comfort after his day of toil which he looks for in vain at his own fireside. The habits of a manufacturing life being once established in a woman, she continues it after marriage, and leaves her home and children to the care of a neighbour or of a hired child, sometimes only a few years older than her own children, whose services sometimes cost her almost as much as she obtains by her own labour. To this neglect on the part of their parents is to be traced the death of many young children. They are left in the house with a fire before they are old enough to know the danger to which they are exposed, and are often dreadfully burned. ... To the habit of married women working in manufactories may often be traced those jealousies and heart-burnings, those quarrels, and that discord which embitter the home of the poor man."

Upon the question of infant mortality in Birmingham at that time (1840) the committee of physicians and surgeons stated that—

"The ratio of infant mortality in Birmingham is very considerable. It greatly exceeds that of the metropolis, and of the agricultural districts, but it is not so high as in some of the large provincial towns. According to the second report of the Registrar-General, it is proportionally greatest in Manchester, next in Leeds, then in Liverpool, and fourthly, in Birmingham; in each of which places more than one half of the total number of deaths registered are those of children who had not attained their fifth year; whilst it is remarkable that in the metropolis the number of registered deaths of children under five years of age is only in the proportion of one to nearly two-and-a-half of the total number of deaths. In the parish of Birmingham, in the year registered from July 1, 1838, to June 30, 1839, the total number of deaths of all ages was 3,305; of which number 1,658 were under five years of age. Of this last number more than one-half died in their first year. In the counties of Gloucester and Oxford, and parts of the counties of Worcester and Warwick, including Aston, but not in the parish of Birmingham, the total number of deaths registered during the same year is 20,309; of which number 7,298 were under five years of age, and 4,380 of the last number had not completed their first year. The want of sufficient and frequent nutriment, and proper care, caused by the absence of the mothers, who are detained from their children, and are engaged in their employments in the workshops, may, perhaps, have some share in causing this high rate of infant mortality in the large manufacturing towns.

"We have but few remarks to offer with regard to the accidents which occur to the manufacturing population of this town. They are very severe and numerous, as shown by the registers of the General Hospital. Many are the consequences of the want of proper attention to fencing in the machinery, which appears to be seldom thought of in the manufactories; and many are caused by loose portions of dress being caught by the machinery so as to drag the unfortunate sufferers under its power. The shawls of the females, or their long hair, and the aprons and loose sleeves of the boys and men, are in this way frequent causes of dreadful mutilations. We think that greater precautions than are at present employed might be adopted by the owners and superintendents of machinery with respect to the points which we have now mentioned.

"One class of accidents is very frequent in Birmingham—severe burns and scalds. So numerous are these cases, particularly the former, that in the General Hospital two rooms are devoted for their reception. We find from the registers of the institution that in the year ending July 1st, 1840, independent of 180 slighter cases received as out-patients, that 130 patients were admitted into the house, having been dangerously burnt or scalded. Of this number 74 were males, and 56 females, and 36 died. Of the 36 who died, 27 were under ten years of age. A great number of these accidents we know to have arisen from the children having been left without proper superintendence."

The subjoined extracts from the burial registries of the large parishes of St. Philip's and St. Thomas's, show the number of burials within the districts for the years 1848, 1849, and 1850, and of the deaths of children under five years of age. The following is the extract from the burial register of St. Philip's Church, from June, 1847, to June, 1850:—

TOTAL NUMBER OF INTERMENTS.

From June, 1847, to June, 1848	914
From June, 1848, to June, 1849	542
From June, 1849, to June, 1850	467
Total	1,923

TOTAL NUMBER OF INTERMENTS OF CHILDREN,
THREE YEARS OF AGE AND UNDER.

From June, 1847, to June, 1848 380
From June, 1848, to June, 1849 248
From June, 1849, to June, 1850 217

Total 845

TOTAL NUMBER OF INTERMENTS OF CHILDREN,
FIVE YEARS OF AGE AND UNDER.

From June, 1847, to June, 1848 441
From June, 1848, to June, 1849 274
From June, 1849, to June, 1850 230

Total 945

The decrease in the number of burials in the year from June, 1848, to June, 1849, as compared with the previous year, is explained by the fact that one-half of the burial ground was shut up during the latter period on account of the crowded state of the churchyard, and that many burials took place elsewhere.

It will be seen from the above that the burials of children in this parish, under five years of age, were, in the year 1847-8, in the proportion of upwards of 47 per cent. of the whole number of burials—that in 1848-9 the proportion was upwards of 50 per cent.—and that in 1849-50 it was 49.25 per cent., and that the average of the three years was 48.6 per cent.

In the parish of St. Thomas's the total number of burials, and of the burials of children under five years of age, for the years 1847, 1848, 1849, and a part of 1850, were as follows. Though not above a third of the inhabitants of the parish bury in this churchyard, the proportion will show the comparative mortality among children, as well as if the whole parish made use of it.

TOTAL NUMBER OF INTERMENTS IN THE CHURCHYARD
OF ST. THOMAS'S, BIRMINGHAM, FROM JANUARY 1ST,
1847, TO NOVEMBER, 1850:—

1847 303
1848 332
1849 308
From January 1 to November 19, 1850 .. 295

Total 1,238

TOTAL NUMBER OF INTERMENTS OF YOUNG CHILDREN,
UNDER THE AGE OF FIVE YEARS, IN THE CHURCHYARD
OF ST. THOMAS'S, BIRMINGHAM, FROM JANUARY, 1847
TO NOVEMBER, 1850:—

1847	112
1848	142
1849	132
From January 1 to November 19, 1850	142
Total	528

The proportions, therefore, of the deaths of young children in 1847 were 37 per cent. of the whole number; in 1848, they were 42.74 per cent.; in 1849, they were 42.85 per cent.; and during the present year, when trade has been unusually brisk, and women have been employed more constantly from their homes, they have been 48.12 per cent. On visiting the infant schools of this parish, and requesting the respected and zealous minister to take at random one of the girls aside and ask her some questions relative to her family, it appeared that she was the sole survivor of eight children, and that her mother went out to work in a factory. A second trial produced a like result. The little girl said that she had six brothers and sisters; that her mother had had fourteen in all, and had lost seven; and that she went out to work every day. The third trial was that of a child who never had either brothers or sisters; but the fourth and last selected from this school-room, without any knowledge of the facts detailed by the other three, stated that her mother was a screw-maker, and that she was the only child left out of six.

From a tabular view of the number of inquests held in the borough for the quinquennial period ending on the 31st of December, 1844, published by the coroner, it appears that out of a total of 1,416 inquests held within that period, 246 were cases of burning, or an average of nearly 50 per annum. The number of fatal accidents from machinery was but 16. On application at the coroner's office for similar information relative to the succeeding period, the returns of which are not yet published, it was stated that the average number of burnings at the present time is from 55 to 60 per annum, including adults. It was further stated that the majority of deaths of young children upon whom inquests are held occurs from their being overlain.

As regards the premature deaths of young children upon whom inquests are not held, and the equally important subject of the accidents not fatal to life, but permanently injurious to the health of body and mind, which result from neglect on the part of mothers, I have no means of obtaining information. The burial registers may show the number of deaths under a certain age, but there are no registries which can show the injuries not immediately fatal, or the number of children whose constitutions are weakened, or who are maimed or lamed, or rendered insane or idiotic, by the neglect of those who should watch over their helpless infancy. In these respects the whole truth can never be known. Enough, however, has, I think, been elicited to show that the employment of mothers in factories and workshops is productive of many and great social evils, of which the premature deaths of young children are far from being the least.

———

LABOUR AND THE POOR.

———◆———

BIRMINGHAM.

[FROM OUR SPECIAL CORRESPONDENT.]

THE EMPLOYMENT AND EDUCATION OF CHILDREN.

LETTER VIII.

Some facts were stated in my last Letter, on the social and moral condition of the women employed in the manufactures of Birmingham, from which it might be seen that the majority of young girls are sent to labour at an age too early to permit them to have received any adequate instruction—that they labour very hard and very long—that their education, for the most part, does not include even the rudiments of writing and arithmetic—that the art of reading, which they imperfectly acquire at Sunday-schools, is very often forgotten in after life—that they pass from childhood into womanhood with but slight moral and no intellectual training—and that their knowledge of religion is but small at first, and is not increased as they grow older. It was further observed that the tastes and habits which they acquire in a manufacturing life unfit them for a proper knowledge of domestic duty and economy, and that their existence as wives and mothers is but too often a long struggle with every kind of misery.

Unfortunately, the system of manufacture pursued at Birmingham, which encourages, if it does not absolutely compel, the employment of children of tender years, is almost equally injurious in its effects upon the male population. Boys as well as girls are sent into factories and workshops at an age when they ought to be at school. Many boys of eight, nine, and ten years of age are employed, not simply at hard, but at unhealthy work, such as bone turning and pearl button-making, and in the innumerable branches of the manufacture of metals; and they work for so many hours in the day that they are unfit to profit after their daily toil is at an end by the instruction which they might otherwise receive. Thus there are in Birmingham many thousands of hardworking and honest children of both sexes whose very industry and usefulness prevent them from receiving the instruction which is freely imparted in workhouses to pauper children, and no less freely given in prisons to young criminals after conviction. The number of these children cannot be precisely estimated. A committee of inquiry, appointed by the parochial clergy, in 1846, stated that the population of the borough of Birmingham could not be estimated at less than 200,000 souls; and of this number they calculated that 32,000 were between the ages of two years and fifteen years, and of these that probably 25,000 were in circumstances to require aid in providing for their education. On dividing again this number into two classes, according to the age at which children are deemed admissible into infant or national schools, it was found that about 10,000 were between the ages of two and seven, and that 15,000 were between the ages of seven and fifteen. In regard to this latter class, they stated that educational provision had been made, either by the Church of England or by other bodies, for 7,749 in daily schools.

It is to the education received by, or the want of education among, these 15,000 children—supposing these to be the numbers of the young workers of Birmingham—that I wish to direct attention in this Letter.

The hours of labour in Birmingham may be considered as a general rule to extend from eight in the morning to seven in the evening, including an hour for dinner—or from eight in the morning to eight in the evening, including two hours, and in some cases an hour and a half, for dinner and tea. It is evident, therefore, that whatever may be the proportion of the 15,000 children between the ages of seven and fifteen who are employed in the manufactures of the town—they are, by the very fact of their being employed for so many hours per day, deprived of the same amount of time for education as is enjoyed by children out of work, as well as by children who are educated at the public expense in the workhouses, the charity schools, and the prisons. While all these have the whole day for education, the hard-working children of both sexes have only the evening, when they are more inclined either to play or to sleep than to vary their bodily with mental labour. They have in addition the Sunday; but as this day is set apart, in the Sunday-schools conducted by the parochial clergy, and by most of the dissenting congregations, to purely religious teaching, the only knowledge they can acquire on that day is of a scriptural character, and does not include writing, arithmetic, geography, or any branch of science or natural philosophy.

If we take the numbers given by the committee of inquiry appointed by the clergy in 1846, we find that nearly one-half of these 15,000 children are unprovided with the means of education at daily schools; and that they must, therefore, either be altogether uneducated, or only receive instruction from the Sunday schools. Taking first the case of the 7,749 for whom educational provision is said to have been made, it would be interesting and important to know how large a per centage of them actually receive the instruction open to them, and what is the amount of benefit they receive. I found it a general subject of complaint at all the schools at which I made inquiries, that the attendance of the pupils was extremely irregular, and that boys and girls of eight and nine years of age were often taken away by their parents and sent to work after they had been in attendance for a month or less. In numberless instances I found the names of children on the books who had only attended one or two days a week, and against their names were the words "gone to work." Of 150 boys in the parochial school of St. Thomas, on the 1st of July in the present year, the average age was only nine years; and the master stated in his published report, "that most of those above nine years of age were in the lower classes, owing to their having been at work up to that time, from about seven to nine years of age;" that of twenty-five boys who were in the first class at the corresponding period of the previous year, only four remained, the others having left school to go to work. He further stated that of the whole number of 150, only seventeen had been in the school for a twelvemonth. We must not take it for granted, therefore, that the 7,749 children whose names have been entered in any one year on the books of a day-school have received instruction, or can be called educated. One day's attendance of a child at school fixes it as an educational unit in the annual statistics of the parochial clergy, or of the dissenting bodies—a fact which must not be lost sight of by those who wish to discover the real state of the juvenile population as regards education.

Whenever trade is bad in Birmingham, and boys and girls of tender years are unable to find constant employment, the attendance at the day-schools increases. When trade is brisk the school attendance invariably falls off, and when it is unusually brisk, and the workmen and workwomen who require the assistance of children work over-hours, the attendance both at day and evening schools is further and more sensibly diminished. Some of the manufacturers, painfully aware of the evils of this state of things, and sincerely anxious to remedy it to the utmost extent of their means, endeavour in various ways to provide education for their juvenile workpeople. Mr. Gillott, the eminent steel pen manufacturer, who employs upwards of 500 girls and women, objects to receive into his factory any girl under thirteen years of age, and he gives the preference to those above thirteen who can read and write, and who bring a certificate of regular attendance at school, as well as of good moral behaviour, from a day or Sunday school teacher, or a clergyman. Many other manufacturers, among whom the names of Messrs. Chance, and Mr. Bacchus, in the glass trade, and that of Mr. Winfield, of the Cambridge-street Brass Works, are the most conspicuous, have established schools for the benefit of their young workpeople, and of the adults in their employ, whose education has been neglected. Others, who have it not in their power for want of means to imitate the example set by these gentlemen, are equally well aware of the vast amount of social evil and ignorance caused by the too early employment of children, and have expressed, both publicly and privately, how gladly they would hail the interference of the Legislature to prevent children under a certain age from being employed in manufactures. The workmen in some of the trades have shown as much zeal in the cause as their employers, and in a manner still more gratifying. Many of them, aware of their own early deficiencies, have devoted those hours which their more thoughtless companions spend in drink and dissipation, to the improvement of their minds. They have not been ashamed to learn the rudiments of reading, writing, and arithmetic, among little boys and girls, and, having conquered all the elementary difficulties, have endeavoured to extend the blessings of education, not only to their own children, but to those of their comrades. In one great glass-house in the town, three of the operatives have established schools in their own houses for the instruction of flint-glass makers, men and boys. They gratuitously teach reading, writing, and arithmetic, and devote the Friday and Saturday of every week to the purpose, those being the leisure days of the trade. Each of the three has about ten pupils.

But it is not the day, but the evening and Sunday schools, which form the main reliance of those friends of education who desire to make the best of circumstances, without stirring the question of legislative interference. Day schools are obviously useless to a juvenile population that is engaged for the whole day at hard work. It therefore remains to show, somewhat more in detail, how far the evening and Sunday schools answer, or can be expected to answer, the end in view, and how far they palliate a great evil which they cannot remove. I have already stated that the attendance at the day and evening schools is always greatest when trade is most depressed. I should also state that, whatever the state of trade may be, the attendance at evening schools invariably falls off in the summer months. The boys and girls, confined for ten or ten and a half hours per day in close workshops—breathing an atmosphere intermingled with bone, pearl, stone, and metal filings or dust—take advantage of the fine summer evenings, not merely to inhale a purer air (of which possibly they do not know the advantages), but to take their recreation in the sports congenial to their age. They have no other opportunities of play. In the winter evenings the school has the advantage of light and warmth, but in summer the streets or the lanes in the neighbourhood of the town have much greater attractiveness. This is the universal experience of all the managers of evening schools for the working classes. One extensive manufacturer stated that about a twelvemonth ago he found that out of seventy women and girls in his employment not quite one-half could read, and that of this number the greater proportion could only read imperfectly. Only four of the number could write. Those who could read and not write had been to Sunday schools, and the four who could write had been to day and evening schools. He hired a room, established a night school, and paid a female teacher to attend and give instruction to the children in reading, writing, and arithmetic; and to the adults in sewing, cutting out, and mending their clothes. The hours of attendance were from six to eight on Monday, and from seven to nine on Thursday evenings. The school was established in the winter of 1849, and the attendance until the middle of March was tolerably regular. But as soon as the days began to grow long, the attendance became gradually more and more scanty. The teacher and the employer remonstrated both with young and old, for neglecting the opportunity of instruction; but remonstrance was in vain. At the end of April, the regular attendants had dropped down to two. Both teacher and employer were discouraged, and before the middle of May the experiment was abandoned. In going into one of the workshops of this establishment, I found twelve young girls engaged under the superintendence of a woman in packing up hooks and eyes in small boxes. Their ages varied from eight to eleven, or twelve. Out of the twelve not one could write well, and three could write very imperfectly. Ten of them knew their letters, and only two could read fluently. The whole of these girls went to one Sunday school, at which 170 girls attended. The forewoman made it a rule to see that the children in her employ went to school on the Sunday. She stated that an evening school was attached to it, but that out of the 170 who attended on Sundays less than 70 attended the evening school on the other nights of the week, so that by far the greater portion of them had no opportunity of learning either writing or arithmetic, or any other branch of study.

In my visits to the various manufactories of the town I have never missed an opportunity, when I have seen very young boys or girls employed, of asking their age and amount of schooling. In the bone and horn button trades, I have constantly seen ragged and wretched boys of eight or nine years of age, who, on being asked the question, have stated that they had never been at any school, and that they did not know their letters. At rolling mills I have put the same question to the same kind of boys, and have received the same answer. Day, evening, and Sunday schools were alike unknown to them. In the nail, screw, gun-lock, and brass manufactures, the same results were apparent; and the less extensive the establishment, the more wretched in attire and appearance, and the more ignorant, were the juvenile operatives.

Mr. Winfield, the eminent brass-founder, who employs from 450 to 500 people, of whom a very small proportion are women, was so painfully convinced of these evils that he established an evening school for his workpeople upwards of six years ago. The charge of admission was fixed at one penny per week. The school has been in operation since the middle of 1844, and Mr. Winfield expects that every boy in his employment shall attend it. The hours of school are from half-past seven to nine every Monday, Tuesday, Wednesday, and Friday night, and the course of instruction includes reading, writing, arithmetic, English grammar, geography, and drawing, with occasional lectures on the principles of mechanics, natural philosophy, and history. Some of the scholars of the drawing-class have passed into the Government School of Design, where they have been the recipients of prizes. The managers and clerks of the establishment and many of the superior and more intelligent of the workmen aid Mr. Winfield in his benevolent design, and gratuitously devote their leisure to the instruction of the boys. The school is not strictly confined to the labouring boys, as all the male children of the workmen are eligible. When the school was first established, it was remarked that scarcely a boy knew his companion except by a nickname; and that fights, both on entering and leaving school, were of constant occurrence. At present the practice of nicknames has disappeared, and a fight does not take place once in three months. There are 130 names on the books, the age of the youngest scholar being eleven, and of the eldest seventeen. The average attendance is eighty. It is found somewhat difficult to secure the attendance of the elder boys, who have not previously been at any school, and it is sometimes necessary to threaten them with discharge from the works in order to induce them to receive instruction. Many lads of sixteen and seventeen learn their letters at this school, never having received the slightest instruction of any kind before they had the good fortune to be taken into Mr. Winfield's employment. The younger boys more willingly attend school than the elder ones, and the men for whom they work hold it out as an inducement to them that their school penny will be paid for them if they behave themselves properly. On visiting this school, to which I was conducted by one of the managers of the factory, I found about seventy boys assembled. The greater portion of them were unwashed, just as they had come from their work in the shops. It was rather a novel sight to see so many dirty faces, but the teacher said that the boys were kept at their work till so late a moment that he was glad to see them to their time, even with all the disadvantage of dirty hands and faces. I was informed that Mr. Winfield contemplated the erection of a swimming bath, and that the idea was so popular among the boys that they made constant inquiries about it, and daily expressed their hope that their benevolent employer would be enabled to indulge them with the luxury. The proceedings of the evening commenced with a hymn. An orphan boy, fourteen years of age—a self-taught musician—placed himself before a small organ, provided by Mr. Winfield for the school-room, and played the Evening Hymn. All the boys accompanied him with their voices, and sang very creditably. After this they were distributed into their usual classes for reading, writing, and arithmetic. I was shown the copybooks of boys who had learned to write at the school; and I put some questions to the upper class, the replies to which showed a considerable proficiency. On making more particular inquiries of the masters and teachers, I was informed that the school laboured under many disadvantages—the principal being that the hours of attendance were not sufficiently long, and that even these few hours per week were constantly infringed upon when trade was brisk, by the men working over-hours, and requiring the boys to assist them.

Most of the boys, they said, preferred the over-work, because they got more money for it, and would rather work than be at school. Another great disadvantage was the physical exhaustion of the boys at that late hour of the evening. It was not at all unusual for the younger boys to drop asleep over their books, and sometimes during the singing of the hymn. No sectarian feeling is exhibited or allowed in the school. Mr. Winfield is himself a member of the Church of England, but no catechism or doctrinal point is introduced. The hymn is sung, a prayer is said, and the Bible is read without comment. Among the boys are the sons of workmen who belong to every Christian church and sect in the town—Church of England, Roman Catholic, Wesleyan, Presbyterian, Unitarian, and others. The master observed that many of the boys were tee-totallers; and on asking those who had taken the pledge to hold up their hands, it was found that there were twenty-nine. On those who were not tee-totallers being asked to declare themselves, thirty-seven hands were held up. A small library is attached to the school, consisting chiefly of Knight's Weekly Volumes. A boy is only eligible to the use of the library for general good conduct, regular attendance at school, when not required for work, and for general proficiency. Only about twenty of them are duly qualified.

The schools established by Messrs. William Chance and Co., the eminent manufacturers of crown and plate glass, at West Bromwich, near Birmingham, are still more extensive. Mr. William Chance is well-known for his benevolent efforts to elevate the moral and social condition of the children of the poor, and he maintains a Ragged-school in Birmingham entirely at his own expense. The schools at Spon Lane, West Bromwich, are of a different character, and are intended for the benefit, not of the ragged and idle, but of the honest working children employed in the neighbourhood, or in their own glass works. The first general schools for the children of the workpeople, and for those of the neighbourhood without distinction, were established in October, 1845, and are located in a very handsome row of buildings, built at the expense of the Messrs. Chance. At the period of my visit they were attended by 190 boys, 80 girls, and 150 infants. The attendance of the boys was reported to be "regular," that of the girls "improving," and that of the infants "good." About one-half of the total numbers came to the school from a distance of three-quarters of a mile to a mile and a half. The weekly charge is 3d. each, for which all books and stationery are provided. The boys are instructed in reading, writing, arithmetic, English grammar, geo-

graphy, and the elements of drawing. The girls receive the same education, except that plain needlework is substituted for drawing. The
schools are open to all sects. No catechism is taught, but the Bible is
read without comment. About one-half are the children of parents in
communion with the Church of England, and the other half are the
children of Dissenters of all denominations, including a few Roman
Catholics. The boys' school was opened about six months prior to
the girls' and infants' schools, and was originally intended for none
but the children of Messrs. Chance's workpeople. Between 60 and 70
were the numbers in attendance. At the end of that time the plan was
extended, and the schools were opened to the public, since which the
numbers have gradually increased. The children of Messrs. Chance's
workpeople form about a third of those in the boys' and about one-
half of those in the girls' and infant schools. Punctual and regular
attendance, cleanliness, and regularity of payment, are the sole conditions imposed upon children who wish to remain in the schools.
In connection with my visit to this school, I may mention that the
following suggestion was made to me in writing by Mr. Talbot, the
master:—

"The thought," says he, "has often occurred to me, that it would
not prove an impracticable thing to have a printing-press in connection
with every parochial school, under the immediate control of the heads
of the parish. Such an instrument might be made largely conducive to
the enlightenment and improvement of the masses of our people. The
art of printing might be, without much difficulty, acquired by our pupil
teachers when they shall become inmates of the training institutions,
and they might instruct one or two of the boys of their future charge,
who might be retained for a year or two in the service and pay of the
school. The press and types necessary for a small weekly, monthly, or
occasional pamphlet would cost about 20*l.* or 30*l.* The articles given
would have a direct and local bearing upon the people of the district
in which the school might be situated. How might the daily letters of
The Morning Chronicle commissioners, for instance, be reprinted and
circulated through such an agency! The children of our schools might
become the vendors of the school magazine and the evening instructors
of their households."

In addition to this school, the Messrs. Chance have established
another in the same handsome buildings, which is strictly confined
to the boys and men employed in the glass works. It was founded

on the 29th of July, in the present year, and opened with 110 scholars, all boys from the age of twelve upwards. No boys under twelve are employed by the Messrs. Chance in any of the departments of their business. The school fee is 2d. per week. For the first month or six weeks no men attended, as there was a general feeling of shame among the totally uneducated, and even among the partially instructed, at coming among boys to learn. This feeling gradually wore off, and by the end of October there were about 40 adults in regular attendance, of ages varying from 20 to 45. The mass of these men could read only, without being able to write, probably from having received no other education in their youth but such as could be acquired at the Sunday-schools. A very few of them could read and write well. Among them I was informed of one who had commenced the study of the French language, that he might be able to read the weekly article in French that appears in *The Morning Chronicle*, on the subject of the Great Exhibition of 1851. There is also one who is taking lessons in Latin, and a third—a gatekeeper, not a glass-blower—who has reached the mature age of 50, is learning Greek, in order that he may be able to read the New Testament in the original. The boys are taught reading, writing, and arithmetic, and the superior class receives instruction in English grammar and composition. Once a week there is an evening lecture on scripture history or general geography. A few of the Frenchmen employed at the works take lessons in English. The hours of school attendance are arranged so as not to interfere with the hours of labour. If a boy does not regularly attend the school, and cannot satisfactorily explain his absence, his conduct is reported to the manager of the department in which he works, whose duty it is to remonstrate with him on his neglect, and to urge upon him the duty of regular attendance. These irregularities appear to be as often the fault of the parents as of the boys; but generally the remonstrance of the manager is found sufficient, as it is understood that positive refusal on the part of the parents to allow the boy to come to the school, or of the boy himself to attend, will be followed by his discharge from the works. A reading-room for the use of the adults attending this school was established on the 1st of October. It is open from half-past six to ten every evening, and is supplied with *The Morning Chronicle* and two other daily papers and seven weekly papers, besides a French daily paper, and the principal monthly periodicals. There is a large open space between the school-house and the canal, which is used as a playground for foot-ball, cricket, and other sports; and if the Messrs.

Chance would construct a swimming-bath, for which they have not only abundance of room, but the facility of an ample supply of water from the canal, the establishment would be as admirable for the physical training as it is for the moral and intellectual improvement of the young glass makers. The school is found to answer its purpose so well, though not self-supporting, on account of the lowness of the school fee, that the Messrs. Chance are about to open another on a similar scale and plan at their extensive glass works at Oldbury, within a few miles distance from Spon Lane.

There seems, as far as I could ascertain, to be a very general impression among the large employers of Birmingham in favour of the education of the young children whom they are compelled, either directly or indirectly, to employ. I should be glad to present a complete list of those who have imitated, or are about to imitate, the example of the Messrs. Chance and the Messrs. Winfield, but after diligent inquiry, I am only able to mention the names of Mr. Bacchus, glass maker; Mr. Middlemore, carrier; and Messrs. Peyton and Barlow, brass and iron bedstead makers; although there are doubtless some other employers in the town who do good in this way without its being generally known. The schools of Messrs. Chance and Winfield are by far the most numerously attended; and supposing that all the other workshops or factory schools afford the opportunity of education to as many hard-working children as they do, it would appear that not above 500, out of the 15,000 of an age to be employed in the manufactories of Birmingham, receive any aid from their employers.

It is evident, therefore, that day, evening, and factory schools accomplish but little towards the education of the industrious youth of Birmingham—and that if the day and evening schools are to be turned to due account, it must be by means of some such legislative enactment for the regulation of the hours of labour of the juvenile workers in metal and other materials, as already applies to the children employed in the textile manufactures of the country. In default of any such legislative interference, the sole remaining means would be to extend the education given upon the Sunday, and to include in it not merely the reading of the Bible and the repetition of the Catechism, but instruction in writing, in the rudiments of arithmetic, in general geography, and in what is commonly called secular knowledge. But as this course would be repugnant to the Church of England, and to the dissenters generally, it is probable that if the juvenile working population of Birmingham are not to learn to write their names until they learn in the Sunday-schools, the ignorance which now prevails among them will be perpetuated. Such are the demands of the town for infant and juvenile labour, that only these two courses are open to those who do not desire that the education of the children of Birmingham should end in their seventh year; for it is scarcely to be expected that employers generally will voluntarily imitate the example of the few large manufacturers who refuse work to children under twelve. It is, therefore, highly necessary that the true cause of the deplorable ignorance in which such numbers of children grow into manhood and womanhood in the most industrious town in the world should be distinctly stated, in order that those who object to the teaching of writing on the Sunday may devote their energies to the only other possible means of effecting the object. Unless one or the other of these alternatives be employed, the more prosperous the town of Birmingham shall become, the greater will be the number of young children of both sexes who will grow up annually in intellectual, and perhaps in moral and religious darkness.

There are three Sunday-schools in the town, the conductors of which have no religious objection to the teaching of writing, geography, and arithmetic, or any other branch of knowledge on that day. These are the Old and New Meeting House Sunday-schools, founded and supported by the Unitarian body; and the Lancasterian Sunday-school, in Severn-street, founded and supported by members of the Society of Friends. No doctrinal points are touched upon in these schools, and they are attended by children, as well as by adults, of all religious denominations. The Old and New Meeting Sunday-schools, which were established in 1787, have effected much good; and in the course of my inquiries into the general condition of the population, I met with many individuals—shopkeepers, manufacturers, and even magistrates of the town—who acknowledged that they were solely indebted to the instruction which they received at one or other of these schools, and which they could not have obtained elsewhere, for all the success which had attended them through life, and for the means of rising from the lowest ranks of the people to their present position of affluence and responsibility.

The Old Meeting Sunday School is divided into five departments. The first is the *Writing Room*, the pupils of which are admitted at the age of twelve, and are taught reading and writing. It is necessary, before any pupil be admitted, that he attend one month regularly as a candidate, and his parents must present themselves before the committee, and pledge themselves to use every exertion that the pupil shall attend regularly, and conform to the rules of the institution.

When sufficient progress has been made by the pupils of the writing room, their behaviour being otherwise commendable, they are transferred to the arithmetic room. Here they are taught the rules of arithmetic, reading, and dictation. The pupils are afterwards transferred to the second adult room, or third department. This consists of pupils from the ages of 16 to 18, who are admitted direct into this room, the age being a sufficient qualification, and are classified according to their capabilities; the pupils from the arithmetic room have a preference, because of their connection with the school in other classes. The instruction given consists of reading, writing, arithmetic, geography, and the History of England.

The fourth department is the *Adult Room*. The age of the pupil must be 18 and upwards. Reading, writing, and arithmetic, as taught to the youngest children, are taught in this department to adults who have received no previous instruction.

The fifth branch of the institution is the superior class: the only qualification for admission is the progress made by the boys or adults. It is necessary that they should read well, write a good hand, understand the elementary rules of arithmetic; and, above all, that their attendance should be regular, and their behaviour commendable. To the branches of knowledge already acquired are added geography, elocution, English grammar, the higher branches of common arithmetic, from practice to decimals, and mensuration. It is from this room that the schools are supplied with efficient teachers.

The present number of pupils in the school is 522, of which there are in the writing room, 185; in the arithmetic room, 119; in the first adult room, 112; in the second adult room, 54; and in the superior room, 52. The average attendance and non-attendance daily, during the year, has been as follows:—

	Attendance.	Non-attendance.
Writing room	120	54
Arithmetic room	87	29
First adult	63	40
Second adult	43	18
Superior room	50	18
Total	363	159

The numbers admitted during the past year to the various rooms were as follow:—

To the writing room	....	95
„ 1st adult	....	49
„ 2nd adult	....	24
	Total	168

The total number of teachers is 106, whose attendance is every alternate Sunday. The average number attending each day is 35. The regular attendance is 70 per cent. of the total number on the books.

Quarterly meetings are held in the various rooms, to receive the reason from the pupils for absence, and if the committee, consisting of the teachers of the room, deem it unsatisfactory, they appoint a teacher to visit the parents, to ascertain the cause, and report to the Society of Teachers.

A "Casual Fund" has been recently formed for the purpose of relieving teachers and families in cases of necessity. It is composed of 67 members, who contribute 1s. a year, or 3d. per quarter.

There is also a sick society in connection with the school, to which the number of subscribers in 1849-50 is 378, being an increase over the previous year of 32.

In the savings club, also attached to the school, the number of depositors amounts to 190. The number of deposits last year was 2,376; the highest being £2, and the smallest 1d. The number of repayments was 350.

There is a library in connection with the school—which on the morning of my visit was so crowded with well-dressed young men, all anxious to obtain books, that I could with difficulty force my way to the table. The number of volumes is 2,319. The number of renewals and exchanges of books during the year was 14,860. The average weekly receipts for reading are 14s. 1½d.

As regards the adults, the following Statement of the ages of persons admitted since January, 1847, will prove interesting:—

38 at 17 years	8 at 24 years	1 at 31 years
37 at 18	10 at 25	7 at 32
22 at 19	9 at 26	1 at 33
19 at 20	4 at 27	11 at 34
16 at 21	4 at 28	1 at 38
10 at 22	2 at 29	1 at 43
12 at 23	6 at 30	

The great bulk of these persons could neither read nor write, but some few of them have made such progress that they are enabled to teach the juvenile classes, and they attend very regularly for that purpose. In my inquiries into the state of the glass manufacture, I met with one very intelligent man, much respected by all the trade, who stated to me that at the age of 27 he was unable to read. He attended the Old Meeting School for two or three years, and he can now read and write a good hand, keep accounts, and express himself correctly both in speaking and writing. The hours of attendance are every Sunday, from half-past nine in the morning until twelve, and from half-past two to four in the afternoon. No payment is received from the pupils, either juvenile or adult. The school is maintained by the contributions of the Old Meeting congregation of Unitarians, the voluntary aid of the public, and the proceeds of an annual sermon. The teachers all work gratuitously, and the only expense is therefore for house-room, and books and stationery. Among the teachers at the present time are two clerks, a gun-maker, a plane-maker, an iron bedstead maker, a brassfounder, a modeller, a saddler, and a pearl button maker, all of whom received their own education at the school. There are no means of knowing the religious opinions of the youths and adults. No inquiry is ever made upon the subject. The parents of the children, the children themselves, and the adults are informed that no creed is taught, but that religious instruction is left to the parents themselves to instil, and to the adults to acquire elsewhere. The following statement, made to me by one of the teachers, to whom I am indebted for the statistics of the school, will show the class of persons who principally receive benefit from it. He said:—"I went to a Church Sunday-school from the age of five to that of twelve, and occasionally to a day-school in connection with it. I went to work in a brass foundry at the age of eleven, at which time I could with some difficulty read the Testament. I was generally employed from eight in the morning until seven at night, but often had over-work till ten at night. I should think that three nights in the week I had over-work. At this time I could not attend either a day or evening school. I was too wearied to go to school, even if I did not work over-hours. I continued, however, to attend the Church Sunday-school for more than a year, during which time the little knowledge of writing which I had acquired in the day-school before I went to work failed me for want of use. I did not know one letter in writing from another, nor any of the figures. I knew nothing whatever about arithmetic or geography, and was in fact utterly ignorant. At the age of thirteen and a half I went for the first time to the Old Meeting School. There I have learned all that I know. I have never been at any other school. I have profited so much myself by the school that I endeavour to show my gratitude by devoting my Sundays to the instruction of others, who are now as ignorant as I then was. I have gone through all the offices in connection with the school, and have been superintendent. I know many persons in Birmingham, holding responsible situations, and occupying very high positions, who were educated here, and they all take an interest in the school, and attend from time to time."

The New Meeting School is conducted upon similar principles, and has been the means of educating almost as many youths and men as the Old Meeting. It may be estimated that at least 20,000 persons have been indebted to these two schools for their education during the 63 years in which they have been in operation.

The Sunday-school of the Society of Friends was established in 1845, and is solely supported by the contributions of the members of that sect. No school fee is required. The hours of attendance are from half-past seven to half-past nine every Sunday morning. The number of pupils on the books at the present time is 170, and the average attendance is 130. One of the teachers ascertained for me the ages of 147 of the scholars. There were 25 under sixteen years of age, 49 from sixteen to eighteen, 32 from eighteen to twenty, 33 from twenty to thirty, and 8 above thirty. Their trades and occupations were—brass casters and founders, 34; shoemakers, 10; tailors, 5; button-makers, 7; silver platers, 7; steel toy-makers, 6; jewellers, 11; glass-makers, 7; lamp-makers, 6; screw-makers, 6; spectacle-makers, 4; scale-makers, 2; engine-fitters, 3; gun and gun-lock makers, 9; stampers, piercers, and die sinkers, 6; painters, 4; printers, 4; book-binders, 2; carpenters, 5; and one porter. Twelve of the scholars were married men with families.

> "The school (says a memorandum forwarded by one of the teachers) is opened by the superintendent reading a portion of the Scriptures. Half the time is employed by the scholars in reading, and the other half in writing. The reading lessons are from the Bible.
> "Many of the scholars have much improved in reading and writing, and in numerous instances the scholars assert that they have derived much profit, directly and indirectly, from attendance at the school. Some in my own class could only just say their letters on entering the

school, who now are good readers, and write a fair hand. I have encouraged some to write letters to me, as many of them much wished for a little instruction in that art. Some of their productions are very amusing—others, even of those who can write tolerably, are not to be understood, being so unintelligibly expressed—but several are clear and sensible, and are always kind and grateful in their expression.

"Those scholars who come to school *quite ignorant* soon get discouraged, and but few of this class remain long.

"As a whole, the scholars are exceedingly well conducted, and often thank the teachers for their exertions. As far as I myself am concerned in the school, I may unhesitatingly add that my opinion of the working classes of Birmingham has much improved during the time I have been connected with the school.

"In connection with the 'First Day' school (Sunday) we have a school one evening in the course of the week, from eight to ten o'clock, to which only scholars of the other school are admitted. About thirty usually attend. They are instructed in reading, writing, and arithmetic. Some learn a little of geography, and have made progress, but their geographical information is generally very small. Lessons for writing are given on the subject of health and sanitary reform. These seldom fail to interest the learners."

It will appear from the above statements that not more than one-half of the children in Birmingham, between the ages of seven and fifteen, receive any instruction at all; and that the education received by the other half is irregular, in consequence of the demand for the labour of children in the workshops and factories, and that, when given on Sundays, it is for the most part incomplete, and includes nothing but reading and religious instruction. The efforts that are made by individuals to improve this state of things show the greatness of the evil which has forced them to bestir themselves, and how much yet remains to be done for the hard-working children of this town. I reserve the subject of education generally for another letter, having purposely confined myself in this to the state of children. I cannot conclude this subject without remarking the precocity in vice which is manifested by the young workpeople of Birmingham. Many boys of fourteen or fifteen years of age are known to spend their evenings in public-houses when not employed in over-hours of work, and may be seen in the streets on Sundays and Mondays smoking pipes and cigars with all the confidence, and fifty times the impudence, of manhood.

LABOUR AND THE POOR.

——◆——

BIRMINGHAM.

[FROM OUR SPECIAL CORRESPONDENT.]

THE MANUFACTURE OF STEEL-PENS.

LETTER IX.

The *Birmingham Directory* gives the names of eighteen steel-pen manufacturers in this town, and one in Walsall, and of eight pen-holder makers. Two of these manufacturers employ nearly 1,000 people; and it is estimated that the others employ among them about as many more. Nine years ago, the trade did not employ altogether above 400 persons. Steel-pens are almost entirely manufactured by women and young girls; and it is probable that out of the two thousand persons or upwards who are now engaged in the business, not above one hundred, or one hundred and fifty, are of the male sex. Men are only employed as tool-makers to keep in repair the tools and machines used in the manufacture, and in rolling the steel to the necessary thickness. In this last operation they are assisted by boys of the age of eight and nine and upwards. The more laborious process of tempering the pens, to be described hereafter, is also performed by men. The manufacture of pen-holders, and that of pen-boxes, which are carried on in separate establishments, give employment to an additional number of women and children, variously estimated at from 200 to 400 persons.

Metal pens are very ancient. "As long," says Beckman in his "History of Inventions," "as people wrote upon tables covered with wax they were obliged to use a style or bodkin made of bone, metal, or other hard substance, but when they began to write with coloured liquids, they employed a reed, and afterwards quills or feathers." But the metal pen, to be used with ink, to write upon paper, is a comparatively modern invention. Gold and silver pens have been known for upwards of half a century; and Mr. Bohn, the publisher, in a note to the article on reeds and quills, or "Writing Pens," in Beckman's "History of Inventions," states that he has in his possession "an extremely

well made metallic pen (brass) at least fifty years old, and with it a
style for writing by means of smoked paper, both in a morocco pocket-
book, which formerly belonged to Horace Walpole, and was sold at
the Strawberry Hill sale." The most eminent manufacturer of steel
pens in Birmingham first tried his hand at his art upwards of thirty
years ago, when steel pens were quite unknown, and manufactured a
pen of silver, to fit into a pencil case. He had at that time no idea
of superseding the quill in schools, offices, and for general use, but
simply to produce an article for the waistcoat pocket. He afterwards
made experiments with iron and steel, and produced a pen very creditable to his skill and ingenuity at that time, but not for a moment
to be compared with the beautiful pens which he now fabricates by
millions. While these original steel pens were very hard, stiff, and
bad, they were also very dear. About the year 1820 or 1821 the first
gross of "three-slit" steel pens was sold wholesale at the rate of £7
4s. the gross. In the year 1830 they had fallen to 8s., and in 1832 to
6s. the gross. A better article is now sold at 6d. per gross. A japan
pen that eight or ten years ago sold at 32s. a gross, is now sold at
1s. 2d., and is far more flexible and serviceable. For many years steel
pens had to struggle not only against the conservatism of the lovers of
the quill, but against their own badness. They spluttered, rusted, tore
the paper, and had so many imperfections that they made way very
slowly. Clerks in offices set their faces against them—schoolmasters
would have none of them, and authors gave them up in despair. Even
within the last five or six years they were so dear that people, though
otherwise satisfied with the improvements which had been gradually
made, objected to their use because they could not be mended; and
various attempts were made by many parties to obviate the objection
by inventing a method of renovating them. They have now become so
elastic, so excellent, and so exceedingly cheap, that people no more
think of mending a steel pen, than they would think of mending a
pin. One factory alone in Birmingham produces them at the rate
of no less than 40,000 gross, or 5,760,000 in a week—very nearly a
million, or 960,000 per working day, or 289,520,000 per annum. A
second establishment, which employs as many people, doubtless produces as great a quantity, so that it may be safely estimated, at the
very lowest calculation, that Birmingham produces 1,000 millions
per annum of these articles. The cheapest pens are sold as low as
2d. per gross wholesale; and the price rises, with the elasticity and
finish of the pen, up to 3s. 6d. and 5s. per gross. There are no

manufactories of steel pens in London, or in any other part of the United Kingdom, although the names of the London dealers which are impressed upon them might lead to the contrary belief. Birmingham produces them all, and one establishment in this town has the distinctive marks of no less than 500 different dealers in all parts of the country, as well as on the continents of Europe and America, for whom he manufactures, according to order. They are exported to all parts of the world; for although the Americans, the Germans, the Belgians, and the French have endeavoured to compete with the people of Birmingham, they have not yet succeeded in producing so excellent or so cheap an article, and in spite of an *ad valorem* duty of 24 per cent. on their importation into America, and of a duty of about 1½d. per gross by weight in France, the French and American dealers send their orders to Birmingham, and have their names and marks stamped upon them. Our continental neighbours, it may be observed, *en passant,* make steel pens subservient to political purposes, not simply in their uses, as other people might do, but in their pattern. The ultra-republican dealers order pens to be decorated with the head of the goddess of Liberty, with the Phrygian cap, or with the words "*République Française.*" The Bonapartists order pens with the head of Louis Napoleon; while the Legitimists strive to render the countenance of the Count de Chambord familiar to the public by the same means. The Italian Republicans also endeavour to keep up the anti-Papal enthusiasm and the spirit of Carbonarism by the like devices.

The great drawbacks to the success of the manufacture on the continent appear to be threefold—first, the necessity under which the foreign manufacturers labour of procuring their steel from Sheffield, and paying for it at a rate exceeding that paid by the Birmingham manufacturers by nearly the whole cost of transmission; secondly, the difficulty of finding skilled tool-makers; and thirdly, the still greater difficulty of finding a sufficient number of women and girls in countries where the services of females are required for so many other pursuits and occupations, of agriculture, trade, and labour, in consequence of the demand made for all the available portion of the other sex by revolutions and wars, and rumours of wars. So many men are withdrawn from the pursuits of industry to play the costly game of the military governments, that women are required in too great numbers for the ordinary avocations of life to permit any considerable number of them to be diverted into the channel of a new manufacture. The chief exports are to America. The next best customers are the French, who require a very delicate and flexible pen, on account of the thinness of the paper which they commonly use. There is also a very considerable export to Germany, which, however, the recent unsettled state of that portion of the continent has to some extent diminished. There are two or three, if not more, manufacturers of steel pens in Paris, but they cannot compete even in their own market with the Birmingham makers. The French pens are both bad and dear. A manufactory existed in Vienna, about two years ago, but it has been closed, and the Austrian dealers get all their pens from Birmingham. There is also a manufactory of steel pens in Boulogne, under the superintendence of an English firm, connected with Birmingham; but I am not enabled to state what kind of article it produces, nor whether the prices are equally low with those of the English manufacturers.

The establishment of the penny postage has no doubt contributed largely to increase the demand for steel pens in England. The growth of the steel pen manufacture has kept pace with the increase in the number of letters passing through the Post-office since that great social reformation was effected. "Without steel pens," to quote the *Household Words* of Mr. Dickens, "it may reasonably be doubted whether there were mechanical means within the reach of the great bulk of the population for writing the three hundred and thirty-seven millions of letters that now annually pass through the Post-office." And greatly as the manufacture of steel pens has been improved by the skill and perseverance of such men as Mr. Gillott, who have devoted their lives, in difficulty and discouragement as well as in prosperity, to bring it to perfection, it is not likely that it has yet reached the maximum of excellence or the minimum of cheapness. Mr. Gillott himself, who has done so much to improve it, considers the manufacture to be yet in its infancy.

A description of a visit to the establishment of this gentleman will afford the reader a sufficient idea of the various interesting processes of the manufacture; of the earnings of the workwomen; of the arrangements made by and for them for their good government and comfort; and of their general social, intellectual, and moral condition. The first steel pens were made in garrets—the manufacturer and his family being the only workpeople. But now they are produced in factories of palatial appearance and extent. That of Mr. Gillott accommodates from 500 to 600 people. That of Messrs. Hinckes and Wells is equally large. Both establishments continue to extend, first to one side, and then to another, of their original location; and that of Messrs. Hinckes and Wells has spread to both sides of the street in which it is situated. Mr. Gillott's factory is considered a model of its kind; and his arrangements for the social welfare of his workpeople being particularly spoken of, I requested the permission—not usually granted to strangers, or to those who merely wish to pass an idle hour in viewing the manufacturing "lions" of the town—to inspect the establishment. It was readily accorded, and every information bearing either upon the past or present state of the trade, or upon the condition of the workpeople, both old and young, both male and female, was freely given.

Interior of Gillott's Pen Manufactory

The first operations are performed by steam power. The sheets of steel, after they are received from Sheffield, are reduced to the requisite tenuity by successive transits through the rolling-mill, operations which are tended by men and boys. When reduced in this manner to the thinness of a steel pen, and to the length of about two feet and the breadth of two inches and a half, or three inches, the sheets of steel are ready for the next processes, which are entirely performed by women and girls. Describing the rooms according to the order of the processes, and not according to the arrangement of the building, the first to be entered is that where the "blanks" are punched out. Ranged in double rows along a large and roomy workshop, with windows at both sides, and scrupulously white and clean, in floor, roof, and walls, are seated from fifty to a hundred girls and women, from the age of fourteen to that of forty and upwards. Unlike too many of the women employed in the manufactories of Birmingham, they are extremely neat in person and attire. They present an air both of cleanliness and comfort seldom to be met with. There is no talking in the room. The only sounds to be heard are the working of the hand press, and the clinking of the small pieces of metal as they fall from the block into the receptacle prepared for them. This process is performed with great rapidity—one girl, of average industry and dexterity, being able to punch or cut out about 100 gross per day. Each division of the workshop is superintended by a tool-maker, whose business it is to keep the punches and presses in good working condition, to superintend the work generally, and to keep order among the workpeople. Much immorality is produced in Birmingham by the inattention of employers, who often appoint improper characters to these responsible situations. They are too often satisfied if they can secure a skilful workman—however immoral and bad his behaviour may be—and do not care whether he be married or single, provided he understand his business. Mr. Gillott, and the larger and better class of employers in general, are more careful, and select married men of good moral character for these situations. When it is considered that the tool-maker has it in his power to procure the discharge of a girl or a woman, it will be at once understood how important it is that the libertine and the profligate should not be placed in situations where they may abuse the trust and the authority confided to them, and how sacred and essential a duty to the workwomen is performed by those employers who direct their attention to this matter, and endeavour to preserve the females of their establishment from the contamination of immoral taskmasters.

The next operation is to place the blank in a concave die, on which a slight touch from a convex punch produces the requisite shape—that of the semi-tube. The slits and apertures which increase the elasticity of the pen, and the maker's or vendor's name or mark, are produced by a similar tool. The arrangement of the workpeople along each side of a spacious, lofty, well-lighted and well-ventilated room, is the same as in the previous department; and the scene presents the same animation, yet perfect order and regularity, as are exhibited in the one previously entered. The cleanliness of the floors in all these rooms is as gratifying as it is remarkable. Each worker cleans her own compartment, or enters into an arrangement with her neighbour to do it for her; and no tax is levied by the proprietor for this purpose, as in the screw-factory, of which one of the girls complained to me, as related in a former letter of this series.

The last operation is that of slitting, which is also performed by girls and women. Previously to this, however, the pen undergoes a variety of processes, in a different part of the factory, and under the hands of a different class of workpeople. When complete all but the slit, the pen is soft and pliable, and may be bent or twisted in the hand like a piece of thin lead. Being collected in "grosses," or "great grosses"—the former containing 144, and the great gross twelve times that number—the pens are thrown into little iron square boxes by men, who perform all the work in this department, and they are placed in a furnace, where they remain till box and pens are of a white heat. They are then taken out, and thrown hissing hot into pails or tanks of oil—a process which cures them of their softness, by making them brittle. When taken out of the oil, they may be broken by the fingers with as much ease as if they were so many wafers. As a great deal of oil adheres to them, they are put into a sieve to drain. There they remain until no more oil will run from them; but, notwithstanding all the draining which they have received, the oil is not effectually removed. To cleanse them thoroughly they were formerly thrown into pits or heaps of sawdust, and stirred about; but as by this process the sawdust became clotted into oil cakes, and was rendered unserviceable, the ingenuity of Mr. Gillott was taxed to discover some means by which a saving both of oil and of sawdust could be effected. He was not long before the thought struck him that, if the pens were made to revolve rapidly in a perforated cylinder, the last drop of oil might be forced out of them; in fact, that the oil might be twirled from the pens like moisture from a mop. The experiment was tried, and succeeded admirably. The pens, after being allowed to drain in the sieve until no more oil would run off them, were placed, apparently dry, but greasy-looking, in the cylinder, and twirled round with great rapidity, until the oil ran off in a copious stream. The mingled sawdust and oil formerly constituted a nuisance, and it was necessary to change the sawdust, and burn it, three or four times a day. It now lasts for a week. By this means—a remarkable instance of the economy of manufactures—Mr. Gillott has diminished his oil account by a sum varying from £200 to £300 per annum. This operation completed, the pens are once more placed in revolving cylinders, where their friction against each other produces the necessary polish. Each pen is thus made to clean and polish its neighbour. The next process is to roast or anneal these brittle articles, and give them the flexibility of the quill, and to produce upon them at the same time the colour which may be desired, whether bronze or blue. The flexibility and colour are both produced by heat, and it becomes a delicate matter so to arrange and regulate it as to attain the exact results desired. From this department they are once more consigned to the female part of the establishment, where, by the operation of the cutting tool, each pen receives the required slit. One girl, with a quick and practised finger, can slit by this means as many as 200 gross, or 28,800 pens in a day. They are now ready for counting and packing, in boxes or grosses, for the wholesale market. This last stage of the business is wholly performed by young girls.

The workpeople are all paid according to the amount of work performed. The younger girls earn from 5s. to 6s. per week, and some of the more expert and attentive women earn as much as 12s. or 14s. a week. The average wages are 10s. or 11s. There is no sub-employing. Every person is directly hired and paid by the manufacturer. The tool makers receive high wages, often as much as £3 or £4 a week. The wages of the men in the steam and fire departments are from 20s. to 25s., or 30s., and those of the boys who assist them from 4s. to 7s.

As regards the moral government of the factories, the following particulars were communicated by Mr. Gillott and by other persons. He takes as much care as possible to prevent the introduction of improper characters, whether male or female. He will not employ children under the age of thirteen or fourteen, and he advises all applicants under thirteen to go to school. He selects in preference those girls who have been to a day as well as a Sunday school, and who can both read and write. It is not possible, however, to insist too rigidly upon the qualification of writing, as so few girls can write as well as read, that he would be short of hands to work his factory if he excluded them on this account. He requires that they should be recommended for good moral conduct, for steadiness, and for cleanliness, by a Sunday-school teacher, a clergyman, or other respectable person, before he will admit them into his employ. He finds, if by any chance a girl of improper character is engaged, that the other girls immediately bring her conduct under his notice, and call for an investigation. If the charge of immoral life is proved against her, she is discharged. Among so many young women cases of the kind will sometimes occur, but they are exceedingly rare, and as a general rule the young women are modest and well-behaved. They marry much too early. On Sundays and holidays the unmarried girls, like most of this class in Birmingham, dress very smartly, but their finery too often is all out-side show—and the silk dress very commonly covers ragged dirt and inferior under-clothes. Mr. Gillott will not allow Saint Monday, but finds a general inclination among the girls to indulge in a holiday on that day. In the fine summer weather he occasionally yields so far to their wishes as to close at five o'clock on Monday afternoon, instead of at seven, the usual hour. The whole of the persons in the factory, men and boys, girls and women, belong to the sick club established by Mr. Gillott. The club is encouraged by him, but it is not imperatively required that the workpeople shall belong to it. He and all his fam-ily, and all the clerks in his employ, pay regularly towards it, and the workpeople, when sick, receive an allowance. The subscription is 3d. a week. The girls have other clubs among themselves, and put by from a penny to twopence and threepence a week, to purchase articles of clothing. There are shoe and boot clubs, shawl clubs, and dress clubs. The favourite club is for the annual "gipsy party," or excursion into the country. The gipsy parties are now very common in Birmingham, and form quite a feature in the social history of the working classes. Almost every class of workpeople in the town have them. They were scarcely known at all about five years ago; but owing to the cheapness of locomotion, and the trips advertised by the railway companies, a taste for excursions has sprung up, and "gipsy parties" occur almost every day, in the summer season. The favourite resorts are Kenilworth, to visit the magnificent ruins of the Castle, and the Clent Hills, from which there is a magnificent panoramic view, extending over an area of sixty square miles, and exhibiting glimpses of the Malvern Hills, the Wrekin, and the Peak of Derbyshire. Mr. Gillott's gipsy party this year was spoiled by the bad weather. That of Messrs. Hinckes and Wells was more fortunate. The girls and women paid a penny a week for a twelvemonth towards it, and the men 2d. a week, their employers contributing a handsome sum. The party mustered no less than 350 people. About 150 stayed away, some because they could not afford the money, and others because they stated that they had no clothes to go in. The party started from Birmingham at seven o'clock on a fine summer morning to Hagley and the Clent Hills to pass the day. They filled 45 cars, which were gaily ornamented with banners and devices, and they were accompanied by a band of music. The whole of the party breakfasted in the open air, in tents, at the

Hagley Arms. They walked in procession up to the Clent Hills, and enjoyed the beautiful view into Wales. Quadrilles and country dances were then got up, and these and other amusements continued until dinner time. The whole party dined under tents in the open air, the band of music playing all the time. It was not a tee-total festival, but the party were very temperate. A copy of the following regulations, neatly printed, was given to each individual before starting:—

"REGULATIONS TO BE OBSERVED ON THE OCCASION OF MESSRS. HINCKS, WELLS, AND CO.'S PLEASURE TRIP, JULY 13, 1850.

"Car, No......

"The holder of this ticket must ride there and back in this conveyance.

"Time of Starting.—Half-past six o'clock precisely; any one being later, will be left behind, and their money forfeited.

"The Road.—In getting out of the cars, to walk up the hills (on the road); you are requested not to mix with other parties, but to keep pace with your own conveyance.

"The Park.—In passing through the park the same order to be observed as in riding; to walk four abreast, and under no pretence to move out of the line; any one seen injuring or destroying the trees, hedges, or plants, will be discharged.

"Clent Hills.—On the hills, dancing and other amusements. You are requested not to roam in small or detached parties, otherwise you will incur the severe displeasure of your employers; at the sounding of the trumpet, the whole to return to dinner in the same order as in first passing through the park.

"Time of returning Home.—Eight o'clock precisely. The same order must be observed in returning as in going. You are requested not to sing, or otherwise make a noise in passing through the streets; and it is hoped that the greatest order and propriety will be observed throughout the day.

"Any one requiring any information, must apply to either of the members of the committee.

"Programme for Dancing.—Triumph, Paine's 1st set, gallopade, Schottische, Circassian circle, Lancers, polka, Spanish dance, circular waltz."

These regulations were drawn up by a committee of the employed and the employers, and were so strictly and cheerfully adhered to, that neither in going nor returning, nor during the stay of the party

on the hills, did there occur a single instance of disobedience to orders, of misbehaviour of any kind, or of drunkenness—a fact as highly
creditable to the employers as to the workpeople.

Upon the whole, the manufacture of steel-pens is exceedingly
well-conducted. The labour is not hard; it is much better paid than
the labour of women generally. Children are not employed in it at too
early an age. There is no sub-employing; all the workpeople are directly responsible to the manufacturers; and the work is not unwholesome. The workshops are light, clean, and well ventilated, and the
principal employers are men who seem to understand thoroughly the
duties which they owe to those dependent upon them for subsistence,
and not to be contented with merely paying them their wages and
taking no further interest in them. The manufacture is already large,
and is daily increasing. The only subject of regret in connection with
it seems to be that, out of so many hundreds of women employed
in making the pens which all the civilized nations of the world use
in recording their thoughts and their wishes, their business and their
affections, so very few can make use of them. They can make pens
by myriads, but they cannot write their own names. At every steel-
pen factory at which I inquired, the number of girls and women who
could read was considerable; but the number of those who could write
was very small. For these girls there is no other chance of education
except at evening and Sunday schools. I have shown in a former Letter the necessary non-success of evening schools; and as the Sunday
schools, with a few exceptions, do not teach writing, the girls who
have not acquired the art before they commenced work have little or
no opportunity of acquiring it afterwards.

LABOUR AND THE POOR.

——◆——

BIRMINGHAM.

[FROM OUR SPECIAL CORRESPONDENT.]

GLASS-MAKERS AND WORKERS IN GLASS.

LETTER X.

The glass-manufacture of Birmingham is divisible into two great branches: the first, that of Crown and Plate Glass, or glass used for windows, for mirrors, and for shades; the second, that of Flint Glass, comprising all other articles for scientific and domestic purposes, and for table use and ornament. There is a third manufacture—that of black bottles for wine and beer, and of soda-water and pickle bottles, but there are no establishments of this kind in Birmingham. Black bottles are manufactured principally at Stourbridge and Wordsley, in Staffordshire; at Hunslet, in Yorkshire; at Leeds, Bristol, Glasgow, Dumbarton, and London.

The Birmingham Directory contains the names of 19 glass manufacturers, 20 glass button manufacturers, 5 glass chandelier and lustre manufacturers, 27 glass cutters, 5 glass engravers, 4 glass mould makers, 15 glass painters, stainers, and benders, and 20 glass toy manufacturers. There is no manufacture of crown or plate glass in the town, but there is one very extensive establishment at Spon Lane, near West Bromwich—that of Messrs. Chance and Co.—which is so closely connected with Birmingham as to form a necessary subject of description in connection with its manufactures.

Hutton, in his History of Birmingham, gives some account, more or less detailed and accurate, of the various branches of manufacture carried on in the town, but he makes no mention of glass. It does not appear that this manufacture was at all extensive in the town until a comparatively recent period. On making inquiry into the subject, I learned from an eminent firm of glass cutters, that "a Mr. Hawker, who kept a glass shop in Edgbaston-street, built a small glass furnace in the same street about the year 1785, and was the first person who made glass in Birmingham. His son afterwards erected some large

works on Birmingham Heath, the same that are now occupied by
Messrs. Lloyd and Summerfield. A Mr. Johnson, in connexion with
a Mr. Shakspear, followed, and in 1798 commenced working a furnace in Walmer-lane, from which they shortly afterwards removed
to the neighbourhood of Soho, and built the extensive works lately
in the occupation of a son of Mr. Shakspear. Previously to 1785, and
for some time afterwards, the Midland counties were principally supplied with glass from Dudley and Stourbridge." Birmingham at the
present time is as celebrated for its beautiful manufactures in glass, as
for its manufactures in metal. Among the various articles which it
produces, independently of crown, sheet, and plate glass—of which I
shall speak presently—are drinking glasses, tumblers, and goblets of
all kinds, decanters, jugs, pitchers, lamp pillars, chimneys, and shades,
candlesticks, inkstands, lustres, gas shades, glass plates and dishes,
épergnes, smelling bottles, chimney ornaments, and a whole host of
minor articles, not easy to enumerate. The flint glass manufacture of
Birmingham gives employment to about 210 glass makers or blowers,
and to about the same number of glass cutters or grinders. The whole
number of flint glass makers in the United Kingdom is about 1,000;
so that upwards of one-fifth reside in and near Birmingham.

The first operation in glass making is technically called "pot-
setting." The pot, which is made of fine white or Stourbridge clay, is
placed in the furnace, and filled with the sand and other materials.
The sand comes principally from the Isle of Wight; the pot ash from
Smethwick, near Birmingham; and the manganese from chemical
works at Liverpool, Glasgow, or London. The pots, according to the
custom of the trade, are set or filled on Friday night, at six o'clock.
By Saturday morning early, the material in the pot is smelted down
to less than half of its original bulk. It takes three "fillings" to fill the
pot, the last of which is put in at ten or eleven o'clock on Saturday
night. The mouth of the pot is then closed up in the furnace, and
remains closed until Monday morning at six o'clock, when it is
considered ready for work. At seven o'clock on Monday morning,
the work of the glass makers and blowers begins. The hours of work
in the trade are peculiar. A first batch of workmen commences
at seven in the morning, and works for six hours, until one in the
afternoon. This is called a "turn," or two "moves," of three hours
each. Another batch or relay of men then relieves the first, and
works from one in the afternoon until seven. This is the second turn
of two moves. The first set relieves these again at seven, and works

for six hours, until one in the morning, when they are once more relieved by the second relay. This is the invariable routine, and five of these turns and a half, or eleven moves of three hours, are considered a full week's work. By this system the men have six hours' work and six hours' rest, and cannot like the operatives in other trades have a full night's sleep, until the end of the week. The ordinary work of the week therefore ends on Wednesday—making twelve hours on Monday, day and night; twelve on Tuesday; and nine on Wednesday. All the work performed on Thursday and Friday is, therefore, considered over-hours, and paid accordingly. Very few of the men work on Friday, and none of them on Saturday. The wages received vary with the skill and dexterity of the glass-blower. There are considered to be four degrees of skill in flint glass making. The work is divided into what are called "chairs," each chair comprising a "taker-in," a "foot-maker," a "servitor or blower," and a "workman." The last-mentioned is the principal man, who sits at his "chair" opposite the furnace, and is assisted by the other men. The "taker-in" is usually a boy; his business is to carry the glass to and from the furnace. The "foot-maker" forms the feet or stands of wine glasses and goblets. The "servitor or blower" blows the metal, and prepares it for the "workman," who gives it the shape required—an operation which, in lamp-shades, decanters, jugs, &c., requires much skill and dexterity of manipulation. The wages of a "taker-in" are 4s. a week, and 3d. each "move," of overwork. The "foot-makers"—generally lads, or men who have not been able to acquire the skill necessary for the fine work—receive from 9s. to 13s. a week, and from 10d. to 1s. per "move" overwork. The "servitor" has from 16s. to 22s. per week, and from 1s. to 1s. 9d. per move extra; and the "workman" has from 28s. to 30s. per week, and from 2s. to 3s. a move extra. The men regularly go through all these gradations, and it is considered that a boy ought to begin the business at ten years of age, if he wishes to become a skilful workman.

The following particulars of the habits of the men, the effect of the occupation upon their health and comfort, the recent history of the trade, the disputes between the employed and the employers, and the means adopted by the operatives to remove the superabundant hands from the neighbourhood, and provide for them elsewhere, were communicated by an intelligent working man:—

"The glass-blowers," he said, "do not consider their business to be unhealthy. Though it is very hot in the glass-house, there is al-

The Manufacture of Glass

ways a great current of air through the works. After working for six hours, we are in a great perspiration. We often perspire through our clothes, and my clothes have many a time been as wet as if I had been wading in a brook. I am not now in the trade, but know all about it, having recently left it to attend to another business. I never changed clothes when I left off work, and yet I did not catch cold. The heat and the perspiration make the men thirsty, and they are obliged to drink a good deal. The perspiration is also very exhausting, and they feed well to keep up their strength. It is a general thing among the men in this trade to have meat for breakfast, dinner, and supper. There is no difficulty in the blowing, so far as strength is concerned. A child could blow, for that matter. The only difficulty is to blow at the right time, when the material is at the proper heat, and to blow it to the exact size required. After leaving off work at the end of the first turn, at one in the day, the men go to dinner, and some of them go to bed till six in the afternoon, and are then able to work pretty freshly till one in the night. They then take another spell of bed; though there are many men who do not go to sleep in the day-time between 'turns,' but look after some other business. Some of them keep public-houses. No man could stand the work if it lasted the whole week—the strongest man could not do it; and generally it may be said that the glass-blowers have the whole of Friday and Saturday to themselves. The flint-glass makers have a very strong union all through the kingdom. There was a great strike among the blowers at one establishment in Birmingham, which began in June or July, 1848, and lasted till March, 1849. The strike was supported by the union, and cost about £1,500. The dispute arose about time, and consequently about wages; and all the blowers of the establishment in question held out for about three months. At the end of that time some of them returned to their work. The proprietor, as soon as he suffered inconvenience for want of men, sent over to France, and procured about twenty-six 'blowers.' The Frenchmen were hooted and pelted in the streets of the town, and rows often occurred. The union offered the Frenchmen 26s. per week each, if they would join the strike, and undertook to pay their expenses back to France, if they preferred to go; but they all refused. The union ultimately gave in to the master's terms. The strike caused much ill-will and ill-feeling, besides costing a great deal of money. Flint-glass makers are generally men who have seen a good deal of the world. When a man is out of work, and cannot procure it in his own neighbourhood, he is paid at a certain rate out of the funds of the union, to travel to the next town where there may be glass works, and from that again still further if no work is to be procured. There are many men now in Birmingham who have travelled over France and the United States, and in every part of the United Kingdom, in search of work. The repeal of the Excise duty on glass is considered a great boon by the working men. They are all very thankful for it. Formerly the trade was in the hands of a few capitalists who had a complete monopoly. If a man offended his employers, for any reason, right or wrong, the master sent a circular to all the glass makers in England, Scotland, and Ireland, and prevented him from getting employment. Men were often kept out of work for as long as eighteen months or two years under this system, and they and their families reduced to the workhouse. These things are impossible now. If the masters declare against a man and refuse him work, the man can set up for himself. For £20, or thereabouts, he can establish himself in a small way and make glass. Even with so small a sum as £10 he may make a beginning in common glass, and may earn enough to keep him, besides having the pleasure and consolation of knowing that he is his own master, and that it is out of the power of any large employer or other person to ruin him. Out of the 210 flint-glass makers in Birmingham there is scarcely a man who has not subscribed something towards the statue of Sir Robert Peel. The working-men consider that it was quite a 'god-send' to their trade when the Excise duty on glass was abolished. The Excise was a great impediment to the manufacture and prevented all improvement. A manufacturer could not try experiments under the old system. Before filling a 'pot,' however small, it was necessary to give so many hours' notice to the exciseman; and the metal in the pot, if it were ever so little, could not be worked off to try an experiment with, unless the whole duty for the pot were paid. This made experiments very expensive, and the consequence was, they were not tried."

Another workman—a strong, hale, man, who looked about six-and-twenty, but said he was six-and-thirty—gave information which corroborated the above statements in most of the particulars. He said, "he had been twenty-seven years in the trade, having commenced as a taker-in at the age of nine, and gone through all the gradations of taker-in, footmaker, servitor, and workman. He earned the highest wages, and worked as hard as any man in Birmingham. He had saved money, and was the owner of several small houses, but he still continued to work as a journeyman, and would until he had amassed enough to retire. He found the work hard, but not unhealthy. He was obliged to feed well, and he usually drank three quarts of porter a day, and thought it agreed with him. He was of opinion that the repeal of the Excise duty, though calculated to be of service to the trade, had in reality injured it—because the men, either from quarrels, or differences of opinion with their employers, or from a desire to become their own masters, set up small glasshouses for themselves, and carried on a trade without sufficient capital. Since the abolition of the Excise duty, many workmen in Birmingham had begun to manufacture glass, but all, or nearly all, of them had failed after struggling for a few months. They produced the commonest glass, at a cheap rate, and depended upon an immediate sale one week to carry on their business for the next. They could not afford to wait, and on Saturday night they forced sales, and offered their glass to the dealers, or 'slaughtermen,' for almost any price, rather than not sell at all. This system operated injuriously upon the whole trade. It brought down prices, and tended to bring down wages. Upon the whole, however, he thought that freedom in the glass trade had produced improvement in the manufacture, and that, with the exception named, it had been of advantage to the employed as well as the employers."

The flint-glass makers' union is represented as a powerful body, but their funds having severely suffered from the drain made upon them by the strike of 1848 and 1849, and the members having long complained of a superabundance of labour and a consequent competition for work among the operatives, which was fast bringing down the price of labour, it was resolved early in the present year to summon a Conference in Birmingham to consider the state and prospects of the trade. The Conference was summoned, as the circular stated, "to determine on the best course to be pursued in removing the vast amount of surplus labour which was prostrating the manufacture, and on the necessary steps to be taken to benefit the condition of the workmen generally." The Conference met at the "Glass-makers' Arms," in Birmingham, on the 13th of July, and was attended by delegates from London, Edinburgh, Dublin, Birmingham, Manchester, Glasgow, York, Bristol, Belfast, Newcastle-on-Tyne, Waterford, St. Helen's, Warrington, Tutbury, Longport, Rotherham, Catcliffe, Haverton Hill (near Stockton-upon-Tees), Dudley and Holly Hall, Stourbridge, Wordsley, Hunslet, and Worsborodale near Barnsley— being the whole of the places at which glass is manufactured in the United Kingdom. At the conclusion of the Conference a dinner of the delegates took place, which was attended by about 150 members. The Chairman "congratulated the members and delegates on their prospects in entering what might be considered a new era in the trade, when the men would be able to make themselves more independent of masters who chose to be tyrants, without running the risk of being left to starve, as they had now organized a system by which not only their rights would be protected, but by means of which they would be enabled to get rid of any surplus labour there might be in the market." At this conference it was resolved that an emigrational committee of the trade should be established, of which the object should be to send the surplus hands to the United States, at the rate of six men per month for six months, or for a longer period if necessary. Many of them have been despatched to Brooklyn, Pittsburg, New Jersey, and Philadelphia, where glass works have been established, and where there is a pretty regular demand for skilled workmen from England. It was also decided at the conference to establish a penny monthly magazine, to disseminate information on all points connected with the manufacture abroad and at home, to uphold the interests of the working men, and to communicate scientific knowledge and information of a nature calculated to improve the morals and elevate the social condition of the general body.

The *Glass Cutters* form a separate trade. The total number in the United Kingdom is supposed to be from 980 to 1,000. Of these nearly one-half are in Birmingham and its neighbourhood—namely, from 200 to 220 in Birmingham, 50 in Dudley, and nearly 200 in Stourbridge. The trade began, about two years and a half ago, to establish a fund for maintaining the members when out of work, each member of the Glass Cutters' Society or Union contributing 6d. a week for that purpose. There was such great depression in the trade during the years 1848 and 1849—consequent, to some extent, upon the large quantities of glass sent into the English market from the Continent, by Continental manufacturers who were desirous to force sales at almost any price—that many hands were thrown out of work, and it was found necessary to increase the weekly contribution, and raise what was called an "extra levy." One hundred and thirty men out of work were at one time on the list, but the average number maintained at the expense of the trade in those years was fifty. The lowest sum paid per week for the support of the unemployed is 4s. 9d., and the highest 10s. The Union also established a "Tramp Society," of which the object was to pay every man out of work a penny a mile to go on the "tramp" in search of it. On arriving at any town where glass cutters are employed, the man in search of work receives a supper, bed, and breakfast. If no work is to be obtained, he is passed on to the next town at the same rate, and receives a similar allowance. If he has to take a sea voyage—from Liverpool to Glasgow or Dublin, or elsewhere—his passage is paid, and he receives 2s. 6d. besides. If he is offered work at any town, and, preferring to go on the tramp, refuses to accept it, the case is represented to the Union, and he is struck off the list. The glass-cutters, like the glass-makers, have established an emigrational committee, to draft off the surplus labour to the United States. This committee, since its formation in 1849, has sent off about twenty men to America. They do not pay the whole cost of their emigration, but give them thirteen weeks' allowance in advance to assist them to go.

Ten hours a day is the usual time of labour in the trade; and there is no system of relays, as in the glass-making. The wages average, according to ability and the number of hours per week, from £1 to £1 14s. No workman is allowed to have an apprentice, or to employ boys under him. The manufacturers are only allowed to take one apprentice for every five men in their employ, the object of the restriction being to prevent the introduction of surplus labour. The system of "agreements"—by which a workman binds himself to work for a certain master—has been attempted in the trade, but it is discouraged by the Union, and there is now but little of it. The discount system has also, to some extent, been introduced. In addition to the "emigration" and "unemployed" funds, there is a "superannuated" fund, from which men, when past work, receive an allowance amounting to two-thirds of that given to the unemployed able-bodied workmen. This fund is partly supported by the profits arising from balls, tea-parties, and other entertainments got up for the purpose. During the last summer, as gipsy parties had become very popular, two of them were organized, and succeeded to the satisfaction of their promoters and the benefit of the fund.

The work of glass-cutting consists of three processes—roughing, smoothing, and polishing. The *rougher*, or *grinder*, receives the glass as it comes from the glasshouse, marks the pattern on it, and cuts it. The instrument used is a circular piece of iron, rapidly revolving by steam power. A stream of wet sand runs continually upon the glass when being cut or ground. The roughing of glass shades for lamps is sometimes performed by women. Before the application of steam power to glass-cutting, the cutter had to pay out of his wages a man or boy to turn the wheel for him; but since the introduction of steam into the manufacture, the masters insist that the men shall still continue to pay for the turning. They take from 12s. to 12s. 9d. per week for the steam power from each workman. In some establishments the "turning," or steam power, is reckoned at one-third of a man's earnings; so that, if a man nominally earns 36s. a week, he only receives 24s. The masters allege that the operative is none the worse for this, as the sum he now pays for steam power he would have had to pay to a boy or man, under the old system, to turn his wheel for him. The masters are represented by the workpeople as very tenacious of their "turning," and determined not to relinquish their hold upon it. The *smoother* receives the article from the rougher, and with a stone— harder or softer according to the nature of his work—smooths all the cuttings, and makes them of a perfectly even surface, but quite dull. The stone employed is commonly called the Warrington stone. The business of the *polisher* is to make all these dull surfaces, which have been cut or ground, perfectly bright. For this purpose he uses pumice or rotten stone. The article is next "puttied" by the polisher, in or-

der to bring out the fine gloss and white colour, so much admired
in cut glass of the most expensive qualities and workmanship. This
"putty" is a white powder, formed by calcining an alloy composed of
equal parts of tin and lead. It forms the base of most enamels, and is
used for polishing metals and stones as well as glass. The workmen
consider the putty used in polishing to be injurious to the hand, if it
gets under the nails. A good workman must be able to perform all
these processes. The men are subject to a disease known as "dropped
hand;" and the trade is generally considered unhealthy. The hands
of the workmen are continually in water, and the workshops are necessarily damp, from the continual flow of sand and water upon the
glass. "The Benefit Societies," to use the words of a member of the
trade, "do not like the glass-cutters, and charge them an additional
rate, much higher than they charge the glass-makers." The disease
called "dropped hand" is by some of the men supposed to be caused
by the poisonous putty used in polishing; but medical men do not
consider this to be the case. They assert it to be caused by the tightness of grasp which the men are compelled to employ when holding
the glass—a tightness maintained for many hours in the day, amid
a constant damp and cold, which impairs the muscular power, and
paralyzes the hand. A glass-cutter stated, in reply to some inquiries
made to him upon the subject, that the "dropped hand" was very common in the trade. "If the men left off work, and took to some other
business, not requiring such pressure by the hand, or the holding of
it in the position to which it was accustomed at the grinding or polishing, they often regained the use of their hands." The case of one
man was cited who had twice been afflicted with "dropped hand," and
twice regained the use of it, after a twelvemonth's cessation of work.
It was stated that he had finally quitted the trade, being apprehensive
that if he again lost the use of his hand he would never recover it. My
informant did not consider that the members of the trade lived to a
good age. The oldest glass-cutter in the town was 64, and there was
no other within ten years of that age.

The operative glass-cutters of Birmingham were formerly known
as staunch Protectionists. One of their body, who has taken a prominent part in the affairs of the trade, and from whom some portions of
the above statements were derived, remarked "that whenever the subject of the Excise duty on glass was expected to come on for discussion
in the House of Commons, many men were sure to be thrown out of
work." The shopkeepers and dealers, apprehensive of a change, kept

back their orders, the manufacturer ceased producing, and labour was discharged. The men consider it a great advantage to them that the Excise duty has been finally abolished, and that no further changes can take place. When Sir Robert Peel introduced his amended tariff, the glass-cutters of Birmingham were afraid they would be ruined by the free introduction of Bohemian glass, and sent a deputation to remonstrate with him. They did not see Sir Robert Peel, but had an interview with Sir George Clerk, at which they explained their views upon the subject. Since that time the men have gradually become converted to the principles of Free-trade. "I for one," said my informant, "have been regularly converted from Protection to Free-trade. The Bohemians, having had no excisemen to interfere with the manufacture of glass, are at present able to beat the English in colour, but they can't beat the English in quality of glass or of workmanship, and they won't much longer be able to beat us in colour. Now that they are quit of the exciseman, the English glass-makers will try experiments, as the Bohemians and French were allowed to do, and if we don't beat them I shall be very much surprised; at all events, we shall be equal to them. From my experience among the working glass-cutters of Birmingham, I should say that Protection is going out of fashion with them. Indeed, there is scarcely a Protectionist remaining among us."

The manufacture of crown and plate glass, and of shades for clocks and figures, employs a much larger number of the men than those branches of the glass trade which have been first described. The establishment of the Messrs. Chance, in Spon Lane, is one of the largest of this kind in England, or in the world, and has lately acquired additional celebrity as the place where all the glass is manufactured for the Crystal Palace of the Exhibition of 1851.

Spon Lane is situated about four miles from Birmingham, on the banks of the Wolverhampton Canal. A journey thither, in one of the "swift passage boats" as they are called, affords the stranger a good idea of the extensive industry of the town and neighbourhood. As the boat is rapidly drawn through the black, greasy water, the bells of the horses jingling on the bank, barge after barge is passed, in transit either to or from the town, laden with bars of iron—with crates of glass—with coils of brass or iron wire—with iron manufactured into almost every conceivable shape for the uses of man—with coal, with lime, with ore, and with other materials. Most of these barges are drawn by horses, some by asses, and not a few by men. I noticed in this short journey no less than five barges to each of which a man and an ass were yoked together. On either side of the canal rise large factories, of which the tall chimneys pour forth such volumes of thick black smoke as to darken the atmosphere for miles around. The Spon Lane works themselves form a huge pile of black buildings on the right bank of the canal. They cover altogether upwards of 20 acres of ground, and give constant employment on the average to about 1,000 people. At present, in consequence of the extra demand for glass for Mr. Paxton's building, the number of workpeople is upwards of 1,200. The glass manufactured here consists of crown, sheet, plate, and coloured glass, and glass shades. It is the only establishment of the kind in the Midland Counties that has been successfully worked. All preceding and subsequent attempts to manufacture crown and plate glass in the district are represented to have failed. It was originally commenced in 1815 by a company of six of the most extensive glass dealers in London and Staffordshire, who carried it on for about seven years with moderate success. The concern was purchased from the old company, in 1822, by one of the present proprietors, by whom, in conjunction with his partners, it has since been conducted with eminent spirit. For ten years the manufacture of crown glass was the only department of the business to which the Messrs. Chance devoted their attention, but in 1832 they introduced the sheet glass and shade manufacture from France and Belgium. The French and Belgians, not having been burdened either with an Excise duty upon glass or a tax upon windows, were far greater producers and consumers of glass in every variety than the English, and consequently were more skilful in its manufacture. It was therefore necessary to introduce French and Belgian workmen in 1832, many of whom have since remained in the country, and many have returned home possessors of fortunes amassed in the service of the Messrs. Chance. The English workmen have gradually learned all the processes, and are fast becoming equal, if not superior, to the French and Belgians. The Messrs. Chance have a smaller establishment at Oldbury, within about a mile and a half of Spon Lane, where they manufacture chemical glass, and give employment to about 400 people.

The Spon Lane establishment is not only noted for the extent of the works, for the quantity of glass produced, and for the perfection to which the manufacture has been brought—but for the excellent social government of the large body of persons employed, and for the means taken by the proprietors to increase the comfort and to elevate the physical, moral, and intellectual condition both of young and old. In the 8th Letter of this series, the efforts made by these philanthropic employers to extend the blessings of education to their juvenile workpeople, and to the children of the married people in their employ, as well as to the poorer children of the district generally, were fully detailed. I shall show in the present Letter what they have done and attempted on behalf of the adult workers.

The various processes in the manufacture of crown and plate glass are too well known to require any elaborate description, but a few words upon the principal stages of the work will not be out of place. The first great operation is that of pot-setting, which is common to the making of all kinds of glass, whether plate, crown, or flint, and which has been already described. The manufacture of crown glass for windows is as simple as it is beautiful. A long iron tube, with a bulb of glass at the end, is put into the furnace until the glass is heated of a white heat. It is then withdrawn, by a workman called the "gatherer," and the glass is slightly cooled. After this the tube is once more directed towards the furnace, and, with the bulb of glass at the end, is inserted into the liquid glass in the pot, and turned round several times, until a sufficient quantity of metal, or glass, adheres to it to form the circular sheet required. The "blower" then applies his lips to the tube, and the molten mass gradually expands into a globe. When by incessant blowings and applications to the heat of the furnace, it has acquired the proper size and shape, being still retained at the end of the tube, a "gatherer," armed with an iron rod, at the end of which is another bulb of molten glass, applies it to the opposite extremity; and the "blower" extricates his tube from the mass, leaving it with a large hole in the middle to adhere to the second rod. The second bulb of glass, thus affixed, forms the well known "bull's eye." The globe, firmly affixed to the rod of the "gatherer" or "servitor," is then transferred to another furnace, in the heat thrown out by which it is made to spin round with immense velocity, until by the centrifugal force it gradually and beautifully expands into a circle of glass, with the bull's-eye in the centre. It is next allowed to cool, and, when sufficiently hard, is tilted gently on end, and allowed to remain until its removal to another part of the premises, to be cut into squares.

The process of the manufacture of plate-glass is even more beautiful and striking. The bulb, or solid globe of glass, which is destined to be made into a square sheet, weighing from 12 lbs. to 14 lbs., is rounded, while in a soft state, by gentle evolutions in a hollow made in a block of wood. When it has thus acquired the proper shape for the blower's purpose, it is again subjected to the action of the furnace. When sufficiently liquid, the blower applies his lips to the tube, and the solid globe expands, and gradually becomes elliptical or elongated. The object of the next process is to increase the elongation. Standing upon a stage, erected over a pit opposite to the mouth of the furnace, the blower swings the metal over his head, and under his feet—the form of the ellipsis becoming gradually more developed. As the glass cools under this operation, it is subjected two or three times to the action of the furnace; and it is swung each time with great dexterity, until the repeated blowings cause the "metal" to give way at the extremity. The stranger cannot avoid a feeling of alarm at seeing the liquid mass swung in this manner, and he imagines that the molten glass will be projected in drops, like water from a mop; or that, if this does not happen, the workman will dash the glass against some of his comrades as they pass to and fro—or knock it into fragments against the stage on which he stands, or against the furnace, which seems in such close and dangerous proximity. But nothing of the kind takes place. Both eye and hand are educated to the work, and the glass speedily assumes the form of a cylinder, open at the extremity, about four feet, or four-and-a-half feet long, and nine or ten inches in diameter. It is then dissevered from the connecting tube on which it was swung, by the application of a string of red-hot glass, and when sufficiently cool is carried away by boys to another part of the building. The transformation of these cylinders into sheets of glass is performed in a very simple manner. The cylinder is cut lengthways, and placed on a moving platform in the "flattening kiln." As the heat gradually permeates it, the cut sides begin to gape, and, with a very slight assistance from the attendant workman, fall gently on to the stone platform, where they lie, and form a plate or sheet of glass, perfectly flat and smooth. They are then allowed to cool, and, when hard enough to be removed, are gently tilted on end, and are fit for all the uses to which they are destined. In this manner were manufactured the glass sheets for Mr. Paxton's industrial Palace. The sudden demand caused the Messrs. Chance to import a number of skilled workmen from France and Belgium; but not one ounce of glass has been imported for the purpose, and Messrs. Chance state that, if the contract had been still larger than it was, they would have been prepared to execute it. The finished glass for Mr. Paxton's building will weigh 400 tons, requiring for its manufacture upwards of 600 tons of sand and other materials, and about 3,000 tons of coal. The average quantity of coal required for the manufacture of glass is eight times the bulk of glass produced, or from 7½ to 8 tons of coal for one ton of glass.

The process of the manufacture of glass shades is very similar to that of sheet glass, except in the ultimate operation of flattening, which is not required. The glass, when brought to the cylindrical form by the swinging process, is inserted gently in a mould, which gives it the shape required for the shade; and the extraneous portions at the edges are removed in the usual way by the application of a string of red hot glass. In this process the French, from long habit, have acquired a dexterity not usual with the English; but within the last two or three years the English workmen have greatly improved, and some of them can produce shades as large and excellent as the French. It is stated that the French workmen are less tidy in their houses than the English, but that, as a general rule, they are far more temperate, abstemious, and economical. Their stay being limited, they endeavour to save as much money as they can, with which to return to their own country. Many English glass-blowers who gain as much as £4 a week, spend it all, but a few are more provident, and several of the men are possessors of freehold houses and bits of land. The French are extremely provident, and many of the "blowers" have as much as £400 or £500, which they leave at interest in Messrs. Chance's hands. The wages of glass-blowers vary according to the skill and powers of the workmen, from 30s. to £6 a week. One French workman, who quitted this country in March last, earned for a long period about £9 a week, and lived upon £2 or less, placing the remainder out in a variety of ways, and to such advantage that, when he returned to France, he took with him nearly 120,000 francs, or £4,800. There is very little drunkenness among the workmen, although they habitually consume large quantities of ale and beer. The Messrs. Chance state that within the last few years there has been a marked and very gratifying improvement in the general character of the men, and that intoxication, formerly common, is now exceedingly rare. The effect of the relay system upon the boys is prejudicial. When boys leave off work at seven in the afternoon, and have to re-commence work at an hour after midnight, they do not as a general rule go to bed in the interval, but amuse themselves in the best way they can; and very often they become dissipated, and frequent beer-shops to smoke, drink, and play at games of hazard. The Messrs. Chance have endeavoured to lessen and prevent this evil, by the establishment of the school and the library mentioned in a former letter.

It is one of the many accusations brought against society under the competitive system, in the writings of Fourier, Considerant, Louis Blanc, and others, that medical men are directly interested in the ill-health of the community; and one of the many advantages which, according to those authors and their disciples, would result from the co-operative system, would be the employment of medical men directly interested in the good health of the community, and in the prevention of disease. This result has been attained in the Spon Lane Glassworks. Every workman, young and old, in that establishment, contributes from a penny to threepence per week, according to his wages, for the support of a dispensary, and of a duly qualified medical practitioner. For this sum they are entitled to medical attendance and medicine for themselves and families. The medical gentleman receives a salary of £300 a year, and devotes his whole time to the patients of the glass works, having no private practice whatever. He attends them in their own illnesses, attends also the midwifery cases of the wives of the workpeople, vaccinates the children, and visits them at their own homes to give them advice which, if duly followed, may prevent disease. If they live in filthy cottages or rooms—if they do not understand the necessity of ventilation—if they suffer stagnant waters to collect about them—if they are dirty in their persons—if they consume unwholesome food—if they allow the necessaries to be choked up—if they suffer their walls to remain too long without whitewash—if they dress unsuitably to the season, and commit, through ignorance, any other offence against the laws of health, he warns them of the evil consequences that are certain to result. One workman, who had had illness in his family for many months, stated that if he had purchased his own medicines, and employed any other medical man in the usual way, it would have cost him upwards of £20, whereas, by this system, he had paid but 13s. in the twelvemonth. This dispensary is found to work extremely well, to be self-supporting, and to give the greatest satisfaction to the workpeople. The Messrs. Chance seem to be proud of the good which it has been the means of effecting—and well they may be.

LABOUR AND THE POOR.

———◆———

BIRMINGHAM.

[FROM OUR SPECIAL CORRESPONDENT.]

THE MANUFACTURE OF SWORDS, MATCHETTS, AND BAYONETS.

LETTER XI.

If we are to believe Hutton, the historian of Birmingham, this town was noted for the manufacture of swords and other weapons of war as early as the time of the Romans. But this is mere conjecture. No certain information upon the subject occurs earlier than the time of Henry VIII., when Leland mentions the town as containing "many smiths, making knives and cutting tools." Little, if any, information upon the subject, beyond these few words (which do not include swords) has reached our times; and it is not known whether the Birmingham makers, or those of some other part of the country, supplied our warlike ancestors with their weapons of offence and defence, or whether they made or imported their swords as well as their guns. So little, in fact, is known upon the subject of the sword manufacture, both of Birmingham and of Great Britain generally, that even as regards Andrew, or Andrea Ferrara—a man whose name was long applied to the best kind of broadswords, principally used in Scotland, but also in England—there is no positive information.

"The name of Andrea de Ferrara," says a note to the Abbotsford edition of the "Waverly Novels," "is inscribed on all the Scottish broadswords, which are accounted of peculiar excellence. Who this artist was, what were his fortunes, and when he flourished, have hitherto defied the research of antiquaries; only it is in general believed that Andrea de Ferrara was a Spanish or Italian artificer, brought over by James IV. or V. to instruct the Scots in the manufacture of sword blades. Most barbarous nations," adds the annotator, "excel in the fabrication of arms; and the Scots had attained great proficiency in forging swords so early as the field of Pinkie; at which notable period the historian Patten describes them as 'all notable, broad, and thin, universally made to slice, and of such exceeding good temper, that, as I never saw any so good, so I think it hard to devise better.'" We learn, on the same authority, that the genuine Andrea de Ferrara swords had always a crown marked on the blades. At the present time it is not known that a single sword is manufactured in Scotland, or anywhere within the United Kingdom, except in Birmingham and Enfield. In the time of Queen Elizabeth a sword was often termed a "fox." In Shakspeare's *Henry V.*, Act 4, Scene 4, *Pistol* exclaims to the French soldier, "O, Seigneur Dew, thou diest on point of *fox*." A similar expression occurs in Beaumont and Fletcher, where *Philaster* says, "I made my father's old *fox* fly about his ears." In the *Two Old Women of Abington* occurs the phrase, "I had a sword, aye, the flower of Smithfield for a sword, a right *fox* i'faith;" and in "The Life and Death of Captain Thomas Stukeley," 1605, we have, "Old hacked swords, *foxes*, bilbos, and iron buckles." Where the "foxes" and other swords used in England at that time were made, does not appear; but a note of one of the countless editors of Shakspeare says that "fox" was a cant word for a sword, so called from a famous sword cutler of the name of Fox. Regarding it as a point not without interest in the history of the sword manufacture, as well as curious in elucidation of the text of Shakspeare—and thinking that probably there might have been some sword manufacturer in those days as famous for his weapons as Manton is for guns in our day—I endeavoured to ascertain whether any tradition of such a sword maker existed in Birmingham, but I could not discover that anything whatever was known of him by the "oldest inhabitants" of the town, whether in the sword trade or out of it. The name of this Fox—if such a man ever existed—appears, therefore, to be as barren of particulars as that of his fellow-manufacturer, Andrea Ferrara. I may mention, however, for the benefit of those who take a pleasure in antiquarian or philological research, that in some districts of Holland and Germany a broad sword is to this day called a "Fuchsel" (a little fox), and that the proper German name for the article is "Fuchtel," apparently derived from the same root of *fuchs*, a fox. It should also be stated that it was in former days—as, indeed, it is, to a considerable extent, at present—the fashion to ornament sword grips, or handles with the heads of birds and animals—foxes, eagles, lions, dogs, &c.—and that possibly the word "fox" may have been applied to swords when manufactured with foxes' heads for their handles. This view of the case is strengthened by a passage in an old dramatist, where a sword having the head of Minerva on the handle is called a "wisdom."

Wherever the swords of our ancestors were manufactured—whether they came from the famous factories of Toledo—which are still noted for the article*—or whether the blades came from Germany, or were forged in London, or any other part of the country—it does not appear that Birmingham, which is now the chief seat of the manufacture in England, and the only seat of the private trade, was at all celebrated for them until long after the middle of the eighteenth century:—

> "Previous to the American war," says Hutton, "English swords fell into disrepute, and application was made, October 1, 1783, for leave to import swords and sword blades from Germany. A member of the Board of Trade (the Earl of Surrey, afterwards Duke of Norfolk) wrote to Mr. Eyre, of Sheffield, to inform him of this fact, and to solicit such information as would enable him to rebut the statements made upon the inferiority of the English blades. The people of Sheffield were

---

* "Amongst the many remarkable things which meet the eye of the curious observer at Toledo, is the manufactory of arms, where are wrought the swords, spears, and other weapons intended for the army, with the exception of fire-arms, which mostly come from abroad.

"In old times, as is well known, the sword blades of Toledo were held in great estimation, and were transmitted as merchandise throughout Christendom. The present manufactory, or 'fabrica,' as it is called, is a handsome modern edifice, situated without the wall of the city, on a plain contiguous to the river, with which it communicates by a small canal. It is said that the water and the sand of the Tagus are essential for the proper tempering of the swords. I asked some of the principal workmen whether, at the present day, they could manufacture weapons of equal value to those of former days, and whether the secret had been lost.

"'Ba!' said they, 'the swords of Toledo were never so good as those which we are daily making. It is ridiculous enough to see strangers coming here to purchase old swords, the greater part of which are mere rubbish, and never made at Toledo. Yet for such they will give a large price, whilst they would grudge two dollars for this jewel, which was made but yesterday,' thereupon putting into my hand a middle-sized rapier. 'Your worship,' said they, 'seems to have a strong arm. Prove its temper against the stone wall. Thrust boldly, and fear not.'

"I *have* a strong arm, and dashed the point with my utmost force against the solid granite. My arm was numbed to the shoulder, from the violence of the concussion, and continued so for nearly a week, but the sword appeared not to be at all blunted, or to have suffered in any respect.

"'A better sword than that,' said an ancient workman, a native of Old Castile, 'never transfixed Moor out yonder on the sagea.'"—*Borrow's Bible in Spain.*

makers of cutting instruments of the more civil kind; Mr. Eyre therefore referred the letter to Mr. Gill, of Birmingham. Mr. Gill memori-
alised the Lords of the Treasury, stating that swords could be made by
him equal to the German ones. In 1786, one of the East India orders
was divided among the English and German manufacturers. Mr. Gill
obtained an order from the board, to have the swords of the two countries tried by a test which reduced the blade from 36 inches to 29, from
hilt to point, by forcing it into a curved state. Four swords only were
rejected, out of 2,654 presented by Mr. Gill; 1,428 were presented by
the German manufacturers, 1,400 were received, and 28 rejected; the
English makers presented 3,784, out of which only 2,700 were received,
and 1,084 rejected. This being in proportion of one to thirteen in favour of Mr. Gill's swords as compared with the foreign ones, and one
to 1,000 as compared with the others made in England."

Birmingham, therefore, owes much to Mr. Gill for its reputation
in sword making, and since that time it has regularly produced all, or
nearly all, the swords required for the home and foreign trade in the
article, with the sole exception of a portion of the infantry and cavalry
swords required by the British Government, which are manufactured
at Enfield. It may be remembered by the readers of these letters that,
in the account of the gun trade, it was stated that in the year 1813
the Ordnance Department established a manufactory of fire-arms in
that village, with the view of checking the prices and competing with
the private manufacturers of Birmingham, as well as of procuring a
supply more rapid and extensive than it was thought the people of
Birmingham could produce in time of war. That manufactory is still
in existence, and is the only place in the United Kingdom, except
Birmingham, where sword blades are now made. The manufacture
of swords did not commence in Enfield until 1821. There is a notion that many swords are made in Sheffield, but the sword makers
of Birmingham allege that this is not the fact. On my asking a manufacturer in Birmingham if he knew how many swords were annually
produced in Sheffield, he arched his eyebrows with surprise, and said
that he had never heard that a single sword was made in that town.
"They make carving knives and scythes," he said, "but they cannot
produce a sword. The Sheffield cutlers occasionally receive a few orders for swords, from people who do not know the town; but they
are always sent on to Birmingham to be executed." The London dealers, in the same way, whose names appear on the hilts of the more
expensive kinds of swords, only mount the sword, or put the blade,

hilt, and scabbard together. The blades themselves are all forged and tempered in Birmingham; and most of the fittings and trappings are produced in the same place. Sheffield, however, though it does not produce the sword blade, supplies the rough steel, or "moulds," from which they are manufactured.

During the war the manufacture of swords is supposed to have given employment to about 1,000 men in this town, independently altogether of the men employed in the manufacture of gun barrels—a branch of business which was then, as it is now, carried on in many instances under the same roof. The British Government not only supplied Birmingham with orders for its own large armies, but for the armies of the allies; and from the time of Mr. Gill's experiment until the last great armament, prior to the battle of Waterloo, it kept the trade in constant activity. Things have now greatly altered. Sword-making, instead of being one of the most flourishing and extensive manufactures in the town, is perhaps one of the least, and scarcely gives employment to a tenth of the number of persons who are employed in making pens. Swords, being large and heavy articles, are almost entirely manufactured by masculine labour; while steel pens are almost entirely due to the lighter, more graceful, and more appropriate labour of women and young girls. The names of only ten sword cutlers, four scabbard makers, and seven embossers, appear in the Birmingham Directory; and it is stated, on the authority of one of the most eminent of these, that the trade, at the present time, including the manufacture of the more peaceful article, the matchett—to be described hereafter—does not employ above 250 people, probably not above 200 or 220. "In fact," said my informant, "our trade does not prosper; there seems to be a curse upon it. It is nothing like what it was within my remembrance." During the war, wages at this trade, though never so high as in the manufacture of fire-arms, were still superior in amount to those received in most of the other trades of the town. "In those times," said another manufacturer, still connected with the trade, "the forgers and filers of sword blades only worked when they pleased. They were not to be commanded. They considered it quite a favour to do a job at all. They could earn as much in two days as would keep them for a week, and work was quite a piece of condescension on their part. At the Birmingham market, when the country people brought in their poultry for sale, the dealers sometimes held on, or refused to dispose of their goods, until the gun and sword makers, or their wives, had made their appearance. They had plenty of money, and always had the pick of the market. When a low offer was made for a duck or a goose, the answer commonly was, 'Oh no, you must wait till the gun and sword men have been.' At the present time things have sadly changed with the sword-makers; and although, like many others, addicted to keeping St. Monday—thus wasting one day out of six—they can barely make a subsistence by working all the week, and are often out of employment for many weeks, if not for months, together." Thirty years ago the orders for swords for the United States gave constant employment to 200 or 300 men for six months in the year. The Americans procured their common swords from Liège, or from Germany; but all their naval, dress, and fine swords came from Birmingham. They were all extremely national in the form and mounting; they were eagle-hilted, and as richly embossed with stars upon the blade as their star-spangled banner is in its folds. The Americans now manufacture by far the greater portion of their own swords, and their orders from Birmingham scarcely give the trade employment for a fortnight. The small trade that remains is principally for the finer and highly-ornamented description of swords. There is a much larger trade with Mexico and Brazil, but there is little or no trade with the Continent of Europe. France manufactures her own. Spain supplies her own wants and those of Portugal—and also, to some extent, those of Italy—from her celebrated factory at Toledo. Russia is supplied from Belgium and Germany; and Turkey takes her swords from Damascus, in her own dominions, or from Tabreez, in Persia. The sword trade of Birmingham is at present mainly supported by the occasional orders of the Government, for sea service swords; by the orders of the East India Company, both for infantry and cavalry; and by a tolerably constant, but not very extensive, demand for cheap and gaudy swords for the African market. The Government sometimes wants as many as 40,000 sea service swords at a time, the manufacture of which, like that of fire-arms, is taken by contract, and, as it appears, at a yearly diminishing rate of profit to the producer. Cavalry swords are also in considerable demand for India, and are made by contract, like those for the Board of Ordnance. The home trade is not otherwise extensive. "There is," said a manufacturer, "an occasional demand for dress and court swords. A royal funeral invariably brings a few orders for mourning swords for court dresses; and since the accession of her present Majesty, and the consequent frequency of levees, drawing-rooms, and court balls, there has been a much greater demand for court swords than there was in the reign of

William IV. Her Majesty's visit to Ireland in 1849 gave employment for some weeks to the sword-makers of Birmingham. We got rid of all our old stock of dress swords that had long remained on hand, and had to manufacture others for the occasion. When her Majesty went to Holyrood this year, orders for swords came up from Scotland, and gave both masters and men a lift. The French Revolution of 1848, which created such a stir in the gun trade, and caused so large a demand from Sardinia, Sicily, and Denmark, had no effect upon the sword manufacture. It looked promising for a week or two. Speculators, who saw how much the guns of Birmingham were in request for the Continent, sent round to the manufacturers to know whether we could supply from 20,000 to 30,000 swords, and within what period we could do so. Some of these agents, factors, or speculators, inquired for as many as 50,000. Day after day inquiries continued to be made—and tantalized the sword-makers with the hope of business. But the flattering prospect soon faded away, and all the revolutions of the Continent cannot be said to have caused the sale of 1,000 swords in Birmingham—no, nor half of that number. There is an occasional order for theatrical swords and daggers, and now and then for a presentation sword of rich workmanship. The swords presented at various times by the City of London and other corporations, to the Duke of Wellington and other great soldiers, were made at Birmingham, either in whole or in part; and one of the handsomest and most costly swords ever manufactured was made by Mr. Mole, of Birmingham, a few months ago, for the Emperor Soulouque, of Hayti. But the trade is very uncertain, and were it not for the matchetts the manufacturers could scarcely live. The military swords are greatly reduced in price, and they do not afford the same opportunity as formerly for any additional expenditure upon them. Up to the year 1820 or 1821 every officer in the infantry or cavalry regiments was allowed to suit his own taste in the pattern and fashion of his sword handle and grip, and there was a constant striving after novelty of design and elegance of ornament to suit the taste of the wealthy. This gave a considerable amount of extra employment. But about the year 1821 a uniform regulation was adopted, by which all the military swords were reduced to one pattern, and this put a stop to all ingenuity and skill in this department. Swords for private use, or for presentation, still afford scope to the taste of the manufacturer. Swords with Latin and other mottoes upon the hilts were common in ancient times, but I do not remember ever to have heard of such a thing in my lifetime."

The steel of which sword blades are manufactured having been received from Sheffield, each "mould," consisting of the materials for two swords, joined end to end, is divided in the middle. The blade is then given to the *forger*, who beats it out upon the anvil to the proper length and breadth, and then hardens and tempers it by dipping it in water, and again passing and repassing it through the furnace as often as may be required. This is a process which requires both skill and care, and the workmen are somewhat better paid than those in any other branch of the manufacture. They make, on the average, from 7s. to 9s. a day. The blade next passes into the hands of the *grinder*, who, seated at an enormous grindstone, similar to those employed in the grinding of gun barrels, and revolving by steam power at a rapid rate, reduces it to the required weight and strength. It is a picturesque sight to see the sword-grinders at their work, although it is scarcely so striking as the severer grinding of gun barrels, which requires larger grindstones and a harder grit. The grinder receives from 6s. to 8s. a day, according to his industry and skill. A good workman will grind from 18 to 24 swords in a day. The blade, having been ground, is proved. Every manufacturer proves his own goods; but the Board of Ordnance and the East India Company have proof-houses of their own, in which they submit all the swords received from the contractors to a second proof. The method adopted is—first, to place the sword with its point on the ground, and to bend it down in a curve from the hilt, to a certain gauge of three or four inches, until it forms a bow; then to strike it on both sides, with all the strength of a strong man, against a stone used for the purpose; and in the last place, to strike it back and edge with equal strength—in short, to subject it to a trial much more severe than any sword is likely to receive in any service to which it may be put. It is stated that swords of Belgian and German manufacture, made at a cheaper rate than those of Birmingham, and of steel that is not so carefully tempered, will not bear the same degree of proof. If there be any flaw in the steel, however trifling, it will immediately show itself, and the blade is sent back to the furnace to be re-forged and re-tempered, and the workman has lost his time, labour, and consequently his wages. If it bears the proof, it is transferred to the hands of the *polisher*, who brings it to the requisite brightness, in the manner usual with those more peaceful weapons— the knives of Sheffield. If the sword be required for the ordinary use of the army, or for sea service, or for the African trade, the blade is now complete. If it be required for the officers of either service, or of the East India Company, or for the finer and more expensive swords for Court suits, or Highland dresses, or any other private purpose, it passes into the hands of the *embosser* and *gilder*. Embossing being a trade of itself, and required for other articles as well as swords, the blades pass from the premises of the manufacturer to various parts of the town, to receive the last finish from the hands of these outworkers. The blades are then ready to be mounted; preparatory to which, however, the other component parts of the complete sword have been in course of manufacture. These comprise the *grip*, the *hilt* or *handle*, and the *scabbard*. The *grip* and the *hilt* are, in the common swords, made by one process. The *hilt* for an infantry officer's sword is first cast in gilding metal, then set to shape and filed by the *filer;* from the filer it passes to the *polisher*, and from the polisher to the *chaser*. The grip undergoes the same processes, and is besides gilt and burnished, and both are then ready for being mounted to the blade.

"About thirty years ago," said a manufacturer, "the hilt of a cavalry sword used to be forged. The forging cost 3s. 6d.; the filing, smoothing, and burnishing, cost 3s. 6d. more. The making alone, therefore, cost 7s. Malleable casting was then introduced, and it took one pound of malleable iron to make a hilt. This cost 5d. only. Instead of 3s. 6d. for filing, &c., no more than 6d. is now paid, and 3d. more is paid for polishing. The hilt, therefore, which thirty years ago cost 7s., may now be had for 1s. 2d. An apprentice at that time could make about 3s. 6d. before dinner by filing a hilt, and all his afternoons were for his own profit. Dozens are now made in the same time that used to be given to one; and as for apprentices, the trade is too bad to warrant any man in binding his son to it."

In the finer descriptions of swords the *hilt* and *grip* are more beautiful and complicated. They are sometimes of gold and silver, and sometimes of the finest polished steel, according to the taste of the purchaser or the ornamental uses to which they are to be put. The harmless swords worn at levees and drawing-rooms, or used in the theatre, or those equally harmless ones which form part of the full Highland costume, are tastefully ornamented, both in grip and handle. A very handsome grip, either of black or white, is made of the hard skin of a fish, called in the trade by the names of the "Nore" and the "Dog-fish." The demand for this beautiful skin is so small that the London merchants, who principally supply it, do not take much interest in the matter, and the consequence is, that scarcities often ensue, and the little that is on hand rises to a high price. The whole stock has often been monopolised by one dealer, who has dictated his own terms; and it is related that a few years ago, when the sword-makers had a considerable order on hand, which they could not execute for want of Nore-skins, and when, to use the words of a manufacturer, "they were regularly hard driven into a corner," a quantity of the precious article was accidentally discovered in a cellar in Liverpool, where it had lain unnoticed and unknown for many years, and by the timely liberation of which they were enabled to execute their orders.

The scabbard for cavalry swords is made of steel, and that for the infantry swords of strong black leather. Scabbard-making is a separate branch of the trade. The cheap swords for the African market have invariably green, red, or yellow leather scabbards, as the negro taste insists upon flaunting colours, and will not tolerate the sober tints that please the people of colder climates. These African swords are brass mounted, having a brass handle and grip, a brass "chafe" at the end of the showy scabbard, and a brass "top-locket." The common swords, in all their various processes, require to pass through from ten to fifteen pair of hands from the forging to the mounting, according to the character of the scabbard and fittings. The regulation swords for the army pass through fifteen pairs of hands. The finer swords for court suits, or for private use at home and abroad, sometimes employ upwards of twenty different sub-divisions of the trade, including the outworkers.

Swords do not find so ready a sale in Africa as guns. They cannot be used in hunting or sporting, and are consequently only of service for the personal adornment of the African kings and chiefs, and occasionally for war purposes. There is a shrewd suspicion, though nothing more, that many of these swords, as well as the guns of Birmingham, find their way to the slave-traders of Brazil, and that the Brazilian slavers take considerable cargoes of these articles to the coast of Africa, where they are bartered for men. A gun for a man, or a sword for a man, used to be a common exchange when Great Britain was a slave-trading nation; and it is much to be feared that the warlike weapons of Birmingham are still largely employed for this inhuman and unholy traffic. Daggers are also manufactured in Birmingham for the African market, but the orders are not large, and seldom exceed a hundred or two hundred at a time. The chief trade appears to be with Guinea and Sierra Leone; but as the orders pass through the hands of London and Liverpool merchants, the ultimate destination of the swords, whether for the legitimate English or the illegitimate Brazilian trade, is scarcely known to the manufacturer.

The *matchett* is an article that is much more extensively made in Birmingham than the sword, and without which the sword trade would scarcely support a hundred workmen. The matchett is an instrument of which the blade very closely resembles that of a sword. Its length is from 18 to 26 inches, and its breadth from 1½ to 2 inches. It is well tempered, but is not quite so flexible as the sword. It has no scabbard or mountings of any kind—nothing but a plain unstained beechwood handle of the commonest description. Matchetts are not used in England at all, but are sent in large quantities to Ceylon and other parts of the East Indies, to the West India Islands, to South America, and to Africa. They are used for cutting down the sugar-cane, and for other agricultural purposes, and are sold wholesale at the rate of a few pence each. The chief labour bestowed upon them is the forging and grinding. The grinder is paid from 1s. 6d. to 3s. a dozen; a rate which, after deductions for mill-power and for the rapid wear and tear of the enormous grindstones, leaves from 6½d. to 8d. a dozen for the mere labour. A steady grinder might grind from 10 to 12 dozen a day, earning from 5s. 6d. to 8s. a day, according to his skill and industry. The Africans use their matchetts, it is supposed, instead of swords, for offence and defence; and the backwoodsmen of South America find them serviceable on horseback in cutting down the thick brush-wood and jungle, or the light overhanging branches of trees. Birmingham produces from 600 to 700 dozen of these instruments per week, pretty steadily all the year round, or between 400,000 and 500,000 per annum.

The bayonet manufacture in Birmingham is not extensive. The Directory contains the names of only five persons in this trade. As sporting guns, and the great bulk of that staple article, the African guns, do not require bayonets, the sole demand is created by the Government and by the East India Company, with an occasional order from abroad. The bayonet trade rises and falls with the orders received for military guns, and, therefore, shared to some extent the transient prosperity caused by the revolutionary doings of 1848. Altogether, it will be seen that these closely related trades are not in a progressive state. In Birmingham, however, but little distress is caused among the working classes by the temporary or even permanent downfall of any particular manufacture. The man who can work in iron or steel can turn his hand to a variety of articles when the demand for any one in particular happens to fall; and there is so constant a demand for nov-elty, and so large a field for the exercise of ingenuity, not only in the manufacture of iron and steel, but of copper and brass, that the steady, sober, and industrious workman need never be for any length of time out of employment. If his services are not required in the production of articles of war, he can try those of peace; and many sword-makers, finding their occupation leaving them, have become for this reason manufacturers of tools and other equally useful articles.

LABOUR AND THE POOR.

—◆—

BIRMINGHAM.

[FROM OUR SPECIAL CORRESPONDENT.]

WORKERS IN BRASS.

LETTER XII.

Birmingham excels in the manufacture of all kinds of brass and gilt articles, bronze figures excepted; and though not the only town in the kingdom where brass is converted into articles of ornament and necessity, it may be called the principal seat of the manufacture. Sheffield, London, Glasgow, and all the other towns where brass is wrought, do not appear to supply much, if any, of the foreign trade in brass goods. It is difficult to convey an idea of the extent and variety of the manufacture, as carried on in Birmingham, or to estimate accurately the number of hands employed; but it may be generally stated that, in all its complex ramifications and divisions, it employs considerably above 6,000 persons. By some, competent to form an opinion, it is supposed that 8,000 would express more correctly than 6,000 the numbers of brass-workers in the town and neighbourhood; and it is admitted on all hands, whatever the actual numbers may be, that not even those great staple articles, guns and buttons, find employment for so large a population.

The following list of the master manufacturers of brass goods in Birmingham is copied from the Directory. Taking them in alphabetical order, there are 16 bell-founders, 13 bottle-jack makers, 190 brass-founders, 78 braziers, 5 bronze powder makers, 34 brass casters, 10 clasp makers (partly in brass), 26 coach lamp, furniture, and ornament makers (partly in brass and partly in steel), 25 cock founders, 4 compass makers, 17 coppersmiths, 7 cornice and cornice-pole makers, 10 curtain-ring makers, 7 bronze wire fender-makers, 28 gas-fitting makers, 8 lamp manufacturers, 43 chandelier and lustre manufacturers (partly glass and partly brass), 1 ecclesiastical ornament maker, 12 lantern makers (partly in brass for ships and partly in tin), 5 letter-clip makers, 14 mathematical instrument makers (partly in brass), 10 brass and metallic bedstead makers, 7 military ornament makers, 4 brass nail makers, 5 brass-headed nail makers, 15 saddlers' ironmongers (chiefly in brass work, though called ironmongers), 19 scale-beam and weighing-machine makers (partly in brass), 17 stair-rod, moulding, and astrigal makers; 26 brass thimble makers, 21 tube makers (partly in brass), 4 brass and copper wiredrawers, and 43 wireworkers and weavers. To these must be added various other trades dependent upon the manufacture of brass; such as lacquer and solder makers, copper and zinc dealers, and metal rollers. But many of these trades are often united in one firm, and their numbers cannot be held to represent the actual number or sub-division of master manufacturers in the town.

Hutton, in his "History of Birmingham," states that the manufacture of brass was first introduced in the year 1740. He estimated the consumption of metal at the time he wrote at 1,000 tons per annum. It is probable that at the present time the production of brass is from five to six times that amount. In so complicated a manufacture, producing such an endless variety of articles, it is next to impossible to make an accurate classification; but the greater sub-divisions of the trade appear to be as follow:—

First, the *general brassfounders*, including the countless articles in brass required by carpenters, builders, cabinetmakers, and upholsterers—articles of which a specification would almost suffice to fill a newspaper. To these may be added all kinds of new articles, which the enterprise or ingenuity of the manufacturer may produce from time to time, to please or create a public taste, or to administer to a public necessity. Among the many introductions of the kind may be mentioned brass picture-frames, to supersede the ancient wooden gilt frames; letter-clips and weights, and other articles for the chamber or the writing-desk; and, more recently, vesta and lucifer boxes. A year and a half ago one workman was able to supply the whole public demand for this useful and elegant article. At that time it was made without ornament, and intended chiefly for the mantelpiece or the office-table. It pleased the public taste; a demand was created for it both at home and abroad; new patterns were invented; enamel and colouring were introduced, and they were made not only for the table or desk, but for the waistcoat-pocket. They are now manufactured in countless thousands to supply a daily increasing demand from Germany, Russia, Belgium, Holland, India, Australia, and North and South America. California is stated to be a large customer. This article is now manufactured in six or seven establishments in the town—some of which employ as many as forty or fifty men. Among other miscellaneous articles which find the general brassfounders of Birmingham in casual or constant employment are brass spittoons, of which great quantities are sent to Mexico and South America; brass tinder-boxes, for the Dutch and Germans, who seem to dislike the more convenient lucifer match, and to "stand upon the ancient ways" of procuring a light with flint and steel; lasso rings, of which many tons are annually exported to South America for steadying the cast of the lasso, and forming the noose; and bells of all shapes and sizes. The cattle and sheep bells of Australia, the United States, and Canada, are produced in immense numbers in Birmingham, besides a large proportion of the hand and house bells required for home consumption. It is related that, not many months ago, a very large order for bells was received in Birmingham, through a London merchant, which gave employment to a number of brassworkers for several months. These bells, amounting to many thousands, were intended for the exterior decoration of the palace of a Malay prince.

The second great division of the brass manufacture is that of *gas fittings and gasaliers*, from the plainest and cheapest to the most elaborate, elegant, and expensive articles. Birmingham supplies a large portion of the home, and nearly the whole of the foreign, demand. It may be mentioned as an interesting circumstance in connection with this branch of trade, and as a proof of the progress of European civilization, that gas and gas-fittings have found their way into Turkey, along with newspapers and steamboats, and that, three or four years ago, the present Sultan gave an order to a Birmingham manufacturer for fifty large gilt brackets, and the same number of gilt standard lamp posts, for ornamenting and lighting the harem with gas.

The third division is that of *candelabra*, and *oil lamps;* and the fourth, that of *brass candlesticks, trays, and snuffers.* Besides these may be enumerated the *brass cock founders*, which is a separate trade. The *manufacture of saddlers' and coachmakers' brass*—that of *brass military ornaments*, and *brass wire weaving and working;* the manufacture of *metallic bedsteads*, and lastly, that of *brass weights* and *brass-headed nails.* There are many other divisions and sub-divisions of the trade, which might be attempted in an elaborate classification; but these will serve to show, not simply how extensive, but at the same time how intricate are the divisions and sub-divisions of the manufacture.

The wages of good workmen in the brass trade vary according to the kind of work. The subdivisions of labour are, first, the *metal maker, smelter* or *strip caster*, whose business is to smelt the copper and zinc, or, in other words, to make the brass. The wages of this class of workmen, who are not numerous, average from 30s. to 40s. per week. The *modellers*, who invent the patterns and work them in clay or wood in the first instance, receive from 35s. to 50s. a week, according to their ability and industry. The *moulders* or *casters* who produce the pattern in metal receive about 30s., but the wages vary, often as much as from 6s. to 8s. a week. The *chasers*, who put the finish to the pattern, and work up the minuter details of such articles as chandeliers and their ornaments, receive, on an average, from 25s. to 36s. a week. The *fitters*, who join the various pieces of chandeliers, lamps, and such articles together, and are assisted in their labour by boys and lads, receive from 22s. to 25s. a week. The *Burnishers*, who produce that exquisite polish, almost, if not superior to gilding, and to which Birmingham brass goods owe so much of the reputation they have acquired in every part of the world, receive from 20s. to 30s. a week. The *Dippers*, whose business is to plunge the brass article, after it has been cast, stamped or chased, into dilute acid, to cleanse it from grease or other impurity, and afterwards into aquafortis, to give it a clear bright yellow colour, free of spots and stains, receive on an average 25s. a week. This is the most unhealthy part of the business. The workmen complain of tightness and oppression at the chest, and are in the habit of drinking skim-milk as a remedy for it.

The number of women employed in the manufacture is considerable, though probably it does not amount to more than a tenth of the whole number of hands in the trade. These consist, in the first place, of the *lacquerers*. The wages of the women in this branch of the business are about 10s. a week, and of young girls from 4s. to 7s. Another description of female workers in the brass trade are the *chargers*, who put the solder on the seams of tubing before it is passed through the furnace to be annealed. They receive from 6s. to 8s. a week. Women are also employed in wrapping paper around the highly-finished and polished goods, and in the packing department generally. Their wages average about 10s. a week. Boys are employed to a great extent by the workmen to assist in the various departments of the business; and many branches of the manufacture, especially those of gas and oil chandeliers, candelabra, and ornamental brass, cannot be properly carried on without their aid.

The number of persons employed in cabinet brass foundry alone has been estimated at about 1,500; but in this, as in other departments, there is a difficulty in procuring an accurate statement, from the fact that a considerable portion of the work is done by jobbing workmen or "garret masters," in their own houses, of whom no accurate account can be made, and also from the circumstance that a very large number of lads and boys are employed by the journeymen, nearly all of them quite unknown and irresponsible to the managers and proprietors. The staple articles of production in the cabinet brass department are castors for chairs, sofas, and tables; hinges of all sorts; door-handles and knobs, bolts, escutcheons, &c.; window fastenings; bell levers, pulls, and cranks; stair-case eyes and rods; brass-headed nails; hat and coat pins; curtain rings; drawer-handles, sconces, table-fasteners, &c. The introduction of portions of ornamental china into cabinet brass goods, such as bell-pulls, and curtain bands, about ten years ago, opened up a new branch of industry, and has given a great impetus to the trade. Glass has still more recently been employed for similar purposes, and has tended to introduce into cabinet brass foundry a more expensive and superior style of workmanship. The character given of the workers in this branch of the brass trade, both by the employers and the operatives themselves, is highly favourable as compared with some other branches of trade. The habits of intemperance, carelessness, and irregularity, which are stated to have formerly prevailed amongst them, only linger among the elder race of workmen, and are fast disappearing among the younger men. The observance of "St. Monday" and all such holidays, is stated to be almost entirely confined to the older hands; "and it not unfrequently happens," said an intelligent journeyman, "that if one of the workmen absents himself from work for drunkenness, he returns to the manufactory amidst the ridicule and hootings of his comrades. The number of teetotallers in our establishment is considerable. In one shop, or department, out of ten men there are six teetotallers. They are not ridiculed and jeered at as they used to be, but on the contrary, there is a degree of shyness observed in bringing in ale to the shop, particularly at eleven o'clock. No drinking fee, such as 'foot-money,' is insisted upon. Nevertheless, it is often voluntarily given, and then the men club together till they get enough to have a supper. On the occasion of a marriage the bridegroom generally gives 5s. or 10s. towards a supper. The men are also inclined to enforce the payment of the 'shifting shilling,' when a man moves from one lathe to another.

These shillings are hoarded up till there be enough in hand to afford a 'jollification;' but these things are becoming rarer and rarer every year."

A large manufacturer, who had ample opportunities of observing the habits of the brassfounders, corroborated the statement of this workman, and stated that "drunkenness was not the vice of the brassworkers of Birmingham. It still haunts," he said, "some of those manufactories in other trades where the work is severe and exhausting; but, except in these cases, the men generally are industrious and sober, and if they are properly cared for they prove good men and good workmen." The stricter discipline and order introduced into the large factories has tended, it would appear, to confirm the temperate habits which of late years have spread so extensively among the superior class of skilled workmen. The number of men who have taken the temperance pledge has considerably augmented within the last few years, and their position among the men has become more agreeable than it used to be; and it is highly satisfactory to learn on all hands that the men never seek to insult their abstaining comrades, but treat them with the utmost respect, and express, on many occasions, a wish that they could follow their example. These are indications not only of a more temperate spirit, but of the kindly and tolerant feeling which appears to be extending among the mechanics of this trade.

There are few apprentices taken to learn the business, the boys employed by the journeymen being only retained during good behaviour, or for the mutual convenience of both parties. The average wages for such assistants, between the ages of ten and fifteen, are from 3s. to 6s. 6d. a week. Between fifteen and eighteen years of age, lads may earn from 10s. to 14s. or 15s. a week, according to their ability. Single-handed, an average workman at the cabinet brass trade, may earn from £1 to £1 4s. a week; with two or three boys under him, he may make from 6s. to 7s. more; and with half a dozen boys, a number often employed by active workmen, some will earn from £1 15s. to £2, or £2 10s. a week. There is no union of this branch of the trade, nor of the trade generally, but the men in most of the large factories, either under the influence of their employers, or because they are aware of the duty and advantage of encouraging provident habits among themselves, have established sick and burial clubs.

One of the best conducted of these clubs was established in 1828, in the large manufactory of the Messrs. Winfield, the gentlemen whose efforts for the education of the boys in their own employ, or in those of their workmen, were detailed in a former letter of this series. It should be stated that the Messrs. Winfield combine several of the branches of the brass manufacture, and produce not only cabinet and general brass goods, but gas lamps, gas fittings, metallic bedsteads, and other articles. The club was commenced in January, 1828, but the rules were revised and amended in January, 1847, by the workmen and masters at a general meeting. The object of the club is to form a fund for the purpose of assisting members and their families in case of sickness or death; and thus to obviate the necessity of making charitable collections. Every man above twenty-one years of age who now works in the manufactory or may hereafter be taken into it, is compelled to contribute. No person is admitted into the club under eighteen years of age. Every member pays into the fund 2s. 6d. as entrance-money, which sum is considered as paid instead of the usual "foot-ale," or drinking-money. Each member pays to the secretary weekly, on Monday morning, the sum of 3d.; and if the claims of the sick members exceed the moneys in hand, each member pays 6d. per week so long as the necessity exists. In the case where any member is unable to work, and brings a certificate from a surgeon, he receives 6s. per week for the space of twelve months, and if he remain ill after that period, he receives 3s. per week so long as he afterwards continues unable to work. No member receives any money from the fund if his sickness arise from fighting or any unlawful disease. On the death of a member the secretary pays to the friend, widow, or relative of the deceased, the sum of £8 towards defraying the expenses of his funeral; and on the death of a member's wife, he receives £4; and on the death of a member's child, £1. In case of the death of a member, each workman pays into the fund the sum of 1s.; in case of the death of a member's wife, 6d.; and on the death of a member's child, 2d., in addition to the regular contribution. If any member strike another, he forfeits to the fund the sum of 5s.; and if proved that the member receiving the blow gave provocation, he is also fined 5s. This rule is always rigidly enforced, but the cases are stated to be exceedingly rare in which it is necessary to apply it. On the Christmas-eve in each year (except when happening on a Sunday), the cash in hand, after reserving the sum of 2s. each member as a fund for any extra claim which may be made upon the society in case of sickness or death, is equally divided amongst the members.

The regulations of this club being drawn up by the members themselves, for their own benefit, are cheerfully obeyed. This and similar smaller clubs in other establishments are the only attempts at Trade Unions in the general or other brass manufacture, with the sole exception of the branch devoted to cock or tap founding, to be hereafter mentioned.

In the important department of the brass manufacture including "general" goods, or builders', carpenters', and upholsterers', and cabinet brass, there are general complaints, not alone among the better class of manufacturers, but among the public, of the inferiority of a large proportion of the goods which are poured into the market. "Slop" brass seems to be as extensively manufactured in Birmingham as slop clothes are in London, Liverpool, and Glasgow; and brass goods for builders' purposes, or for furniture, gradually become lighter, thinner, and less serviceable, in consequence of the ruinous competition of numerous small, and some large, manufacturers, and of the effect upon the market of the dealings of men who cannot afford to keep their goods over the Saturday night without forcing a sale among the factors or merchants. The very name of Birmingham threatens to fall into discredit in the markets of the world for the wretched articles which, under the name of "cabinet brass," find their way to the retail dealers, both at home and abroad, and of which it is difficult to say whether the dishonest competition of men who have capital, or the ruinous trading of men who have none, is the most active cause.

The following statements, derived from masters as well as operatives, throw some light upon this system, and the extent to which it has been carried:—"There has," said a journeyman well acquainted with the trade, "been a reduction of 2d. a set made in the wages paid to the workman for socket castors within the last fifteen years. Many of the castors that are now made are quite unfit for use. They are about one-half the weight that is requisite for a good serviceable article for a chair, or sofa, on which a man may expect to sit down without breaking it. There is a large proportion of bad articles made in the trade. Men are paid better for good articles, and are less liable to lose money by spoiling them altogether. The difference in a workman's weekly receipts on good and bad work would amount to at least 5s. The demand for good work is better than it was three or four years ago, but articles are still made which are quite unfit for use, and are a positive disgrace to the town. About six years ago men worked at these light castors for about 14s. 6d. or 15s. a week. About 14 years ago, window fastenings, &c., were made at 2s. 3d. a set, which are now made for 1s. 3d. or 1s. 6d. a set. Bell cranks are also made by the 'garret-masters' for one-half of the fair and regular price, to the great injury of the trade generally. The articles are lighter, and every way inferior, and cannot stand ordinary wear and tear."

On the same subject a manufacturer stated:—"A general depreciation has been going on for several years in cabinet brass articles. There are, however, exceptions; and the goods manufactured for the houses of the wealthy, for which a good price is paid, are as substantially made as ever they were. In some instances, it should be stated, goods which were formerly made with a great quantity of metal, admit of reduction without deterioration. Too much metal was formerly used in some cases, but generally speaking the reductions in the weight of metal are effected at the cost of the durability and excellence of the articles. The ordinary easy chair and sofa makers in London—the slop furniture makers, as they are called— use the very worst castors; and contractors for house furnishing also purchase the cheap and inferior slop articles. Year by year the articles are made lighter and lighter. In twenty years the difference has been very great. I believe that castors, similar to those which thirty years ago were sold at 6s. a set, are now sold at from 3s. to 4s. a set, and the higher priced was in reality much the cheaper article of the two. A great deal of the cabinet brass trade is done by 'little men,' who take the work to their own houses. It requires very little to commence business as a cabinet brassfounder. A vice, a lathe, a few files, and a few turning tools are enough to start a slop-worker, and either alone, or with a little assistance, he is able to turn out a quantity of work, which he will sell to the 'factors,' or, as some call them, the 'slaughtermen.' Factors who purchase a large quantity of goods when they have no present demand for them, expect as a matter of course to receive them at a lower rate than ordinary customers. If a factor takes goods from a slop-man, he does so very often when the only object in making the purchase is to get the goods cheap and retain them till he can make a large profit. He knows that the garret-master cannot do without money on Saturday night, and that he will sell at any price as the night wears on. The great manufacturers also work against each other, often, I think, most unfairly. In the face of such competition, the only honest chance of clearing much by an article is to make it novel and striking in design, so that before it is pirated or remodelled by others a sufficient quantity may be disposed of at a remunerative price."

"I have remarked," said another manufacturer, "that a general reduction of 10 per cent. has taken place within the last seven or eight
years in the weight of all cabinet brass goods, while on some of the
common articles of manufacture the reduction has been about 30 per
cent. The principal cause of this reduction has been the growing competition among manufacturers, factors, and small makers, or 'garret-
masters.' Factors, striving to undersell each other, try among the manufacturers to procure a reduction in their prices; and, failing in this,
they purchase the flimsiest work that is offered cheap, until the legitimate manufacturer is compelled to reduce his prices in order to
obtain a market for his goods. The workman is the first to feel the
effects of the reduction, and if he cannot realize his former profits
by increasing the amount of his labour, he will either suffer a considerable loss, or 'scamp' his work in order to do it more quickly. A
few years ago the demand for cheap inferior work was very great, and
produced large quantities of wretched goods, quite unfit for service.
The slop chair and sofa makers in London and other places still continue the demand for these articles. The castors for chairs and tables
which were made thirty years ago were fully one-third heavier than
the articles made at present, and a good castor as made now by the respectable trade is almost double the weight of the slop articles. Those
who try to compete with the garret-masters, must grind down the
wages of their men to the last penny, and must save every possible
half ounce of metal. It is a bad system altogether, and all the worse
because there seems to be no remedy for it."

I now come to the next most important branch of the brass manufacture, which is that of lamps and chandeliers, including gasaliers and gas-fittings, chandeliers and candelabra, and oil, candle, and
spirit lamps. Some of the manufacturers produce no gasaliers or gas-
fittings, and others produce nothing else; while a third description
combines all these branches, as well as general brass-work. From
1,400 to 1,800 persons are believed to be employed in this trade. As in
the general brass trade, the workmen receive fair and constant wages,
and are assisted to a great extent by juvenile labour. "The 'gang' system," said a manufacturer, "is the only one which can be satisfactorily
adopted in a large establishment, because of the infinite variety of
work required to make a lamp. There may, for instance, be a score
of men occupied upon different parts of one lamp-burner, and these
being placed under one person, the work is greatly facilitated. The
lamp trade suffered very much after the panic in 1846 and 1847, but

is now reviving. Any man who knows his trade can get from 20s. to 25s. a week. The heads of the gangs make from £2 to £3 a week. One man in our employ has invested his savings so well that he is the owner of eleven small houses. Another has built seven houses. Many workmen within my knowledge have shares in railways, and have made other investments of their savings. The men are willing to work, and they live soberly. Drunkenness is not the vice of the brass-workers of Birmingham, though there are many trades in which the workmen are very intemperate. These are principally trades in which the work is given out, and no regular factory discipline is observed, or where the actual work is of the severest description, and the men seek relief from their exhaustion in drinking. It has been found that the introduction of steam or water power for the heaviest part of the work tends to improve the condition of the men, and to reform their vicious habits. At present almost all the heavy work is done by mechanical power. The fine work depends upon the skill of the workman in the use of his tools. The use of fancy glass pillars for table lamps and chandelier ornaments has greatly increased of late. In the manufacture of these, the Bohemians excel the English. Their introduction into the lamp trade has given it quite a new feature. It is only three or four years old, and is certainly a result for which we have to thank Sir Robert Peel, for his wise abolition of the excise duties on glass, and the reduction of the import duties. I know but little of the glass trade, but I dare say the English glass will soon equal the Bohemian. The prices of lamps have not been reduced by the introduction of glass in their manufacture. Camphine lamps were at first favourably received, but became unpopular because they were not well understood. The trade is now reviving. There is a large export of candle and oil lamps to North and South America. All those grand and flaring patterns which you see are for the southern markets. People in warm climates will have brilliant patterns and colours; red, green, gold, and blue, are more esteemed than the soberer tints which please the people in the more northern latitudes."

The following information on the lamp and chandelier trade, the rate of wages, and the condition of the operatives, was communicated by an intelligent working man:—"An average day-workman gets about £1 1s. a week. The wages of the piece-workman differ according to his ability, and to the number of men or boys working under him. A workman has ordinarily from three to six persons working under him, called his 'crew.' By the aid of his crew he may earn from

35s. to £2 a week. Boys between ten and fifteen years of age, serving thus, earn from 2s. 6d. to 8s. per week, according to their ability; lads from fifteen to eighteen years of age earn from 8s. to 12s. a week—or, if skilful workmen, they may get about 14s. a week. Some men of inferior skill work under others till they are twenty-five or thirty years of age, or older. There are some manufactories in the town where the crew, or gang, system is not admitted. I do not know of any instance where the boys composing a crew receive much attention from the proprietors, except in the case of Messrs. Winfield, whose school is well known. I hear constantly of parents who desire to get their boys into Messrs. Winfield's establishment, because of the existence of the school. The wages now given for such work as gas-fittings are less than they were ten years ago. During the last year trade has been unusually brisk, and although the ordinary wages have remained the same, the men have been enabled to gain considerably by over hours. In some establishments the price of gas-fittings and lamps has fallen, but in these there has been a corresponding reduction in their intrinsic value. Generally, it may be said, a great reduction has taken place in the quantity of material used in the manufacture of various articles. In superior work there is an increase of the skill and labour devoted to it, and the lightness of the articles in superior work is not so much to save metal as to give them a light and neat appearance. The heavy-chandelier trade is somewhat stagnant. There has been a great change in the character and habits of the workmen themselves within the last ten years. They are, as far as I can judge, much better behaved, and are in fact better men than they used to be. Some of the old hands seem incurable, and constantly live in distress and poverty, although they might live well and comfortably on the wages they receive. It seems to me that much of the misery of working men is caused by their wives, who do not sufficiently understand household economy and general management, and have not the art of making home comfortable. Factory girls make bad housewives. The men expect to live well, and to have butcher-meat once a day, properly cooked and served, otherwise they become discontented and irregular in their habits. Much good might, I think, be done by the cheap publication of works upon household economy, to teach the wives of the workmen a better system of household management than they ever had the means of learning from experience; but then, unluckily the wives of working men are for the most part ignorant even of the alphabet. The working classes would generally be more comfortable if the women were better taught; but bad wives make bad husbands, and the evil extends from them to their children."

Within the last ten or twelve years the attention paid to designs has greatly increased. The constant demand for novelty of pattern has obliged manufacturers to make considerable efforts to procure the services of able modellers and draughtsmen in their establishments, and at present scarcely any other means of extending his trade is left to the manufacturer, but to surpass his competitors in novelty and elegance of pattern. Most of the larger establishments in Birmingham have from two, three, to four modellers in constant employment; while designs are frequently received from chance artists, who, without adhering to any one branch of manufacture, supply ornamental designs for all kinds of metallic work. The School of Design, from which it is to be hoped that additional advantages may be reaped, has hitherto been of little use. The pupils are stated to manifest a much greater partiality for landscape drawing than for decorative art.

One of the most interesting sights in Birmingham is the pattern and model room of Mr. Messinger, a visit to which conveys a striking idea of the ceaseless activity of the trade, and the constant production of novelties of design, in chandeliers, lamps, candelabra, bronzes, and miscellaneous brass articles. The room, which is about seventy-two feet long by eighteen broad, is covered—walls and roof—with patterns of brass articles—and along the whole range a series of tables are laden with similar articles, from patterns which have been produced for a few shillings, to those which have cost hundreds of pounds to invent. In this room are the accumulated patterns of forty years. Among the patterns of brackets and chandeliers, are some of which, according to previous agreement no second copy was ever produced; among others, a beautiful chandelier for Windsor Castle, of which pattern her Majesty is the sole possessor, at a price enhanced, as a matter of course, by the whole cost of the design and model, which is alone estimated at a very considerable sum. On asking the proprietor the number of patterns in his room, he declared his utter inability to form an opinion, but stated that there must be, including paper-stands, chimney ornaments, letter-clips, match-boxes, inkstands, and a whole host of minor articles, in addition to chandeliers and candelabra, "some scores of thousands." The cost of their production was stated to be nearer £40,000 than £30,000. The English modellers produced the greater portion of these designs, those elegant and expensive articles alone excepted in which the human figure was introduced. In this branch of decorative art it was stated that "the English were fifty years behind the French."

"In this branch of the brass manufacture," said a workman who had been nearly forty years in the trade, "there is much jealousy between those who work at one article and those who work at another. The man who makes most money looks down on the rest. One man will not insist upon the same rate that others will, and of course this diminishes the friendly understanding among the men. The men compete with each other. There is no book of prices to which masters and men can adhere, and consequently no discount when prices decline, as there is in some trades. The great variety of articles and of prices, and the constant novelty of design and manufacture, render it impossible to make a book of prices. About one hundred tons of brass are manufactured per annum in our establishment. The articles now made are much lighter than they used to be about twenty or thirty years ago, though the work is as good as it was then, and there is a much greater elegance of design. The change in the character of designs for lamps and general brass-work began to be visible about ten years ago, and since then the variety has been very great. It is now found necessary to keep modellers and draughtsmen on the premises of the principal manufacturers. Two modellers and one draughtsman are generally found to be sufficient, but designs are constantly being received from persons who sell them, but who are not regularly employed for the purpose. This branch of the pattern business has only been known within the last few years; such a thing as hawking about designs in that manner was not heard of twenty years ago. The only part of our trade which is considered at all unhealthy, is the casting, yet the men do not generally complain. Dipping brass into *aqua fortis* is pernicious, but the men are cleaner and more careful than they used to be; and the objections offered by benefit societies against the admission of brass founders are disappearing. The brass founders have no benefit society or union among themselves; and do nothing for their mutual improvement and advancement, as the glass makers and other trades have done. They are too much divided, and know too little of one another. A union was attempted a few years ago, but the number of members never exceeded fifty or sixty, and it has since been discontinued."

It does not appear that the same causes which have tended to deteriorate other branches of the brass trade have operated much upon the manufacture of lamps, chandeliers, and gas fittings. The amount of capital required to start in the business, the expense at which it is kept up, the large premises required, and the high rate of wages, have kept the small garret-masters out of the trade, and thus the large manufacturers have been enabled to maintain the superior character of their goods, and, consequently, the rate of the workmen's wages.

Another department of the brass-lamp manufacture, which is considered a separate trade, is that of *ship lamps and scuttles*. This branch of the lamp trade is principally carried on in the spring and the end of summer. Ship lamps are made in several of the large ports of the kingdom, including London, Liverpool, and Glasgow. In Birmingham the number of persons engaged in the trade is estimated by a manufacturer at not more than thirty men and boys, who produce in the course of the year about 5,000 lamps. They are made for ships of all countries, and are extensively used by the American packet and emigrant ships. They are now sold at one-fourth of the price charged 20 years ago, but it should be stated that they can be produced with much greater facility and at less expense than formerly. The great increase of emigration has led to a corresponding increase in the demand. Few lamps, of a cheap or common sort, were produced previous to the year 1846 or 1847. On those now produced less work is bestowed, and they are slighter than the old lamps, though stated to be quite as useful. The increased facilities for manipulation are such that, although the workman receives considerably less money for each lamp produced, he is yet able to do so many more in the course of a day that his wages are not diminished, but, on the contrary, are often higher than they were 20 years ago.

The next great subdivision of the manufactures is that of *Brass Candlesticks*. There are large numbers of makers of these articles in Birmingham, some of whom devote themselves to standard or parlour candlesticks, and others to the small, flat, bedroom candlesticks. Though both of these articles are generally made in the same establishment, the manufacture of one or other of them usually predominates, yet in no case to the entire exclusion of other brass goods. Candlesticks may form but one department of an establishment in which half a dozen branches of manufacture are carried on, or it may be the staple article made amidst a hundred minor objects. The number of persons engaged in the trade is considerable; one manufacturer estimated them at 300, and another at 500 hands. The number of women employed is very small, and in bedroom candlestick making the proportion of boys required is not so much as one boy to each man. The introduction of gas into more common use in England has had the effect of decreasing very materially the manufacture of candlesticks required for home consumption, but its effect upon the foreign markets has not yet been felt in any degree by the majority of the manufacturers. In one establishment, where a large quantity of candlesticks have long been made for home and foreign consumption, the decrease in the home trade has been about one-third, while there has been an increase in the foreign trade of about five times the amount made twenty years ago. It is to the foreign markets that manufacturers principally look for large orders, and particularly to North and South America and the West Indies, where the importations are very great. "The greatest quantity sent out," said a manufacturer, "go to the River Plate and to Mexico. In Mexico these goods are hawked about the streets as knives and such ware are in this country. Great quantities of spittoons are sent to Mexico. Within a few years the price of spittoons has been reduced from 30s. to 18s. a dozen, and are made by some of the garret-masters here for no more than the workman's wages would amount to for a good article. Where and how they get brass I cannot imagine. Brass egg-cups have been made in enormous quantities within the last five years. Turkey is the principal market, where they are used to hand round cups of coffee. One order given was for 16,000 dozen of them. Great quantities of small candlesticks," said the same gentleman, "are made, often so light and fragile, as to be unfit for supporting the weight of a candle, but being of the size required, though not half their proper weight, they are packed up and sent to their destination without once being seen until they are delivered to the foreign importer." A gentleman who had entered the bedroom candlestick business only about three years ago, said that within that time some of the articles had been reduced to half their previous weight, and that they were being made thinner and lighter every year, wherever any further reductions in their calibre were possible. These reductions are represented to have been made principally in the manufacture of candlesticks which were originally of an inferior description. In the better class of standard candlesticks the application of steam to the lathe, and the facilities in manipulation which have been introduced, have enabled the manufacturers to produce three times the quantity of candlesticks that could be produced formerly, and to reduce the price of good articles so much that they are now sold for less than was formerly paid for dressing them.

One of the workmen in an establishment where the better description of candlesticks are made, stated, from personal recollection, that though he had now to make a greater number of articles in a week than formerly, for the same wages that he received twenty years ago, he made as much money now as then, and with less bodily fatigue than when the lathe was turned by the foot. An average workman will make 25s. or 26s. a week. Among the manufacturers of inferior work, the principal difficulties to contend with are the competition of garret-masters, and the low prices necessarily offered by factors to people who force sales when the market is over-stocked. So little machinery is required to start the manufacture of light bed-room candlesticks, that two or three workmen out of employment may, by clubbing their small means together, produce a considerable quantity of goods in the course of a week. If they force a sale, as they commonly do, at the end of the week, they receive much less money than they could be made for by the legitimate manufacturer. As there are a large number of garret-masters engaged in the manufacture of inferior candlesticks, their influence upon the general market is very considerable. A manufacturer, who was principally engaged in making articles of a second-rate character, said that one in his position had little chance of competing with the "slop" maker, except by producing from time to time a new and popular pattern. As long as the die remained unpirated, their articles commanded a sale at remunerative prices, but some pushing garret-master soon contrived to sink a similar die, and, by under-selling the original manufacturer, to bring down the price of the article.

There are still a number of important branches of the brass trade to be described, which must be reserved for a second and concluding letter.

LABOUR AND THE POOR.

BIRMINGHAM.

[FROM OUR SPECIAL CORRESPONDENT.]

WORKERS IN BRASS (CONCLUDED).

LETTER XIII.

There are various divisions of the manufacture of brass, of which no account was given in the preceding Letter of this series. I now proceed to notice the most important of those which remain.

Brass Cock Founding is an extensive manufacture in Birmingham; but there appears to be so much mutual jealousy between masters and men that it is extremely difficult to procure information from either of them on any point connected with the trade. I found that if inquiry were made of an employer, however intelligent he might be, and however well disposed towards the working classes generally, he seemed to jump to the conclusion that something hostile was meant to the master cock-founders, and his lips were sealed in an instant. If a similar inquiry were made of the workmen, the same degree of mistrust was exhibited, and more than one expressed his belief that such inquiries could have no other object than the reduction of wages.

Even in so simple, and, as might be imagined, so harmless and neutral a matter as the number of hands employed or supposed to be employed, an eminent manufacturer refused point-blank to give any information, or to refer me to any intelligent workman in his service who might be able to afford it. Some of the men were equally close, and were fearful apparently of some concealed and nefarious design in the mere asking of the question. The following particulars, however, were derived, but not without considerable difficulty, from a few persons in the trade, unconnected with each other, who became aware, after a little explanation, that an inquiry of this kind could have no other object than the welfare of the working classes. If there should be any inaccuracy in their statements, it will be due to the mistrust alluded to, and to the excessive jealousy both of the employers and the employed—a jealousy which was not exhibited by any other trade of the town.

It would appear that the trade of Brass Cock or Tap founding gives employment to about 180 men, and to about the same number of boys and lads. A few women are engaged in making the "cores" or moulds for casting the cocks. The trade is not peculiar to Birmingham, but is carried on to a considerable extent in London, Manchester, Leeds, Sheffield, Glasgow, and other large towns. There are twenty-five recognised cock-founders in Birmingham—whose names appear in the Directory—and there are believed to be about twice that number of small or "garret" masters, who prefer working for themselves to serving as journeymen in the manufactories of large employers.

A combination was established among the masters about a quarter of a century ago, for the purpose of keeping up and regulating the prices, but it was broken up after being in existence for eight or nine years. It was found that many of the manufacturers did not adhere to their own rules, but secretly attempted to force business by underselling each other. The combination has not since been revived.

About the same time there was a partial strike by the men, but they were defeated by the masters, and returned gradually to their work. A union was shortly afterwards formed by the men, by means of which they succeeded in obtaining terms from the masters more liberal than those which they had previously enjoyed. A list of prices was agreed to, which, after being for nearly 18 years in operation, was ultimately discontinued. After this, although the list of prices remained the same, a system of exacting discount on the rate of wages was commenced; and by the year 1845, according to the statement of a manufacturer, in some cases a discount of 25 per cent. was taken from the men's earnings. This, with an additional charge made on them of a per centage on their wages for the rent of the manufactory, made the deduction, virtually amount to 30 per cent. on their earnings. This led to a reorganisation of the union in 1845, by which the men succeeded in abolishing the discount charged on their prices, and in restoring to use the list which had been agreed to in 1824. This list continues in use at present; so that the men are paid at precisely the same rate of wages as they were twenty-six years ago. With a boy—and by a rule of the union no journeyman can have more than one boy to work under him—an average workman can earn from £1 5s. to £1 10s. a week. Single-handed, he can earn from £1 to £1 5s. a week. Taps for the foreign market, it is stated, are generally inferior to those made for England; and the wages earned in the manufacture of foreign goods are fully 2s. a week less than are earned upon more substantial work. How such a system will ultimately affect the reputation, not only of Birmingham, but of English manufactures generally, should be thought of before the market is entirely lost. While the rate of wages has continued nearly the same for so long a time, considerable reductions have been made in price. The manufacturers, forced by competition amongst themselves, have introduced a rigid system of economy in the application of material. An old workman said that the manufacturers of the present day made their profits out of savings that would have been despised by the masters in his younger days.

Upon the character of the brass-cock workers the opinions of those most competent to judge varied very considerably. One manufacturer, who employs a considerable number of men, and has long been in business, stated that "irregularity and drunkenness were but too general among them, and that they observed St. Monday to a considerable extent. Most of them might make more than £1 5s. a week, but he had known an expert workman make 12s. by five o'clock in the day, and then leave off work to go and enjoy himself. It is," he said, "the ruin of the trade here that the men are fonder of drinking than of working. It often happens—in fact it is general—that the family of the workman who can only earn 24s. a week is better off than that of the man who can make £3 in a week. The quick man is apt to idle away half his time, and to acquire habits which lead ultimately to his total ruin." Another manufacturer, who had lived in more immediate contact with the workmen, spoke more reservedly respecting their character. "The union," he said, "had a direct tendency to bring the men a good deal together, and as they met in public-houses, it led to drinking and dissipated habits. They were, he thought, not altogether so steady, as a class, as many others of the trades in the town; but they were steadier than the casters and the pearl button makers. He could not say that they absented themselves so much on Mondays as the men in some other trades. Among the young hands there was a great and decided improvement, which every day became more visible."

The union numbers about 130 members. There are three or four large manufactories in Birmingham, besides various small makers, and garret masters.

Another important branch of the brass manufacture in Birmingham is that of *brass weights and measures*. This manufacture is carried on extensively in many towns of England, but principally at London, Birmingham, Bilston, Wolverhampton, and Bewdley. The nicer manufacture of standard weights and measures for the various boroughs of England was, until lately, confined to London. All weights and measures made for boroughs and towns—in order to test the accuracy of others—must now be subjected to inspection at the Exchequer. The advantage which brass weights have over those made of iron is, that they can be made with more exactness, and that they do not corrode. In Birmingham there are from 50 to 70 workmen employed in this manufacture, which is gradually increasing with the increase of population, and is seldom subject to other fluctuations than those produced by an occasional examination in a town of the weights and measures employed in trade, and by the attendant demand for measures more exact. The foreign and colonial trade has never been very extensive, although the United States, Canada, and Mexico, are supplied to some extent from Birmingham. Weights are also made, though not in large quantities, for other countries, including Holland, Spain, Russia, and Italy. For France and the Channel Islands a limited quantity has also been supplied.

About seven or eight years ago, large quantities of "manillas"—which are coins, or rather weights, resembling the old Roman ring coin—were made at Birmingham, and sent to the Gold Coast, where they were in great demand for trading with the natives. A brass tube of various lengths has since then been substituted for the ring coin; but the demand for both of these has for the present ceased. During last year one manufacturer in Birmingham is stated to have made upwards of 30,000 sets of troy and avoirdupois weights, of which nearly two-thirds were to weigh gold in California. Considerable reductions have been made in the price of weights and measures within the last few years. "So lately as five years ago," said a gentleman engaged in the trade, "the prices were from 15 to 20 per cent. higher than at present, and corresponding reductions have been made in that time in the wages of the workmen. This has been owing to the competition among the manufacturers, to the facilities which steam and ingenuity have afforded for the rapid production of these articles, and to the influence of small makers upon the general market. The application of steam or water motive power to turning the lathe, &c., gives the large manufacturers an advantage over their smaller brethren, but the general character of the work is so simple that it can be carried on pretty extensively at very little expense. Any reductions that are made must come out of rent and wages, for the weight and quantity of material used must necessarily remain unchanged."

Another manufacturer of weights and measures, of a high standing in Birmingham, complained that, except by sending to the Founders' Hall at London, there was no means of having the accuracy of troy weights officially tested. This, he said, was not the case with avoirdupois, or other weights, which could be inspected and adjusted in provincial towns. The expediency of providing similar means for testing troy weights he urged very strongly.

The manufacture of *military ornaments* is the next branch of brass work that requires notice. During the revolutionary war, and for some time afterwards, this trade was exceedingly brisk, and all the hands were fully occupied. An old workman, who had been engaged in the trade at that time, said that, without working over time, he could then make from 25s. to 30s. a week, and by working more than ten hours a day, he could increase his wages by 5s. or 10s. a week. "There was so much to do that the men often worked day and night, yet could not supply the demand, and this although a part of the trade was supplied by the ordinary brass founders of Birmingham." For about twenty years the trade is represented to have been generally very steady, except within the last two years, when there has been considerable depression. The manufacturers state that they are obliged to devote their attention to other articles, or they would be unable to retain the number of hands which they formerly required for making military ornaments alone. The ornaments made for the British army are fewer than formerly, and appear to be diminishing annually. The cavalry regiments and the artillery have not yet lost many of their decorations, but both men and officers in the infantry have been stripped of their superfluities of dress within the last few years. Among the more recent changes have been the loss of the "frock-strap;" the plain epaulet which was worn upon the shoulder of an officer's undress coat; the brass chain by which the soldier's cap was fastened under the chin; the brass breastplate which was fastened upon the soldier's belt, &c. These and similar changes have operated detrimentally to the manufacture of brass military ornaments. The supply for the Indian army has also diminished, more especially within the last eighteen months, but it gives fully as much employment as the regular British army.

The other standard claimants for military brass ornaments are the regiments stationed in the colonies, and the yeomanry regiments of England. A good many orders have lately been received from South

America. Naval ornaments were formerly made for the navy of the United States, but this demand has lately ceased.

The value of the articles now made for the use of the rank and file of the army is estimated at about 40 per cent. less than that of the ornaments made during the war, and in some cases the reduction in value has been even greater. The ornaments made for officers' dresses have generally maintained their price, though within the last twenty years there has been some reduction, more especially in the ornaments used for undress clothing. The wages of the workmen have undergone no material change for many years, and at present they average from £1 to £1 5s. a week. The majority of the men are day workers, though paid according to their ability. The total number of workmen employed in the trade is about 150—about the same, it was said, as was employed about twenty years ago.

The *Mathematical Instrument* manufacture is another branch of the brass trade that is carried on at Birmingham. Under the general title of mathematical instruments, are usually included mathematical-drawing instruments, optical instruments, surveying instruments, astronomical instruments, and goniometrical instruments for measuring the angles of crystals. According to the Birmingham Directory, there are fourteen makers of these at Birmingham, each of whom devotes himself more especially to one department of the trade, and to others generally. The number of workmen and boys employed does not exceed 60. It may, however, be said that for the most part the mathematical instruments produced at Birmingham are of an inferior character to those made in London, and that the more scientific and expensive class of instruments are either not made at all in the town, or are made in such small quantities as not to form an essential feature of the Birmingham trade. An intelligent workman, who appeared to be conversant with all the work done in Birmingham in his own trade, stated that he was aware of only three workmen in the town who were engaged in what he termed "first-rate work," and that these were fully able to supply the demand. There were others who in part assisted these workmen, but they were the only persons who could make instruments as perfect as those manufactured in London. The demand for first-class goods would appear, however, to be on the increase in Birmingham, and it was agreed on all hands that a great scarcity of able workmen was felt. The demand for good surveyors' instruments, during the time of the railway mania, was so great that one maker stated that he could have sold "any quantity" at that time. The increased demand lasted only for a few months; but public attention being directed to the study of geometry and other branches of mathematics, cases of instruments for the use of schools have been much more in demand since that time than they were previously. It is also stated that railway engine drivers, and other workmen employed in the manufacture and management of locomotives, are now generally possessed of mathematical instruments, and that this has further tended to keep up the demand. Both in London and Birmingham the increase in the manufacture is stated to have been considerable within the last ten or twelve years, but the makers seem to be generally of opinion that some part of the London trade is passing to Birmingham, and that the increase has been much more than is simply in proportion to the increase of population. Within that time, the number of makers in Birmingham has been doubled, and a corresponding increase has taken place in the number of workmen employed. As in other branches of the brass manufacture, competition has led to greatly reduced profits, and this has led to the production of inferior articles at a cheap rate. The demand has been increased both for the home and foreign markets, but the great portion of the instruments manufactured for the foreign trade are of the slop description. The foreign trade is estimated at two-thirds of the whole. The reduction in the value of these articles within the last thirty years is stated to be about 35 per cent.; and within the last 12 or 15 years, 20 per cent. But good instruments have maintained a steady price during that time, and no tendency to reduction is remarked. Such improvements as have been made within the last 20 years in the manufacture of mathematical instruments have been chiefly in the style of getting up, and in the process of putting the parts together.

When the articles are of a superior character, these improvements are very marked, and it was allowed by manufacturers and workmen that the instruments of this kind which are now made are very superior to those ever made before, even in those instances where there has been a considerable reduction in price. The worst class of goods are, however, made upon the old system, and to produce the greatest possible number at the cheapest possible rate is almost the only consideration of their makers. Many of these cheap instruments were said by one of the workmen to be quite unfit for practical purposes. The principal market for cheap goods is America, and second to it Australia and the colonies. For some years France and Germany have been striving to compete with the English makers in this trade, but, bad as the English slop goods are, it is asserted that French instruments are no better. They are described as having a more elegant finish, but as being less durable, and quite as expensive as those made in England. A manufacturer, who was also a workman, said that the jointing of French-made instruments was faulty, and liable to become loose with a little use, and he did not think that, as a general rule, they were so accurate, so steady, or so durable as English instruments. "When French instruments are good," said another manufacturer, "they are very good, and when bad they are very bad; and in both cases they are as dear as our own." German instruments were generally considered as truer than the French, and of better manufacture throughout, but as dear as English articles.

The decrease that has taken place in the value of common goods was nowhere attributed to the influence of Continental competition, but to the competition among manufacturers here. Their increasing number leads to greater competition, and the wages of the workmen have been lowered more and more, according as manufacturers of cheaper goods multiply. This reduction is, however, less marked than in many other branches of the brass trade, and prices for the last two years have been tolerably steady. A workman who has been engaged in this manufacture for nearly 30 years stated that, about 20 years ago, the average receipts of a workman engaged upon average work were about 27s. or 28s. a week, and that a man of corresponding ability, at corresponding work, at present makes from 20s. to 24s. a week. At common and cheap work, the average receipts are about 20s. a week. The best workmen at the best work now make about 30s. a week. There is no union among the workmen. As a class they are represented as sober and industrious, and several manufacturers stated that their best workmen were, in all other respects, the best men in their employment. A considerable degree of talent, taste, and ability, is required, and the workmen possessing these qualities are generally well-educated and respectable people.

The manufacture of *metallic bedsteads* is another department of the brass trade—though it includes to some extent the manufacture of articles in iron. The use of metallic bedsteads in barracks led to their adoption in private houses, and about fifty years ago they began to be constructed of iron in considerable quantities. The manufacture now gives employment to about 500 persons in Birmingham, and their number is steadily increasing. The domestic demand for these articles, though very considerable, is not equal to that from abroad, particularly from South America and the East Indies, whither large quantities are annually exported. They are most popular in warm climates. They are made in various shapes, such as four-posted, tent, half-tester, and stump bedsteads, formed of iron, brass, or japanned iron. Articles of a more costly kind are occasionally plated with silver, and the japanned bedsteads are often ornamented with groups of flowers or gilt scrolls. The greatest demand is for the four-post painted iron bedsteads. The competition in the manufacture has been considerable, and has already led to reductions in prices; improvements have also been introduced in the mode of construction, which have further tended to lower the price. Within twenty years the reduction is estimated to have been about 25 per cent. A diminution in the workmen's prices, of about 10 per cent., has taken place in that time. The average receipts of the workmen are about 25s. a week. The head of a "gang," who may have several journeymen and boys working under him, generally clears for himself about £3 a week. Boys receive from 4s. to 10s. a week.

The manufacture of *brass nails* for chairs, sofas, travelling trunks, &c., was an important and thriving trade in Birmingham, about ten or twelve years ago. There were then as many as thirteen manufactories in full operation; but the use of brass nails in articles of furniture has almost wholly ceased in this country, and the old-fashioned black trunks, set round with brass nails, have been superseded by the lighter leather portmanteau and carpet bag, and such nails are no longer used by cabinet makers. The effect has been to drive nearly all the manufacturers out of the field, and the four or five makers who remain in Birmingham and carry on business, rely almost entirely upon the South American trade for the sale of their goods. Another effect of the altered and falling condition of the trade, has been, for the sake of economizing wages, to substitute the labour of women for that of men in the manufactories. The only exception is in such work as casting and dipping, which is too severe for women, and is still performed by men. Girls and women only are employed in stamping, burnishing, weighing, and packing the nails. A considerable number of young children are employed in sorting the nails, placing their spikes in perforated pans preparatory to lacquering, and such other light work as they are able to do. In one establishment, which affords employment to about sixty-five persons, there are only six men. The number of persons of all ages engaged in the manufacture is about 300, of whom at least 250 are women and children. A woman's average receipts for a week's work are about 7s. or 8s. One of the manufacturers said that if a girl worked from 7 a.m. till 7 p.m., except during meal hours, for six days in the week, she might earn about 12s. a week; but work was irregular, and was not always to be obtained. The children, of nine years and upwards, earn from 1s. 6d. to 2s. a week.

A hale old workman, who had worked as a caster since 1815, stated, in answer to inquiries, "that the wages of the men had come down very much within his recollection. When he first began to work for himself, he could, he said, if steady and hardworking, earn about £2 10s. a week, independently of what he paid for the assistance of boys. No change had taken place in the manner of doing the work. About fifteen years ago, a caster, having three boys under him, could earn about 30s. a week, but at present he could only earn about £1 a week. Manufacturers, in consideration of the low rate of wages, generally allowed the men to manage two or three 'shops,' a shop consisting of about three boys." "No union," he added, "had existed among the men since about 1824, when the masters entered into an agreement among themselves for the purpose of keeping up the selling prices. This induced the men to frame a list of prices higher than those they had been receiving, and they established a union for that purpose. The masters met the proposition half way, and this, after some negotiation, satisfied the men, and the union was broken up. The union of the masters was also speedily dissolved, in consequence of competition against one another, and their secret underselling."

In this branch of the brass trade, as in many others, it was stated that the men do not like working on Monday, and that they will do three times as much on Friday as on Monday, or even on Tuesday. "Almost all their earnings," said a workman, "are at the end of the week."

The manufacture of *Saddlers' Ironmongery and Coach Furniture* is another important trade. The number of persons engaged in it in Birmingham, Walsall, and the neighbourhood, is estimated at about 1,000 men and boys. These articles include iron, steel, and plated, as well as brass goods. The amount of work done is almost equally divided between the foreign, colonial, and home markets. Canada, the United States, Mexico, South America, the East and West Indies, Australia, and Italy are the principal customers. In France, Russia, and Germany, the demand is limited, on account of the high import duties—particularly in France. One of the principle makers of these articles in Birmingham stated that the goods sent to the United

States "were either of the best or of the worst description; the middling articles being made by the Americans themselves. Large quantities of 'riding gear' are sent to South America and to Australia; for the former, the articles are very showy, and highly ornamented, but generally inferior: the harness and coach furniture, on the other hand, are not only showy and elaborate, but of first-rate quality. For the Australian market the articles preferred are what are called in England 'country goods,' in contradistinction to the fine work made for London; they are good in quality, and serviceable. The character of the articles made is stated to have improved of late years, and there is now comparatively little of the inferior work made which was so general a few years ago. This is accounted for by the fact that there is at present ample work for all those engaged in the legitimate trade, and there is consequently less disposition among the workmen to hawk inferior goods about the country. At present there is a scarcity of workmen in Birmingham and there are few garret masters, but whenever there is a scarcity of work the men immediately begin to manufacture for themselves, and to undersell the large manufacturers. The tools required for making saddlers' ironmongery are neither numerous nor expensive, so that a man may very easily commence business for himself. Great numbers of journeymen have at various times done so; and this, together with the readier methods of working which have been introduced, and the competition among the larger manufacturers, has had the effect of reducing the prices." In some of the articles most abundantly used, it is stated that this reduction has amounted to nearly 50 per cent. within the last twenty years. The reduction within that time on the price of first-class goods has been estimated at about 10 per cent. A corresponding decrease has taken place in the prices paid for making these articles, but it was generally admitted that, by means of the increased facilities for manipulation which had been applied, the workmen do not earn less in the course of a week than formerly. The average receipts of workmen are from £1 to £1 5s. a week, according to industry and ability.

The effect of the railway system upon this trade has been to divert a portion of it into another channel. Manufacturers who have lost the large orders formerly caused by stage and mail coaches, now produce trimmings for railway carriages, and vast quantities of these are now made in Birmingham by the coach and harness furniture makers.

Wire making and *drawing* is a business which is mainly connected with the brass manufacture. There are eight or nine makers of brass and copper wire in Birmingham, who give employment to about 120 or 130 men and boys. According to the estimate of a very extensive manufacturer, about 30 tons of brass wire are made every week in the town, or 1,560 tons per annum—a quantity 50 per cent. greater than that of all the brass manufactured in Birmingham at the close of the last century. One establishment alone, it was stated, had, upon a very pressing occasion, drawn and rolled 17 tons 18 cwt. of brass and copper wire in the course of a week. The trade is a good deal dependent upon the price of copper, as a large proportion of the wire made for foreign markets must be made at a price which can be remunerative only when the metal is cheap. According to some estimates two-thirds, or according to others about one-fourth, of all the brass wire made in Birmingham, is appropriated to the manufacture of pins; and a large portion of the remainder is converted into hooks and eyes. After leaving the hands of the maker, the wire is further drawn out by "weavers," who prepare it for making bird-cages, sieves, &c. Considerable quantities of brass wire are sent to the Continent, to India, Africa, Mexico, and South America. The quantity of wire now produced is double what it was about twenty years ago. The expense of starting in business is so great as to keep men of little capital out of it, and the profits are represented to be very "fine," so that a large trade is required to repay the expense of commencing. There are thus very few slop makers in the trade; but the competition among the manufacturers already engaged in it is represented as very considerable. About twenty years ago a manufacturer started in business and commenced by striking off about 30 per cent. of the profits, and since then it was stated that about 30 per cent. more had been taken off. Another manufacturer stated, that within his recollection prices had so greatly fallen that brass wire which cost 2s. 3d. a pound about twenty-six or twenty-seven years ago, now sold for 8½d. a pound, and had been once as low as 7½d. Improved machinery has, however, come into use since the days of high prices, and the demand has very greatly increased. The struggle is now, as in almost every other department of the brass manufacture, to make everything cheaply and speedily. To effect this, great improvements have been made in the process of manufacture and in the machinery applied. Foreign competition has to some extent affected the manufacturers, inasmuch as it has limited the demand. Belgium and the United States make their own wire and their own pins. The demand in Holland and the north of Europe is stated to have been interfered with by the Belgian and German manufacturers. The Germans have made much progress in the art, and have enticed several able workmen from this country.

Within the last ten or twelve years the rate of wages has undergone little change. The average receipts of the workmen at present are stated to be about 20s. a week, though they vary, according to the ability of the workmen, from 14s. to 30s. a week. The casters are better paid than other workmen in the trade, and one of the manufacturers said that a short time ago a sober and intelligent caster, who had worked for nearly thirty years in his employment, had saved sufficient money to enable him to purchase property which yielded nearly £3 a week.

The *Brass Thimble* Trade—the last of the great subdivisions of the brass manufacture which it will be necessary to notice—is estimated to employ about 200 persons, of whom a large majority are boys and women. The proportion of men varies according to the manner in which the manufactory is conducted. In some cases the men are said to number one-third of the whole, and in others it is stated that men are only employed as tool-makers, and to superintend the work-shops, in the same manner as in the principal steel pen and Florentine button manufactories. About 25 or 30 years ago thimbles used to be cast, but they are now formed by light presses, which can be managed by women; and since steam power has been applied to turning the lathe, boys can do nearly all the rest of the work except keeping the tools in order. By these mechanical improvements able-bodied men have been gradually thrown out of employment. Several attempts have, however, been made to check the too great introduction of boys and women into the business. In 1830 a union was formed, for the purpose of restricting the number of boys employed, of maintaining the prices then paid, and of watching over the general interests of the members. But the men, it appeared, were too jealous of each other to agree upon the basis of their union, and in less than a year the project was given up. The average receipts of the men about the year 1830 would have been from 25s. to 30s. a week supposing that they worked for six days in the week and for ten hours a day, which, it was admitted, was rarely done. The attempt which had been made to form a union had no effect whatever upon the prices paid to the men, or upon the number of boys employed; but prices were gradually reduced, and year after year a larger number of boys and women were introduced. In 1842 another effort was made by the men to form a union, but with no better success than before. No attempt has since been made to resuscitate it. Boys and women largely preponderate in thimble making; and it was stated by a gentleman whose name appears in the Directory as a thimble manufacturer, but who has gone out of the trade, that a boy now makes, by the aid of machinery, more thimbles in a week for 5s. or 6s. than an able-bodied man could have made for 25s. thirty years ago.

The reductions made in the price of thimbles has been proportionate to the cheapness and facility with which they can be manufactured. The strength and weight of the thimble, when it was cast, rendered it expensive, and they were sold by weight; but since the recent improvement the price has fallen 20 per cent. The rate of wages varies in almost every establishment. In some cases, a man does not earn more than 12s. a week; and the average of his wages cannot be estimated at more than from 15s. to 21s. a week. Women earn from 7s. to 9s. a week, and boys and girls make from 2s. 6d. a week upwards.

Upon a review of the brass manufacture generally, it may be stated that, as regards the workpeople, it offers advantages possessed in few other trades. So numerous are the articles to be produced, and so similar is the skill to be exhibited in them all, that when any branch of the trade declines, the workman can betake himself to another without difficulty. Hence the workpeople have seldom or never to complain of distress or want of employment; and if a working man has a turn for mechanical invention, he can, if sober and prudent, soon raise himself from the position of a journeyman to that of a master manufacturer. Such instances are frequent in all the trades of Birmingham, but in none more so than in the multifarious branches of the brass manufacture. The great evil is the extent to which the production of "slop" articles is carried—an evil which, if it be not checked, bids fair to seal up against Birmingham goods some of the most important and profitable markets of the world.

LABOUR AND THE POOR.

———◆———

BIRMINGHAM.

[FROM OUR SPECIAL CORRESPONDENT.]

HEAVY STEEL TOYS.

LETTER XIV.

"The manufacture of iron in Birmingham," says Hutton, "is ancient beyond research—that of steel is of modern date." The historian, having given this information, follows it up with a disquisition upon pride, and ends his article by stating that "from this warm, but dismal, climate (Birmingham), issues the button which shines on the breast, and the bayonets intended to pierce it; the lancet which bleeds the man, and the rowel which bleeds the horse; the lock which preserves the beloved bottle, and the screw to uncork it; the needle, equally obedient to the thimble and the pole." This, with a statement that a person of the name of Kettle introduced the steel trade into Birmingham in the seventeenth century, is the whole of the information derivable from his pages on the ancient state of this important manufacture in the town. In this department of the inquiry it will thus be seen that little aid of any value is to be derived from the labours of Mr. Hutton.

The trade at the present day may be divided into the two great branches of Heavy and Light Steel Toys. In the first is generally included the manufacture of edge tools. The word "toy" is a sad misnomer as applied to nearly the whole of the articles in the heavy department of the business. Birmingham was called by Edmund Burke "the toy-shop of the world;" but whether he knew the kind of articles that were included under that designation by the people of the town, or whether he meant by toys such articles of jewellery and nicknackery as go by that name elsewhere, it is not easy to say, nor is it perhaps of importance to ascertain. The title, however, has stuck to Birmingham, and it will doubtless continue to be called the "toy-shop of the world" for generations yet to come. The list of what are called the heavy steel toys includes, according to the index to the pattern-book of one of the principal manufacturers, nearly 600 articles. Among the number may be specified the tools and implements used by carpenters, coopers, gardeners, butchers, glaziers, upholsterers, farriers, masons, plumbers, coachmakers, millwrights, mineralogists, saddlers, harness makers, tinmen, shoemakers, weavers, wheelers, and wire drawers; besides bodkins for tailors, spatulæ for surgeons, ships' augers, and a whole multitude of minor and most hetero-geneous articles—such as corkscrews, sugar-tongs, sugar-nippers, boot-hooks, button-hooks, door-scrapers, calippers, compasses in countless variety, from three inches to twenty-four inches in length, pinking-irons, curling-irons, dog-collars, dog-chains, dog-whistles, tweezers, lobster crackers, cheese tasters, champagne nippers, tinder-boxes, and tobacco stoppers. Among other strange articles formerly included under the term of steel toys, were tomahawks for the North American Indians—but this article is no longer in demand, though a few specimens are preserved in the town as curiosities. The great distinction between the heavy and the light steel toy seems to be, that the one is useful, and the other ornamental; that the heavy steel toys are used as tools in trades, or in the household; and that the light steel toys are devoted almost exclusively to the adornment of the person.

Another misnomer, as applied to the heavy steel trade, is, that very little steel is used in the manufacture—by far the larger proportion of the articles being made of iron. In some articles—such as choppers, cleavers, mincing-knives, trowels, &c., steel and iron are intermixed. Between two thin sheets or layers of iron, is inclosed a sheet or layer of steel of the same size, and these three are put into the furnace and welded together. The effect of this is to have the edge of the instrument always of steel and the sides of iron; and thus to combine great solidity with the requisite sharpness and hardness of edge. Inferior articles—of which, unfortunately for the credit of the town in foreign and colonial markets, considerable quantities are made by some "go-a-head" manufacturers, of more energy than honesty—instead of having the layer of steel right through, from edge to back, have only a very thin line of steel, which is worn away after two or three sharpenings, when the instrument becomes useless. Other articles, in which no steel is used, are "case-hardened;" by which process a tool of iron becomes as hard on its exterior surface as if it were steel, and yet preserves the solidity of iron. The process is very simple. The article to be case-hardened is placed in a mass of bone-dust or filings from the button, knife-handle, and other factories; and then placed in the furnace till it is of what is technically called a worm-red heat, in which it is allowed to remain for a few hours, according to its size or quality. It is then taken out and plunged into cold water—when the surface, which, before the process, was too soft to resist the file, is found to be so hard that the file will make no impression upon it. The articles which give employment to the largest number of hands in the heavy steel department appear to be hammers, of which there are from 200 or 300 varieties for different mechanical trades—each of these being again subdivided, according to their size and weight, into eight or ten kinds, weighing from two ounces to three pounds. The next most important articles are shoemakers' tools, which are exported in countless thousands to North America, the Cape, Australia, and other colonies, besides being in constant demand for home consumption. Sugar nippers are also made in very large quantities—not only for the home, colonial, and American, but for the continental trade, especially with Germany.

Although the great manufacturers produce the whole of the articles included under the general name of heavy steel toys, as well as edge tools of various kinds, it happens in this, as in other trades, that a manufacturer, from long-established connection and the devotion of particular care to the production of one article, gains a reputation for it superior to that acquired—or indeed acquirable—by any other person. Some firms are renowned for the peculiar excellence of their shoe-pincers, which fetch a higher price in the markets of the world than the pincers made by any other firm; others, again, are celebrated for their hammers; others for hatchets; while another has such a reputation for trowels that competition with him is all but useless. In this trade, it may be of importance at the present time to state that large quantities of heavy brown paper are used for packing the articles both for the home and foreign demand. Many of the manufacturers use from two to five tons of paper per annum for this purpose alone, and thus pay to the Government, at 1½d. per lb., a tax of from £28 to £70 per annum. In the export trade, in which the articles must be better and more thoroughly packed than in the home trade, this tax operates as an export duty to that amount, and places the manufacturer at a disadvantage, compared with his rivals, the German, Belgian, and French producers, who are not subject to it. The duty operates in another way upon the manufacturer in his trade, as the pattern books are large, heavy, and expensive, and weigh upon an average from 2 lbs. to 2½ lbs. At this rate he pays from 3d. to 3¾d. paper duty for every copy of his book which he places in the hands of his travellers for the purposes of his trade.

The names of thirty-two makers of heavy steel toys and tools appear in the "Directory;" but Sheffield and Wolverhampton, as well as Birmingham, carry on an extensive manufacture of these articles. Birmingham, however, enjoys by far the largest share of the trade, except in the manufacture of edge tools, which is principally seated at Sheffield. The articles known as "Lancashire tools," though greatly resembling heavy steel toys, are considered as a separate manufacture, the seat of which is Warrington. The number of persons employed in the trade in Birmingham is estimated at from 800 to 900, men and boys, of whom about 360 or 400 are engaged in the manufacture of edge tools. No women whatever are employed in the production either of heavy steel toys or edge-tools—and only a very few boys under the age of ten or twelve. The staple articles of the trade are in constant, great, and increasing demand, not only for the home market, and for the supply of mechanics in every part of the country, but for Canada, Mexico, the United States, the West Indies, the Cape, the East Indies, Australia, and New Zealand. There is not an emigrant ship that leaves London or Liverpool that does not carry away a large assortment of these articles, either for domestic, trading, or agricultural purposes—as, for example, to make and mend the shoes and clothes of remote settlers—to fell the primeval forests, or to construct log-huts and their necessary furniture.

The trade includes workers both in iron and wood—the latter department being almost as important, and employing as many hands, as the first, for every tool must have a handle. Both branches of the business are usually carried on under one roof. In each there is a minute sub-division of labour, but more especially in the manufacture of the tools themselves. A common pair of shoemaker's pincers undergoes twelve distinct processes from the first rude block of iron to the ground and polished tool. Hammers, compasses, sugar nippers, and other articles undergo quite as many, and some of them more. The workmen comprise forgers, filers, and grinders, with their assistants, chiefly boys and lads. The trade is generally considered healthy, with the exception of the grinding and polishing, which is hard and exhaustive, if not dangerous work. The men sit upon blocks, or 'horses,' before the great grindstones turned by steam-power—common to

this as to the gun-barrel grinding and other trades—and wet-grind
the pincers, the hammer heads, the hatchets, and other tools.

At present the average receipts of the heavy steel toy makers are,
for a forger, about 25s. or 26s. a week; and for a filer, if paid by the
day, about £1 1s. a week, or, if paid by the amount of work done,
from £1 to £1 6s. Some of the most skilful and industrious workmen
earn as much as £3 10s. a week; but this is in peculiar branches of the
business, to excel in which a man may have devoted the best part of
his life. Generally, the wages of the trade have undergone little variation within the memory of the oldest hands. Whatever be the price
of corn, the wages of their skill remain the same. Another cause of
this steadiness is, that the introduction of machinery into the ordinary branches of the manufacture has been partial, and that the work
continues to be done almost entirely by hand labour, except grinding
and polishing, and the turning of the wood handles. This has not
only had the effect of keeping up wages, but of maintaining steady
prices throughout the trade. In some of the principal establishments
in Birmingham, there has scarcely been any alteration in the scale of
prices for some of the chief articles of manufacture for upwards of
half a century.

The absence of costly machinery—for £4 or £5 is money enough
to start a maker of common articles in business—has had the effect
of inducing a considerable number of workmen to commence manufacturing on their own account, but they are confined to such articles
as gimlets, corkscrews, brad-awls, &c. The number of these small
makers, and those whom they employ, is said to be greater than that
employed in the larger manufactories, but their influence upon the
makers of superior goods seems to be very insignificant, as both manufacturers and their workmen describe themselves as being in as good
a position as ever they were.

About six years ago the English were subjected to the apparently
formidable competition of the German manufacturers. Large quantities of cheap German goods were imported, and at that time much
fear was entertained lest they should be able to undersell the Birmingham makers; a stimulus was thus communicated to the trade, and
additional care was bestowed upon all the goods made, so as to produce better articles than those made in Germany, and at as low a price.
The result was that the Germans were fairly beaten out of the market,
and the Birmingham manufacturers say that they have now no fear of
any Continental competition. Belgium is said to be the only country

whence any serious rivalry may be expected. A few heavy steel toys are even exported to the Continent, and Germany is largely supplied with saw-sets from this country. This brush of national rivalry had no effect whatever upon prices, or upon the general demand.

The maintenance of wages has been influenced more or less by various other circumstances; but principally by an arrangement made between masters and men in the year 1833, after a strike, which, as regards some of the manufactories, lasted for a considerable time. The following account of the strike, and of the circumstances which led to it, was given by a very intelligent workman, who took an active part in the dispute:—"About the year 1823 wages were about the same as they are now, but the demand for skilled labour was so great that in 1824 the men were induced to meet together and to demand an increase of wages. They asked an increase of 4d. on every shilling which they earned. The masters were eventually induced to grant 2d. per shilling extra, and with this the men were satisfied. In 1825 this increase was disallowed, and a system of exacting discount from the earnings of the men, on the plea of badness of trade, began to be practised by the manufacturers. In the course of two years this discount amounted to more than 10 per cent. and it was rigorously exacted in most manufactories in the town. In one establishment no discount was exacted till the year 1833. When the manufacturer attempted it, the men resisted, and called a meeting of all the steel toy workers of Birmingham and the neighbourhood. The meeting was held, and a partial strike of that establishment was resolved upon, to resist the discount system once for all. Although no provision had been made for such an event, the men very generally left their work in a few days afterwards. In a short time not a hand was at work, the men trusting for pecuniary assistance to the general trade. This was liberally granted, and the strike continued, both at Birmingham and Wolverhampton, for about three weeks. After this an arrangement was come to, by which it was agreed that three months after the men returned to their work, they should receive the full value of their earnings without discount. The period of three months was fixed, because the masters were under contract to supply the factors, at the diminished rate, with certain orders which it would take that time to execute. A few men held out until those three months had expired, rather than allow the discount system to continue even for that time. A list of prices was then agreed upon, which continues to be acknowledged at the present time by men and masters. At Wolverhampton the strike lasted longer than at Birmingham, and was maintained by those steel toy workers who had employment at Birmingham, at rates varying according to the necessities of the families thrown out of employ. In some instances, the Wolverhampton workmen who had large families were paid as much as 22s. a week, and single men had 8s. a week. The Birmingham men out on strike received from 4s. to 8s. a week from the other trades in the town. The strike did not extend to the edge-tool makers. At present the men are very well contented with the wages they receive, which are as large as they used to be, with the additional advantage that bread, and living in general, is much cheaper. Numerous improvements have been made in the trade, by which a greater quantity of goods can be produced in a given time. The iron is better prepared, and by improvements in the art of forging the filer's labour is simplified, and rendered easier. After the strike of 1833 a club, or union, was formed among the men, which continued to exist for about two years; but as trade continued good, and no subject of complaint existed against the masters, the men became careless about paying their subscriptions, and it was discontinued. Since that time no attempt has been made to revive the union."

Fashion influences even this old and steady trade. Articles are occasionally demanded in greater numbers than usual, and a rise in their price takes place in consequence. As an instance of this may be cited the extraordinary demand for pinking irons, created a short time ago by the popularity of flounces for ladies' dresses. About thirty years ago pinking irons were only used for ornamenting the hems of shrouds, but lately they were applied to the purpose of cutting the fringes of flounces into circular, pointed, Vandyke, and other patterns. A skilful workman stated that for about two years he had been occupied almost entirely in making pinking irons, and in that time he had made with his own hands about 100 gross (14,400) of them, and had earned on an average about £3 a week at this work. He was sorry that flounces had gone out of fashion, but hoped they might "take a turn again" in spring or summer.

With regard to the moral and social condition of the heavy steel toy makers, a marked improvement is generally admitted to have taken place within the last ten or twenty years; so that, although the manufacturers have yet to complain of occasional irregularity in attendance during the early part of the week, and of a disposition to inebriety among those engaged in the heaviest parts of the trade, there are yet indications of a better spirit among the men, and unmistakeable evidence of more provident habits among the younger portion of them. The following statement, made by one who had worked at the heavy steel toy trade for nearly forty years, may be considered as affording a fair general view of the whole trade, although made with especial reference to one of the oldest establishments in the town— that of Messrs. R. Timmins and Sons—in whose service the narrator has been for upwards of thirty years:—

"So far as I know of the trade, I believe that the workmen are in a better condition now than they were thirty-six years ago, which is nearly as far back as I can remember. They are more provident for themselves and families than they used to be, and are in all respects better members of society. Their habits are more cleanly, and their tastes and feelings more refined; there is also less hard drinking than formerly. Gipsy parties are got up frequently among the men of this manufacturing district during the summer season. They have, I think, been the means of creating among the men a love of out-door exercises and sports. The favourite games are cricket and archery, and the men possess bats, wickets and balls, bows, arrows and targets in common. In summer the men turn out to play two or three times a week, and often sacrifice a Monday afternoon to the exercise of these sports, which, at all events, is better than drinking away the Monday, as thousands do in Birmingham. There are about 120 men and boys in this establishment, and nearly all of them participate in these sports. At present the men are consulting whether they shall have a gipsy party in summer as usual, or whether they shall make a trip to London to see the Great Exhibition. The feeling is in favour of London and the Exhibition, and I have no doubt but the men will make considerable sacrifices in order to gratify their wish. These gipsy parties I think have the effect of spreading a feeling of good-will and cordiality among the men, and they become better acquainted with each other. Within seven or eight years a Friendly Fund has been established among the men working in this manufactory, into which each man pays 2d. a-week; from the fund thus collected a workman receives 5s. a week when confined by sickness; at the death of a child he receives 10s.; at the death of his wife he receives £1; at his own death his widow receives £2 for funeral expenses. Nearly every one of us—and, in fact, I believe every one—subscribed towards the monument to the memory of the late Sir Robert Peel. We considered him the working man's best friend for repealing the corn laws. Our employers did not ask us to subscribe; but we got up the subscription quietly among ourselves. We paid about 30s. or £2 amongst us."

Birmingham Town Hall & Statue of Sir Robert Peel

In reference to the management of this establishment, one fact deserves to be stated, for its important bearing upon the social and domestic comfort of the workmen. About fifteen years ago the Messrs. Timmins resolved to try the effect of an experiment, often urged by philanthropists, of paying the workpeople at a reasonable hour on the Saturday forenoon. It was urged against this change, by those who wished to make no alteration in the old customs of the trade, that, if the men were paid by twelve or one o'clock on the Saturday, they would leave their work for the remainder of the day. Messrs. Timmins, however, persevered with the experiment, and paid their men before the dinner hour. The result proved that they had not misjudged their workpeople. The men came as regularly to their work as usual, and have continued to do so from that time to the present. Now and then, on a fine Saturday in summer, a man asks permission to leave work, that he may go and "do a little gardening to amuse himself;" but even this is not asked when trade is brisk, and when his services are required. They generally express their gratitude for the accommodation of receiving their money at an hour which enables their wives to go to market in proper time, and to lay in their week's stock of provisions and their Sunday's dinner; and they acknowledge that its effect is to keep them away from the public-house on Saturday night. At some establishments, where men have to loiter about for an hour or more after their work is done on Saturday before the books and the accounts for wages are made up, they resort to the public-house to "kill the time;" and often acquire habits of intemperance which they never shake off, to the injury of their health as men, of their efficiency as workmen, and too often of their social and domestic happiness. Six or seven other establishments in different trades in Birmingham are known to have adopted this plan, and, it is stated, with the same beneficial effects upon the character and comfort of the men and their families.

In close and very secret connection with the manufacture of heavy steel toys, is that of Housebreakers' Instruments, which is carried on at Birmingham by men who are known by reputation to the police. Many of the implements used by the burglars of London, and by those expert hands who try their fortune more particularly in the county of Surrey, are the legitimate tools necessary to carpenters and other mechanics. The centre-bit and the crow-bar, or wedge, for instance, may be included in the number; but in addition to these may be mentioned the "steel bars," the "gouges," the "ripping chisels," the "picklocks," the "skeleton keys," the "pocket jacks," and other implements which are set forth and described in George Cruikshank's recent pamphlet, entitled "Stop Thief." The respectable manufacturers do not supply such notorious articles as these; but even they are stated to receive occasionally an order for an odd looking instrument, which they suspect cannot be intended for any good or lawful purpose, although they have no means of ascertaining the fact. The extent of this trade cannot be known; but a decent-looking, tradesman-like man, of jovial appearance, standing at the door of a public-house, in company with two or three men known to the detective police as reputed thieves, was pointed out to me by an officer as a thriving manufacturer in this particular branch of business. But Birmingham supplies an antidote to the bane of this secret manufacture, and produces large quantities of handcuffs, manacles, leg-irons, chains, and other similar gear, for securing the safe custody and punishment of offenders against the law. The names of four master manufacturers in this line appear in "The Directory:" the trade being distinct from that of heavy steel toys, although some of the handcuff makers occasionally produce articles which are included under that head. This branch of trade gives employment to about twenty-five persons only; and they supply the prisons of all England and Wales, if not of Ireland and Scotland, with these grim paraphernalia of offended justice. The ordinary handcuff for felons is also exported to the United States and to the British colonies, being used in the Southern States for slaves as well as for felons, and in the Northern States and the colonies for felons only. Of about 4,000 pairs of manacles annually produced in Birmingham, about one-half are understood to be supplied to merchants for the foreign and colonial trade. The trade, however, has other ramifications, and the Birmingham makers supply not Justice alone, but injustice and tyranny, with these cruel implements of coercion. Merchants of London and Liverpool who trade with Brazil and Cuba, occasionally favour the manacle and leg iron-makers with an order for a few hundred complete "suits" of chains for the unhappy slaves in the middle passage. The "suit" includes a heavy iron collar, of which the ring is from five-eighths to seven-eighths of an inch in diameter, and weighs about two pounds; and manacles for the wrists and legs, with corresponding heavy chains. The whole suit weighs about fifteen pounds. They are made as roughly and cheaply as possible, the slave holders and slave traders not caring to incur any great expense. They are not only formidable, but unsightly articles, and are painted black, to save expense in polishing, and to prevent rust. The average annual demand for this unholy purpose, a few years ago, or until 1848, was about 2,000 pair of manacles. Since 1848 the demand has slackened, and scarcely 250 pairs have been made. They form part of the regular furniture of the Brazilian slave ships.

The manacles and chains for the English prisons are lighter and more elegant in make, and much labour is expended upon them. Their weight has been greatly reduced within the last twenty years. They are fine specimens of workmanship when new, and are as highly polished as steel toys. Like most other articles of manufacture, they have been reduced in price by competition and by the readier methods of making them which have been introduced; but they do not seem to have been generally deteriorated in quality—the diminished weight having in all probability made up for the deficiency in price. The old long-linked leg chains are not now made for the prisons of England, but they find a market in Brazil and Cuba. They consist of two or more long links, connecting the locks round the ankles with a ring attached to a belt, which is fastened round the waist. One

of these old leg irons without the ankle-locks weighed about 7 lbs.
Leg-irons are still made in considerable numbers, but, as it is not
thought necessary in our times to treat felons with the brutal severity
so common in days gone by, they are manufactured of a lighter
description altogether. A chain is substituted for the links, and they
have lighter foot-locks. They weigh, without the foot-locks, about
2¾ lbs., and about 5 lbs. altogether. The heaviest chains for felons
which have been lately made are those for convicts at Norfolk Island,
some of which have weighed as much as 14 lbs. They are frequently
riveted round the foot, so as to be removed only when the prisoner
is finally released. The average weight of convict irons is from 4 lbs.
to 7 lbs. These irons are never used in our gaols. The heaviest used
in England are for conveying prisoners from one station or gaol to
another. They are called travelling irons, and are taken off when the
prisoner is placed in his cell. The organization of the present police
system gave a considerable impulse to the manufacture of handcuffs,
and many districts had to be supplied altogether with the article, and
others had to procure an additional stock. Among the orders now on
the books of one of the principal manufacturers was one for several
dozen of small handcuffs for "ladies."

The price of handcuffs has fallen about fifty per cent. of late years,
the principal cause of which was the change which was made about
eight years ago in the mode of their manufacture. Previously to that
time the socket of the handcuff, in which the lock moved, was made
from the barrels of old guns, and the rest of the cuff was welded on;
but by a much simpler process, which is now adopted, the forger
makes a barrel from a piece of iron beaten flat, punches such holes
as are necessary, and hammers the whole into the required shape, in
much less time, at less expense, and more efficiently than by the old
system. A forger will now make about a dozen pairs of handcuffs in
a day, about one half of which can be filed by one person, and put
together by another in a day.

One department of the fetter and manacle trade, which forty or
fifty years ago employed many hands in Birmingham, is now all but
extinct. It will be gratifying to philanthropists, and especially to that
section of them who take lunatics under their peculiar care, to learn
that few chains or manacles are now manufactured for lunatic asylums.
The demand began to slacken about fifteen years ago, and has been
gradually diminishing from year to year. At the present time the manufacturers scarcely receive half a dozen orders in a twelvemonth, and

such orders as arrive are for single sets or "suits." Even these are of the lightest possible construction.

It may be mentioned, in connection with this branch of trade, that thumb-screws have recently been made by more than one manufacturer of chains and manacles in Birmingham, and, at least in one instance, it would appear that they were for actual use. About seven years ago an order was received for two dozen thumb-screws, and it was understood that they were for some of the States of South America, but for what purpose the manufacturer could not ascertain. The order came from a merchant in London, and was accompanied by a pattern "thumb-screw," which was the first the manufacturer had ever seen.

The Edge Tool Manufacture, which is often combined in the same factory with that of the heavy steel toys, and is classed by some as part of the same trade, includes such articles as axes, adzes, bills, bill-hooks; Carolina, Demerara, and West India hoes; Columbia, Boston, Mamottee, Spanish, and Portuguese hoes; Spanish and Biscay shovels, grubbing hoes, pick-axes, wedges, ploughs, spades of all kinds; the heavier gardening tools, draining tools, and generally such agricultural implements as are not complicated enough to come under the head of machinery. The pattern books of an extensive firm contain the descriptions and prices of 45 different kinds of axes, including 14 different varieties manufactured expressly for the American market, ornamented with the American eagle, and designated by such names as the Kentucky wedge axe, the Yankee axe, the American slinging hatchet, the New Orleans axe, &c. There are about 12 varieties of adzes; 26 of bills and bill-hooks; upwards of 70 of hoes for all climates and soils; and spades and shovels innumerable. The names of 12 master manufacturers appear in the Directory, and the trade is estimated to afford employment to between three and four hundred men. Birmingham, as already stated, is not the only seat of this manufacture, but its trade appears to be greatly on the increase, at the expense of that of Sheffield.

The following account of the past and present state of the manufacture was given by a small manufacturer:—"Between thirty and forty years ago there were not more than four makers in Birmingham, and I think there were only three. They made the same sort of tools that are made now, and perhaps as good for practical purposes, though not so neat or so well finished. About thirty years ago the number of men and boys employed in the trade was under a hundred.

A union has existed among the men for about ten years. Within thirty years prices have been reduced by about 20 per cent. on nearly all goods, and about 50 per cent. on plantation hoes. Readier methods of working have been introduced, so that, although a reduction of 50 per cent. has been made in the price of hoes, a man can make a good many more in the same time. The reduction in the receipts of a man working at hoes is about 25 per cent. The men are, however, as well off now in point of fact as ever they were, for living is cheaper, and they can find the same amount of comfort for less money. Prices have been further lowered in fact by the improvement that has been made in the quality of work. People are better judges of a good article now than they used to be, at least in our trade, and they will only purchase good things. The German competition five or six years ago had the effect of lowering prices and of improving the workmanship in our manufactures, for it was by making better articles that we drove them out of the market. The Germans cannot make such good work as the English; and we have not suffered any loss in the trade from their competition. Prices did not return to their old scale when we regained the market, but have had, as I think, a tendency to fall ever since. Within my recollection there has been a great change in the character of the Birmingham workmen, and in that of workmen generally in every part of the country. The improvement within 30 years is wonderful, and teetotalism has done a great deal of it. Even the amusements of the men have changed for the better. When I was a young working man, nothing was thought of by the workmen but cock-fighting, bull-baiting, rat-worrying, and such like; but these things are not popular now, and thereby, I say, the country is improved. The young men of the present day are better educated than they were when I was a youth. They go to the Town Hall on a Monday night to hear music for 3d. Nothing of that sort was known 30 years ago, but the men spent their nights at the ale-house. When I was a young man I never saw games of cricket played by the workmen, or anything of the sort, except foot-ball, and that was not common. Within the last twelve years these manly and healthy sports have become quite popular, and I hear of clubs being formed among the men for the purpose. Education is a great thing for the working classes. I wish they had more of it. A little is better than none. The more book-learning a young man has, the better workman he becomes. I am sure of that. I was a pretty tidy workman in my youth, but the young men of the present day beat me out and out. I think the general condition of Birmingham and of England is likely to become more prosperous than ever it was. Australia is already a large market for our edge tools and for manufactures of all sorts, and it will soon require as much from us as America used to take."

Turning from the opinions of this hopeful old gentleman to those of a workman, on the condition of his craft, the reader may compare their statements. The question as regards the condition of the workmen and manufacturers at Sheffield, to which he alludes, is one of much importance to both towns:—

"I left Sheffield to come to Birmingham about 13 years ago, because work was slack there at the time. The strikes among the workmen are very numerous at Sheffield. In times of good trade a grinder will make three times as much at Sheffield as at Birmingham. They can make £3 a week there. A good deal of the heavy edge-tool trade has come to Birmingham and Wolverhampton. I should think that the reason of this is, that iron and coal are cheaper here than at Sheffield, and also that the Sheffield unions are opposed to the introduction of machinery in the trade. Light edge-tools are better made at Sheffield than at Birmingham, and the greater part of the light garden hoes used in this country are made in the former place. Machinery is much more extensively employed at Birmingham than at Sheffield, and the prejudice against it is so strong at Sheffield that I have known an instance of a man being obliged to leave that town because he substituted a bellows for the ordinary blow-pipe used for soldering. He could do the work much quicker by means of the bellows. The tilt hammer, which is moved by steam or water power, does away with the necessity for employing a striker, and workmen at some sorts of work will make as much money in the course of the week by employing the tilt hammer as with the aid of an assistant, while he is enabled to produce a larger number of articles at a lower rate. Heavy work is paid about one-third less at Birmingham than at Sheffield, but in consequence of the use of machinery it is less exhausting. In those departments of the trade in which manual labour is employed, the Sheffield workmen are much better paid than those of Birmingham. Ever since I have known Sheffield there has been strife between masters and workmen, and as soon as orders come in briskly the men strike for the prices they had in 1810, when a list of prices had been formally agreed to by men and masters. But when trade slackens, the masters 'put on the screw' and reduce wages as much as they can. The men come and offer themselves at lower wages rather than suffer themselves to be brought to the workhouse. Unions are much more general there than at Birmingham. I was once obliged to leave a place in consequence of not belonging to the union of the trade in which I worked at the time; but it was not the trade to which I had been brought up, and the men took care to inform me that I was looked upon as an interloper. I had been out of work for some time before entering that business, but was obliged to leave it. I have seen nothing of that sort in Birmingham. There have been several attempts made to form a trade union among the edge-tool makers in Birmingham and the neighbourhood since I have come here, but they have never succeeded. The men do not understand unions here so well as in the north, and the trade lies in a very large circle, so that the men cannot be often and readily collected together. In Sheffield I have known the children hoot a workman in the streets who did not belong to the union of his trade. I dare say the trades unions of Sheffield, by keeping up the high price of labour, have helped in some degree to drive the trade from the town; but iron and coal are cheaper here, and I believe that to be the principal reason why the Birmingham trade has increased so much of late. Prices have been steadily decreasing in this trade. Some articles—as, for instance, the Brazil hoe—are now sold for the same money as was paid for making them 20 years ago. The men are obliged to work harder, and more hours, than formerly, and such relaxation as they have is in the ale-house or in sleep. As far as I know they have no games such as cricket, ball-playing, jump-ing, and foot-racing, which are comparatively common at Sheffield, where, on a Monday afternoon, when little or no work is done, the men of one establishment challenge those of another to a game of cricket, or something of the sort, and spend the evening pleasantly in this manner. At Sheffield the workmen turn out two or three times a week to indulge in these sports. This may be the case in Birmingham also, but I never heard of it. As to the effect of unions, I am at a loss to balance their advantages and disadvantages in my own mind. The workmen are better paid wherever they exist, for in bad seasons they do not get less than elsewhere, and in good seasons they get more. But there are evils connected with them, the worst of which is 'rattening'—that is, destroying the property and tools of their op-ponents—an evil which I believe is always to be traced more or less to the unions; but if they could be carried on without violence, I believe trades' unions would be a blessing both to masters and to men."

Tilting Steel

The abominable practice of "rattening," to which this working-man alludes, does not appear to be much known in Birmingham. It is deplorably common in some towns, and instances are known in which injury has been done to the heavy grindstones to cause them to "fly," and to maim and kill the workman.

Another workman, at an extensive establishment which combines the manufacture of heavy steel toys with that of edge tools, said— "The introduction of machinery into our trade has relieved us of a great deal of hard work, and has not only increased the number of articles made, but has increased the number of workmen employed. I do not know how many men are employed now, or how many there were twenty years ago, but I should think at present they are nearly ten to one. The wages have, however, been reduced by the introduction of machinery. A fair workman at ordinary work, twenty years ago, could make £4 or £5 a week, if he worked every day and for ten hours a day—out of which his striker would receive at the rate of 7s. or 7s. 6d. in the pound; at present, an average workman makes about £2 10s. a week, and pays his striker at the same rate as formerly. I used to receive about 30s. a week as striker when I was a young man. I find living much cheaper now than it used to be, and perhaps I get on as comfortably on the reduced wages as most of the men did on their high wages twenty years ago. I have no doubt, if the men were more steady and industrious, they could get on very comfortably. The Sunday-schools have done a great deal for the men in the way of education, and far more of them can read and write than in my day. I mean the Old and New Meeting Sunday-schools; where writing is taught on the Sunday. The Church schools and Methodist schools object to teach writing on that day. Yet, with all the enlightenment of working men, they do not seem to improve as much as they ought to do. They could lay out their money to ten times better advantage than they do, if they would think a little more. Many of those who might, if they liked, earn the highest wages, are the most dissipated; and I believe that I can show a sovereign for every shilling that many a man has who can earn much more money in a week than I can. But then I am careful, and I fancy I know what I am about."

The department of light steel toys—employing a great number of hands, and including the manufacture of an immense variety of articles for which Birmingham in past or present time enjoyed, and still enjoys, a reputation—yet remains to be treated of, and will form the subject of another letter.

LABOUR AND THE POOR.

———◆———

BIRMINGHAM.

[FROM OUR SPECIAL CORRESPONDENT.]

LIGHT STEEL TOYS.

Letter XV.

The Birmingham Directory contains the names of fifty Light Steel Toy-makers. Like other trades in this town, that of Light Steel Toy making is divided and sub-divided into a great variety of branches. Some of the manufacturers confine themselves to the production of one or two articles out of the many. Others produce all the trinkets commonly called Light Steel Toys, as well as many of the more substantial articles belonging more strictly to the Heavy Steel department. Many of the Light Steel Toy manufacturers call themselves snuffer-makers; others are known as fancy chain manufacturers, and makers of steel watch-keys and steel watch-hands. The Directory, besides the names of the fifty Light Steel Toy-makers properly so designated, contains the names of six fancy steel chain makers, forty-four snuffer makers, eleven skate manufacturers, seventeen key ring makers, ten clasp manufacturers, twenty-three watch-key makers, and twenty-three watch and clock-hand makers. Among the articles manufactured by one of the first houses in the trade, are chatelaines, watch chains, neck chains, keys, seals, purses, purse springs, slides, and beads, reticule springs and fittings, waist buckles, knee buckles, latchets (a kind of shoe buckle with steel springs, worn with the Court or fancy dress), dress swords, steel buttons for court suits, button hooks, boot-hooks, nutcrackers, corkscrews of all kinds, steel tassels, tags, and fringes, bodkins, stilettos, swivels, brooches, spectacle frames, knitting and netting implements, necklace snaps, steel snuffers, bracelets, pocket-book locks, snaps, &c. Unlike the heavy steel toy trade, which formed the subject of the preceding letter, the manufacture of light steel toys is subject to constant fluctuation. At the present time it is supposed to afford employment to about 1,000 persons, including about 300 women and children. Some manufacturers allege, however, that not above 600 persons are employed; but from a comparison of various statements, and from other means of information, I believe that the larger estimate is the more correct one. One article alone, the shoe buckle—and which, except for Court suits, is almost wholly out of fashion—once gave employment to upwards of 5,000 persons; and its production formed the staple trade of the town. At the present time, not half-a-dozen persons are employed in shoe and knee-buckle-making, and even these are engaged for the greater portion of their time upon other articles.

Birmingham has been long the principal seat of the Light Steel Toy Trade; although London was its original birthplace in England. It was introduced into London from Milan and Germany. The London manufacturers appear to have had sufficient influence with the Government of Henry VII. to procure an act prohibiting the importation of light steel toys. An act passed in that reign decreed that no "merchant strangers" should bring into "the realm of England to be sold" any men's girdles, points, purses, pouches, pins, knives, hangers, tailors' shears, scissors and irons, tongs, "fire-forks," gridirons, cocks, keys, hinges, beaten gold or silver horse-harness, bits, stirrups, buckles, chains, candlesticks, curtain-rings, clasps for gloves, spoons, chains, and a whole host of similar articles, which at the present day in Birmingham are classed under the head of Light Steel Toys. It would seem, however, that the act was in reality inoperative for the purposes intended, and that although it prevented the importation of foreign goods, it did not prevent the immigration of large numbers of Milanese and German workmen, who congregated together in the outskirts of London, and produced large quantities of steel goods, of a better workmanship and at a cheaper rate than the English. The celebrated riot which took place on the first of May, 1517, which is known in the history of London as "Evil May-day," had its origin in the jealousy entertained against these strangers by the London 'prentices. "There were such numbers of foreign artificers in London," says Hall, in his "Life of King Henry VIII.," "that the English could get no work."

It is not clearly known at what period the trade was transferred from London to the Midland Counties; but in the middle of the eighteenth century Birmingham, Wolverhampton, and Walsall had attained so great a reputation for light steel toys that they supplied an immense home and foreign demand, and employed considerably above 10,000 persons in their production. Buckles alone, as already stated, gave employment to half that number.

The well-known Matthew Boulton, of the Soho Works, long before the illustrious Watt became his partner, was the head of the most eminent firm of steel toy-makers in the world, and acquired in that trade the fortune which enabled him, in conjunction with Watt, to make the steam-engine so wondrously available for the advantage and civilization of mankind. But wars on the one hand, and changes of fashion on the other, deprived the Birmingham and Wolverhampton manufacturers, first of the foreign, and afterwards of a large portion of the home trade; and steel toy making, instead of being the most important of the manufactures of the town, as it was between fifty and sixty years ago, is now of only fourth or fifth-rate extent. The "foreigner" appears to have ever been a formidable competitor in these light and graceful articles—the buckle always excepted; and at the present time the French manufacture large quantities of elegant and serviceable steel trinkets at a price far below that at which the Birmingham makers can produce them. The one article of small beads for purses supplies an illustration of the French superiority. The Birmingham manufacturers allege that they cannot produce such beads under 6d. a gross; while they can be imported from France and sold in Birmingham at 2½d. for a dozen gross. In the production of steel watch-chains the French have also an advantage over the English; and an eminent maker of light steel toys, in showing an article of this kind, large and massive to suit the present fashion, but beautifully polished and wrought, alleged that he could import it for 3d., but could not manufacture one in Birmingham for six times the money. The French makers are quite aware of their superiority, and jealously preserve the secret of the processes they employ, at least from the knowledge of English workmen or employers, or those likely to be in their confidence.

The following statement upon this part of the subject, and that of light steel toys generally, was made by a manufacturer, formerly in the employ of Boulton and Smith, at the Soho works. The firm of Boulton and Watt, at the same place, confined itself to the manufacture of steam engines. James Watt was never engaged in the steel-toy trade.

"Great improvements have taken place in the character of the steel toys made within the last twenty years, as well as great changes in the mode of making many of them. In the manufacture of fancy steel toys, such as light chains, guards, beads, &c., we are fairly beaten by the French; but the demand for them has increased, and we make more now than we did formerly. In some articles we cannot compete with the French with any hope of success; as, for instance, in the manufacture of small beads for purses, &c., which are imported from France, and sold here for about 2½d. a great gross, but which we cannot make under 5s. 6d. a great gross. I cannot account for their superiority. It is said that there are villages in France in which beads are manufactured and strung together by the young children in almost every house, and in this way they may be made cheaper than we can make them. The difference in price is enormous, and there is not sufficient difference in the quality to account for it. Large beads, which vary from one-sixth to one-half of an inch in diameter, can not only be made cheaper in this country than in France, but, after all expenses, including a very heavy import duty, are paid, we can sell them fifty per cent. cheaper in France than the French themselves can make them. For designs in our lighter steel toys we are much indebted to the French, as they have greatly improved upon us, and the trade has, by that means, been better kept up. We can make the ordinary light toys better than the French, but we cannot make fine filagree work, pierced ornaments, beads, &c., so cheaply.

"Steel buttons for Court suits have always been, to a certain extent, in demand, but very few of them are now made. Last year the demand was better than it was for four or five years previously. It was remarked that, immediately after the imposition of the income-tax, the demand for these and similar articles fell off unprecedentedly; but whether from the operation of that tax, or from other causes, I do not know. The depression lasted for several years. People do not seem to buy Court suits now, but to hire them for the occasion. When the Queen went to Ireland an order was received from a house in Dublin for 36 sets of Court-dress buttons and buckles; but it was countermanded, and only 3 sets were made. The reason was, that the Jews were in the market, and sent over immense quantities of old Court-dresses, and lent them out for the Queen's levee and drawing-room.

"During the years 1826 and 1827 the demand in this country for steel buckles for waistbands and bracelet clasps was very great, and continued for at least four years. The demand would, without doubt, have continued much longer, but that the market became deluged with cheap inferior articles which destroyed the dresses on which they were fastened. Had articles of good quality been made, the demand would, I have no doubt, have lasted till the present day. But this is the old sin of Birmingham, and ruins one trade after another.

"Three or four years ago the demand for fancy steel buttons for ladies' and childrens' dresses was so great that the men often worked till ten and eleven o'clock on Saturday night; and buttons which had been lying for 40 years in the warehouses, uncalled for and unknown, were readily disposed of at high prices. Orders were received for as many as 400 grosses at a time. Anything in the shape of a steel button was readily sold. I, for one, was enabled to dispose of all the old steel buttons in my shop. But even in this case the slop manufacturers and unscrupulous traders came into competition by making inferior trash, and the trade soon fell off again. For fine fancy toys the demand is quite recent, and there are few workmen who care to do anything at it. They have to be educated to it. If we had the means of getting up the most tasteful and beautiful steel toys, such as the French produce, there would be no difficulty in disposing of them. Inferior articles have gone down in price very much, and the best sort of work has deteriorated. We do not make so much fine work as formerly. Buttons, for instance, which used to be made for 6s. a set, are now made for 3s. They look as well, but are in reality of an inferior description. For good steel toys wages are nearly as good now as in 1824 or 1825. Less is paid for each article, but by readier methods of manufacture the workman can make up the difference by increasing the quantity produced in the same time. The average weekly receipts of a steady mechanic range from 18s. to 24s."

Another manufacturer said: "Steel buckles are now made in considerable quantities for ladies' dresses. They were introduced a few years ago from France where they were worn extensively. Their introduction into this country gave a stimulus to the trade which has continued till the present time. A large number of hands are employed upon them. Steel brooches have also become fashionable and are somewhat extensively manufactured. Steel chains for gentlemen's watches and for ladies' chatelaines are made in large quantities. A few years ago there was a very great demand for steel buttons for ladies' dresses for the same purposes to which buckles were applied, and they are still used in considerable numbers for children's dresses. The demand has decreased. Should the steel button trade revive, it would be of immense benefit to the steel toy trade, as it gives employment to great numbers of workmen. About twenty years ago there was a great demand for clasps for ladies' wristbands and sashes, and the demand is now reviving. There is always a demand for light-steel toys of some sort or other, and within twenty years the number of persons employed in the trade has been nearly doubled. I should think that there are now from 800 to 1,000 pair of hands engaged in it, of whom a large proportion are women and children. The work is light and healthy. The men do all the heavy work, such as casting, filing, &c. Their wages are about £1 1s. a week, varying according to the ability of the workmen. There is a considerable improvement visible in the general conduct of the men, though they are still negligent of work upon Mondays. There has been very little or no change in the prices for making goods within the last twenty years, but the selling prices have been considerably reduced in consequence of the prevalence of slop working. At present there is a scarcity of workmen, and they consequently receive good wages. Women earn about 8s. a week, and boys and young girls 2s. 6d. a week and upwards."

This manufacturer exhibited a few sets of the ancient steel buckles and steel buttons for Court suits, and contrasted them with the modern latchets and buttons used on similar occasions. The former were of exquisite workmanship, as every part was made by hand; the steel—curiously inlaid or let in—glittered with a splendour almost equal to that of diamonds. The price of such shoe buckles ranged from 10 guineas to 50 guineas a pair. The modern latchets are stamped and plated with silver, and are sold at about 16s. a pair. The knee buckles afforded the same contrast. The ancient ones, elaborately wrought, sold for a guinea a pair; the modern substitutes, quite plain, sell for 1s. 6d. The steel buttons of our ancestors were of equal costliness and beauty, and sold at a guinea, and even as high as five guineas each. The steel buttons on Court suits, used at the present time, sell for 9d. each. The former were made by hand, and the studs on them were let in by hand and separately riveted. The modern ones are stamped, and very inferior in appearance.

One branch of the steel toy manufacture, to the production of which some manufacturers devote themselves exclusively, is that of steel watch keys. Upon the subject of this trade, the following information was communicated by one of the principal employers:—

"My business is principally the manufacture of steel watch-keys and pipes for watch-keys, but I also make other toys. There is a scarcity of workmen at present for watch-key making, though the number of those engaged has not diminished for twenty years or more. Steel watch-keys have long been made at Birmingham. One of the oldest description of those now made is a jointed key, technically called a 'Johnnie Wap,' which is principally in demand among agricultural labourers and country-folks. This key is made on the same principle as the ordinary eight-day clock key. Its price has kept up better than any other sort of key. When I was an apprentice I have heard old workmen say that they used to get as much as a guinea for making a dozen joint keys, but now there is seldom more paid for making a gross of them. Keys can be made much more quickly and cheaply now than 40 years ago; probably a gross can now be made in the same time that was then required to make a dozen. Within 20 years the reduction in the price of some sorts of keys is as much as 50 per cent. The average receipts of a workman at present are from 18s. to 22s. a week. I could employ many additional workmen at present, but there is a scarcity of good ones."

Among light-steel toys, as already mentioned, are included steel clock and watch hands, which are made to a considerable extent in Birmingham. The number produced has of late years become very small, as brass ones answer the purpose as well, and are produced at less expense. About three grosses of clock hands or more are said to be made weekly in Birmingham, and of these scarcely three dozen are steel. For two or three years the clockmakers have been subject to great competition from America, where good clocks are made at very little cost. As they are imported in a finished state, the clock-hand makers of Birmingham find their trade considerably checked in consequence. These American clocks are superseding the Dutch and German clocks, as they are neater and more compact. Steel watch hands are made at London, Coventry, and Prescott, in as great quantities as at Birmingham, but the total number produced is said to be not greater than is annually imported from France and Switzerland. The number of workmen engaged in the trade in Birmingham is only about twelve, who produce on an average about three dozen of watch hands per diem each. If we suppose each of these four English towns to produce the same quantity as Birmingham, we should thus have 144 dozen of steel watch hands made every day in England, or more than half a million per annum. This is exclusive of gold hands, which are used in great quantities. Competition, at home and abroad, has reduced the price of watch-hands by about 20 per cent. within the last ten years; but as the workmen employed in the trade require more than ordinary skill and experience, and only good workmen can be employed, the effect of this reduction upon the rate of wages paid has not been so great as in other trades. An average workman, engaged upon the plain watch-hands usually required, makes from £1 2s. to £1 10s. a week throughout the year; and a good workman who is engaged upon more elaborate work earns from £1 5s. to £1 10s. a week. A first-rate workman may earn 30s. a week and upwards.

A branch of the light-steel toy manufacture, which has of late years very much decreased, is that of steel snuffers. Twelve or fifteen years ago there were many manufacturers in Birmingham who devoted themselves exclusively to this branch of trade. By the introduction of patent candles that require no snuffing, and by the more extensive use of camphine and oil lamps, as well as of gas, the trade has so greatly fallen off, that the whole of these manufacturers have been compelled to extend their business into other channels. "The difference," said a gentleman who formerly made large quantities, "is enormous. Many thousands of grosses used to be made, but now our orders are daily growing smaller. Country dealers that formerly ordered eight or ten gross at a time, now give orders, at rare intervals, for a single dozen or half-dozen. A few snuffers are still in demand for bed-room candlesticks, and the foreign and colonial trade keeps up, but to nothing like the extent that I knew it twenty years ago. Patent lamps for patent candles, or for oil and spirits, are all the rage at home and abroad, and I expect to live to see the day when such a thing as a pair of snuffers will be looked upon as a relic of past times, and of the imperfect civilization of our fathers. I can form no precise idea of the number of snuffer-makers that have been thrown out of work, or have betaken themselves to other trades in consequence of the decrease of the demand, but I should say from 200 to 300 at the very least."

The origin, progress, and extinction of the buckle manufacture of Birmingham would form a curious episode in the history of fashion, and would also be valuable in a commercial point of view. The following particulars in connection with it, from the time when the buckle gave employment to thousands of hands, to the present day, when half-a-dozen people can meet the whole demand, may prove serviceable to any future collector of materials for a more complete history. At the time when Hutton wrote his "History of Birmingham" the buckle was in the height of its fashion. In a slight article upon the subject he says:—

"The beaux of the age of the Stuarts ornamented their lower tier (meaning their shoes) with double laces of silk, tagged with silver, and the extremities were beautified with a small fringe of the same metal. The inferior class wore laces of plain silk, linen, or even a thong of leather, which last is yet to be met with in the humble plains of rural life. But I am inclined to think the artisans of Birmingham had no great hand in fitting out the beaux of the last century. The revolution was remarkable for the introduction of William, of liberty, and the minute buckle not differing much in size and shape from the horse-bean. This offspring of fancy, like the clouds, is ever changing. The fashion of to-day is thrown into the casting pot to-morrow. The buckle seems to have undergone every figure, size, and shape of geometrical invention: it has passed through every form in the whole zodiac of Euclid. The large square buckle, plated with silver, is the *ton* of the present day (1781). The ladies also have adopted the reigning taste: it is difficult to discover their beautiful little feet, covered with an enormous shield of buckle; and we wonder to see the active motion under the mass of load."

The following details upon the subject appeared in the *Birmingham Chronicle* of February 14, 1824, communicated by Mr. Luckcock, formerly a buckle manufacturer:—"About the year 1778 an impulse was given to the article, which had hitherto been stationary, by the introduction of an entirely new mode of plating—that of casting the buckle upon the silver in moulds prepared for the purpose; and the substance consisted of tin, with the addition of such other metals as should give it greater hardness and durability. The facility of working this preparation, and the uncommon beauty which was thereby attained, soon extended the trade infinitely beyond its former limits, so that about the year 1788 there were not fewer than from four to five thousand pairs of hands employed in the town and neighbouring districts, in this article, which seemed to bid defiance to any change of fashion or caprice to remove it from being one of our most staple articles of employment and profit. Fashion was wonderfully active, and its extremes, no doubt, operated to produce its own destruction. The Spanish buckle, long and narrow, was enlarged to such a size as in some instances to require a pad to prevent it touching the ground on each side of the instep. The Italian taste covered the foot from the instep to the toes in a beautiful oval or octagon form, while the English style was generally oblong, about four inches by three for men's size, and proportionably smaller for the ladies. Much ingenuity was displayed in the different inventions of the chapes, which, for the large sizes, were so contrived that the shoe should first be buckled by the small strap belonging to it, and then a large false one should be attached to the double chape, so as to cover the whole.

"To any young person of the present day, the size and elegance of some of these extremes, would appear incredible, and more especially in connection with the low rate at which they were manufactured and sold. Some of the largest of them were placed on iron frames, stamped into rich patterns, with scolloped edges, innumerable piercings, the whole surface repaired and beautified by the hand of the chaser, and covered with silver as rich and white to the eye as if the whole substance had been of that material, with large, highly dressed, and blued double chapes—and the wholesale price to come within the compass of half-a-crown a pair. And, again, these same patterns, by being fine cast and silvered, were turned out most beautiful to the eye at about 1s. a pair; but were only the wear of a day, being shorn of their beauty if once splashed with dirt.

"On the other hand, many were made of extravagant value. The jeweller, the silversmith, with the steel workers—the ornamental workman, with his gilding, his spangles, and his various ornaments—all seemed to vie with each other who should produce the most tempting article to the man of fashion or of wealth. Steel buckles, being considerably in demand, were often as high as twenty or thirty shillings a pair.

"For about ten years the trade was in its prime, and the ten years following witnessed its gradual decline and total dissolution."

The following details, more minute than the information given by Hutton, or by any other person who ever wrote upon the buckle, as far as I have been able to ascertain, were communicated to me by a respectable old gentleman, upwards of eighty years of age, who worked at the trade in his youth, and who, to a memory remarkably clear, united a great interest in all that related to the profession of his early days. He was represented as a "storehouse of anecdote" in connection with the manufactures of the town, and he was certainly a fine specimen of the intelligent English workman. He had been not only a buckle maker, but a gun-lock maker; he had worked at the Soho Works for the firm of Boulton and Smith, at the time that Watt was a partner—had been engaged in various other mechanical trades, according as fashion varied—had also kept a public-house—and, till within the last six years, had regularly worked as a journeyman, when he had retired to pass the remainder of his days in decent competence. He appeared quite delighted at the idea that any one in these times should take an interest in the ancient shoe buckle, and he communicated his information with much perspicuity. The following details were derived from his conversation, and in answer to questions put to him at various times. "The shoe buckle," he said, "is believed to be a Dutch invention, and it had a 'run' for upwards of a hundred years. Bilston was the first place in England where it was manufactured, and it was afterwards introduced into Birmingham. Many fortunes were made out of it at Bilston before the Birmingham people took it up; and one named Jukes, originally a butcher, was especially noted when I was a boy, seventy years ago, for the large fortune he made by buckles in a very short space of time. I had an uncle at Bilston who made his fortune at it about the year 1775, and when he retired he sold his business to Messrs. Wilmer and Alstone, of Birmingham, who, to the best of my recollection and belief, were the first people who ever made buckles in this town. It soon became a 'roaring' business; and Birmingham may be said to have lived by shoe and knee buckles from 1780 to 1790. Many thousands of people were employed, and I have heard that 8,000 or even 10,000 hands were at one time engaged in the various factories, large and small, that abounded in Birmingham, Walsall, Bilston, and Wolverhampton. We supplied the whole world with shoe buckles—Holland, Germany, France, Italy, Spain, America, and England, Scotland, and Ireland. Both men and women wore them, and even the little children had buckles to their shoes—I mean the children of the rich. The children of the poor wore clasps. Mechanics worked with buckles in their shoes, and indeed all kinds of labourers, except those who followed the plough, wore them. Trowsers were not known in those days, nor for a long time afterwards, and boots were not invented; indeed, I don't think I ever saw either boots or trowsers, and I certainly never wore either, until long after the battle of Waterloo. The prices of buckles ranged from five to ten guineas down to a shilling a pair. The best were made of steel and silver; some were even set with diamonds; and it was very common for people to wear paste or Bristol stone buckles on Sundays. Great numbers were made of plated ware. But if you want to know more particularly the various descriptions of buckle, an old song, which I used to hear the workmen sing in the public-houses when I was a boy, will give you as good a notion as anything I can say. It was made by a journeyman buckle-maker, who was 'a bit of a poet,' and worked for a gentleman named Tutin, or Tutan, the inventor of a composition metal, something like Britannia metal in the present day, and which, after his name, was called Tutinia, or Tutania metal. The song, so far as I know, has never been in print, and I never met with any person of late years who knew anything about it except from me. It must have been made near upon seventy years ago." The old gentleman then recited the following:—

> "By mechanical invention
>   Many wonders have been wrought;
> But the buckle trade to mention
>   Far outstrikes all common thought.
>
> "Constantly as patterns vary,
>   Happy he who well can scheme,
> Plan, project, strike out, and carry
>   Fashion to the full extreme.
>
> "Some for pinchbeck—some for plated—
>   Some for soft white—some for hard—
> But every one is over-rated
>   With Tutinia when compared.
>
> "But all to one old soul must truckle,
>   He whose wit his brain-pan clips,
> Who makes a song and shapes a buckle,
>   While the pipe's between his lips.
>
> "So farewell to vain disputing—
>   Of this evening make the most—
> 'Friendship, Freedom, Trade, and Tutin,'
>   Round the globe, shall be the toast."

"The pinchbeck buckles," he continued, "were made of a white composition metal, of which brass was the principal ingredient. The soft white buckles used to be called *tommics*. They did not last very long, but looked very bright when new, and were sold very cheap. The plated buckles were much worn for a long time. They were made of iron, first tinned and then silvered, and were stamped or pierced out. There was but little workmanship in them, but they wore tolerably well. Buckles soon grew monstrously large, especially for men, and reached right across the foot from sole to sole. They almost covered the foot, in fact, and were much too large for comfort in walking; but fashion reconciled people to them, as it will to anything however ridiculous. The silver buckles used to be sold by weight, and the chape, whether of iron or steel, used to be weighed in with them. The French war interfered a good deal with the foreign trade in buckles. The Spaniards used to take immense numbers of very large and very expensive buckles from us, but that demand fell off, after the French revolution, and the French demand came to nothing. I never heard of a deputation to the Prince of Wales on the subject of buckles, but I heard of the button-makers, when they went to London to induce the Prince to wear gilt buttons, and that he remarked to a member of the deputation that it was odd he should ask him (the Prince) to wear gilt buttons, when he (the manufacturer) wore covered ones."

It may be observed, however, although the narrator did not remember the circumstance, that a deputation waited upon the Prince of Wales, in 1791—when there was great stagnation in the buckle manufacture on account of the loss of the foreign trade, and also of a partial change of fashion consequent upon the introduction of the shoe-string—to induce his Royal Highness to appear in public with buckles. The Prince, having heard that many thousand individuals were in distress in consequence of the change, informed the deputation that he would not only wear buckles himself, but order all the members of his household to do the same. The royal example was not altogether nugatory, and the trade revived to a considerable extent. A similar story to that of the button maker and the Prince is related of a member of this deputation, who is said to have appeared with shoe-strings when urging upon the royal attention the superior claims of the buckle. Which of the two stories is the original one it is difficult to determine. "The fashion," continued my informant, "began to change about the beginning of this century, but even then many fortunes were made out of the business. At the Soho works, Mr. Matthew Boulton introduced the patent buckle or latchet, which interfered a great deal with the old-fashioned buckle. Boulton and Smith employed some hundreds of hands in making latchets, and built very large workshops for this branch of the trade. These workshops were afterwards converted into the famous Soho Mint, where nearly all the British money was coined for many years. I worked at the buckle trade in the year 1810, when the Princess Amelia died. It was a very considerable trade at that time; and I remember that much distress was caused in some branches of the trade by the general mourning that was ordered for the Princess. Everybody, male and female, wore black buckles; and a great business in black buckles was consequently created at the expense of the general buckle trade. The wages of the workmen were good. A *chaser* got from 30s. to 40s. a week single-handed; and if he had the assistance of two or three boys, he might make £4 a week. The *bottomers*, who filed the bottoms of the buckles, got from 20s. to 30s. a week single-handed. No women were employed in the trade. A buckle went through a great number of processes in all, and was not begun and completed in Birmingham. The forging was principally done at Darlaston, and the chapes were almost exclusively manufactured at Bilston. The filing, chasing, and putting together were the work of Birmingham. A workman was a workman in those days. Hands were scarce, on account of the war, and the men were very independent in their whole behaviour. They would not work unless they pleased; and a good hand could always obtain employment at a good price. I cannot precisely remember when buckles went out of fashion, but it was after the death of the Princess Amelia. So many slop buckles—regular trash—were made, that people got tired of them. The plating wore off—and a spatter of mud was sometimes sufficient to ruin a fine-looking buckle that had been put on new a day or two previously. Shoe-strings, being more economical, began to be worn; and long before buckles went quite out of fashion, the waiters at inns, and servants generally, used to be known by their shoe-strings. The shoemakers did a good deal to drive the buckle out. When the fashion began to change, they did their best to encourage it, for the straps to fasten the buckle took a good deal of leather as well as workmanship—both of which were saved by the introduction of shoe-strings, while the price of shoes remained the same—the whole difference in the expense going into the pocket of the shoemaker. I remember that great indignation was aroused in Birmingham when it was made known that the Prince Regent had finally discarded the buckle, and had been seen in public with shoe-strings. The buckle never recovered itself. If I may so say, it never held up its head in the world again—it was quite ruined and done for. The working men in the buckle trade hissed whenever the name of the Prince was mentioned. Hundreds, if not thousands, of men were thrown out of work. I remember that a party of them, having nothing else to do, hired a donkey, and led the animal about the streets, with shoe-strings tied about its hoofs, and ribbons about its legs, to ridicule the new fashion, and to implore charity at the same time. Whenever a man or woman appeared with shoe-strings in the streets of Birmingham, he or she was hooted by the children, and by grown-up people too. The cry was *'Lick-dish! lick-dish!'* or *'Dog-robber! Dog-robber!'*—meaning that a person who wore shoe-strings could only be a waiter at an inn, or a 'flunkey.' By 'dog-robber' was meant a man who picked bones after other people had done with them—in fact, a waiter. There used to be constant rows and disturbances in the streets, got up by the unemployed buckle-makers. But it was all of no use. The buckle trade was done for. Fashion had changed, and boots and trowsers were coming into vogue, to deprive it of all chance of revival. The men gradually went into other trades—some of them went into the saddlery buckle making—but that was poor work in comparison with that they had been accustomed to. Some became carters and porters—some went to the workhouse—and many, being skilled in metal work, went into the brass trade—or to other branches of the heavy or light steel toys. I went into the gun-lock business, but I never afterwards found a trade that I liked so well as buckle making."

In corroboration of the statements of this venerable and intelligent working man, the following, from a still more ancient member of the light steel toy and buckle trade—the oldest man in Birmingham— will be found of interest. The narrator is upwards of 92 years of age, and is still able to move about his little house in the suburbs of the town. He always wears a pair of large and handsome buckles in his shoes, which he manufactured for himself in the days when the buckle "was the only wear." He remembers almost all the principal fluctuations which have taken place in his trade for the last seventy or eighty years. His ideas are strongly impregnated with a love of the "olden time," especially of buckles, and with a hearty hatred of steamboats and railways, which he declares have brought the country to the verge of ruin. "Before the first French revolution," said he, "the light steel toy trade was the best in Birmingham, and one-half the town was dependent upon it. By the revolution it was nearly annihilated, for the principal part of the trade was with France, Spain, and Portugal, and all orders were suspended, for the two latter countries were supplied through France. When Napoleon came to power he prohibited all English steel toys from being imported into France, and from that time the French began to manufacture steel toys, and to supply their own markets. The workmen in Birmingham were obliged to give up the work, and to turn to other trades. I myself took to gardening for awhile, and then, when the war was going on, I worked at military ornaments. I made sword-hilts among other things, and I have known sword-hilts to be made which were valued at £30 each, without either blade or scabbard. The steel toys made when I was an apprentice were much the same as those made subsequently, such as watch-chains, 'middle pieces,' for hanging seals and keys for watches upon, scissor-hooks, steel scent-bottles, ladies' hooks for the work-table, &c., and of course the shoe-buckle and steel latchet, which were the staple articles of manufacture. These and all other articles made were infinitely superior to anything made at present—indeed, there is nothing but rubbish made now—stuff that I would not pick out of the dirt, and should be ashamed to work at. There were few watch-chains made in my day which did not bring in from 5s. to 10s. each, but now they sell them for less than half the money. For three years I remember working at nothing else but scissor-hooks for ladies. Wages were not so high sixty or seventy years ago as now, but provisions and house-rent were not so dear. For the best butchers' meat in Birmingham we paid only 2d. or 2½d. a pound, and we had 14 lb. of bread for a shilling; coals and other fuel were also much cheaper, and for 5s. I could have a better pair of shoes than I can now have for 10s. I began working as a journeyman for 12s. a week, but I could live pretty well for 7s. or 8s. a week. A good tool-maker for steel toy work at that time could make from 15s. to 20s. a week, and a good cutter and filer could make nearly 30s. a week, but to do this they must have been able workmen and must have worked over time. Generally speaking I should think that the workmen seventy years ago made about 12s. or 13s. a week regularly, and no more. At that time the usual hours for work were from six a.m. till seven p.m. in summer, and from seven a.m. till eight p.m. in winter. But now-a-days the men are such lie-a-beds that they cannot get to work, even in summer, till nearly eight o'clock. Our sports used to be cock-fighting, bull-baiting, skittle-playing, quoits, foot-ball, leapfrog, &c. But nearly all these manly amusements have passed away, and we see nothing of them among the young men. We used to have a 'wake' (a fair) in every parish of the town once a year, and with these and the neighbouring wakes there used to be one nearly every month, which the working men of Birmingham could attend. There was generally a bull to be baited at these wakes, and a great deal of drinking and fighting. There is less fighting now than in my day, for the young men now-a-days have not courage to fight as they used to do; but I think there is more drinking now-a-days, and the people are ob-liged to take to fourpenny ale instead of sixpenny, in order to keep within compass. The usual way of spending a jolly evening among the workmen some seventy years ago, was to go in parties to a public house, two or three miles out of town, where they played at skittles and drank ale, while cabbage and bacon were being cooked for their dinner. This was done very frequently. I used never to have anything to do with bull-baiting, or rat-worrying, or anything of the sort, and never 'backed' a cock but once, and then, only for sixpence. But I know that these sports were very common among the workmen, and were more talked about and thought of than such games as foot-ball, 'foot and horse shoe' (leap-frog), or prison bars, which were more popular among boys and young lads. These games have also disappeared here, for Birmingham has grown so big now that 'the fellows' have no ground to 'kick' upon. I was once laid up for a short time when a youth, from having sprained my shoulder while playing. There was no sick or relief fund among the men at that time, so I had to 'fight it out' for myself as best I could." "The buckle trade," continued this venerable buckle-maker, "was a great blessing to Birmingham, and if it were to be revived it would give employment to thousands of workmen. The use of the buckle was first done away with in the army, as it was found among cavalry soldiers that the buckles on their shoes caught the stirrup when they were mounting or dismounting, and frequently occasioned mischief. This was the commencement of its disuse, and in a very short time the buckle trade became confined to supplying country orders and America, and then sunk altogether. But the buckle is the only efficient shoe-tie, and preserves the shoe much longer than tape or ribbon. The first great revival of the steel toy trade was when Queen Charlotte appeared in Court with steel latchets on her shoes, and having her dress adorned with steel buttons and slides. This set the trade in motion, and steel toys of all sorts became highly fashionable; but the demand did not extend beyond this country, and sunk again in about five years in consequence of the wretchedly inferior quality of the articles made. The buckle, I firmly believe, would have been worn to this day if it had not been for the quantity of cheap trash that was made to disgust the people with this noble article of trade. I am convinced that nothing is so handsome for the leg and foot as knee-breeches, a sound shoe, and a good buckle. They beat all your boots and trowsers for beauty—yes, and for convenience, too."

A few particulars as to the present state of the buckle trade in Birmingham will conclude this branch of the subject. The demand for shoe-buckles is chiefly for articles of silver, which are worn by the Queen's coachmen, and by the coachmen of the nobility on State occasions. There is but little demand for silver or fine steel buckles for Court suits, in consequence of the system of hiring court suits, by which the old articles are made to do frequent service. Occasionally an order is received for one solitary pair of handsome shoe or knee-buckles from a new peer, or for a plain pair of silver or plated buckles for a farmer of the old school. Now and then an order comes from Edinburgh or from Dublin when the Queen or the Lord-Lieutenant holds a levee. These orders—at least for the silver articles—always find their way to one manufacturer, who is known to the trade; and this gentleman stated that "the last of the buckle-makers," who manufactured largely, and made a fortune by the trade, died about sixteen years ago. There is a more considerable trade in common steel buckles, which are still required for knee-breeches by grooms, and by old-fashioned people, and also for fastening spur-straps and other purposes.

In conclusion it may be stated that the light steel toy trade fluctuates considerably, and that it has no greater opponents than some of the manufacturers, who, in their over eagerness to become rich, get up showy but inferior articles in imitation of better goods that happen to hit the public taste. The old term of disparagement implied in the words "Brummagem ware," though not deserved at the present day by most of the important trades of the town, affects some of the articles included under the general name of light steel toys, more especially those intended for adornment of the person.

"This business," said a manufacturer, "is not one in which people embark their capital now. It has been improving for five or six years as regard the quantity made, but prices have fallen within that time, and slop and inferior work has very much increased. A considerable revival of trade took place in 1846 by the demand for buckles and buttons for ladies' and children's dresses, which continued till the end of 1847, when the same causes operated against the respectable trade, namely, the inferiority of the articles produced. Articles were made thirty or forty years ago of the very best workmanship, but people want everything so cheap now that really good articles cannot be provided. A general reduction of about 25 per cent. in the prices of steel toys has been made within the last thirty years, but an equal reduction has taken place in the wages paid for making them, and a still greater in the quality of the articles supplied."

LABOUR AND THE POOR.

BIRMINGHAM.

[FROM OUR SPECIAL CORRESPONDENT.]

TIN-PLATE, JAPAN, AND BRITANNIA METAL WORKERS.

LETTER XVI.

Birmingham and Wolverhampton are the principal seats of the manufacture of articles of tin plate. The larger proportion of the hands are employed at Wolverhampton, where they amount to about 270 men and 100 boys, exclusive of japanners and of the women employed in the warehouses and in the packing of the goods. The number of hands in the trade at Birmingham is about a third less than that of Wolverhampton. The tin plate itself, which is wrought up in these two towns and the neighbourhood into a great variety of useful articles, is chiefly manufactured in South Wales. There are also manufactories at Wolverhampton, Bilston, Gospel Oak, Cookley, and Willden, but none is made in Birmingham or in London. The trade is a new one, even in the midland counties. It is estimated to give employment in the district immediately around Wolverhampton to between 400 and 500 people; and in South Wales, to at least three or four times that number. There is a continual home demand for tin plate, while there is an equally large demand for exportation. From the port of Liverpool, between the 1st and 13th of January last, the export of tin plate amounted to 5,636 boxes. Each box contains 225 plates, so that the export for this period was 1,268,100 plates. By far the larger proportion of this supply was for the United States; 2,163 boxes being destined for New York, 1,000 for New Orleans, 365 for Boston, and 850 for Philadelphia. Tin plate, it appears, is largely used in America for the roofing of houses. The other places that take the largest quantities are Calcutta, Bombay, Rio Janeiro, Valparaiso, California, Naples, and Lisbon. The export of this particular fortnight is somewhat under the average, but if estimated at a corresponding ratio for each fortnightly period during the year, the total export of tin plates of British make, through the port of Liverpool alone, would amount to 146,536 boxes, or 33,000,000 plates per annum. The average value of a box of tin plate is 30s.—making the value of the annual export from Liverpool, not far short of a quarter of a million sterling.

A short description of a visit to the works of Messrs. Baldwin, of Wolverhampton, will convey to the reader some idea of the processes of this interesting and important manufacture. The "mill" of the Messrs. Baldwin is what is called a "single" mill, and employs 80 men, women, and lads. A double mill would employ exactly double the number of workpeople. The two constituents of tin plate are iron and tin. The first process is to convert the rough blocks of pig iron into sheets, sufficiently thin for the purpose of being manufactured into those culinary and domestic articles for which the article commonly called tin, but which is in reality tin plate, is required. The iron, after being puddled in the usual manner, passes through the rolling mills till it is compressed into a sheet of several feet in length. While still red hot it is dexterously doubled or folded over, like a sheet of paper, by a workman; again passed into the furnace, and again under the roller, and so on, by successive repetitions of the process, until the original sheet has been eight times folded and rolled. It is then cut into squares or blocks by the steam shears; and when sufficiently cooled, the blocks, which are about a third of an inch in thickness, are handed over to boys, who bend the corners somewhat after the fashion with which a bank clerk uses a pile of bank notes, when he wishes to count them; and then rapidly "split" or separate them into the eight thinner sheets of which they are composed. The next operation is that of "pickling" the plates in vitriol diluted with hot water, to take the scale off, and whiten them. But even after this has been done, the iron sheets are far from being ready to receive the thin coating of the more precious metal, which gives them their name and usefulness. The men who preside over the vitriol tubs, having done their part, transfer the sheets to women, whose business is to rub them slightly with sand, and then to dip them in cold water to remove all traces of vitriol. The poor iron is treated with as much cruelty, and goes through as many processes, before it becomes a tin plate, as John Barleycorn is represented by the poet to have undergone, before his blood became transmuted into the liquor "which warms the heart of man." After they have been cleaned from the vitriol, the plates are placed in a furnace for eight or nine hours, to be annealed; but as the annealing dulls the brightness which the vitriol gave them, they suffer the process of cold rolling, to give them once more the necessary polish. But cold rolling, it appears, though an essential process, has its inconveniences, amongst the most considerable of which is, that it hardens the plates too much. To remedy this last evil, they are once again placed in the furnace, and once more annealed for a few hours, until they are as soft as required.

This, however, is not the last process. There is still a fault to be remedied. The rolling mill requires grease, to go as agreeably as it should; and a portion of grease adheres to the plates after they have issued from it. To cure them of this they undergo what my cicerone called "a mild pickle of vitriol." A short course of acid probation suffices—at the end of which time they are almost ready to receive the coating of tin. One process alone remains, which is somewhat puzzling to the uninitiated in the mysteries of tin plate making. As soon as the mild pickle of vitriol has cleaned them from grease, they are greased again by being plunged into a cauldron, either of boiling tallow or of palm oil, where they remain for a quarter of an hour. Close to this cauldron of boiling grease, and superintended by another workman, is a boiler of molten tin, about two-thirds filled with the metal, upon the top of which bubbles a scum of oil or tallow, of the colour and consistency of chocolate. A workman, called a "tinner," dips the plate into the tin, and leaves it there for ten or twelve minutes, at the end of which time the tin adheres. He then passes it to his companion, called a "washer," who rubs the surface gently with a brush, so as to remove all superfluous tin, and to produce a perfectly even surface. These are the chief operations, and the plates, having passed through the hands of the male workmen for the rougher part of the business, are finally transferred to the female branch of the establishment, to be cleansed from the tallow and palm oil that may adhere to them, and to be afterwards polished, sorted, and packed. They are cleansed by being gently rubbed in "sharps," a kind of bran or husk. The "sharps" used for the purpose become greasy after a little use, when they are sold to the neighbouring farmers to feed pigs, for which purpose they are much sought after by pig-keepers, and are greatly relished by the animals. After being cleaned, the plates are polished by women, who lay them singly on a piece of sheepskin with the wool on, and rub them over with another piece of the same material. One woman has been known to polish in a day as many as fifty boxes, or 12,250 sheets, for which the rate of payment is one halfpenny a box, or two-shillings and a penny for the day's labour. One man is able to wash with the brush, dipped in tin, about half that number per day on the average, while a very industrious workman will be able to manage 30 boxes, or 6,750 sheets. The plates, after being lightly polished in this way, are sorted; the inferior, or spoiled, ones are cast aside, and the good ones are arranged into boxes of 225 each—ready for the merchant and the tin-plate worker—for the foreign and the home manufacture. The wages of the men average from 25s. to 35s. or £2, and of the women from 7s. to 10s. or 12s. per week. The trade is much on the increase at the present time, and good hands can always find employment.

The tin is received from Cornwall in blocks weighing from 3¾ cwts. to 4 cwts., and is worth about £90 a ton. A ton of pig iron is worth about £4, and is converted into tin plates worth about £32 a ton. The tin used in a ton of plates is worth about £9; leaving £19 for the labour and the waste of metal in passing through so many fires. The last item is calculated at about £2 on the ton; thus leaving about £17 per ton for labour—or 52 per cent. on the whole value.

The principal articles manufactured of tin plate are, pots, pans, kettles, and culinary utensils of various kinds; tea-trays, tea-urns, teapots, coffee-pots, toast-racks, beer-jugs, water-pans, canisters, dish-covers, candlesticks, cash-boxes, lanterns, shower-baths, foot-baths, slop-pails, coal-scuttles, coal-vases, plate-warmers, patty-pans, jelly-moulds, cake-moulds, tart pans, &c.

The tinplate workers appear to be divided into five classes, namely, stampers, tinners or dippers, finishers, makers up, and burnishers; but of these the first and last have only lately acquired any importance in the trade. "They are not considered to be tinplate-workers," said a member of the union, and are not admitted to the privileges of the trade. "There are," continued the same informant, "from 170 to 200 tinplate-workers in Birmingham, exclusive of stampers and burnishers, who number from 40 to 60 men. There are a good many apprentices and boys in the trade, but not more than is considered fair by the workmen. They number about one-third of all employed. There is no rule or understanding amongst the men of the union by which they wish to control the masters in the number of boys engaged; but it may be said that by the introduction of stamping and burnishing into the trade, about twenty-five years ago, boys are enabled to do work which used only to be done by men; for these new departments of the trade facilitate finishing and do away with skilled labour to a great extent. With respect to the boys, the only complaint that we journeymen make is, that the master gives as much as possible of the best-paid work to boys, and as much as possible of the worst-paid work to men. He thus makes an additional profit for himself; for though the boys appear to be paid for work done at the same rate as the men, a discount of 50 per cent. is retained off their wages. There is a union or society of tin-plate workers in Birmingham in connection with the unions at Wolverhampton and elsewhere. Discount to the amount of from 10 to 15 per cent. has been deducted from the wages of the workmen in Birmingham for about three years, but means are now being taken to do away with this bad system—of which all the men complain—and to establish a general net price in the trade. For about twenty years prices have been decreasing in Birmingham, principally on account of the great competition among the employers, and no doubt from the readier methods of manufacture which have been introduced within that time. Teapots are now better made for 2s. than they could have been made thirty years ago for 10s. each. About twenty years ago the average receipts of an ordinary workman were about 30s. a week. Many workmen now earn fully as much; but a few years ago an average of the receipts of the tinplate-workers in Birmingham was taken for the National Association of United Trades, when it was found that the average wages of the men throughout the year were only 15s. a week, except in one establishment, where they averaged 17s. 3d. a week. It is true that the average was fixed as low as possible, because the men were obliged to pay a certain per centage upon their earnings, as thus estimated, in order to support the interests of the general body. Yet I think the average was correct for the whole year round."

For the last few months there has been considerable agitation among the members of this trade, in consequence of a strike that took place in Wolverhampton, and which was supported by the tin-plate workers of, but did not extend to, Birmingham. The object of the strike was to secure a uniform list of prices: in fact, to compel three manufacturers in Wolverhampton, who had for many years been paying their workmen a rate of wages thirty per cent. less than was paid by other employers, to raise the wages of their hands to the rate considered equitable by the men, as well as by the old-established and respectable firms. The workmen also complained that the three employers alluded to, and one of them more especially, had induced the men to enter into "one-sided agreements"—in other words, to contract to work for a term of years at the usual prices of the trade, stating that they punished the men for breaking the contract, if they neglected their work, but did not, if they consented to work, pay them as much as they might have earned from other employers. The cause of the tinplate workers was espoused by the National Association of United Trades in London, a body under the presidentship of Mr. T. S. Duncombe, M.P., and having for its object the protection of the working men of all trades throughout the country against oppression and unfairness on the part of employers. This association appears to have been the means of preventing many strikes, by bringing about mutual explanations and concessions on the part of masters and men. Towards the middle of December, all, or nearly all the hands of these three employers being out on strike, except those who were under contract, one of the manufacturers appealed to the mayor and magistrates for protection in the conduct of his business, alleging that the men still in his employ were subjected to insult and annoyance. The mayor invited the two delegates of the United Trades' Association, who had been sent from London to watch the case, to be present at the hearing with two workmen from the complainant's factory, and with two, working at the higher rate of wages, from the older establishments in the town. The mayor, after patiently listening to the evidence on both sides, passed the judgment of the bench upon the case, and said "that since the repeal of the Combination Acts the working classes had the fullest right to meet and discuss their interests, and to be advised by whomsoever they pleased, but that they had no right to interfere with others by coercion or insult. With reference to the Book of Prices, the magistrates had nothing to do with it unless assented to by all parties; nor was it by any meeting or printed book that the price of labour could ultimately be adjusted. That must depend upon the varying state of trade and other circumstances. In the absence of exact terms, the magistrates could know nothing but the market price of work for the time being. And this brought them to the question whether the complainant was bound to pay that price? It appeared that all the workmen usually employed by him had left his manufactory, except those who were under written contracts. By these contracts he engaged to pay each workman such wages as he paid the men not under contract in his manufactory; but if they were all hired, to what standard could the magistrate refer? Those not under contract could remain or not, as they pleased, and a manufacturer could employ them or not, as he could afford; and it was one of the objections to long agreements for service, that if wages rose, and those hired were bound to work for less than their fellow-labourers, discontent was sure to arise. The magistrates, therefore, always regretted to see agreements for long periods, and always had an objection to commit upon them, unless absolutely necessary. The question, however, was—What rate of wages was such an employer bound to give under existing circumstances to men who had signed agreements?" The magistrates then asked to whom they could refer for the market price of the day—whether to the list of the houses paying the lower, or those of the houses paying the higher rate? They ultimately decided to refer to the latter as the standard of value; for this, amongst other reasons, that if a workman were not bound by contract, he might go to those houses and obtain the highest rate. "This, they thought, would be the rule adopted in courts of law, and they hoped this expression of their opinion would terminate the unfortunate differences which had arisen." Six of the magistrates present, and one absent, concurred in this decision. But it was not acquiesced in by the three manufacturers. The men still remained out on strike, and a portion of these employers, with a view of dispensing with their services, brought over a number of French tinplate workers to supply their places. These, however, did not long remain in Wolverhampton; but, disappointed, perhaps, on the one hand, and subjected to annoyance on the other, they were induced after a while to return to their own country, all their expenses being paid by the United Trades' Association. This strike became a matter of great interest at the last municipal elections for Wolverhampton, and two members of the old town-council, known for their opposition to the demands made by the workmen for the higher rate of wages, were defeated in the wards for which they stood for re-election, and their places were supplied by two gentlemen known to be as strongly in the workmen's favour. Each man thrown out of employment by this strike received 12s. 6d. a week, and the cost for the first six months of its continuance was upwards of £500. This strike is not yet ended.

It will be seen from this statement that the system of "agreements," or contracts, into which working men are induced to enter, and by which they bind themselves to work for one employer, upon certain conditions, for a stipulated time, is one of which complaint is made. The following is a form of these agreements:—

"COPY OF AGREEMENT.

"Memorandum of a Contract made this .... day of ...., 18......, between A. B., of &c., and C. D., of the same place, &c. as follows:—

"The said C. D., in consideration of the wages and covenants, on the part of the said A. B., to be paid and performed, doth hereby hire himself unto, covenant, contract, and agree to work for and serve the said A. B. for the term of three years, to be computed from the .... day of .... next, as his hired servant, in the trade or business of a ...., and also for, during, and until the full end and term of six calendar months after notice by him given in writing to quit the said service after the expiration of the said term of three years, during all which said term and terms he the said C. D. shall and will diligently, well, and faithfully serve the said A. B., and also shall and will regularly attend in his manufactory or workshops at Wolverhampton aforesaid during the usual hours of work, and in all respects conform himself to his directions therein, and also shall and will take care of and return all tools and materials entrusted to him, and make or execute and deliver all such descriptions of work as may from time to time be directed by the said A. B. in the best way that he the said C. D. is or shall be capable of. And the said A. B., in consideration of the contract and service aforesaid, doth hereby for himself covenant and agree with the said C. D. that he the said A. B. shall and will find and provide the said C. D. with full and regular employment in his service during the aforesaid term and terms, and also shall and will, on the Saturday in every week, pay or cause to be paid unto the said C. D. the following wages, namely, the same prices for his work which he pays to other workmen in his manufactory, or such prices as may hereafter be agreed upon by the said parties; and also, if he the said A. B. should, at the expiration of the said term, or at any time afterwards, be desirous of discharging the said C. D. from his service, he shall and will first give him one month's notice in writing to that effect. In witness whereof the said parties have hereunto set their hands the day and year first above written.

(Signed)

"Witness E. F.

his
"C. ✕ D.
mark.
"A. B."

The act legalising these contracts is known as the Act of the 4th George IV., cap. 34, and under its provisions a workman who fails to perform his contract, by neglecting his work, or absconding from his employ, is imprisoned with hard labour for any period not exceeding three months; or, in minor cases of complaint by an employer, the magistrate may simply order the defendant to return to his work and pay the costs of the application. Such agreements may be verbal as well as written, if there be sufficient proof to satisfy the magistrate that they were really entered into by the parties. In cases of dispute in a trade, or of a strike, as in the case of the tinplate workers, these agreements may be made the instruments of much hardship. The two following cases occurred during the progress of the Wolverhampton strike, which is still unhappily subsisting. A man in the employment of a master paying the lower rate of wages, being under agreement to serve for three years, absented himself one day for two hours from his work without permission. His employer cited him before the magistrates, and the case was proved against him. The man alleged in his defence that he had attended before the magistrates to hear a case against his employer, under the impression that his evidence would be necessary. He admitted that he had not been subpœnaed for the purpose. His employer pressed for a conviction, and he was sentenced to three weeks' imprisonment and hard labour in Stafford Gaol, which sentence he duly underwent. Another case, which occurred under similar circumstances, may be cited to show the manner in which working men deprive themselves of their natural liberty by these agreements, and the hardships that may be inflicted upon them by the law, under the yoke of which they put themselves without sufficient forethought. In this case, a tin-plate worker, of Liverpool, seeing placards on the walls that men were wanted in Wolverhampton, and being ignorant of the strike, applied for employment at the address given, and was hired upon condition of entering into an agreement to serve either for two or three years. The precise period is not stated, but it is immaterial. He left his wife and children at Liverpool, and proceeded to Wolverhampton to fulfil his contract. Here he soon learned the true state of the case, and found his position not quite so comfortable as he anticipated. In the midst of his dissatisfaction, he received a letter from his wife in Liverpool, stating that one of his children had died, and that another lay dangerously ill; she required his immediate presence, and he started accordingly, without saying a word to his employer. Information was sent to the police at Liverpool, and the man was arrested on his return from a carpenter's shop, where he had been to procure a few boards to make a coffin for his dead child. His wife also lay ill; but, in spite of his remonstrances and her agonized entreaties, he was taken away in custody to Wolverhampton and locked up all night in the police cell. He was brought before the magistrates in the morning, and the irritating circumstances of the strike acting on the mind of his employer, a conviction was pressed for. The magistrates appeared loth to act in such a case—but having no alternative, the man was ordered to return to his work immediately, and to pay the expenses, amounting to between three and four pounds, or in default to be committed to prison for a month with hard labour. The employer offered to let him work out the amount of costs by weekly instalments. I am not able to cite any instances in which convictions have been obtained for breach of verbal agreements—but I am informed by working men that in Staffordshire such convictions are far from uncommon.

The following particulars upon the general condition of the tin-plate manufacture, and of the extent to which dishonest competition and the production of "slop" articles has tended to injure both the employers and the employed, as well as the public, were given by a manufacturer in Birmingham:—"Twenty years ago," he said, "tin goods were nearly all made by hand labour, but machinery has since been introduced in the manufacture of many parts of the articles. As good a teapot can now be made for 20d. as could be then made for 3s. or 3s. 4d. The increase in the number of articles of all descriptions now made is very great. In such articles as dish covers, which used to be made by hand labour, the use of stamping machines has been introduced, by which the articles are made much more quickly and cheaply. The dies for such articles are often cut on the premises. The old mode of planishing has been done away with to a great extent, and the articles are now turned on a lathe and burnished. This process has also tended to reduce prices.

"Competition among the manufacturers has had a large share in causing a reduction of prices. Within twenty years the number of manufacturers of tin plate goods has been quadrupled in Birmingham, and, in cases where machinery is not absolutely necessary, the large manufacturers find great difficulty in competing with the small masters, who can sell for journeymen's wages, and have little expense for rent, and none for steam power. The small masters sometimes sell goods at a profit far less than they could earn as journeymen workers in a large establishment; but they have also the chance occasionally of finding a good market for their goods. Besides, men like to be independent—and the feeling is natural. It must be owned, however, that one result of the entry of men without capital into the trade, has been very largely to increase the quantity of the cheapest kinds of goods. These 'slop' articles do not contain above half the quantity of material that was formerly put in them; and the workmanship is as bad as the stuff. The factors or merchants take advantage of the competition, and hawk a large order about from one manufactory to another to ascertain where it can be most cheaply executed, and to screw down the maker to the lowest price.

"The demand for cheap goods comes both from home and from abroad, but is largest in the foreign market. The Americans import the tin plates and make their own goods, and place a high duty on English manufactured tin plate. The Americans are improving in the quality of their goods, but they cannot yet produce such first-rate articles as the English. The principal foreign markets for manufactured goods are the West Indies, the Cape of Good Hope, South America, and Germany.

"Wages have been nominally reduced, but in reality the men are as well off as ever, especially at the present moment, as the trade is very brisk, and good hands can find constant employment. Any man who keeps steady can do well. A good workman can easily make 30s. a week: a middling workman can make about 20s. a week. In some departments of the trade the men can earn £2 a week; but they lose time during the week, especially on Mondays, and perhaps what they actually receive averages no more than from 17s. to 25s. a week.

"A good many boys are employed in the trade as apprentices to the manufacturer. They make from 4s. to 10s. a week, according to their age. The proportion of apprentices to men is about one-fifth. The union has great power in Birmingham, though the strike at Wolverhampton did not affect the masters here. The Birmingham men have paid out a great deal of money in consequence, in order to support the men of Wolverhampton. There has been no cause of complaint, and no disposition to strike at Birmingham."

Another manufacturer said, in reference to the same subject— "The quality of articles made of tin plate in Birmingham has long been deteriorating. Good articles do not sell now-a-days. There is a run upon common and cheap articles. The factors require that the manufacturers should make goods at a certain low rate, and to do this it is necessary that the manufacturer should make them very much lighter, unless he chooses to lose money, which is not very likely. There are some articles which used to be made in great quantities for which there is now no demand at all, or very little—as, for instance, stewpans, strong fish-kettles, &c. A factor will seek over the whole town to find out where he can get an article a fraction of a farthing cheaper than formerly; and it sometimes happens, from want of judgment or from some other cause, that manufacturers sell articles at an absolute loss. It must be confessed, however, that this is not a common occurrence. Articles are sometimes made so light that they are quite unfit for use; and instances have been known where large quantities of such goods have been purchased and afterwards sent back to the same or to another manufacturer to be cobbled up for use.

"The wages of the men vary from 15s. to £2 a week, according to their industry, punctuality, and ability. An ordinary workman will make about 25s. a week. Those men who earn most money generally spend it as fast as they get it, and many of those who cannot earn more than 15s. a week are more respectable in appearance and in their general habits than those who can earn three times the money. There is, however, a considerable and palpable improvement among the younger race of workmen. Instead of paying a large sum for 'footing ale' when a workman enters an establishment, he now pays a small sum into a sick club; and the custom of borrowing money from the manufacturers for drinking and other purposes immediately upon entering, has been quite discontinued. Things are very different now from what they used to be 20 or 30 years ago.

"Work is very regular, and except occasionally at Easter or Christmas, it is never very slack.

"Work is done more quickly than formerly, and a greater quantity is made. Britannia metal goods have to some extent superseded tin plate articles in such wares as teapots. About forty years ago most large tin-plate manufactories had, at least, one shop, which was devoted to making teapots only; but since that time, one of the most extensive makers in England found so little trade that he could not give employment enough to one workman.

"The use of Britannia metal has greatly influenced the tin trade. It interferes principally with the tea and coffee pot, and with better tin goods generally, because very common articles are made in Britannia metal, by no means equal to the best tin, but which can be made cheaply and slightly, and very light, so that hot water pulls them into all sorts of shapes. The tea-pot trade was at its height about 40 years ago, and at its lowest ebb about 20 years ago. Since then it has greatly revived, so that at present there are more tin plate tea pots made than ever there were made before. They are also much cheaper. Forty years ago it was common to give 3s. 6d. for making a tea pot, and now common tea pots are made for 3d. each. Some parts of the tea pot are now made in two minutes, which used to require an hour in making upon the old system, and these parts are also better done now. Though superior articles can be made at present, there is much more trash made. Tea-caddies can be made by dozens now, in the time and for the price that they used to cost singly. The weight of the caddies was about four times what they weigh now. They resembled cabinet-work more than tin-work in their fine execution, but those made at present are mere rubbish; but, notwithstanding all this, there has not been such a surfeit of bad work as to create a demand for better articles; but I have no doubt the public will be disgusted in time.

"Great quantities of tin-plate goods are sent abroad. The Germans are behind us in the manufacture of such goods. They cannot make first-class articles to be compared with ours, though they can beat the English in making cheap and common articles. French tin-plate articles are exceedingly light and neat, but are inferior to the English goods for wear.

"The strike at Wolverhampton did not affect Birmingham at all. But all along the prices paid at Birmingham have been better than at Wolverhampton; about the same, in fact, as the men are now asking at Wolverhampton. There has been a union amongst the tin-plate workers for a very long time—certainly for more than fifty years. The men are paid according to a list of prices which has been drawn up, but the discount system has long been in operation in Birmingham, and is so at present, though not to such an extent as it was carried at Wolverhampton. It is not objected to at Birmingham, and amounts to about ten per cent."

In close connection with the manufacture of articles of tin plate is the japan trade, which was introduced into Birmingham so early as the year 1740, by the celebrated John Baskerville the printer, who made a large fortune by it, and afterwards lost it in the printing trade.

Under the general name of japan-workers are included those who work at japan-varnishing, polishing, ornamenting, and "finishing" iron and tin-plate and papier maché goods. These processes are carried on upon the same premises, but are considered to be separate trades. They are supposed to give employment to between 600 and 700 persons in Birmingham, of whom about two-thirds are women and young children. The variety of articles japanned and ornamented, both in the tin-plate and papier maché trades, is far too great to admit of specification; but as the present inquiry is more directed to the articles which have immediate reference to the manufacture of tin-plate goods, a few of the staple articles generally made and japanned by the makers of tin-plate goods may be mentioned—namely, baths of all sorts, trays in every variety, toilet services, consisting of pails, washhand basins, jugs, foot-pans, &c.; coal-scuttles, spittoons, garden watering pans, plate warmers, bronzed tea and coffee urns, dressing cases, &c. &c. Of the articles made, a great portion is for the American trade, and the demand for home consumption is large and steady.

The appearance of japanned work is almost as varied as the articles upon which it is used; sometimes it is ornamented in imitation of wood, marble, or tortoiseshell; sometimes it displays birds, fruit, or flowers, painted in gaudy colours, or a fine copper-plate engraving may be transferred upon it. In the best papier-maché work the designs painted or transferred to the japanned surface are selected with much taste, and are admirably executed. In all cases the work is elaborately varnished and polished. Nearly the whole of the work, except painting or printing the designs upon the articles manufactured, is performed by women. The process through which a japanned and ornamented tea-tray is put (and it is almost the same with all other articles) is simply as follows:—After the iron is formed into the required shape and size it is rubbed with a particular sort of stone, procured from Bilston, until it becomes smooth; it is then handed to a woman, who lays on one or two thick coats of colour mixed with varnish, and places the tray in a stove to dry; it is then varnished three or four times and again thoroughly dried, after which it is rubbed, smoothed, and polished, and prepared to be handed to the printer's room, where it is ornamented according to the design required. The design is engraved upon a copper plate, and the impression is taken by rubbing into the cavities of the engraving an oily composition which adheres in the form of the design to the paper pressed upon it. The printed paper is laid upon the tray and rubbed with flannel, so that the oily substance adheres to it. The paper is then lifted off, and gold, silver, or bronze dust plentifully scattered upon the mixture as it stands in the tray. This is rubbed with flannel, and all the details of the design are thus brought out and as accurately transferred as if the tray itself had been subjected to the ordinary process of printing from the copperplate. The colours are then made fast by varnishing and drying, after which the tray is smoothed by rubbing it with rotten-stone, and finally polished with the naked hand. All the painting, varnishing, and polishing is done by females, and as in giving the last polish to superior tin-plate and Britannia metal wares, so also in japanned work, a soft female hand is necessary to communicate that exquisite polish which we find on these articles when new and exposed for sale. It is stated that the females employed in polishing the best goods never engage in the rougher household duties—such as scouring the floor, or even handling the broom, lest their hands should lose the soft touch which is necessary to give the last beautiful polish to those articles of manufacture. In the japanning and ornamenting of very common trays, or articles of toilet service, upon which the ornaments are large, gaudy, or of various colours and hues, the process is different from the above. The ornaments are simply then painted upon the japanned work, in the old-fashioned and ordinary style of painting; the designs are made according to the taste of the person engaged upon them, or from some popular pattern, which may not perhaps have changed for the last half century.

For the most part those engaged in japanning and its various branches of polishing, ornamenting, and finishing, are paid according to the amount of work they do, and in some instances the women are allowed to take in assistants in the same manner as is commonly done by men with regard to boys. Where a woman has a girl working under her, she is represented to earn about 15s. or £1 a week; or single-handed, about 12s. a week. The men receive on an average about £1 5s. a week single-handed. The following statement was made by a workman in an establishment, not confined to japanning, but including the general manufacture of articles of tin-plate, in which more than 300 persons are employed:—"The only union among the men here, is for the maintenance of a sick club; each man pays 4d. a week into the club, and when unable to attend work because of illness, he is entitled to 10s. a week. When any member of a workman's family is ill, a modified sum is allowed to defray expenses. Whatever surplus remains at the end of the year is divided equally among the men. Although there are more women than men employed in this part of the establishment there is no sick or relief fund amongst them. I do not know why, but it is unusual in Birmingham for women to establish clubs of this sort among themselves. One reason may be that as all the girls make a little money, they are married very young. Most of the women here are married."

It will have been observed from the statements of the manufacturers of tin-plate articles that the Britannia metal trade is, to some extent, a rival. The staple articles of production in the Britannia metal trade are tea and coffee pots and spoons, which latter are made in Birmingham in very large numbers. This metal is known also by the names of "Prince's metal" and "white metal," but most commonly it is called "Britannia metal." The ingredients from which it is compounded are the best block-tin, antimony, copper, and brass—the proportions of each varying according to the purpose to which it is to be applied. The compound is poured into casting irons, so as to give it when cold the form of a slab, fifteen inches long by six inches wide, and one inch in thickness.

The principal seat of the manufacture of this metal is in Sheffield, where it was commenced upon a large scale by two individuals named Jessop and Hancock, about the year 1770. At Birmingham there are about 300 men, women, and young persons of both sexes employed, and the number is annually increasing. Since its first introduction into Birmingham, the trade has undergone a variety of changes, the principal of which was the introduction of a process technically termed spinning, by which the lathe was brought into requisition, and the amount of work performed in a given time greatly increased. To this work steam has been applied in most of the larger manufactories. A spindle is made rapidly to revolve in a horizontal position, and a wooden chuck is fixed upon it, or a model of so much of the article to be formed as will allow the metal to slip off the wood after it has been closed upon it. A piece of sheet metal is cut of the required size, which is fixed upon the revolving chuck, and gradually pressed by the workman till it is bent over to the required shape, without either crumpling or laceration. In this manner the upper and lower parts of the body of a circular teapot are made. The lid and the bottom are generally stamped; the spouts and handles are cast, and the whole of the pieces are then soldered together, and sent to be burnished and cleaned. As stated above, the principal articles manufactured in Britannia metal are tea and coffee pots and spoons; but, besides these, there are made all kinds of measures for liquids, candlesticks, dinner services, decanter and bottle-holders, ink-stands and bottles, &c., and a great variety of smaller articles which were formerly made in silver or in German silver.

The following statement respecting the history of the trade in Birmingham was derived from a gentleman who had been engaged in the trade at Sheffield, and who came to Birmingham more than 45 years ago:—

"About 40 years ago there was only one manufactory of Britannia metal here, and the number of persons of all sorts employed in it at that time was only about fifty. Gradually the number increased to about 65 pairs of hands, and other manufacturers entered the trade, though very few of those now engaged in it have served their apprenticeship to Britannia metal working. The work about 40 years ago was almost entirely carried on by stamping from dies, and as the expense of dies was very considerable, it was long before small manufacturers had acquired sufficient influence upon the trade to affect either the manufacturer's prices or the rate of the workman's wages. By the process of spinning the metal upon the lathe, a workman was enabled to do considerably more work in the course of the day than he could have done upon the old principle; but I should not estimate the increase of work made in a week by one workman at 50 per cent.; the principal advantage is, that the expense of dies is saved, and a greater variety of patterns can be obtained at very little additional cost. The natural effect of the general adoption of the principle of 'spinning' was to reduce prices, and it further tended to facilitate the production of cheap and inferior articles. Although these find a ready market, they are generally unfit for use, and derive their apparent weight and solidity from the use of lead and plaster of Paris, and not from genuine metal. The largest number of teapots that I ever produced in a week, at the time when stamping was in use, was 84 dozen; but to do this I had nearly thirty pairs of hands employed. At present a good workman will make and put together about a dozen average teapots in one day. The expense of starting business is not so great now as it used to be before spinning was introduced, and the number of 'small men' has greatly increased.

"All the work is not done by spinning, but in some cases it is stamped as formerly; for such work the small men generally apply to others who work 'out,' and when they cannot afford to have a lathe, and the necessary apparatus for spinning, they also employ outworkers for this part of the business, and only put the parts together themselves. These 'little men,' having no capital, have injured the Britannia metal trade; but as they only make the commonest articles, they have scarcely affected the price of really good articles. A teapot, for instance, of the best kind, costs as much now as it did 40 years ago. For some work, such as finishing the goods, the rate of wages is as high as ever it was; and, in general, the men, though they receive less for each article they make, by readier processes in the work can make such an additional number of articles as yield them about the same amount of money in the course of a week as they earned previously."

Upon the subject of the cheap inferior articles, to the manufacture of which several persons, and particularly those possessing little or no capital, have resorted, the following testimony was given by another person in the trade; and was afterwards confirmed by others:—

"Within the last few years a great many little men have come into the field, and have brought down prices as well as filled the market with trash. Some of these men make teapots of so inferior a kind that they are quite unfit for use; but in order that they may appear to be of good, substantial material, and of sufficient weight and strength to procure purchasers, they put a false bottom to the article, and fill the intermediate space with heavy clay or plaster of Paris. If one of these teapots be filled with hot water, and carried across the room, the weight of the bottom pulls it to pieces at once, or draws it out of all shape. The new way of making tin teapots has tended to check the manufacture of these trashy Britannia-metal pots, because they can be made much cheaper and better in tin, notwithstanding the use of clay and other 'dodges' to make Britannia wares cheap. A cheap tin article is infinitely better than a cheap article of Britannia metal; but for good and durable manufactures, or for the best sort of work, nothing is better than Britannia metal."

The number of persons employed in the trade is from 200 to 300, about 100 of whom are men. The men have long been formed into a union. The following statement was derived from one of the members, and appears to be correct in the details of figures and dates:—

"There are about 90 or 100 men and boys in the trade in Birmingham, of whom about 40 men are members of the union. The union is strictly allied to that of the Britannia metal-workers in Sheffield, which has more than 200 members. The Birmingham branch of this union has been in existence for about twenty years. Before that time two attempts at union had been made here; but in both cases dishonesty among those who had charge of the cash led to its discontinuance. We do not consider those engaged in making Britannia metal spoons as connected with our trade, except as working in the same metal. They have no connection with our union, and all our interests are separate and distinct. There have been several partial disagreements between the masters and workmen in Birmingham, but there has never been a general strike of the trade here. Long after the trade had acquired a footing in Birmingham the men continued to be paid by the 'piece,' but the system of paying men by the day gradually spread among the manufacturers, although piece-work is still the most general. About three years and a half ago it was considered advisable by the union to return to the system of paying by piece-work, and arrangements were accordingly entered into to effect this object. A list of the prices paid at Sheffield was procured, and, with very little modification, was adopted by the Birmingham union and by several of the principal manufacturers; but it has been broken by some of these manufacturers, and was never adopted by others. By these prices the workmen are at present enabled to make about the same weekly sum that they earned twenty years ago, due allowance being made for recent facilities in the process of making which have been introduced. One of the rules of the union is that no apprentices shall be admitted by the men, except they be sons of journeymen already employed. The number of these is thought to be sufficient to supply the demand for extra hands, but at times when the demand is unusually great the men may allow the master to take in boys who are not sons of journeymen. On such an occasion, some years ago, in Birmingham, the union allowed each master to take in one boy. This law of the union has been productive of unpleasantness in several instances in Sheffield; and about eight years ago a misunderstanding also arose upon the subject between one of the oldest manufacturers in Birmingham and his workmen, which led to a strike in his establishment of all the men employed. This manufacturer, however, did not concede the point, but at once engaged the services of other men and boys, whom he instructed in the trade, and thus held out against the workmen, who were thrown back upon their union for support until they found employment elsewhere. Another law of the union is that in times of difficulty and scarcity of trade its members should work short time rather than that any one should be thrown out of employment, and in 1848 this was carried out so inflexibly, that many of the men only received one-half as much money as they earn at present, or when trade is brisk. By such trials as these we are bound together by sympathy and good-will. There is no rule of the union which forbids a master to employ other workmen than members of the union, but in an establishment where unionists are employed they do not and will not associate with any others except members of their own body, which is pretty much the same as forbidding them to work in that establishment. For the most part I should say that the best work is got up at those manufactories where members of the union are employed, for they will not make the common trash which is got up at some of the 'scab houses,' or small manufactories, but prefer to make good and durable articles, as these pay the labour better than others."

LABOUR AND THE POOR.

——◆——

BIRMINGHAM.

[FROM OUR SPECIAL CORRESPONDENT.]

DIE-SINKERS, MEDALLISTS, COINERS, &C.

LETTER XVII.

The arts of die-sinking, medalling, and coining must give employment, directly and indirectly, to many hundreds of persons in this town; but it is difficult to form an exact estimate of the number. In the department of die-sinking, the Directory gives the names of 77 master manufacturers, of whom 17 are die and press tool makers, 49 die-sinkers, and 11 die-stock and screw-plate makers. This art, though carried on extensively at Sheffield, London, and elsewhere, has its principal seat at Birmingham. Dies for plated goods are made at Sheffield in greater quantities than in any other town in England; but it appears no other dies are sunk there. The dies produced in London are principally for jewellers and seal makers, though other sorts are also made. At Birmingham die-sinking is divided into three distinct branches, namely, the "heavy department," or that for brassfounders' goods, chandeliers, cornices, cornice ends, curtain bands and pins, lamp pillars and stands, coffin furniture, &c.; the "light department," or that for coins, medals, buttons, seals, labels, fancy goods, &c., and the department for plated goods, such as dishes, and covers, &c.; of these, the two first are by far the most extensively carried on, and particularly the second, in which the Directory enumerates about thirty masters, many of whom have commenced business but very recently.

Within the last twenty years this art has been greatly improved in all its branches, in consequence of the greater demand that has arisen for fancy articles of domestic use and adornment. "Previous to that time," said a manufacturer, "it mattered very little what the design was for brass goods so that the article answered its purpose; but there is now a constant craving for novelty, and manufacturers are obliged to send out new designs with their travellers at least twice a year. This fact, together with the improvements made in stamping, have had the effect of producing a superior style of die-sinking, and designs are now daily executed in steel which some years ago would have been pronounced impossible. This has been particularly the case in dies for cornices, lamps, and general brass work. The die-sinkers generally admit that they feel themselves deficient in the art of design, and inferior in it to the French; but as regards execution in cutting steel for heavy dies, their belief is, that the English workmen have a decided superiority. This does not apply to medals and light articles. They maintain, however, that the French goods do not show so much distinctness and *crispness* in the execution as the English. This is sometimes attributed to the longer practice which English workmen have had in heavy steel cutting, although some are of opinion that the prevalence of stamping from cast-iron dies among the French is the real cause of their inferiority. The die-sinkers themselves invent the greater part of their designs, but they are frequently indebted, and particularly of late years, to chance designers for their models. Modellers hawk their designs about, and a few are occasionally procured from the School of Design. Great hopes are entertained that this institution will in the course of time turn out some good artists in the service of manufactures of every kind, but as yet it is too young to have produced any appreciable effect."

Die-sinking, in its finer departments, for coins, medals, buttons, &c., has been less subject to fluctuations in demand and in prices than most trades. Greater skill has been attained in the execution of dies, but no readier methods of workmanship have been introduced. The whole is done by hand labour; but so much intelligence, steady application, attention, and delicacy of touch are required, that a good workman commands large wages. Many of those who have served an apprenticeship to the higher branches of die-sinking, are, at the expiry of their seven years, often unable to do more than the commonest work, and are frequently obliged to turn to some other trade requiring less skill and attention. For tool making they are in some measure prepared by the practice of die-sinking, and to this trade most of those who fail eventually turn their attention. On the other hand, a good die-sinker generally finds it to his advantage to commence business for himself, whenever his capabilities have been made sufficiently manifest; for it requires little capital to start with, and very few die-sinkers in Birmingham employ more than three or four journeymen. The work is so delicate, and the effect of the slightest handslip so ruinous, that the master die-sinkers prefer doing as much of the work as possible themselves, and leaving to apprentices or inferior workmen only such rough work as may be safely entrusted to their care. This will account for the fact, that while the Birmingham Directory enumerates nearly fifty master die-sinkers, there are not more than from 100 to 120 pairs of hands directly employed in the general trade. In some businesses—that of tin-plate working, for instance—many of the manufacturers sink their own dies on the premises, and the number of these is not included in the calculation. About two-thirds of the hands employed are apprentices, many of whom receive no wages for about three years, and in numerous cases a premium is paid upon entry. The manner in which they are treated depends of course upon the temper and character of the employer. In one instance it was stated that the master was so jealous lest his apprentices should learn more of the business than was strictly of service to himself, that he took every means of impeding their acquaintance with its more advanced branches, in order that they might not have the power subsequently to commence business in opposition to himself. But this is an exceptional case. The saving effected by the employment of apprentices is sufficient to account for the large number of them employed in the trade, but there is a difficulty in procuring skilful workmen, and any others are more likely to bring loss to the employer than assistance. A first-rate journeyman die-sinker may earn as much as £3 10s. a week. The average receipts are from 25s. to 30s. a week. They vary much according to the ability of the workmen. Almost without exception the men are engaged by the day, as the great variety of dies made—no two of which are the same—and the length of time required for their execution, render piece work inconvenient for all parties.

The reductions which have taken place in the wages of the men within twenty years have been small as compared with those made in other trades, and these reductions have been only in the commonest work. Such articles as are required in great quantities have been considerably reduced in price, but the more elaborate work fetches as good a price as ever. Dies for livery buttons may be taken as an example of the reductions which have been made in prices. The work is neither very good nor very bad, and the demand is extensive and regular. Within twenty years these dies used to cost £1 1s. and they are now sold for 15s. Such reductions as have been made in the prices of articles have been chiefly owing to competition among the die-sinkers, and to the low prices offered by the manufacturers requiring the dies.

One of the most interesting of the trades of Birmingham in connection with die-sinking is that of the manufacture of coffin ornaments and furniture. These ornaments are either of iron, tin plate, or brass. Birmingham contains nine master manufacturers of these articles, who supply nearly the whole of the United Kingdom; the only other factories being one in Bristol and one in Dublin.

This trade has undergone little change in its character since the days of Boulton and Watt, who carried it on to a large extent at the Soho works, and were the first to change the mode of manufacturing the ornaments from punching the brass to stamping it by means of a die. This simplified the process, and reduced the prices to about 1-5th of what they had previously been. Within the last few years the perfection to which die-sinking has been carried, has enabled the manufacturers to apply a great deal more taste to the articles produced than was ever before practised, and the Registration Act has tended to increase the attempts made at beauty and originality by giving the power at a small outlay of preserving the designs unpirated. The designs are principally supplied by the die-sinkers, and by chance designers, who carry their drawings about for sale.

The nine manufacturers of ornaments for coffins, in Birmingham, employ from 200 to 230 persons, principally women and boys. The proportion of men is only about one-fourth. Their work is rather heavy, as the stamping of the coffin plates requires the application of great strength. In one of the principal establishments in the town there is a screw-press of forty ton pressure, for the larger and handsomer coffin-plates, which requires the united efforts of two men to turn. The work of the females is principally confined to lackering and varnishing. The outlay for material and die-sinking constitutes the principal expense. A good workman will earn from 25s. to 30s. a week; the girls and women earn from 6s. to 10s., and the boys or youths, from 11 to 18 or 19 years of age, earn variously from 2s. to 20s., according to their strength and ability. The men are principally engaged as day workers. The trade is liable to very little fluctuation, as the consumption is regular, except during the prevalence of any violent epidemic. The cholera of 1848 kept the trade exceedingly busy, besides enabling the manufacturers to dispose of their old stock. The following particulars of the trade, communicated by an eminent manufacturer, may prove interesting, as showing the changes of fashion, even in death, which the competition among the undertakers and the dealers in these articles of lugubrious finery causes from time to time. They also detail some national and local peculiarities in the matter of burial ornaments, showing that there is a style in the house of the dead, as well as in that of the living, which requires to be humoured by the enterprising manufacturer who desires to make a fortune or a reputation by his business.

"We use in this establishment," said he, "about forty tons per annum of cast iron for coffin handles alone, independently of other materials. There is a constant demand for handles of a new pattern. Our travellers find it quite useless to show themselves with their pattern-books at an undertaker's unless they have something tasteful, new, and uncommon to produce, to tempt the buyers. There is the same demand for new patterns in coffin plates and furniture as there is in handles. The undertakers, I suppose, like to turn out their jobs handsomely; for I question greatly whether this constant demand for novelty comes from the relatives of the dead. They either are, or affect to be, too much afflicted to look after such matters themselves. They give their order in general terms, and the undertaker, like any other tradesman anxious for the reputation of his craft, exerts all his ingenuity to do the thing as well, or better, than any other person in his business. It is noticed here that the orders for Ireland are chiefly for gilt furniture for coffins. The Scotch also are fond of gilt, and so are the people in the west of England. But the taste of the English is decidedly for plain black. There is a constant demand from Wales for a mixture of black and white. The weight of metal used upon coffins varies in different places, and depends to some extent upon the wealth and rank of the deceased. The average weight may be from 3½ to 4 lbs.; but sometimes the coffin handles alone weigh as much as 6 lbs. In London more metal is used upon coffins than in Birmingham, and it forms a considerable portion of our trade to supply the metropolitan undertakers with black, white, and brass nails. From 1,500 to 2,000 ornamental nails are often used in London upon one coffin; and I have known as many as 3,000 employed. The average is at least 1,000 nails—weighing perhaps about 4½ lbs. In Birmingham, and generally throughout England, such nails are seldom used; but coffin lace, both black and white, is employed instead. This 'lace' is formed of very light stamped metal, and is made of almost as many patterns as the ribbons of Coventry. All our designs are registered, as there is a constant piracy going on, which it is necessary to check.

Handles, plate, and lace are all registered; and I have often paid as much as £20 to a modeller for a design for a plate, perhaps some new combination of angels, weeping willows, and heads of cherubim. Women and children are very useful in the ornamental part of the work. Girls of fifteen or sixteen are the most useful workpeople we have; they do far more work than full-grown women, and do it better. Their fingers are more supple and nimble, and I think they are more tasteful than women in what they do. Their work is chiefly the lackering and blackening of portions of the pattern, which are mostly of a dull and of a bright black intermingled. The lightest complete set of coffin furniture for infants does not weigh above eight ounces, and the heaviest about 9 pounds. Pauper coffins contain about 10 ounces of metal only, while the average weight for middle class funerals is above 3½ lbs. The annual number of deaths in the United Kingdom exceeds, I believe, 400,000, and taking the average weight of metal upon their coffins at 3½ lbs., it would follow that 1,400,000 lbs. or 625 tons of good iron, tin plate, and brass are annually buried with the British people. We have no foreign trade whatever for these articles, but we supply India, Australia, Canada, and the other colonies."

An important branch of the business of die-sinking is that for medals. A remarkable increase in the number of medallists has taken place within a few years at Birmingham. One of the most eminent of their number stated that there were only five or six medallists in Birmingham about five years ago, and that he can now count as many as nineteen, a large proportion of whom had commenced business within the last twelve months. A coronation, or the laying the foundation stone of a great public building, usually creates quite a stir in the trade. Victories, such as Trafalgar and Waterloo, formerly provided work, but the trade at present depends more upon Wesleyan and Temperance medals, and medals for presentation for prizes, for agricultural shows, schools, clubs, &c.

Mr. Paxton's Crystal Palace, and the extraordinary and growing popularity of the Exhibition, have also called the ingenuity of the die-sinkers and medallists into requisition; and one enterprising firm has turned out some hundreds of thousands of cheap medals within the last few weeks, containing a very accurate representation of the building, and a suitable inscription. The popularity of Jenny Lind also gave the die-sinkers and medallists employment, and some hundreds of thousands of a light brass medal, with the head of Jenny on one side, and a laurel wreath on the other, have been distributed in every part of the civilized world where she has made her appearance. There is not only a home, but a foreign demand for Birmingham goods of this class. Several medals lately produced have been eminently successful on the Continent, particularly one in imitation of Ary Scheffer's well-known painting of "Christus Consolator," and another commemorative of the death of Schiller. Two beautiful medals were lately issued by the same firm to supply an order from a French house—one of the President of the Republic, and the other of General Cavaignac. The sale in France was very great; and the medal of Louis Napoleon is represented to have pleased the President so well, that he ordered a considerable number of them for distribution among his friends.

One of the most celebrated portions of the famous Soho Works was its mint, whence immense numbers of medals, or nearly the whole of the copper coinage of the kingdom, were formerly issued. As an establishment for coins the Soho Works were not much employed during the present century, but beautiful medals continued to be issued by the successors of Messrs. Boulton and Watt till the year 1830, or even later. This establishment, after having lain for many years in a partially neglected state, was finally broken up in the spring of 1850, and every portion of the once multifarious business of this firm was discontinued, except that of the manufacture of steam-engines, which was removed to Smethwick, near Birmingham, where it is now carried on by the representatives of Messrs. Boulton and Watt. A few extracts from the catalogue of the second day's sale at the Soho Works, which took place on the 30th of April, 1850, will show the description of articles upon which, at the end of the last and the beginning of the present century, the die-sinkers of Birmingham were employed, and in which many hundreds of men found constant occupation. The proprietors of the Soho Works not only undertook coining for the British, but for foreign Governments; and the firms in Birmingham which devote themselves to this business at the present time imitate their example, as will appear hereafter. Among the lots sold on the day specified were medals, beautifully executed, representing "The Assassination of the King of Sweden," "The Restoration of the King of Naples," "The Final Interview of Louis XVI. with his Family," "The Execution of the King of France," "The Slave-trade Abolished," "The Union with Ireland," "The Marquess Cornwallis," "The Battle of Trafalgar," "The Emperor Alexander," "General Suwarrow," "The Battle of Seringapatam," "The Birth of the Dauphin of France," "The Restoration of George III. to Health,"

"Queen Charlotte," "The Battle of the Nile," "The Peace of 1802," "Lafayette," "Jean Jacques Rousseau," "The Death of George III.," "The Death of Matthew Boulton," "The Visit of the Duchess of Kent and the Princess Victoria to the Soho Works, in 1830," and several others. The dies of those medals—many of the earliest of which were executed by the celebrated Küchler—obtained high prices. Besides the dies and specimens of the medals, the dies for British, foreign, and colonial coins, and early proofs, were also put up for sale, and included farthings, pence, and halfpence for the British Government, forty-two different coins for the French Convention, and copper money for Buenos Ayres and the East Indies, with tokens innumerable.

There is at present no regular trade in coining, and no body of men dependent upon it entirely for subsistence. "For a whole year," said a gentleman who combines the business of medallist with several other trades, "there may be nothing whatever done in coining, and then perhaps comes an order for a few tons of copper coins from India, or some of the tropical islands. None of the coining for the English Government is now done here. All coins made for foreign countries must be legalised by the Government, either in London or by their agent in Birmingham."

During the year 1850 a good deal of copper coin, for Bombay, was made in the town. Mr. Ralph Heaton, who purchased many of the Soho dies and presses, made no less than ten tons of what is called "cock money," an Indian coin, bearing a cock upon the obverse; and a second order for a similar quantity was received by another manufacturer. These coins are very small and light, from 230 to 260 of them constituting a pound weight; so that the twenty tons comprised nearly 10,500,000 coins. Pence and copper coins are also made for the West Indian Islands.

"About five months ago," said a manufacturer, "the Pope required estimates from Birmingham for making 2,000 tons of copper coins, of which the largest should be about three times the size of an English penny, and the smallest rather larger than a farthing; but it does not appear that any of the estimates have yet been accepted. Inquiries were also made about two months ago respecting some Chinese money which it was intended to make in this country; but no definite proposals seem to have been made, and nothing further has been heard of the matter."

A few of the old workmen employed by Messrs. Boulton and Watt, in the days when the Soho Works were in full activity and renowned throughout Europe, are still in existence. The following statement was made by one of them:—"Coining was first commenced at the Soho Works in 1787. They had then eight cutting out presses and eight coining presses, by which about 60 pence, 70 halfpence, or about 80 pieces of Indian coin, called 'cock money,' could be produced in a minute. Great quantities of Indian coins were made. Some are still made at Birmingham, but the Soho Company fitted up a mint for Calcutta, by which a large portion of the manufacture was transferred to India. This mint consisted of 19 cutting presses and 13 coining presses. The money made was principally copper, and generally very thin and small. The number of persons employed in this department of the Soho Works was not great. There were about 14 or 15 women engaged in 'cutting out' the copper; 2 men in attending to the machinery; 16 boys and 2 men in the coining; 7 or 8 women in 'lapping up' the coins; 4 or 5 women in milling; 2 men in turning the machines; and 6 men in annealing and shaking—in all 12 or 13 men, about 27 women, and 16 boys. The presses used at the Soho Works were exactly the same as those used at the Royal Mint at London, and just as effective. There was always a risk attending an overworking of the presses, so that no more than 60 pence a minute could be produced with safety. About 24 tons of pence a week were the usual quantity produced when the presses were in full operation, which was in the beginning of the present century, for about twelve months at a time. The coins were examined and weighed by agents from London. James Watt did not trouble himself much in the business, except with the engineering department. The dies for the coins were sunk principally by Messrs. Küchler, Droz, and Wyon, the inventor of the present Royal Mint die-sinker. Mr. Watt was very busy generally at the manufactory, and he came very regularly. Mr. Boulton used to take a great interest in the manufactory, and in those engaged in it. He had a series of rules drawn up for keeping the boys in order, and he supplied each of them regularly with duck trowsers and blue jackets, and all their dress, so that they were exceedingly tidy. The trowsers were changed and washed twice a week. They had all slippers to put on at the Mint. He gave the men and boys an allowance of beer every day at five o'clock. The Mint was kept in perfect order, and every kind of care was taken of the health and morals of the people."

"Birmingham," said another aged and intelligent mechanic, the same, whose account of the shoe buckle, and all the changes of fashion which it underwent, was detailed in a previous letter, "had a bad character for false money, when I was a young man. There were many coiners of false copper, silver, and gold money. Wolverhampton was, perhaps, still worse than Birmingham; but Bilston was the worst place of all, and actually swarmed with coiners of bad money. Almost any kind of rubbish used to pass as copper money, fifty or sixty years ago, button tops, tokens, or any round bit of metal. And all this made the trade of the false coiner more easy. The trade was carried on so openly, that I often wondered at people's hardihood, considering the severity of the punishment on detection. They imitated the old copper halfpence of George II., and fried them in brimstone to give them an antique appearance. If anybody was detected in imitating the gold or silver coinage, it was called a 'spiritual' business, because it touched his life; but if it were for copper money only, it was called 'temporal,' because he was in no danger of the gallows for that. Those were the slang expressions of the town. Executions for coining were very frequent in the neighbourhood. I have known as many as three and four people strung up together at one time for that offence. The makers of false copper money used to be burnt in the hand and imprisoned, and I believe they were sometimes transported. A great deal of what was called 'workhouse money' used also to be coined in Birmingham. There were workhouse pence, sixpences, and shillings; or they might be called 'tokens,' or 'promises to pay,' for those amounts. The coiners forged these as well as the coin of the realm. The large manufactories in all parts of the country used to issue tokens to pay their workmen with, most of which were made in Birmingham, Bilston, and Wolverhampton, and the forgers would not even let these alone. A good deal of coining of false silver money is still carried on hereabouts, I have no doubt. It is a much easier business than it was, and can be done with less risk of detection than formerly. I worked at Boulton and Watt's, and, though not in the coining department, knew a good deal of what went on there. Mr. Boulton coined many hundreds of tons of copper money for the British Government, and silver money also. I remember once that the firm had a large order to melt down some tons of Spanish dollars and re-coin them into English five-shilling pieces. It was during the Spanish war, when the British cruisers used to lie in wait twice a year to capture the galleons bearing the tribute from Mexico to Spain. The dollars came to the Soho Works in waggon-loads, and a guard of soldiers was regularly stationed at the Mint for the whole time during which the order was in progress. Mr. Matthew Boulton was a great friend of the sober and clever workman in every department of his business. He always rewarded merit, and would 'buy any man's brains.' The next Mr. Boulton did not push the business as his father did; his fortune was made; he had more money than he could spend, and was seldom or never seen about the place."

The establishment of the Royal Mint on Tower-hill, by which the Soho establishment lost a valuable portion of its trade—the constant changes in the fashion of other articles produced—the total cessation of the demand for others which formerly employed hundreds of men, such as the shoe-buckle and the latchet, added no doubt to the circumstance that the proprietors had made their fortunes, and were less careful than they might otherwise have been to extend their trade into new channels when the old ones ran dry—all conspired to deprive the "Soho" of its ancient renown in miscellaneous goods, and to confine the business to the one great department of engine-making, for which, in its new locality at Smethwick, it still preserves all its reputation. The final breaking up of the Soho establishment in the spring of 1850, consequent upon the death, in June, 1848, of James Watt, Esq., of Aston Hall, the son of the illustrious man to whom we owe the improvement of the steam-engine, scarcely received any notice at the time from the metropolitan press. For this reason the following account of a visit paid to it during the progress of the sale may not be uninteresting to the readers of these letters, especially as it serves to complete the history of a once important and still interesting branch of the manufactures of Birmingham:—"James Watt and Matthew Boulton," says the writer, a gentleman to whom I have been indebted for much information connected with the brass trade in all its principal departments, "were benefactors not to their country alone, but to the world. While of the one, in the language of the most erratic statesman of the day, it can be said that in very truth he did 'enlarge the resources of this country, increase the power of man, rise to an eminent place among the illustrious followers of science, and the real benefactors of the world;' of the other it could be said with equal justice that he infused into the ornamental metal manufactures of his locality a better spirit, that he discovered and rewarded merit wherever it was to be found, and that not a few of the most celebrated art workmen of this and time past owe their fame and existence to the fostering care and generous discrimination of Matthew Boulton.

"It was not without regret that I visited the Soho Manufactory on one of the days prior to the sale, and pacing along its extensive courtyards, noticed the grass-grown surface, the dilapidation and decay fast stretching their fingers over this, at one time, busy and bustling hive of industry, the focus from whence emanated so much of what at one period was deemed excellent in manufactures. Silence prevailed throughout the buildings, once thronged with so many hundreds of workmen of various kinds, the halls echoing no more the multifarious sounds arising from blows given by lusty and brawny arms dealt right willingly on stubborn metals. I was aware that some years ago the greater, or rather the entire, portion of the plated ware trade in connection with the Works had been dispersed by public sale, still I did not know that so much of the establishment was dismantled and tenantless, while the external marks of decay, as already remarked, were observable enough. The internal traces of the same destroying agent were equally discernible; water trickled down the walls, there were plasterless ceilings, patched windows, empty cupboards, extinguished smithy hearths, rusty iron implements, spindles which had not been turned for years, and which would have shrieked for very pain had you made the attempt; wooden models of long since executed and forgotten engines and machines lay about, abandoned to the efflorescence of mould and the ravages of the worm. To add to the whole, here and there an old grey-haired servitor, who had known the establishment in its days of pride, might be detected pointing out to an inquiring visitor some explanation of the peculiarities of a piece of mechanism furbished up for show and sale. One of the most celebrated portions of the manufactory in its days of active operation was its Mint, and the skilful mechanical appliances which the ingenuity of its proprietors had united for the facilitation of the speed in producing and perfecting the 'pennies' issued therefrom. The total disposal of this portion by public sale afforded an opportunity of learning, by inspection, what these were, and wherein their merit consisted. It is not too much to say that, if automic and almost semi-intelligent labour and regularity denotes in machinery the existence of mechanical skill, here then was it shown to perfection. It would be unfair and impossible to contrast its external form and finish with the elegant machine work, spick-and-span new, fresh from the lathes and planing instruments of Manchester and Patricroft; but here unquestionably might be detected the embryo excellence which has now evolved into maturity and full fruition, and led to the acknowledged and really substantial character of English mechanism. It is this consideration which lends to earlier efforts so much of what is interesting and valuable. In connection with the Mint, it will readily be supposed that the operation of die-sinking would be carried on simultaneously, and one of the departments was devoted to the display of the matrices or dies from which the medals or coins were produced. Prominent among these the collection distinguished by the name of the Works might be observed. These consisted of mementoes referring to events which took place when 'George the Third was King,' when every other day brought the news of a battle and a victory, and when the scaffolds of France were red with aristocratic blood. Yet there was not awanting memorials of a gentler and more pleasing kind, recording the abolition of the slave-trade—the proclamation of peace—the visit of Victoria and the Duchess of Kent to the Soho Mint in 1830.

"In connection with the coining operations, I examined the rolling mills employed in the reduction of the metal used in the manufacture of the blanks from which the coin is made. This portion was in a sadly dilapidated condition, the surface of the rolls being deeply marked by the progress of oxydation. Following out the order of production, the cutting-out presses warranted a critical examination, and the means by which motion was given to the screw carrying the punch was exceedingly clear. Equally so the very ingenious mechanical appliances by which the self-feeding coining press brought forward the blank to receive the impress, and the ingenious operation by which it was passed out after the blow was given. The means employed to mill the edge of the piece, in the manner of our gold and silver pieces, were also shown; the rate of production being somewhat about sixty per minute. Motion was communicated to the whole by water-power, the water being forced up by means of a steam-engine.

"Of the tools in use in connection with the Mint, though excellent in their day, they contained but little of which we do not see better in any ordinary engineering establishment. The same might be said of the steam-engines, were it not that they are useful in marking the progressive advance of this wonder-working machine into the perfection of the present day."

LABOUR AND THE POOR.

—◆—

BIRMINGHAM.

[FROM OUR SPECIAL CORRESPONDENT.]

GILDERS, PLATERS, AND ELECTRO-PLATERS.

LETTER XVIII.

Birmingham was once the most celebrated town in England, if not in the world, for the production of gilt toys and mock jewellery. These departments of trade appear to have given employment, at one time, to almost as many persons as buttons do at present; but the over-hastiness of manufacturers to grow rich, and the keen competition to which they were driven by supposed necessity on the one hand, and by real cupidity on the other, soon deteriorated the manufacture. The markets of the world became glutted with inferior articles. Gilt toys were made, of which the gilding tarnished after a few days' exposure to the weather—a "Brummagem" article became a word of contempt— the fashion for gilt toys went the way of all fashions, and manufac-turers turned their attention to newer branches of industry. Perhaps, among the various slop articles that have been produced in this town, and the inferiority of which has tended to affix a stigma upon its repu-tation from which it is but slowly recovering at the present time, none have been productive of more mischief than the trashy articles of gilt and silver plate, especially the former, which it lavished upon the mar-kets. Small manufacturers produced these goods in almost incredible quantities for a long series of years, till disgusted purchasers could tolerate them no more. A guinea, an iron pot, a little fuel, and a gar-ret, were all the stock-in-trade required. With these the maker of "Brummagem" ware was set up in business; and his guinea, beaten out into gilding, covered trinkets representing a hundred times the original value of the gold employed upon them.

The manufacture of gilt toys is now, and has long been, in a de-clining state; but it still finds work for 200 or 300 people, inclusive of many small masters, who work in their own houses, and employ the labour of their wives and children. The trade is very much divided.

One man devotes his whole time and attention to buckles, another to ear-rings, a third to clasps and snaps, a fourth to chains, a fifth to brooches, a sixth to bracelets, and so on, through the long list of articles that come properly under the designation of gilt toys.

The following particulars of the trade were communicated by a gentleman who served his apprenticeship to the manufacture, and who at present holds an important position in one of the oldest firms in Birmingham:—

"Few of the Birmingham fancy trades have undergone greater changes within the last twenty or thirty years than that of gilt toys. About the year 1815, from all I can learn or remember, there were from 800 to 1,000 persons engaged in the trade, and now I should think that there are not more than 250 or 300 persons employed in it. The principal reason for this diminution is perhaps that fashion has ceased to recognise many articles, such as comb ornaments, clasps for ladies' bags or purses, &c., which were formerly in great demand, and has also, to a great extent, limited the demand for many other articles, the manufacture of which used to employ a considerable number of hands. Other toys, of which we now make little, are still in request, but are more generally plated with gold, and not gilded as they used to be. Inferior plated toys can be made even cheaper than gilt toys, but the quantity of gold put upon them is so small as to be almost inappreciable, and upon many of the so-called gold-plated toys I have no hesitation in saying that there is not a particle of gold. They are merely polished brass. It is astonishing how eager the dealers are to procure cheap goods, and how little attention they pay to their quality. They seem to think that any trash is good enough to make a profit by. Lowness of price and appearance are the only considerations, and manufacturers are consequently obliged to deteriorate more and more the quality of the articles they make in order to come within the dealers' prices. The natural consequence of this unwholesome craving for cheap articles is that the public at last become disgusted with the trash that is palmed off upon them, and cease to purchase. I have every reason to believe that the gilt toy trade has been reduced to its present low state in consequence of the bad quality of these cheap articles; and it is no wonder that fashion changes when producers take such pains to frighten it away.

"In accounting for the decline of the gilt toy trade I should state, however, that the number of ornaments now made from ivory, silver, and other materials, has aided very considerably in promoting its fall.

When purchasers, after repeated trials, discover that they have been imposed upon by sham articles, they naturally try something else; and steel, silver, iron, and other materials come in for a share of their patronage. The trade has also suffered very much from the importation of toys from France. They are admitted into this country at a very low duty, and are sold here at a cheaper rate than they can be produced at in Birmingham. The duty imposed by the French Government upon the importation of English gilt toys amounts to a prohibition. We look upon this as a great hardship, as in the manufacture of many articles we could successfully compete with the French in their own markets, as they do with us in England in others. Still, I make no complaints of free trade. It is the only principle; and, sooner or later, I have no doubt that France will imitate the example of England in this respect, and then, if we cannot compete with the French, we shall give up the struggle, and turn our attention to some other branch of manufacture. Another reason why this trade has declined—and it is as strong, perhaps, as any I have given—is the want of education of a suitable kind amongst the workmen. A knowledge of drawing and design is invaluable in gilt toy making. I am every day reminded of its importance by the inferiority of our English workmen, and I think it would be well for employers to require these qualifications of every boy whom they take into the trade. With proper attention to drawing and design, in which the French so infinitely excel us, I think that a little spirit and energy among the manufacturers would enable us—considering the immense facilities for working complicated and minute articles which we possess, especially since the invention of electro-gilding—to raise the gilt toy trade to a position of much greater importance in Birmingham than it now holds. A first step has been taken by the recent establishment of the Government School of Design; and I anticipate that in future years, all the manufactures of this town will derive advantage from it. The gilt toy makers here appear to me to be as prudent, enterprising, and intelligent as other manufacturers, but they cannot of themselves bring the trade back to its former flourishing condition, considering the mischief which has been done by the glut of trash. I remember, when I was an apprentice, the agent in London of the firm which I served used to meet the Birmingham coach a short distance from town, in order that he might receive a few hours earlier the articles which were sent up from the manufactory. The demand was very steady and quiet whilst it lasted, and there was no fear of accumulating too much stock.

Occasionally we had a bad year, as in 1817 or 1825, but they were few and far between, till the cheap mania set in with great virulence, and reduced it to that state of ruin in which it now is."

The following statement was made by a manufacturer who has had long practical experience of the trade:—"The manufacture of gilt toys has been declining in Birmingham for many years. About 25 or 30 years ago, when I was an apprentice, there were about six large manufactories of gilt toys in the town, and now there is not one of any great importance. In this establishment very little business is now done compared with what was done in former years. One reason for the decline of the trade has been the introduction of the art of plating goods with gold, by which the use of gilt has been in a great measure superseded. Plated goods resemble gold much more than those which are gilt. Another reason is that many of the articles upon which the gilt toy trade formerly depended have now ceased to be fashionable. I would instance ear-rings and necklaces in particular. Ear-rings are scarcely worn at present, and where we sold thousands at one time, we do not now sell dozens. A considerable part of the trade has also gone to France, whence large quantities of gilt toys are annually imported. The French can make the commoner articles at a much cheaper rate, and of a more elegant design than we can; but in the manufacture of good ordinary toys, the English have a decided superiority. In England we do not employ our best hands, who might compete with the French, on gilt toys, but set them to the superior branches of gold and silver jewellery. The French, on the contrary, employ the newest and most beautiful patterns for mock as well as for real jewellery, and their cleverest hands find work in both trades. But, notwithstanding all this, there have been such decided improvements within the last few years in the gilt toy trade of Birmingham, that for the future I do not think we need fear competition with France. Even at the present time, if it were not for the heavy duty, I have no doubt but that we could export large quantities of goods into France itself. Our style would be novel on the Continent, as theirs is in this country; and if we had similar privileges in France to those which the French enjoy in this country, we should be able to do a large trade there. We are much indebted to the French for improvements in our designs. We are obliged to copy French patterns because we have none of our own; but when we do so, we can not only make the articles as well as the French, but considerably cheaper. The French are constantly inventing something new and taking to the eye, and we cannot keep pace with them in this respect. It is their peculiar genius, I suppose, and besides, their modellers and designers have been brought up to it. We have made some improvements in our designs within 25 years, following the French at a long interval. But we have been obliged to do so to preserve ourselves from being utterly beaten out of the field. The public have not purchased gilt toys so readily as they used to do, and we have been compelled to coax them, by bringing out new, pretty, and enticing articles very cheaply. Yet, notwithstanding all our improvements and all our inventions, the trade has fallen off immensely. Most of the old houses have passed away. At present there are not a third of the persons in Birmingham who are in any way, even indirectly, employed in this trade, compared with what there used to be. Of these a considerable number are women and young persons; but the proportion of female labour has of late diminished in consequence of the increased amount of skilled labour required. Stamped or pressed work finds less favour among the public now; it is, of course, cheaper and commoner than the work wrought by hand labour. More work is now exacted from the workman for the money which he formerly received, and, indeed, there are many articles for making which the workman was paid 2s. 6d. some 30 years ago, for which he now receives only 8d. or 9d., and the article is better made now than it was then. In such cases readier methods of making the articles have facilitated and cheapened their production. The cheaper we can make gilt toys, the more does our trade increase; for we receive much of the trade which would otherwise go to France. We used formerly to supply the French market with gilt toys, but the last war put a stop to that trade; and since then the French have not only supplied themselves, but, as I have already remarked, compete successfully with us at home and in the American and other markets. Some thirty years ago there were several manufacturers of gilt toys in Birmingham who severally gave employment to upwards of 100 workpeople; but I am not aware of any maker who employs a quarter of that number at present."

"In the number of persons employed in the trade," said another manufacturer, "there has been a large diminution within thirty or forty years. When I was an apprentice, which is about thirty-five years ago, there were about 2,000 men, women, and young persons employed; and at present I should not think that there are more than 150 persons directly engaged in the legitimate gilt-toy trade in Birmingham. The number of gilders, stampers, piercers, finishers, and every one connected with the trade in my youth, could scarcely have been less than 4,000 persons of all ages. The number of gilt toy makers began to diminish seriously about twenty years ago, and the number of men employed in it fell off rapidly; they were glad to get anything to do, and I knew several who became bailiffs and lamplighters; others were able to turn to other trades more or less connected with that in which they had been previously engaged. The average rate of wages among the men now employed is from £1 to £1 10s. a week. I have one man in my employ, who, if he had constant work, might, by working overtime, make £3 a week without much difficulty. Others make only 12s. or 13s. a week."

In addition to these statements, it may be mentioned that the trade is immensely sub-divided. A small toy, as, for instance, a bracelet, has to go through the hands of a dozen different artificers before it is fit for use. Nearly all the glass and pebble ornaments come from Germany. The cameos are all procured from France, but a duty of 10 per cent. is put upon them; so that the English manufacturers cannot make the articles so cheaply as they otherwise might.

Most of the old gilt-toy makers are stated to have turned their attention to jewellery, but those who still carry on the business are occupied in mounting brooches, buckles, bouquet-holders, &c., and these articles are all either electro gilded or plated.

Before describing the extent to which the new and beautiful adaptation of electricity to the plating and gilding of metals has been carried at Birmingham, and the influence of the discovery upon the domestic and ornamental arts of this country, it will be necessary to state a few particulars of the old plating trade. This manufacture, though extensively carried on at Birmingham, is not peculiar to that town, as Sheffield, long before the discovery of electro-plating, was celebrated in every part of the civilized world for the perfection to which the art had been carried by its manufacturers, and the extent of the business which they transacted. In Birmingham, at the present time, the trade gives employment to from 300 to 400 persons. Of these about two-thirds are women and young persons of both sexes. The advantages of electro-plating are, however, so apparent in all articles requiring beauty of design or much elaborate or complicated workmanship, that there are very few, if any, makers of plated goods in Birmingham, who do not partially make use of the new process.

The articles which are most usually plated according to the old manner are trays, tea or coffee services, urns, dish-covers, candlesticks, snuffers and snuffer-trays, candelabra, bottle-stands, liqueur frames, wine-coolers, cigar-holders, &c.; in all of which, it will be observed, there is little complicated work, or work usually ornamented with much deep carving or engraving. These articles are mostly, if not entirely, plated upon copper.

Having procured the plated metal, which is rolled to the size, strength, and thickness required, the maker proceeds, as for instance in the formation of a large tray, to cut it into the proper shape. If the copper basis be plated on both sides, the material is worked as if it were all of one metal; but many articles are tinned on one side and plated with silver on the other. As in this case the plate cannot be dipped into a pot of liquid tin, in the usual manner of tinning plates, a portion of tin in a liquid state is rubbed over the bottom of the plate. The tinned side of the plate is then laboriously beaten upon a steel anvil, by which means it is planished, and the pores of the metal are closed. When the silver side of the tray is polished in this manner, the hammer used is covered with thin layers of tin, German silver, and cloth, as an ordinary hammer is considered too hard for the purpose. The edge of the tray is formed by hammering it round a bar of steel, and the whole is polished by beating it with a hammer either upon one or upon both sides. To polish both sides at once the plate is put upon a steel anvil and beaten with a hammer, on the face of which are fixed a piece of bright, hardened steel, some common brown paper, and a strip of black cloth. The ornaments which we see chased and cut upon trays, urns, and other plated goods, are executed with great care and skill, although the designs are frequently of a very incongruous character. The small quantity of silver which is generally put upon the solid foundation of copper obliges the engraver to work with great attention and care, as, by a single slip of the hand, or by too heavy a blow, the baser metal may be revealed. Those engaged in this work are consequently better paid than the ordinary hands, and some of the more dexterous among them earn from £2 to £3 a week. The chasing is for the most part done by means of small punches, of innumerable shapes and sizes, adapted to every variety of pattern which may be ordered, or suggested by the artistic ingenuity of the workman. The last operation in the making of a tray, or of almost any article of plated silver, is that of burnishing it. This is wholly done by women, who use polishing-stones for the purpose, and moisten the plate now and then by the application of soap suds.

The following statements regarding the trade were made by a manufacturer of plated goods, who, till within a few years, had himself worked as a journeyman in a manufactory in Birmingham:—

"The trade was very much affected by electro-plating, the invention of Mr. Elkington, which was the means of throwing it open to parties who had little or no previous connection with the silver-plating trade; as, for instance, brass fitters, spoon makers, Britannia-metal manufacturers, knife and fork makers, &c., all of whom, by means of the electro process, can have their goods plated with as much ease as any other articles. The trade was wonderfully increased by this invention, which, like every other real discovery, has done good to the trade in the long run. No doubt it affected injuriously at first those who had been long in the trade, but I go on in the old way as long as it will repay the trouble, and if I can get no orders for it, then I go into the new way, like my neighbours. I now make use of the electro depositing principle, though, a few years ago, I scarcely used it in any case. So far as I can judge, there are about 300 men in the old trade, exclusive of women and children, and of electro-platers; but the various kinds of plating are now so mixed up one with another that I cannot speak with certainty as to the number of those employed in each. There was once a society, or union, among the men, but I believe it was utterly broken up about five years ago, and it has never been revived. The object of the union was to secure a list of prices which should be adhered to throughout the trade; but this object was not attained, and the union never prospered. While it was in existence, the men in one establishment struck against some new regulations which were about to be introduced, and a good many of the workmen held out, and began business for themselves rather than submit. There are a great many small men, or garret-masters in the trade, though it requires some £50 or £60 to start in a good way. This has of course increased the competition—brought down the prices of good articles very much, and has been the means of causing vast quantities of light, unsubstantial articles to be made. Good articles are successfully imitated immediately upon their production, and sold for half the legitimate price. The wages of the workmen have been very much reduced within the last twenty or thirty years. At present they receive on an average from £1 to £1 5s. a week, whilst, when I was an apprentice, about twenty-five years ago, men of ordinary ability might earn from £3 to £4 a week. The wages of the women employed average from 9s. to 12s. a week."

In corroboration of this statement regarding the flimsy and unsubstantial character of some of the slop-work now perpetrated in Birm-

ingham, may be cited the instance of a pair of small plated candlesticks, recently manufactured. On putting the complete candlesticks
into the scales it was found that their weight was 24 oz. On taking
them to pieces, as those who know the secrets of the trade can easily
do, it was found that the base of the candlesticks was composed of clay
and other heavy material, covered with a thin and wafer-like coating
of metal; and on weighing the metal without this clay and rubbish,
which had been stuffed in to make the articles appear massive, it was
found that it amounted only to 2 oz.! The roguery sometimes carried
on in this trade is perhaps one reason why many workmen showed
themselves so averse from communicating any information either as
regarded their wages, the union which formerly existed among them,
or the "slop" system still prevalent. In one establishment of some pretension the men refused point-blank to speak of themselves or of their
trade in any relation whatever. The views of a manufacturer, who was
himself a practical workman, and who plates goods both after the old
mode and the new, may, however, serve to illustrate the opinions of
the respectable portion of the trade:—

"I believe there are about 1,000 pairs of hands employed in the
silver-plating trade, but only about one-third of these work according to the old system of plating. Of the whole number, about two-
thirds are women and young persons of both sexes. I do not think that
there has been any increase in the number of persons employed since
Mr. Elkington's invention has been in operation; but more work can
now be done by the same number of persons in a given time than was
possible twenty years ago. The proportion of women has increased,
because now a man can keep a greater number of women fully employed. As to the quality of the work made at present, I think there
has been an improvement even in the bad work. Good articles are
better both in style and quality than they were formerly, and there
have been great improvements made in the elementary parts of the
trade. Ten years ago we did not know how to plate German silver
goods, and we can now do so by the old mode as well as by electro
plating. The designs used are very superior to those which were commonly used even ten years ago, and they are daily being improved. I
have had a few from our Government School of Design here. I do
not know what may be said by others in the trade, but my best articles are made for the North American market. The Americans used
to cry out for nothing but the very commonest articles which could be
made, but I suppose they have had a surfeit of trash, and have turned

to good articles. At present we send better goods to the United States than we make for this country. Few, if any, articles are made so badly as they were a few years ago, which is, perhaps, partly owing to this change of opinion in America, for they used to take very bad articles. At present the weekly receipts of my workmen average from £1 5s. to £2, whilst twenty years ago workmen in this trade rarely received £1 1s. a week. I do not know how to account for this, except by the fact that good workmen are scarce. The same may be said of the women employed, who receive considerably more than they did twenty years ago. It is true that both men and women do more for what they get than formerly, and the women have not only additional but harder work now in consequence of the introduction of electro plating; for although the silver may be deposited as equally as by the old method, yet it is much rougher, and consequently more difficult to burnish. The silver deposited by the electro process upon such plain work as dish-covers is so rough that we are often obliged to hammer it. Indeed, when it is possible, we always hammer these goods before sending them to be burnished. This is not the case with rolled metal. More silver is used, I think, in plating goods by the electro depositing principle, and certainly the goods require more subsequent dressing than when made from rolled metal. This invention has greatly tended to increase the demand for plated goods."

The discrepancies between the above statements of two manufacturers, both of whom are practically acquainted with all the details of the business may, perhaps, be reconciled by supposing that each has devoted his attention to a particular class of articles—the former to cheap and unsubstantial goods, and the latter to articles more expensive and durable.

The introduction of the electro process, which may well rank among the most useful and beautiful inventions of our age and country, has already effected a revolution in the plating trade, and brought within the reach of persons of moderate fortune articles of a style and excellence formerly only attainable by the most wealthy. To the Messrs. Elkington belongs the credit of making electricity available to the arts of manufacture in gold and silver. They were not the originators of the idea, but they were the first to bring it into practical operation. In the year 1840, amid discouragement and opposition of every kind—amid prophecies of failure—and amid the enmity (open or disguised) of most of those engaged in the old plating trade, they began to manufacture by the new process.

Manufacturers and vendors were alike opposed to the change. All sorts of objections were started, and the silversmiths positively refused, in many instances, to take the articles into their shops, even to retail them at a profit. But these and innumerable other difficulties were ultimately powerless to obstruct the progress of the art. The wonderful nature of the agency by which the result was effected excited curiosity; but when it was seen that the operation was so simple and so unerring—that the most elaborate articles could be plated with as much perfection as a common sheet of metal—and that for beauty and elegance electro-plated goods were fully equal to articles chased in solid silver or gold, a demand for them began to arise. As early as 1841 the business had assumed considerable importance, and in the year 1842 the Messrs. Elkington found constant employment for as many as 300 people. The manufacture has since gone on increasing; and the patentees now employ upwards of 500 hands; they are extending their works, and the manufacturers in Birmingham and Sheffield, licensed by them to use their patent, amount to upwards of thirty, of whom those resident in Birmingham are supposed to employ from 300 to 400 persons, in addition to those on their own premises. The principal advantages of the electro-plated goods are that they are manufactured in the same manner as silver, the ornamental parts being chased in solid metal, and that, where joints are necessary, none but hard solder is used; that the base is composed of a purified white nickel metal, of great durability, and of the same colour as the exterior; that the union of the surface and base is perfect, forming one body; that the plating on the more prominent parts is, from the nature of the process, stronger than on those parts less exposed to wear; that every description of style, however elaborate, and whether embossed or engraved, can be plated with the same facility as a plain surface; that with moderate care these goods will last from ten to twenty years, and that they can be replated when injured or worn (which, under the old processes, could not be done), at a comparatively trifling expense.

A few words will explain the process by which these results are effected. The articles, or parts of articles, having been wrought up with as much care as if they were of solid gold or silver, and having undergone from first to last all the processes from the moulding to the chasing and putting together, are brought to the plating department. Here a powerful electric battery is raised. In front of it are ranged several tanks or troughs filled with a dark-looking fluid, of the colour of strong tea. The fluid is a solution of silver formed by dissolving an oxide or salt of silver in cyanide of potassium. The articles desired to be coated are attached to a wire in connexion with the positive or zinc plate of the electrical apparatus, and immersed into the solution—a plate of silver, in connexion with the negative or copper plate of the apparatus, forming the opposite pole, which plate is dissolved and transferred to the article by the current of electricity passing between them. The length of time required for the operation depends upon the body of silver desired, and also upon the proportional amount of silver in the solution. The arrangement is the same in all electrotype processes.

The solutions of gold are also formed by the same agent as the solutions of silver, and the arrangement is in all respects the same; but, in consequence of a less proportion of gold being usually required, the operation is completed in much less time; for whereas the silver requires from five to ten hours to complete a strong plating, the gilding requires a period only of from one to five minutes, and the articles become perfectly coated after being immersed even for a few seconds. The scientific visitor to the works may look with admiration, but the non-scientific visitor will mingle wonder with the admiration which he bestows upon the process. If he handle the electric-wire, it is as if he handled an ordinary piece of copper. If he use the end of it as a pen, and write upon a sheet of iron, he will see brilliant sparks of electric fire following every letter that he forms; and if he immerse the end of the wire in the solution, it will begin to froth and boil as if the metal were red hot. If the article to be plated or gilded remain in the solution of silver or gold without being attached to the wire, the solution is powerless; but attach the wire, and the fine spirit of electricity begins to do its bidding, and to convert the fluid into a solid crust upon the object submitted to it. This art is yet in its infancy, and the full extent of the powers of electricity to administer to the pleasure and the service of mankind are, perhaps, as yet unimagined even by the most enthusiastic of dreamers and inventors, or by the most hopeful of the philosophers who set no limits to the future progress of science.

The show-rooms of Messrs. Elkington and Mason contain specimens not only of electro-plated articles, such as *epergnes*, candlesticks, candelabra, vases, and countless other objects of domestic use and adornment of modern and of antique art, but of new adaptations of the electro-process to the service of the sciences. They exhibit beautiful specimens of the vegetation or growth of copper by electrical agency; of iron coated with zinc or copper; of flowers and shrubs, with all their delicate anatomy and tracery, coated with metal, and thereby rendered imperishable; and of birds and insects coated and preserved by the same wonderful but simple means. Leaves and flowers of gold and silver are thus manufactured, nature being made to form the basis of art in a manner hitherto unknown. Flowers and shrubs, insects, and other natural objects which it is wished to preserve, are coated with zinc, copper, silver, or gold. Where the coating is of the less valuable metals, it may be painted of the colour of nature; and the specimens by this means may be preserved for centuries. So delicate is the operation of the electric current that even a spider's web may be plated with gold or silver.

The workmen employed in this beautiful manufacture are, as might be expected, of a superior class. It was remarked by an intelligent manufacturer in another branch of trade, that he always found men who worked by mere manual labour, and with ordinary tools, inferior to those who made use of steam power. The complicated machinery, and the regularity of steam power tended, he thought, to make the men regular as well as intelligent. The electro process seems to have exercised a similar, if not a higher, influence upon the character of the workpeople. From an examination of the time-book of Messrs. Elkington, it appears that out of the 500 persons in their employ, not two, on the average, were absent on any Monday, or on any part of a Monday, during the year—a fact very remarkable in Birmingham, where the working classes make it a constant practice to neglect their work on that day, and where it is a common complaint among employers, especially when trade is brisk, that men sacrifice not only the Monday, but too often a portion of the Tuesday, to drinking and idleness. Ten years ago the platers are represented as having been "a rough set," but those employed in the superior branches necessary for the finer beauty of the electro process, bear the highest character, not only for regularity and sobriety, but for their provident economy. Great numbers of them save money. They have no union of the trade, but they have founded a sick and burial club, and have it in contemplation, in conjunction with their employers, to establish a school for their children and for the boys engaged in the manufacture, and a library and reading room for themselves. It is to be hoped that no circumstances will arise to prevent the realisation of a design in every respect so praiseworthy.

LABOUR AND THE POOR.

———◆———

BIRMINGHAM.

[FROM OUR SPECIAL CORRESPONDENT.]

INDUSTRIAL AND RAGGED SCHOOLS.

LETTER XIX.

The great and constant demand for the labour of young children in Birmingham—where it is of frequent occurrence to send them to the button, screw, lock, and toy factories at so early an age as seven years—renders the educational question one of peculiar interest. Although manufactures absorb so many thousands of them, and prevent them from obtaining much, if any, education, except Sunday-school teaching, in which writing, arithmetic, and geography are not included, there is a class of children, even in this busy town, whose parents cannot, or will not, find employment for them, whom they are unable to send to school, and who consequently prowl about the streets, picking up for themselves an education in vice and crime, if in nothing else. As in most of our large towns, the attention of the humane and benevolent, and of the friends of education, has been strongly directed to this class; and several Ragged Schools have been established for their benefit. The word "Ragged" is not, however, in much favour, either among the promoters of the schools, or among the parents of the children; and out of four such establishments, which is the whole number in the town, only two preserve the obnoxious designation. The most important of these schools is called the Free Industrial School, and owes its existence to the indefatigable exertions of the Hon. and Rev. Grantham M. Yorke, the rector of St. Philip's. Early in the year 1846 a minute investigation of the condition of the poor of this parish was instituted by Mr. Yorke. In this inquiry it became apparent that "by far the larger proportion of the inhabitants of the district belonged to a class either too poor to pay for their children at the National Schools, or too ignorant to value the benefit of instruction for their children, or too selfish and careless about the matter to make any sacrifice to procure it for them. Multitudes of ragged, dirty, and disorderly children swarmed in the streets and courts, while the parish schools exhibited a comparatively meagre attendance. Although considerable improvements were effected in the organization, teaching, and discipline of those schools, yet they failed to attract scholars from amongst those 'melancholy multitudes,' the children of the 'dangerous classes.' In this state of things it was determined to open a room for the reception of ragged children, free of charge." After a time it was found necessary to engage larger premises, where the attendance amounted very soon to about 200 children of both sexes. A large proportion of the "ragged scholars" were weak and unhealthy, through the want of sufficient food, and it was found that in consequence their mental efforts were feeble, and their attention languid and painful. It was determined, therefore, as far as means would allow, to supply them with food; and accordingly a dinner of soup and bread, or of rice and milk, with a piece of bread, was supplied to the whole school three times a week. The system adopted for the education and training of the children was based upon that of the Industrial School at Aberdeen, and of the Ragged School in Pye-street, Westminster. Two industrial classes for boys were formed, in 1847— one under a tailor, and the other under a shoemaker, and about thirty pupils were distributed between them. A class was also formed, about the same time, of the elder girls, in which plain needlework and knitting were taught. The reasons for setting the children to this kind of work were stated by the promoters of the school to be the actual condition of the children to be employed. "They were found clothed, or but half-clothed, in miserable rags; many of them without shoes and stockings; most of them filthy in their persons and habits; growing up, therefore, not merely in want of the decencies of life, but in an almost brutal disregard of them, without self-respect, without industry; too often taught and trained to depend upon the shifts of cunning and dishonesty for a livelihood, and to become, in process of time, plunderers by profession, the worst pests of society, and an equal expense to the public, whether pilfering them at large, or maintained at their cost within the walls of a prison, or in the penal colony, the ultimate destination of many. Such being the condition and the prospects of the class of boys especially assembled in such schools, the main object of their industrial training, at the first, seemed to be not so much to teach them a trade by which to gain a living as to employ them beneficially to themselves and their ragged companions; making their hands useful in ministering to their own necessities, and turning their own ingenuity and quickness and manual skill to account, in causing their rags to disappear, and in improving their own outward appearance and substantial comfort, so as to create a new feeling of self-respect, and a new desire for those advantages which were placed, for the first time, within the apparent reach of their own industry."

The school, affording such solid and intelligible inducements for the attendance of neglected and half-famished children as food and warmth, soon began to increase; the rooms hired from time to time were found to be too small and otherwise inconvenient, and it became, therefore, the desire of those chiefly interested in the experiment to obtain funds sufficient to erect, or to alter and arrange, a building suitable to the full working out of the system contemplated. In September, 1847, the first meeting for the consideration of a permanent plan took place, at which the amount of funds announced as previously collected for the purpose of erecting an Industrial School Building was £472. In April, 1848, the fund had increased to £763, and the chairman of the committee announced that the governors of King Edward's School, "viewing with favour the project of an industrial school to educate the children of very poor parents free of charge, and considering it in some sense an extension of their own system (which the terms of their own charter and acts of Parliament precluded them from making directly), had agreed to a grant of land as a site for a school building and play grounds for the Free Industrial School in Gem-street."

In consequence of the increasing importance of the school, and the widening prospects before it, it was next resolved that the chairman should put himself in communication with the Secretary of the Committee of the Council on Education, for the purpose of obtaining a grant of money for building. The Government gave a favourable reply to the first application; and the committee proceeded to obtain plans and estimates. These being approved of by the Privy Council, their lordships voted a grant of £495 towards the erection of "school-rooms, work-shops, laundry, wash-house, kitchen, and master's house." The grant was reported to the committee in 1848, but it was not until 1849 that the building was commenced. On the 12th of April, of that year, the inscription-stone over the principal entrance was publicly laid by Mr. M. D. Hill, the Recorder of Birmingham, whose public position in the town, and his lifelong efforts in the cause of education, pointed him out as the most fitting person to inaugurate the institution. The building was completed sufficiently to admit of the school assembling in it at the commencement of 1850. In the mean time, ample funds for the purpose had been supplied by means of a bazaar held in the Town-hall, in the summer of the preceding year; and on the 14th of March, 1850, the first meeting of the General Managing Committee of the school met to receive a report of the original building committee, signifying the completion of the work in every department.

Such is a slight sketch of the origin and history of the Industrial School. It is now in full operation, and consists of three departments. 1. A day school for boys and girls above seven years of age. 2. Industrial classes for both sexes, with the same limitation as to age. 3. An asylum for deserted and orphan children.

1. The first includes all the children attending the school; the sexes being taught in separate rooms under a schoolmaster and schoolmistress. Reading, writing, and arithmetic, together with biblical instruction, and (unless in any particular case prohibited by the parents) the Church Catechism, form the staple of the instruction given in the day school. The outlines of geography and English history occasionally form an additional subject of instruction to the first class of boys. Singing also forms a variety in the school instruction. In this department of the school no food is given.

2. The Industrial department is at present limited to 50, viz., 30 boys and 20 girls, which number is always kept up by promoting day scholars to the vacancies made by children leaving this department of the school. The fifty working children attend their industrial classes from two to five in the afternoon. These children remain for ten hours a day in the school, and receive two meals, viz., dinner at half-past twelve, and supper at five. The insufficient amount of subscriptions and donations at present precludes the possibility of feeding a larger number of children. The boys' employments, as already stated, are tailoring and shoemaking. The larger portion of the clothing and shoes they make are sold at nominal prices to themselves, and they have been always encouraged to put in from time to time a penny or a halfpenny into a clothing fund, by which means they accumulate in a longer or shorter time, as the case may be, enough to purchase a jacket or pair of trowsers or shoes, or under-clothing made by the girls; and when the subscriber is a working boy, subscribing for his own work, he obtains the article at a lower price, in consideration of his labour.

In a letter from the master of the school, addressed to the Rev. Mr. Yorke, it is stated:—

"I have read at different times reports in which the children of Ragged Schools are represented as joining in open rebellion against their teachers, where swearing was their common talk, even in school, and confessed robbery their daily practice and delight. I am unable, thank God, to furnish anything of this kind. With due consideration for the ignorance and wretchedness in which the children have been generally brought up, I have always found them as obedient and as sensible to kindness as children even of a better state. They always appear to me as one happy family whilst together, delighted to sit, sing, pray, read, eat, work, and play with each other; and I believe few are the cases where the child does not know, from his own feelings, when he does evil as well as when he does well. One general effect this school has had most certainly—that of bringing up the children in habits of industry and cleanliness."

It appears from the published report of the committee, that very little of the work of the children has been sold out of the school during the last twelvemonth; the fact being, though not so stated in the report, that the slop tailors of London and Liverpool can supply the Birmingham cheap clothes shops with better articles at a much lower price than the Industrial School—employing unskilled, and consequently inexperienced, labour—can be expected to do. There is at present a considerable stock on hand, which can only be sold at a loss; and the managers of the school—aware of the uselessness of competing with the regular slop trade, and aware also, it would appear, of the very questionable benefit, either to the boys themselves or to society, of teaching them trades which are already so enormously overstocked with hands as only to afford the starvation wages of nine or ten shillings a week for twelve or fifteen hours' labour per day— have determined to discontinue the tailoring work, except at stated intervals, when the boys will be taught to mend their own clothes. The work to be substituted is that of basket-making; but this is rather to teach the children habits of industry than to turn their labour to commercial account. The minutes of the Committee of Council for the year 1846 held out an expectation that annual gratuities would be given to work-masters in proportion to the number of skilled working lads they could produce. A communication, however, was recently made to the committee by the Inspector of Schools, to the effect "that the Committee of Council were, on reflection, disinclined to give encouragement to classes in which any sort of industrial labour but that employed in the cultivation of the soil was taught." In a district such as that around Birmingham, swarming with manufactories of every kind, and intersected by railways and canals, land is seldom for sale, and when it is, it fetches too high a price to be within the reach of a charitable institution so young and so utterly unendowed as this is. But it is obvious that until work can be found for the children which shall be remunerative, the principles on which the school is founded will not have a fair trial, and that the only kind of labour not objectionable is that recommended by the Educational Committee of the Privy Council. There seems, however, but little present prospect that any land will be obtained for the purpose.

The Industrial School is located in a very handsome building, in the Elizabethan style, and is a great ornament to the town. Whether the benevolent intentions of its founders and supporters—however great the amount of good they are instrumental in performing, and however great the amount of evil they may prevent—are of much value in an educational point of view, will appear hereafter. I shall present the subject in a more complete form if, before entering upon this question, I describe the other Ragged Schools which have been established for the same class of children. The Free Industrial School differs from every other in Birmingham. It is the only one at which food is given, and also the only one at which work of any kind is taught to the male scholars. Another peculiar feature in connection with it is the "Asylum," intended to accommodate fifteen or twenty boys, and the same number of girls, of the deserted or orphan class. "The committee are anxious that the public should understand that any such children will be received, if otherwise qualified, upon the payment in advance of £8 per annum, for which sum the committee undertake to lodge, board, clothe, and educate them from the age of seven to fifteen years inclusive. It is hoped that benevolent persons feeling an interest in any particular child will willingly pay this small sum, and thus provide a fund for the support of the general establishment. Any child residing within a radius of two miles of the parish church of St. Philip's is eligible for admission to this department."

The income of the school may be estimated at present as follows:—

From annual subscriptions	£135	0	0
Collections	100	0	0
Endowments promised, but not yet received	60	0	0
Sale of clothes, &c.	30	0	0
	£325	0	0

The expenses are at present about £30 per month. It will be seen from the above that the income is inadequate at present, but there is no debt, and the managers hope by renewed exertions to increase their subscription list, and to obtain collections to make up the deficiency.

The next "Ragged School," situated in Windmill-street, is mainly, if not entirely, supported by the benevolence of one individual—Mr. William Chance, a magistrate of the town, and a partner in the plate, sheet, and crown glass works, at Spon-lane, near Smethwick, so celebrated at the present time for the manufacture of the glass for the Industrial Palace in Hyde Park. Poverty is the only qualification for admission to this school. No food is given, and no work is taught, except sewing to the girls. There are about two hundred scholars.

Another Ragged School, in a different part of the town, was founded some time ago by the same kind-hearted gentleman. It is situated in Legge-street, but its character has lately been entirely changed. So great an objection was felt to the name Ragged School on the part of many very poor but very respectable parents, that they would not allow their children to attend it. Under the circumstances, it was determined to try the experiment whether, by abolishing the unpopular name, and demanding at the same time a small money payment from each child, the amount of attendance might not be increased. The result, so far as is yet known, has justified the change. At the end of the year 1850, up to which time it was strictly a Ragged School, at which gratuitous instruction but no food was given, the average attendance was about 135 scholars. The school opened on the 4th of January on a new system. It was designated simply "The Legge-street Day School," and a school fee of 1d. a week was demanded. In five weeks afterwards the average attendance had risen to 150. Most of the old scholars remained, and brought their weekly pence, and many parents who had preferred to keep their children at home or allow them to run idle about the streets, rather than let them attend a "Ragged School," have regularly sent them since that period, and regularly paid the fee demanded.

The third school was established by the rector of St. Martin's parish, and is still called by the old name. It is situated in Well-lane, and is divided into two branches—one for infants under six, and the other for children above that age. Poverty and residence in the parish are the sole qualifications for admission. No food is given, and no work is taught to the boys. The average attendance of boys between the ages of 6 and 14 is about 146. The average attendance at the infant school is 130.

The last is "the Little Anne-street Ragged School," established in the year 1846, with an average attendance of 100 children.

The master of Mr. Chance's Ragged School said, in answer to inquiries as to the average amount of schooling which a child received: "The attendance is extremely irregular. The parents keep their children away for the most frivolous occasions, and do not seem to prize the advantages offered to them. They are all little boys here—the eldest is not above eleven. Trade has been very good during the last twelve months, and I have not been able to keep the children sufficiently long to do much good. Boys and girls of seven and eight years of age are often taken away to go to work after they have had a week's or a month's instruction—which is next to useless to them. Reading, writing, arithmetic, geography, and easy lessons on the History of England are taught; and if then children attended long enough they might receive the rudiments of a good education. They go to work for a few months, and when they are thrown out of work for any cause they often return to the school, but they generally forget in the interval all that they have learned. I find them very well-disposed children. Some of them are the children of tramps and vagrants passing through the town, who come for a week or two and then disappear, and we never afterwards hear of them. Others are the children of hawkers and pedlars, who come occasionally to the district. Their attendance is too irregular and too short to be of any value. Others are the children of widows and poor people in the town, who are too glad to get a shilling or eighteenpence a week out of their labour, to keep them at school for a day after they can get employment of any kind."

On desiring to question some of these children, and to ascertain whether they were of the class of children for whose benefit in other large towns it has been deemed advisable to establish Ragged Schools, a little boy, ten years of age, was called up. He was represented as a very regular attendant at the school. It will be seen from the statements he made that he was scarcely of the class for which Ragged

Schools were originally instituted. He said, "I have no work to do in the day, and I come to school. I go to work in the evening from 6 till 10. I work at a druggist's, and get two shillings a week. I can write a little. I know as far as three times three in the multiplication table. I have money in a money-box. I pay to the clothes' club. I have a suit of Sunday clothes much better than these I have on. I paid for them out of my own money."

Another boy, of 11, said: "I have worked at steel brooches. I filed them with a heavy file. The boys and big lads in the shop beat me because I was too little. They made brooches and buckles red hot, and burned me with them. I got 2s. a week. I was absent a year from school, and forgot all I learned. The master of the shop sent me away because the boys hit me and I used to cry. I then worked at carpentering, and got 1s. 6d. a week, and 3d. pocket-money. I bought sweetstuff with that on Sunday. I have 4s. in my money-box. I am saving it to buy clothes."

A third boy: "I am going on 9. I worked at Florentine buttons for 1s. a week before I was 7. Mother took me away because I did not get enough money, and I went to a gilt-toy maker's to link chains, and got 2s. a week. The big boys knocked me about. They throwed me on the floor often, and punched me on the belly—hard. Mother took me away because the lads would not let me alone. I can read a little. I can't write. I shall go to work again as soon as I can get a place. I would rather be at work than at school, if the lads would not beat me."

Similar results were obtained by questioning the children of the other Ragged Schools. At the St. Martin's school, a sharp-looking child of ten years of age said—"I have worked at great lots of things. I don't know how old I was when I began. It was a good while ago. I worked at spectacles first, and got a shilling a week. I afterwards worked at brass cocks. I brushed them, and emptied the sand out. I was not strong enough to do it. I got a shilling a week for that. I was strong enough for horn buttons, and went to that; and worked a long while at it. I got a shilling a week, and a penny for myself. The men used to hit me, and master would not let me have any breakfast because I did not do the work well enough. I can read a little. I have been at school a fortnight. I shall go to work as soon as I can."

The master of this school complained of the thoughtlessness of parents who would not allow their children to have the advantage from the school which they might obtain. He alleged that, even when trade was bad, and when there was not the excuse of profitable work for the children to justify the parents in taking them from the school, they were kept at home to run errands or to nurse a baby. On washing days, at the end of the week, the attendance invariably fell off, because the mothers, being engaged over the washtub, required the elder children to take care of the younger ones. The children often stayed away for a week or a fortnight at a time. The average attendance of the children could not be above three or four months. Of the 195 children whose names were on the books, only one had been above a twelvemonth an attendant at the school, and he was a cripple and deformed, and could not get work like other children.

The master of the Legge-street Day School, in which the principle has been adopted of making the children pay for their instruction—a principle that might well be applied to the majority of the children in the other establishments—stated, as the result of his experience, that since the penny fee has been demanded, the parents do not so often take their children from the school on frivolous excuses as they used to do. They seem to think that if it be worth while to pay for schooling, it is worth while to make the children attend regularly. Out of 764 children admitted into this school in two years and two months, the average attendance of each was but four months.

The "Free Industrial School" is situated in the worst part of Birmingham—a part inhabited by low lodging house-keepers, where thieves, vagrants, and tramps resort, and where the poorest class of Irish herd together. In this district, therefore, the children exhibit more of the unhealthiness consequent upon poverty and neglect than in the other parts of the town. In the other Ragged Schools where no food is given, and where no inducement is held out to the children to attend, except that of gratuitous instruction, I did not notice any of the squalor or weakness which led the Rev. Mr. Yorke to establish the Industrial School on the principle of both feeding and instructing the children. On the contrary, the children at all these schools looked plump and hearty. Many of them were ragged enough in their attire, but there was no symptom of starvation about any of them; and it will have been seen from the statements of the little workers given above (children taken at random from the crowd) that they were not of the class for whose benefit Ragged Schools have been established in other towns. They were, for the most part, children who had been trained to work for their living, and not beggars and pilferers. The result of the experiment at the

Legge-street Day School, as far as it has yet evolved itself, seems to show that in a town like Birmingham, where children can earn even so little as a shilling a week, more scholars would be obtained, and more permanent benefit would be conferred, by making them pay a nominal sum for instruction than by receiving them gratuitously. Whether any great amount of good can ever be done in such a town, where the labour of infants is more immediately valuable to themselves and to their parents than an education which shall fit them for the proper discharge of the duties of citizenship at a later period of their lives, is a wide and important inquiry. In Birmingham the prosperity of manufactures is the educational ruin of the children of the poor. The child of the pauper, or the infant convicted of felony, has a better chance of education than the child whose parents exist just above the limit of pauperism, or than the child who works like the infants whose little histories are sketched in this letter. There is no remedy for this evil within the reach of private benevolence or exertion. The utmost that can be done by the present agencies that can be brought to bear upon it is to diminish it by such efforts as have been made by the founders of the Industrial and Ragged Schools. Such efforts may perhaps lessen the extent of a great social evil, but they do not, and cannot eradicate it.

LABOUR AND THE POOR.

BIRMINGHAM.

[FROM OUR SPECIAL CORRESPONDENT.]

AMUSEMENTS OF THE PEOPLE.

LETTER XX.

The working men of Birmingham and the manufacturing districts of Staffordshire were notorious during the first twenty-five years of the present century—and, indeed, to a much later period—for the brutality of their sports. On Saturday afternoons in the open air, during the whole of Sunday in public-house tap-rooms, and again on the Monday at their usual haunts in the outskirts of the town, dog-fights, cock-fights, bull-baitings, badger-baitings, bear-baitings, and pugilistic encounters were the favourite amusements of the operative classes, and of some portion of their employers. Much of the ancient love for these and other demoralizing exhibitions still exists among the uneducated portion of the workmen and small manufacturers; but the law has prohibited cruelty to animals, and rendered it difficult as well as dangerous for those who crave such coarse indulgences to indulge in them; and the growth of a taste for music and for reading has aided the efforts of the law, in rendering such exhibitions comparatively rare. Before describing the more rational amusements of the working classes in the present day, or noting the vast improvement which has been effected in the tastes and manners of the people, an account of the rougher sports of thirty or forty years ago—derived from the recollections of two gentlemen holding official situations in the town, and whose duties brought, and still bring them into contact with assemblages of the people, and with offenders against the laws—will no doubt be perused with interest by the public of Birmingham and its neighbourhood, as well as by that larger public who delight to trace the progress of civilization in the refinement of manners. "The popular sports in Birmingham," said one of these gentlemen, a man of much experience and of excellent memory for local facts, "were, till within about twenty-five years ago, bull-baiting,

cock-fighting, badger-baiting, and bear-baiting. These were the great
favourites of the working men. A sort of arena was fitted up for these
and other sports, which consisted of an inclosure containing about
2,500 square yards of ground. The workmen and other young men
of the town used very frequently to assemble here for playing at foot
ball, leap-frog, and other games of the sort; but cock-fighting and
more brutal amusements were more popular than healthy games. The
cock-fights often lasted for two or three days, and were attended by
thousands of people. Contests were got up between two counties,
as for instance between Warwickshire and Worcestershire, each side
being presided over by some gentleman or nobleman of the respective counties. There was a covered part of the inclosure set aside for
cock-fighting, in which a pit was dug for the cocks, and seats were
ranged round, so that the fight could be seen by all around. There
were generally two or three grand '*bouts*' in the course of a year, and
parties came from London, and greater distances, to witness the con-
test. The number of cocks brought forward on these occasions to
support the credit of the respective counties or towns in which they
were reared varied considerably, but generally, on grand occasions,
about ten pairs of cocks were pitted against each other before dinner,
and ten pairs in the afternoon, with a little badger-baiting or other
sport by way of varying the entertainment. On a smaller scale there
used to be some cock-fighting carried on almost every Monday afternoon in public-houses in and around the town, and in winter still
more frequently. The 'main,' or prize contended for, varied according to the circumstances of the principals or the number of cocks
produced. Many noblemen indulged in the sport, and made money
by it, and the workmen thoroughly understood the rules of the game,
and betted on the result of a fight according to their means, or even
beyond them, if we take the authority of the ballad of 'Wednesbury
Cocking,' an old song which is still popular among the country folks
around Birmingham, and often sung by the older workmen of the
town. Badger-baiting was almost as common as cock-fighting, and
was carried on principally in an open space of ground in Smallbrook-
street, on which a church is now being erected. A hole was dug in
the ground, in which the badger was placed. There were generally a
good many dogs ready to attack it in the hole, and one by one they
were allowed to try to dislodge the badger, the owner of each dog
paying a stipulated sum for the privilege of running his dog at the animal. Bull-baiting was a more costly, and consequently a rarer source

of amusement. One bull was often baited on three or four successive Mondays. There was generally a baiting match at the three great
'wakes,' or local fairs, held annually at Birmingham. Chapel wake
was the best for sports of all kinds, and an unusual amount of bull-
baiting, cock-fighting, badger-baiting, dancing, singing, and sight-
seeing, was there indulged in. A good wake often lasted for three or
four days, commencing on Sunday and terminating on the following
Wednesday. Monday was, however, the principal holiday, and those
who came from the country to participate in the wake generally selected that day. In almost every public-house music and dancing were
carried on in the evening, and towards noon the whole town swarmed
out in the streets to witness the sports. The Birmingham wakes are
still held. They follow each other with only an interval of about a
week. The three great wakes are those of Deritend, Bell, and Chapel,
and there are two others, namely Ashted and Edgbaston. They are all
held during the months of July and August. The difference between
'wakes' and fairs is, that the former are not attended by vendors of
wares from the country, but are wholly confined to the people of the
town, who erect stalls and tents much in the same way as country dealers do at a fair. For about twenty years the wakes have been gradually
falling off in importance, and are likely to become almost extinct in
a few years. The gipsy parties got up by the workmen of most of the
principal manufactories of the town have, I think, tended as much
as anything to diminish their importance, as the men save up their
spare cash to be spent then, rather than spend it as they used to do,
in bull-baiting and cock-fighting, or in dancing at the wakes. Both
bull-baits and cock-fights, however, are still indulged in on the sly,
by workmen of the old school; but their number is fast diminishing."

A few extracts from the popular ballad of the "Wednesbury Cocking," alluded to by this gentleman, and selected as far as decency will
admit, will show the extent of the brutality formerly prevalent, but
which is now happily passing away. The ballad was written by one
Owen Probyn, a notorious "cocker," who frequented all the wakes in
and around Birmingham:—

"At Wednesbury there was a cocking,
    A match between Newton and Scroggins;
The colliers and nailors left work,
    And all to old Spittle's went jogging.
To see this noble sport,
    Many noble men resorted,
And though they'd little money,
    Yet that they freely sported.

"There was Jeffory and Golborn from Hampton,
    And Dusty from Bilston was there;
Plummery he came from Darlaston,
    And he was as rude as a bear.
There was old Will from Walsall,
    And Smacker from Westbromich come;
Blind Robin he came from Rowley,
    And staggering he went home.
            * * * * * *

"The morning's sport being over,
    Old Spittle a dinner proclaimed,
Each man he should dine for a groat,
    If he grumbled he ought to be d——d,
For there was plenty of beef,
    But Spittle he swore by his troth,
That never a man should dine,
    Till he'd eat his noggin of broth.

"The beef it was old and tough,
    Of a bull that was baited to death,
Barney Hyde got a lump in his throat,
    That had liked to have stopp'd his breath.
The company all fell into confusion,
    At seeing poor Barney Hyde choked,
They took him in the kitchen,
    And held his head over the smoke.

"They held him so close to the fire,
    He frizzled just like a beef steak,
Then threw him down on the floor,
    Which had like to have broken his neck.
One gave him a kick on the stomach,
    Another a kick on the brow,
His wife said "throw him into the stable,
    And he will be better just now."

"Then they all returned to the pit,
    And the fighting went forward again,
Six battles were fought on each side,
    And the next was to decide the main.
For they were two famous cocks,
    As ever this country bred;
Scroggins' a duck-winged black,
    And Newton's a shift-winged red.

"The conflict was hard on both sides,
    Till brassy wing'd black was choaked,
The colliers were nationly vexed,
    And the nailors were sorely provoked;
Peter Stevens he swore a great oath,
    That Scroggins had play'd his cock foul;
Scroggins gave him a kick on the head,
    And cried, yea G— d—n thy soul.

"The company then fell in discord,
    And a bold fight ensued,
Kick, ——, and bite was the word,
    Till the Walsall men were subdued.
Ralph Moody bit off a man's nose,
    And wish'd that he could have him slain,
So they trampled both cocks to death,
    And they made a draw of the main.

"Some people may think this is strange,
　　Who Wednesbury never knew,
But those who have ever been there,
　　Won't have the least doubt but it's true;
For they are savage by nature,
　　And guilty of deeds the most shocking;
Jack Baker whack'd his own father,
　　And so ended Wednesbury cocking."

The following particulars relative to cock-fighting and bear-baiting, and the cruel and disgusting sport of bull-baiting, for which Birmingham used many years ago to be the most notorious place in England, were derived from the second of the two gentlemen already alluded to. It may be first of all mentioned, for the information of strangers to Birmingham, that one of the principal open squares of the town is still called the "Bull-ring," and that it derived its name from having been the spot where bulls were legally baited for the amusement of the populace. Hutton in his history states that one John Cooper, who had lived about two hundred and fifty years prior to the time at which he wrote, obtained three privileges from the lord of the manor of Birmingham—"that of regulating the goodness and price of beer, that he should, whenever he pleased, bait a bull in the Bull-ring, and that he should be allowed interment in the south porch of St. Martin's Church." "His memory," adds Hutton, "ought to be transmitted with honour to posterity for promoting the harmony of his neighbourhood (in the matter of beer), but he ought to have been buried on a dung-hill for punishing an innocent animal."

"The last time that a bull was baited," said my informant, "was in 1811, during the Chapel wake, which commenced upon the Sunday after St. Bartholomew's day. Upon this occasion the bull broke loose from the stake to which it was tied, and endeavouring to escape, the animal ran down a lane, which was crowded with people to see the baiting. In the rush of the people to escape from the bull, a child was crushed to death, and an old woman very seriously hurt. This precipitated the abolition of bull-baiting in Birmingham considerably before the general Act, by which this and other cruel sports were prohibited, was passed by the Legislature. The great times of bull-baiting and other sports were Easter, Whitsuntide, and during the wakes, when the workmen had holidays. Bulls were baited every Monday or Tuesday during these festivities, and sometimes the sport was indulged in

The Bull Ring & Nelson Statue

every day for a week or more at a time. At the country wakes it was quite common to have three or four bulls to bait, and on one occasion, in the year 1798, I saw no less than seven bulls placed in a row to be baited on a level piece of ground close to a church in the neighbourhood of the town. The ground was about 150 yards long by about 40 yards wide. Generally, when a bull was baited at a country wake near the town on a Monday or Tuesday, it was brought into Birmingham on the Wednesday afternoon and baited again. These were chance baitings, however. The regular matches were got up during the holidays or wakes in town; and to procure a bull it was customary for the workmen to club together a sufficient sum to purchase one. The animal was brought forward early on the Monday of the wake, and whoever had a dog paid 6d. or 1s. to let it have a fly at the bull. The proceeds went to pay for the bull, which was sold after the baiting. The dog, when let loose, flew directly at the bull, and was either tossed in the air or it succeeded in fastening itself upon him, either by the nose or ear, or some other part. If tossed, the owner immediately ran forward to catch the dog, and if uninjured it was encouraged to have another *fly* at him. Sometimes the dog seized the bull by the nose and 'pinned' him to the earth, so that the beast roared and bellowed again, and was brought down upon its knees; the people then shouted out 'Wind, wind!' that is, to let the bull have breath, and the parties rushed forward to take off the dog. This was no easy matter, and beating, pulling, the application of cold water, and other remedies were often for a long time ineffectual. The best way of loosening the dog was attended with a little danger; its owner went forward, accompanied by another person, and lifted the dog by its tail, while the other put its paw in his mouth and bit it as severely as he could. The dog, feeling the bite, let the bull go, and turned to attack its new enemy, but the moment the hold was loosened the master swung his dog round, and carried him off in triumph, while the bull breathed a little before the next encounter. The first baiting took place early in the morning, and lasted for about an hour; after breakfast the bull was again brought out, and baited for about the same time, and in the afternoon and evening the scene was repeated, so that the bull was generally baited for about four hours a day. The intervals were filled up with cock-fighting, badger-baiting, or bear-baiting. By practice some of the bulls became so conversant with baiting, that when in the fields or passing through a town, the boys had only to cry out, 'A lane! a lane!' to make them immediately assume a posture of defence and paw the ground impatient for the attack. These were well known in the neighbourhood, and I remember at least five noted 'game' bulls. They became so expert in defending themselves that even two dogs at once had no chance of success with them. I have seen such a bull toss a couple of dogs as lightly as a man might play with a couple of balls. A premium was frequently offered to the man who could produce a dog able to touch one of these game bulls. In this there was real sport, and it was much less cruel than hunting a fox with a pack of hounds, or spurring horses almost to death at a race.

"There was a large black bear called 'Old Nell,' which stood the brunt of war for several years in Birmingham. Scarcely a Monday passed by on which Old Nell was not brought into the yard in Coleshill-street, to be baited. Her mouth and nose were protected against the dogs, or rather, she was muzzled to prevent her from biting them; the dogs flew at the ears, neck, or breast of the bear, which, on the other hand, tried to grasp them within her paws and crush them to death, or blow down their throats till they were almost suffocated. During wakes or festival times Old Nell was baited for two or three successive days, and did not appear to be much the worse for it.

"Cock-fighting and badger-baiting were the most common of the by-gone sports. They were indulged in almost every day in some part of the town, and much time was spent in training cocks to fight. On Monday there were almost invariably several pairs of cocks brought into the yard usually appropriated to such sports. The workmen of the town who were fond of 'cocking' bred 'fowl' themselves, and two workmen were always ready to bring their cocks to fight for a 'main,' which was just whatever money they could spare more than was necessary to pay the owner of the yard for the use of the pit. Noblemen and gentlemen frequently fought for a 'main' with their cocks, and the amount of it varied according to the number of cocks brought forward. It was frequently forty or fifty guineas, and on a grand occasion as much as 100 guineas were staked upon the result of the fight. Considerable care was required to arrange the preliminaries to a cock-fight. The birds had to be 'trimmed,' that is, to have their wings clipped and dressed, and to have the spurs well adjusted for service; and it required an experienced hand to 'set' the birds properly on to fight, and to manage them while the combat was going on. Spurring a cock was a very important duty. The spurs were sometimes made of steel, but silver was preferred, as the blow from silver was considered to be less likely to be fatal. Both had disadvantages, however, as the steel frequently broke and the silver was liable to bend and double up, if the blow were not dexterously struck. The spurs were from two inches and a half to four inches in length. If badly put on, the cock ran a chance of choking itself with the spurs in the course of the fight. Out of fifty lovers of cock-fighting, there was scarcely one who knew how to spur a bird, or to set or handle them at a fight. A good deal of gambling used to be carried on at cock-fighting, as the issue was generally very uncertain. I have known several instances in which a cock had apparently killed or utterly subdued its antagonist, and stood crowing over it, when the vanquished one suddenly started up and struck the other such a blow as proved fatal.

"Cock-fighting decreased a good deal before the passing of Martin's bill for the prevention of cruelty to animals, but it is still carried on pretty freely within doors and in secret. About ten years ago there was a cock-fight in Birmingham, but the police interrupted it, and apprehended about 100 persons. They were all brought before the magistrates and bound over not to offend again either as spectators or principals. So long as fox-hunting, coursing, and horse-racing are allowed by law, I do not see why cock-fighting should be forbidden. It was intended by nature that cocks should fight. Look at two cocks brought up in one brood; they will not fight so long as they belong to that brood, but separate them for some time, and then bring them together, and they will fly at each other's eyes the moment they meet. Now, in hunting, it is not enough that the horse strains itself to the utmost, with a good will, but the rider must keep digging his spurs into the poor beast's side to make him go faster, till at last he falls down quite brokenhearted. But two game cocks will by themselves fight till one or the other is killed, and nature has given them 'pluck,' strength, and activity for fighting. I dare say you will not agree with me about cock-fighting, but these are my opinions. Prize-fighting among men was always rare at Birmingham, though there was plenty of unprofessional boxing at a wake or fair in the town. Mondays and Tuesdays were the favourite days in the week for settling quarrels, or for making them, and the yard in Coleshill-street always saw plenty of fighting going on. There is very little fighting now compared with what there used to be in former times.

"Badger-baiting was almost as popular and as common as cock-fighting. The badger was put into a hole dug in the ground, or into a box, and as many dogs as were brought forward were allowed, one by one, to 'have a worry' at it. The badger was a serious enemy to encounter, and frequently bit and lacerated the dogs very severely. I remember once an imprudent fellow taking a badger that had been two or three weeks dead, putting it into a box, and collecting around him several persons with dogs. One by one the dogs had a 'worry' at the dead badger, and the fellow had stuck pins and small nails in its head, so that the dogs came from the encounter torn and bleeding as if they had been bitten. The trick was, however, discovered, and the impostor soundly beaten."

A specimen of the bull-baiting songs of the Birmingham people, which are still popular, and sold in large quantities, may not prove uninteresting. A few extracts from the ballad of the "Darlaston Wake Bull-baiting" will suffice. Darlaston is a manufacturing town in the neighbourhood of Birmingham:—

" Of all the diversions in life,
    There is one among the rest,
It exceeds all others for fun,
    Was allowed to be the best.

" All those who delight in a bull,
    To see it will go many a mile,
  If you go to Darlaston Wake,
    You may see it in the highest style.

" Old Mockist a bull did provide,
    And one of a rare good sort,
  He bought him at Tipton-green,
    And there he made rare good sport.

" For they were all pleased to the heart,
    And swore at a terrible rate,
  To think they were indulged with a bull,
    To accompany Darlaston Wake.

" A lane! a lane! was then cried,
    For a dog was going to run,
  When Wats he slapt at his nose,
    And so the sport begun.

" The bull how he caper'd and jump'd,
    Old Wats to spread his fame,
  I'll swear, says Willenhall Dick,
    That this is a rare good game.

" To collar him straight he went,
    And brought him to the stake,
  They drank success to the bull,
    And so begun the wake.

" Tom Biddle he roared out amain,
    'If I may speak my mind,
  There shall but one run at a time,
    And so it will give the bull wind.'

" 'A lane,' again it was cried,
    For Foster's Smut to run,
  The bull broke her back the first put,
    And for it she made a sad moan.
          * * * * * * *

" 'A lane,' once more was cried,
    For Ball was going to run,
  He pin'd him so fast by the groin,
    Which caused them rare good fun.

" For he held him there so fast,
    Which made the bull to roar;
I'll be hamper'd, says Darlaston Tom,
    If the like we e'er see any more.
            * * * * * * *

" They ran two dogs at a time,
    Which made the colliers to loof,
There was about forty brave fellows,
    Whacking away their buff.

" The bull they lock'd in the stable,
    The matter to settle then,
And there was a straight young lad,
    That challenged every man.

" He found himself quite big with fight,
    And challenged the company round,
So Biddle the cudgels took up,
    And fought him for a crown.
            * * * * * * *

" The fight it being now over,
    And Biddle he bore the sway,
Then straight to the tavern they went,
    In mirth for to spend the day.

" The beef they knock'd in them apace,
    And liquor they drank amain,
And when they'd well stuff'd their guts,
    They had the bull out again."

The following particulars, referring to a period which the younger race of mechanics remember, were communicated by an intelligent workman in the chandelier and gas-fitting trade:—

"The ancient sports of the Birmingham working men are not yet forgotten, and have not fallen into total disuse. About fifteen years ago or less, dog-fights used to be got up every Monday, and there are a few still in the summer time, when the men do not think much of walking a few miles out of this overgrown town to some quiet part of the country. There was a regular cockpit about twenty years ago, built in the open air, on purpose for the sport and for dog-fighting. It was suppressed by the magistrates. I was one of forty taken into custody by the police for attending it. We were all tied together with ropes round the body or arms, two by two, and were marched in procession through the principal streets of the town as an example, and then brought before the magistrates. The ringleaders, who actually got up the cock-fight, were fined, and the rest of us, who were spectators only, were discharged. The workmen are still to some extent fond of cock-fights. The fights are got up in public-house parlours, fitted up conveniently for the purpose. On Shrove Tuesday especially there are great numbers of cock-fights in tap-rooms and parlours, to which the admission is by ticket, at 3d. and 6d. each. I think, however, there has been less of this amusement during the last five or six years than there used to be."

Within the last few years Birmingham has attained considerable reputation for its encouragement of music; and its triennial musical festivals are well known and appreciated. Of these, however, it is not consistent with the object of these letters to speak. The popular love of music, which has been much extended in every part of England, and which forms, indeed, one of the most interesting characteristics of the present age, has seized all classes of the people in this town, and the purveyors of amusement have not failed to administer to it. No singing and dancing license is requisite in Birmingham, and the keepers of gin-shops and public-houses vie with each other in providing dramatic and musical entertainments for their customers. In the gin-shops—where no accommodation beyond a bench or two, or a seat before a barrel which serves as a table to put the liquor upon, is provided for the guests, and where in consequence the larger portion of the company have to stand at the bar and partake of their drams—it is not uncommon for the proprietor to hire a few fiddlers and banjo players, who sit in a kind of orchestra, overlooking the crowd, and make music from seven or eight in the evening until midnight. In one establishment of this kind, I was amused at seeing four men with blackened faces in a raised orchestra, smoking long clay pipes and playing the fiddle. In another, a fat boy was exhibiting his obesity, taking advantage of the intervals in the musical performances to go his rounds, accompanied by his "keeper." But the tavern entertainments are of a higher class than is provided in the gin-shops. In many of these musical houses there is a regular stage on which farces and ballets are performed. At Christmas time they get up pantomimes, and incur considerable expense in their production. One of these rooms is fitted up to contain upwards of 1,000 people, and is very handsomely decorated. Here the working classes resort with their wives and children, and have the enjoyment of a dramatic performance quite as good as would be provided for them at some of the minor theatres of the metropolis, together with those coarser enjoyments of smoking and drinking which are prohibited in the regular theatre. The price of admission is 3d. and 6d., according to the seat occupied, and the amount is returned in ale, beer, spirits, and tobacco. The number of young lads and boys in their teens—workmen on their own account, earning their own wages, and responsible to nobody—who attend these places, is perhaps unparalleled out of Birmingham. The precocity in vice of these boys is one of the most melancholy results of the manufacturing system in this town. Factory girls of an age quite as tender, accompany them to such places, and sit for hours—especially on the Saturday, Sunday, and Monday evenings—drinking with their companions, and imbibing the odour of tobacco smoke, demoralizing to every woman who is accustomed to it. On Sunday, when no dramatic entertainment is allowed, psalm tunes and other sacred pieces are played upon the organ. Some of these instruments are not only large and handsome in appearance, but powerful and rich in tone. In one public-house the proprietor stated that he had expended upwards of £800 upon his organ for Sunday evening performance, and there is no reason to doubt the truth of the assertion. The company is almost as numerous on Sundays as on the other nights of the week, and is composed of the same classes who frequent it at other times. The smoking and drinking form, it must be confessed, a strange accompaniment to the psalm and hymn tunes; and the conversation of the guests, if truly reported, would doubtless form an accompaniment, if possible, still more strange, incongruous, and improper.

It may be said that a stranger to a town sees these things under a peculiar aspect, and with a feeling of curiosity different from that with which they are regarded by the inhabitants. It is possible that familiarity may lead those who have been spectators of such scenes all their lives to regard them with more indifference than a person who, in the fulfilment of a duty, undertakes to describe them; but that the Sunday evening amusements of the populace in Birmingham have not escaped local notice, the following street ballad will suffice to show. The Birmingham poet and satirist, whoever he may be, who has described the scene at "Vauxhalls," meaning the old and new gardens of that name in the outskirts of the town, has depicted from the life, and without exaggeration. The ballad is of the class of wall literature, and comes from the press of a person who provides Birmingham with ballads by the yard, like the purveyors of similar compositions who have made the "Seven-dials" of London notorious. A few stanzas are omitted, on account of their indelicacy:—

VAUXHALLS ON SUNDAY NIGHT.

"I'm going to sing a little song,
I hope my subject's nothing wrong,
So list and I'll tell of many sights,
Seen about Vauxhalls on Sunday nights:
One half of the Brummagem people or near
Between four o'clock and ten their way wend there;
All other walks are deserted quite,
For the Vauxhalls on Sunday night.

"Old bachelors there are strutting away,
Joking with the girls so gay,
And sour old maids, too, there you'll find,
With their puppy dogs trotting behind:
And soldiers in red coats so gay,
With factory lasses are marching away,
Talking of how they can drink and fight,
Round about Vauxhalls on Sunday night.
　　　　* * * * * *

"There the young widow tired of a single life,
And wishing again to become a wife,
You'll see with many a roguish leer,
Fishing for another husband so dear:
From one to the other place reeling along,
Singing 'I'm a gent,' or some such song;
You'll see young swells in paletots white,
Round about Vauxhalls on Sunday night.

"There's married folks whose clothes are up the spout,
    And who by day-light can't stir out,
    At night brush up their seedy togs,
    Polish their boots and off they jogs;
    The wife envelops herself in a cloak,
    The husband his coat buttons round his throat,
    With his hat well greased he looks spicy quite,
    Round about Vauxhalls on Sunday night.

"Then what loving couples each other meet,
    On Sunday night dressed up so neat,
    And not wishing to be observed by all,
    Will courting get in Old Vauxhall;
    And under the shadow of those trees,
    Lawks!—how they will each other squeeze.
    If those trees could spell what tales they'd write,
    About Old Vauxhall on Sunday night.
                    *   *   *   *   *   *

"But the worst sight there that me annoys,
    Is to see such lots of naughty boys,
    Who instead of being with their mammas,
    Are strutting about there smoking cigars;
    And there's little girls there about twelve years old,
    Walking and talking with them so bold,
    And doing that wot isn't right,
    Round about Vauxhalls on Sunday night.

"There's trades and mechanics jogging along,
    With snobs and tailors to fill up the throng.
    But I think I'd now better finish my ditty,
    And to say any more it would not be witty,
    Should you doubt the truth of what I've sung:
    Before you attempt to say I'm wrong,
    Go yourselves and take a sight,
    Round about Vauxhalls on Sunday night."

An attempt, which has been happily successful, has been made
to provide a superior entertainment for the working classes on the
Mondays, on the evening of which day their habits lead them more
than on any other to seek for amusement. The circumstances out
of which it arose deserve to be recorded as highly creditable to the

Vauxhall Gardens, Saltley

working classes themselves, with whom the idea originated, and to the authorities of the town. It may not be generally known that the noble town-hall of Birmingham, containing one of the most magnificent rooms in England, is adorned with an organ of splendid proportions and of great beauty and power. In the year 1835, this organ being nearly completed, the building was placed under the conservancy and management of trustees, and in order that the public might have the pleasure of hearing this instrument properly played upon, they obtained permission to have the use of the hall on Thursdays from one to three o'clock, providing that the performances should not interfere with the use of the hall if wanted for public purposes. The admission was fixed at 1s. In 1836 the organ was taken down and greatly enlarged, and placed nine feet back in a large recess provided by adding to the north end of the hall. In 1842 great additions and improvements were made to the instrument. In the autumn of 1844 memorials, very numerously signed by the workmen employed in several of the large manufactories, were addressed to the committee of the General Hospital, and to the Town Commissioners, requesting "that the organ might be made accessible to the working classes one or two evenings in the week, at a low charge." The commissioners having granted the use of the room for this purpose, the trustees cheerfully consented to the request of the memorialists, by way of

experiment, for three months, at a charge of 3d. for admission to
an organ performance of an hour and a half. At the first performance, Monday, Nov. 18, 1844, there were 1,100 persons present, and
on the succeeding Monday 1,700. At the end of three months the
trustees felt justified in believing they might safely continue this rational gratification, as the receipts produced a small surplus over the
expenditure, the conduct of the people was extremely decorous and
satisfactory, and the entertainment was greatly appreciated. In April,
1845, it was thought advisable to add to the attractions of the organ
some madrigal and other vocal music for eight to twelve voices. A pianoforte was purchased, and although the expenses were considerably
augmented, improved receipts followed—not an immaterial point, although, with the trustees, secondary to the desire to produce a good
moral effect by affording agreeable amusement within reach of the
humblest classes. In 1848 a pianoforte, constructed especially to suit
the large dimensions of the hall, by Erard, was placed in the orchestra, and opened by Madame Dulcken. A concerto or other piece, ably
played, has since formed an attractive feature in the scheme, in lieu
of an interval of ten minutes heretofore allowed between the first and
second parts of the concert, which was usually the occasion of some
confusion by persons leaving their seats to perambulate the hall.

The organ is very ably displayed every Monday evening by
Mr. Stimpson, in four or five pieces calculated to exhibit its power
and sweetness. The entertainment also includes a well-played piece
on the pianoforte, glees, duets, madrigals, and other vocal pieces
(and occasionally the choruses of Handel, with a numerous choir),
with the National Anthem. All these compose a concert of no small
interest, which concludes at half-past nine.

The attendance (affected by bad weather in winter, and by the
competing attraction in summer of the Botanical Gardens, which are
open on Monday to the working classes at one penny each), fluctuates from about 400 to upwards of 2,000. On the whole the effect is
said to have been very encouraging and useful in cultivating the taste
and improving the manners and habits of that class which forms the
bulk of the audience; and, in a pecuniary point of view, it has been
the means of enabling the trustees to keep their great organ in constant tune and repair, besides leaving a small balance, which is added
to the receipts of the triennial festival for the benefit of the General
Hospital.

One other point in connection with the amusements of the working-classes in Birmingham remains to be stated. Formerly, when the town was not half so large as it is at present, and before the railways cut up the neighbourhood, and took possession of the vacant land in the immediate vicinity on which to erect their stations and approaches, the better class of working men used to be fond of renting small plots of garden ground. These plots were let out by large landed proprietors, and produced a high rental. They were called "guinea gardens"—a guinea being the sum usually paid for a plot of an eighth, and sometimes for a sixteenth, of an acre. Here working men built themselves little summer-houses of wood and brick, where, on the fine summer evenings, and on Sundays, they retired to smoke their pipes, and where they often took their wives and children to tea. They were fond of growing their own vegetables as well as flowers, and these little bits of ground were so much in request that, although the holding was precarious, and the tenant liable to a six months' notice to quit, the good-will of one of them has often been sold for as much as £20 or £30. The expansion of the town on all sides has almost swept the whole of them away, and the goods station of the London and North-Western Railway occupies the site of many scores of them. Only a few now remain, in the neighbourhood of the two Vauxhalls; and it is likely that these will be speedily swept away by the rapid extension of streets, factories, and railway stations. The working men of Birmingham cannot obtain land for any such purpose at the present time, and, more unfortunate than the dwellers in other large towns, they do not possess the privilege of a public park of any kind. But the railways, which have been instrumental in depriving them of their little plots of garden ground, have to some extent made them amends. Cheap excursion trains run on all, or nearly all, their holidays during the fine season, and convey them at almost a nominal rate to every popular place of resort in the beautiful county of Warwick, and sometimes into Shropshire or Wales, or as far as Liverpool to inhale the sea-breezes of the Mersey, and to visit the novel spectacle, to an inland population, of the splendid line of docks in the great seaport of the west. Gipsy parties, as will have appeared from some previous allusions in this and other letters of the series, have also become exceedingly popular among the working classes of late years. In almost every large factory, and in the small ones besides, the men and women, the boys and the girls employed, club up their money for an annual "gipsy party." There are not wanting persons in the town who set their faces against the practice, and allege that the gipsy parties are the occasions and the opportunities of vice and immorality; yet it seems harsh to condemn the innocent desire of an annual trip to the country for an occasional abuse which may result from it. Some of the largest manufacturers in the town—men who employ from 350 to 500 persons each, and who devote much of their care and attention to the social comfort and improvement of their workpeople, and who ought to be qualified to form an opinion on such a subject—speak in the highest terms of approval of the gipsy parties, and not only contribute largely to the funds, but attend themselves, with the members of their families. As already observed, the total absence of public parks, where the people can enjoy daily or weekly a gulp of fresh air—and especially in a town incessantly filled with smoke from countless factory chimneys, as Birmingham is—renders it imperatively necessary for the health of the population that no additional and unnecessary impediment should be placed in the way of their natural enjoyment in the open air. Those who object so much to the "gipsy parties" of the people forget this fact, and are somewhat too much inclined to look for more virtue in the poor than they exact from the more comfortable classes of society, and to draw so strict and narrow a line for enjoyment that the poor would for the most part be excluded from its circle. It is surely better that the people should indulge in their rural excursions—even although prudery might, at rare intervals, be justified in looking offended at some of the incidents that cannot fail to occur when large numbers of the young of both sexes are congregated together for the purposes of relaxation from incessant toil—than that they should be cooped up from month to month, and from year to year, within the smoky precincts of the town, and thereby be driven for amusement into the far more demoralising and debasing gin-shop and public-house singing-rooms, where so many cheap attractions are held out to tempt them. The experience of all the greatest employers, and of those who mix most intimately with the working classes, seems to show that the expectation of, and the preparation for, the annual gipsy party or excursion, exercises a beneficial influence upon the people in a factory for the whole of the year, and that the scene and its enjoyments tend in a high degree to encourage kindly feelings, and to improve the mind, character, and temper of the people. They are for the most part temperate; and they include dinner and tea in the country, a band of music, a walk on the hill or in the woods, and a dance on the grass. Some of them are tee-total festivals, at which not even smoking is allowed. The alleged evil results are so rare that diligent inquiries have failed to authenticate them.

In conclusion, it may be mentioned that a club or Institute, composed entirely of working men, has recently been formed for the encouragement of athletic sports in the town. It is called the "Athenic Institute," bears the classic motto of "*Mens sana in corpore sano,*" and is under the presidency of Lord John Manners. The Institute labours under the disadvantage of having no plot of ground upon which it can carry out its objects, and the members are compelled, both by the great expense of procuring land for their purpose, and the difficulty of procuring it within a reasonable distance, even if they had the means, to amuse themselves with gymnastic exercises under the cover of a roof. To make amends, they vary their entertainments by tea-parties, balls, dramatic meetings, and occasional lectures on subjects of literary and social importance. A reading room, and rooms for mental improvement classes, are attached to the institution, which seems to be little known in Birmingham, but to be deserving of encouragement by the class for whose benefit it was organized.

LABOUR AND THE POOR.

—◆—

BIRMINGHAM.

[FROM OUR SPECIAL CORRESPONDENT.]

CLUBS OF WORKING MEN AND THEIR FAMILIES.

Letter XXI.

There is perhaps no town in England in which the principle of association for mutual benefit, real or supposed, is carried to so great an extent as in Birmingham. Persons of both sexes and of all ages belong to sick and benefit clubs—to clothing clubs, and to associations of other kinds for almost every purpose for which a club can be devised. Even infants of two or three years of age are taught to club their half-pence, for medical attendance, or for the purchase of Sunday finery. Any one who walks along the streets, and looks at the placards on the walls, or the bills in public-houses, coffee-houses, and other shop-windows, may see at a glance from these announcements how deep a hold the club system has taken upon the affections of the people. In Birmingham the associative principle, if not worked out upon any great or comprehensive plan, is carried into a multiplicity of minor channels. The father of the family clubs for his Trade Society, or for the Odd Fellows, or for a Sick and Burial Society, or perhaps for the Freehold Land Society, or for a Money Club, or for a Watch and Seals Club, or for an Excursion Club. The mother joins a Medical Attendance Club, or a Coal and Coke Club, or a Flour Club, or a Shawl Club, or a Silk Dress Club, or, at Christmas time, a Pudding Club, or a Goose and Gin Club; while the children, if at school, bring their fortnightly halfpence to a Sick Club, or a Clothing Club; or if at work in a factory, contribute at a specified rate to the club of the establishment, to which it is a rule for every person, young or old, male or female, to belong.

Birmingham has long been noted in this respect. Hutton, in his History, states that in his time "thousands of the inhabitants were connected with clubs—and that to be otherwise was unfashionable. Some of these clubs," he adds, "boast the antiquity of more than a century." A continuation of his History, published in 1835, states the number of benefit societies in the town in that year to have been upwards of four hundred, containing about 40,000 members.

"The general custom of these clubs," says Hutton, "is to meet at a public-house every fortnight, spend a trifle, and each contribute six-pence, or any stated sum, to the common stock. The landlord is always treasurer, or father, and is assisted by two stewards, annually or monthly chosen.

"One of these institutions is the Rent Club, where, from the weekly sums deposited by the members, a sop is regularly served up twice a year, to prevent the growlings of a landlord.

"In the Breeches Club every member ballots for a pair, value one guinea, promised of more value by the maker. This club dissolves when all the members are served.

"The intentions of the Book Club are well known;—to catch the productions of the press as they rise.

"The Watch Club has generally a watchmaker for its president, is composed of young men, and is always temporary.

"If a tailor be short of employment, he has only to consult a land-lord over a bottle, who, by their joint powers, can give birth to a Clothes Club, where every member is supplied with a suit to his taste, of a stipulated price.

"Thus a bricklayer stands at the head of a Building Club, where every member, perhaps, subscribes two guineas per month, and each house, value about one hundred pounds, is balloted for as soon as erected. As a house is a weighty concern, every member is obliged to produce two bondsmen for the performance of covenants.

"There are several hundreds of money clubs for sums of £5, £10, £20, £25, £50, £80, and £100; various sums are contributed weekly, fortnightly, or monthly, according to agreement. The shares are generally sold to the best bidder, and interest paid from two-and-a-half to five per cent. by the purchasers to the end of the club. Bonds are, of course, required for the repayment of the money. The cash thus collected and thus disposed of must amount to a very large sum, not less than £100,000 per annum.

"The last I shall enumerate is the Clock Club. When the weekly deposits of the members amount to about £4, they cast lots who shall be served first with a clock of that value, and continue the same method till the whole club is supplied, after which the clockmaker and landlord cast about for another set, who are chiefly composed of young house-keepers. Hence the beginner ornaments his premises with furniture, the artist finds employment and profit, and the publican empties his barrel."

But since the time at which Hutton wrote, and the continuation of his history was published, the number of clubs has very largely increased. If there were 40,000 club members in 1835, there are in all probability 60,000 or 70,000 in 1851. It is not possible to present a perfectly accurate list; but a general view of the working men's clubs in the town will show in what a variety of ways the principle of association is tried, and how much might be done by working men for their mutual benefit, if they could forget their mutual jealousies, and learn to combine for their self-elevation in domestic comfort.

Beginning with the children's clubs, and going upwards to the clubs of heads of families, the "Medical Attendance Club" of the General Provident and Benevolent Institution claims the first notice. All the members of this club under fourteen years of age pay a penny a fortnight, which payment entitles them to medical attendance, advice, and medicines, whatever their illness may be. The little children of five and six years of age, attending the infant schools in the various parishes of the town, bring their fortnightly pence to the teacher; and often, when asked, seem to be quite aware of the purpose for which the money is contributed. The club is generally admitted to have had a most beneficial effect in diminishing the rate of infant mortality in the town; for it is the interest of the managers to prevent disease, and not to make a "business" of it, as druggists and apothecaries too often do, by pampering it, and pouring in unnecessary medicine to their patients. The committee of this club, in their annual report, have more than once drawn attention to some remarkable facts connected with it. The fifteenth annual report, for 1848, says:—"The number of members, during the year 1848, was 2,147; and although they were of all ages, from three weeks to upwards of sixty years, 12 deaths only occurred during the year, or 1 in 180, in a population in which the average annual mortality is 1 in 39. The case," it is added, "appeared still stronger if observation were confined to the previous six months, in which there were only three deaths, or 1 in 715; and during the last three months, in which the general mortality was so greatly increased, there was only one death among 2,147 members—a result that could only be explained by the additional fact that the patients of the institution were always enabled to obtain regular professional assistance in the commencement of their illness, instead of losing their time and aggravating their disease by begging for hospital and dispensary notes, or endangering their lives by resorting to druggists or domestic remedies."

The following Table, showing the rate of mortality among 884 children, under six years of age, who have joined the club during the last fifteen years, will show its advantages more clearly as regards the juvenile members. Nine-tenths of these children joined the club during the last five years:—

Age.	Number who entered the Institution at each age.	Number who entered on each age while in the Institution.	Total who entered at or on each age in the Institution.	Number who passed to the next age in the Institution.	Number in the Institution at each age on the 30th of June 1850.	Number who left the Institution by ceasing to pay at each age, being at that time alive*.	Number of deaths at each age.
Months from							
0 to 1 ...	1	...	1	1	...	...	...
1 to 2 ...	27	1	28	28	...	...	...
2 to 3 ...	33	28	61	59	2	...	...
3 to 6 ...	89	59	148	134	13	1	...
6 to 9 ...	67	134	201	179	16	4	2
9 to 12 ...	73	179	252	218	23	9	2
Years from							
0 to 1 ...	290	...	290	218	54	14	4
1 to 2 ...	156	218	374	214	122	29	9
2 to 3 ...	138	214	352	222	100	25	5
3 to 4 ...	128	222	350	213	104	28	5
4 to 5 ...	105	213	318	199	98	19	2
5 to 6 ...	67	199	266	170	72	21	3
6	...	170	...	...	170†	...	...
Totals	884	...	...	...	720	136	28

* No members are excluded from the club until after they have been six months in arrears with their contributions; but as it would be impossible to ascertain in many instances of removal, &c., whether they were dead or alive at the date of their exclusion, the numbers in this Table are all taken from the date of their last payment, when it must be quite evident they were alive.

† These numbers refer only to those children who having entered the institution under six years of age, have passed that period while in the institution.

Among the women's clubs, in addition to the sick and burial clubs, the most important are divisible into two great classes—those which are instituted in the large manufactories, and which every person connected with them, male or female, is expected to join; and those which are instituted for the purchase of articles of household necessity, or personal adornment, at the wholesale price. In the first class of clubs are generally included a sick fund and an excursion or gipsy-party fund. In the second are clubs for the purchase of shawls, bonnets, winter and under-clothing, shoes, &c., by weekly payments of a few pence each person. The husbands, quite as often as the wives, are members of clubs for the purchase, at more reasonable rates than the retail shops will allow, of those two great essentials to the comfort of a home—cheap fuel, and cheap bread and flour. The Clothing clubs are generally private, and are managed without printed rules; but the Coal and Coke clubs, and the Bread and Flour clubs, are conducted upon larger principles, and are governed by a regularly drawn up and printed code of laws, certified in the usual way by Mr. Tidd Pratt.

The first two rules of the Birmingham Coal and Coke Company, an institution established in January 1850, state that the objects of the society are to purchase coal and coke wholesale, and retail them as cheap and good as possible to members only. The shares are not transferable, but the investment of each member is employed for his or her sole benefit, or that of the husband, wife, child, or kindred of such member. No part is appropriated to the relief of any other member or person whatever. Any person desirous of becoming a member of the society must be proposed at one of its meetings, and is admitted, if approved, by a majority of the members present. The amount of the shares is ten shillings each. No member is allowed more than one share, nor can receive more coal or coke than is necessary for his or her own (or family's) use. Any member who sells or otherwise disposes of any coal or coke received from the society, may, on conviction of either of the above offences, be fined ten shillings for the first offence, and excluded on a repetition of it.

If any member of the society dies, no right or benefit of survivorship can be claimed by the surviving members, but the interest of the deceased member belongs to his or her legal personal representatives, whether male or female, who are allowed to derive as much advantage, according to the rules of the society, as the deceased member would have derived if he or she had been alive. And such representatives may vote and act in all cases whatsoever, as the deceased member whom they represent might, if living, have voted and acted. Only one executor or executrix, or one administrator or administratrix, is allowed to vote for a deceased member; and if more than one claim to vote, the senior has the preference.

The rules of the "Birmingham Flour Society" are exactly the same as these, except that the shares are £1 each.

These clubs chiefly hold their meetings at temperance hotels and coffee-houses, and pay nothing more than the rent of the room in which they assemble—a sum ranging from 2s. 6d. to 3s. 6d. per night. No inducement is offered to the members to spend money. Of a less respectable and less useful class of clubs, to which women contribute, are the "goose and gin clubs." These, as their title sufficiently implies, are invariably held in public-houses; their ostensible object being to enable poor families, by a small weekly payment, to obtain once in a twelvemonth, or oftener, what is to them a luxurious dinner. The real object is to draw custom to the public-house. The geese that the poor purchase by this means are dear in every sense, present and future.

The Building Societies are chiefly supported by respectable mechanics, and their meetings are mostly held at temperance hotels and coffee-houses. Their object is to enable each member to erect or purchase a house or houses, or some other freehold or leasehold property, from a common fund raised by the voluntary contributions of the members. The contributions vary in different clubs. In some it is 5s. for every share per fortnight, until the sum of £120 is realised for each share, and an equal proportion for half and quarter shares. In others the contributions are ten shillings per share per fortnight until the sum of £240 be raised. Whatever the contribution and amount of share may be, as often as the required sum is raised it is put up for sale. Every member who has not received his share or shares, or part of a share, is entitled to bid; and the share is awarded to the member who offers the highest premium for it, by ticket. If two or more members offer the same premium the bidding is repeated, and the one offering the greatest advance is declared the purchaser. No member can receive money until the land, building, or other premises offered as a security is approved of by the committee, in conformity with the recommendation of the surveyor.

At the termination of the society—that is, when each member has received £120 or £240, as the case may be, on every share he holds in the society—the securities are given up, and a receipt endorsed thereon, which, by statutory enactment, has the effect of revesting the property in the mortgagor, without putting him to the expense of a re-conveyance.

"By way of illustration," says the prospectus of one of these clubs, which has now been in operation seven years, "it may be stated that a person, on purchasing one share of £120 for which he pays five shillings per fortnight—

Will pay, per annum, in contributions	£6	10	0
Interest at 5s. per share, per fortnight	6	10	0
Premium, say £20, divided into ten years	2	0	0
Total payments, per annum, for one share of £120	15	0	0
The £120 invested in a house or houses, will yield, say 10 per cent. per annum, or	12	0	0
Which deducted from the £15, will leave every year a balance of	£3	0	0

only for the member to provide for, over and above the rents; which sum being continued for the term of ten years (the utmost period the society may be expected to last), he will have contributed to the funds of the society the sum of £30 only, and will then have his deeds delivered up to him, with a receipt of the whole £120 borrowed, and will thus become possessed of a dwelling-house or houses, worth £120, for the trifling sum of £3 per annum, paid during the period of 10 years. But should a more advantageous purchase be made—say to pay 12 per cent.—the party would actually become possessed of property unencumbered, and worth £120, for nothing at all on the dissolution of the society. And this is no imaginary case; for many instances of this kind are known in the societies now in operation."

These clubs, of which the number in the town is estimated at above a hundred, are continually dying out in the natural course, and are as continually being revived under new names. The rules of the whole of them are very similar, and differ only in minor details, as in the amount of shares, the fortnightly payments, and the fines for non-payment of interest or contributions. There is considerable rivalry among them in the inducements which they hold out to persons desirous of becoming members. Some of them adopt what they call an equitable adjustment of the rate of interest, in other words;—if a member has been subscribing five years for one share, of £120, at 5s. per fortnight, so that he has paid into the funds of the society nearly £33, and then gets his share advanced, value £120, although in fact he withdraws his own £33 and borrows only £87, he pays interest on the whole £120, and continues to do so although he reduces the principal by every subsequent periodical subscription. This is considered an injustice, and some of the newly established building clubs make a yearly reduction in the amount of interest, in proportion as the principal is redeemed. It seems to be admitted on all hands that these clubs are highly useful in promoting economy among working men, and in tending to their elevation from the ranks of the mere day labourer into those of the capitalist. One result, not quite so agreeable, which has not been so much noticed, is that they tend to cover the town and its outskirts with small and mean houses and cottages, built without any pretension to beauty, and very often of the flimsiest materials, or without proper regard being paid to the requirements of health and decency. The building societies of Birmingham, if they were united in one grand scheme for improving the dwellings of working men, might, with the ample means at their command, and if the operation of the window tax did not to some extent interfere with them, build palaces for work-people, instead of hovels. The principle of association in this respect has never been carried out as it might be; and there seems no reason why working men, raising such a considerable capital every year by their fortnightly payments, might not build dwellings for themselves on a scale far superior to all that has hitherto been attempted for them by sanitary reformers and their friends of the richer classes—and why they might not combine with these improved dwellings, baths and washhouses, reading rooms and lecture rooms, as well as a great common kitchen, and other luxuries and conveniences, which the rich, and even the comparatively poor of the upper and middle classes in London and elsewhere, command by means of their social and political clubs.

The objects of the Freehold Land Society of Birmingham have excited so much discussion, and are so well known, as not to call for more particular description in this place. Similar clubs or societies have been established in every considerable town in the kingdom. The Birmingham Society, the parent of them all, numbered 2,023 members at its annual meeting in November last, possessing among them 2,927 shares. The gross receipts of the year amounted to £11,533 6s. 10d. "The historian of the nineteenth century," says the report, "shall record the pleasing fact, and hand it down to future generations, that the Freehold Land Societies reformed the British House of Commons, and that the honour of their origin belongs to the 'working men of Birmingham.'"

With regard to the vast numbers of sick and burial clubs in Birmingham—small clubs, for the most part, and governed on defective principles—the following table, drawn up by the officers of the General Provident and Benevolent Institution for the Working

Classes, shows very painfully how little they are to be depended upon. It was drawn up by the officers of the society after a visit to the Birmingham workhouse, and refers wholly to the paupers in that establishment.

Name of Ward.	Number of Paupers.	Average Age.	Parish.		Whether in Sick Clubs.		Average number of Years in Sick Clubs.	Reasons of leaving Club.	Ceased Paymts. from.	
			Birmingham.	Elsewhere.	Yes.	No.		Club broken up.	Shortness of work.	Leaving town.
Young able-bodied men	24	36¼	24	0	4	20	4	1	3	0
Middle-aged able-bodied men	35	50¾	32	3	17	18	6½	10	4	4
Old able-bodied men	36	70¼	33	3	25	11	12½	18	9	4
Infirmary	24	46	22	2	10	14	11½	8	2	0
Bed-ridden patients	19	64¾	17	2	16	3	13¼	13	5	2
Old men's sick ward	14	77½	12	2	7	7	22¼	11	0	0
Total	152		140	12	79	73		61	23	10
Or, omitting the young able-bodied men's ward, in which the paupers from idleness are chiefly to be looked for:—										
	120		116	12	75	53		60	20	10
From this statement are excluded those who have been in the army or navy, casual paupers, and Irish.										

"These statistics," as the report observes, "present facts which speak loudly for themselves. In a few instances removal of residence has caused the forfeiture of the benefits which the members had commenced to insure; on some a similar loss has been inflicted by want of work; but the constant failure of their clubs has been the cause which, in a vast and pitiable majority of cases, has consigned to the workhouse the aged and the sick, and mingled by a harsh equality the industrious with the idle, and the provident with the reckless, in the miseries and degradation of a common pauperism." The Provident and Benevolent Society endeavours to remedy these evils—not alone by a properly graduated scale of payment from the members, but by the charitable contributions of the rich in aid of the funds. It combines a "Medical Attendance and Medicine

Club," already spoken of in connection with the young children of the working classes, but the benefits of which extend to people of all ages; a "Sick-pay, Annuity, and Funeral Society," an "Independent or Extra Pay Club," for securing the ordinary weekly income of a family when work is slack, or altogether wanting, and a Savings Bank. Several smaller provident institutions have amalgamated with this, which, at the time of the publication of its last annual report, included 5,105 members, of whom 4,251 were insuring medical attendance, 3,514 a sum at death, and 3,504 weekly pay in sickness. The age of the members in the Medical Attendance Club ranged from one month to 68 years. Of the children 1,463 attended Sunday schools.

But the most numerous class of clubs in Birmingham are the "money clubs"—associations which are no doubt occasionally productive of good, but which, it is much to be feared, are still more frequently productive of evil. Out of the 1,290 taverns, public-houses, gin-shops, and beer-shops, which are reckoned to exist in Birmingham, there is scarcely one—the taverns and gin-shops, which do not amount to above a tenth of the number excepted—which does not hold a money-club at stated times. These clubs are for the most part got up by the landlords, with motives and objects which are clear to the meanest capacity; but others, got up by working men for mutual convenience, and as an investment of money, are held at temperance hotels and coffee-houses. There are £5 clubs, £10 clubs, £12 10s. clubs, £20 clubs, £25 clubs, £50 clubs, and £120 clubs. They are conducted upon similar principles to the building-clubs; and the money or share subscribed for is put up for sale by auction among the members in the same way—the only difference being, that the purchaser of the money is not obliged to spend it on a house, but may make whatever use of it he pleases. The purchaser must find two bondsmen to join in a promissory note for the repayment of the amount by the usual weekly, fortnightly, or monthly instalments. Birmingham, as is well known, abounds in ingenious mechanics. Many a man working at the bench or the lathe as a journeyman has an idea of an improvement in the mechanism with which he labours—or invents some new article which he imagines will make his fortune if he can carry out his scheme—or discovers some new process likely to be advantageous to himself and to his trade. All he requires is money. In these circumstances, if he has not been a provident man, beforehand with the world, the money club is his only available resource; and such men have frequently been known to give these clubs £18 or £20 for £50; in other words, to receive £30, and incur a debt of £50, repayable by weekly instalments. Those who know the working classes, and the private history of some of the cleverest among them for mechanical contrivance, report that many a useful invention has been brought to maturity by this means, although, in some instances, unfortunately not rare, the improvident man of genius has afterwards been compelled to part with his invention for a trifle, to an employer more ignorant and less ingenious than himself—and very often for no other reason than to be released from his liability to the money club. These clubs are also the resource of improvident working men, when their wives are confined, or when the quarter's rent becomes due, and they have not the means of paying it; and very often, also, the young workman, on contracting matrimony, has no other means of procuring furniture than the purchase of a share at the "Money Club." "This system," said the keeper of a temperance hotel, "has increased greatly within the last seven years. Indeed, all kinds of clubs are on the increase in Birmingham. The money clubs that meet in public-houses used to be called 'Spiggot clubs.' Money clubs are held not only in temperance hotels, but in private houses. A man may subscribe for a share, a half share, or a quarter share. The secretaries receive 6d. a quarter from each member for keeping the books, looking after defaulters, and attending to the general business of the club. Many young working men who are expert at figures, or who can write a good hand, make more money as secretaries to clubs than they can make at their trades. I know some who are secretaries of four, five, six, and even eight clubs, and who make it their regular business, and attend to nothing else. Some of them make as much as £100 per annum, or even more, in this way. There are good as well as bad points in the money-clubs, and although it would be better for working men to save their money than to buy loans at a high rate, I know many respectable tradesmen who have been enabled to set themselves up by these means in businesses that do not require much capital. One reason why these clubs are so numerous is that the banks do not afford accommodation to working men. They will have nothing to do with small accounts and small people. The banks with whom the money of these clubs is lodged charge commission for receiving it, and some of them will not receive such deposits at all, on the ground that it gives them too much trouble. At the end of the club, the money in hand is divided among all the members. The £10 clubs last eighty nights, and the £50 clubs on an average three years; but the duration depends to a great extent upon the amount realized by sales of money. The utmost I have ever known to be given were £24 for £50, and £60 for £120. In the panic of 1847 and 1848 very large sums were offered for loans, and there were a great many defaulters. Prices are now much lower."

One of the newest clubs of working-men in Birmingham has been constituted under the patronage of several of the most eminent manufacturers in the town, for the purpose of enabling the members to visit the Great Exhibition of the present year. This club was founded in November last. The following extracts from the prospectus will show the feeling of its promoters towards the Exhibition, and the means by which they propose to meet the expenses of a visit to London:—

"We are upon the eve," they say, "of a grand epoch which is about to unfold its mighty consequences to the world, and at the dawn of which the nations shall gather together, and concentrate their aims and desires upon one great object. The thoughts of every nation are directed to this important subject, which is of paramount consequence, as the commerce of the whole world will be sensibly affected by it. We speak of the Great Industrial Exhibition, which is at present exciting so much sympathy from the great mass of mankind, while some few narrow-minded egotists are meeting it with suspicion and distrust. The people of Birmingham, then, as citizens of that country which has challenged the world to this industrial rivalry, and as artisans whose products have filled the whole world with admiration—should be especially interested in this subject, and ought to be present at this vast concentration of design and industry. It is for this object that the above society is to be formed, and we beg to call the attention of the people generally to the following considerations.

"To small manufacturers and clerks this society will afford an admirable opportunity of visiting the Exhibition, and it is of the greatest importance that they should endeavour to witness the improvements of other nations over their several manufactures. To foremen and artisans generally, it is absolutely necessary that they should attend the Exhibition, and endeavour to gain some practical advantage therefrom. To pleasure-seekers and others this society affords every facility, by enabling persons to realise a sufficient sum to maintain them respectably in the metropolis for a week, ten days, or a fortnight. The subscriptions are:—For a £1 10s. share, 1s. per week; for a £3 share, 2s. per week; for £4 10s. share, 3s. per week; so that the society will last between seven and eight months, and will terminate about next July."

Before concluding the subject of the clubs of the working classes, the public-house "sweeps" ought not to be forgotten. They are exceedingly numerous in Birmingham, and are the growth of the last four or five years. The following placard is selected from a mass of about a hundred of such documents, gathered from the gin-shops and public-houses of the town. It will be seen that the "enterprising landlord" piques himself, in his postscript, on the benefit which his lottery has been the means of conferring upon "very poor but deserving persons!"

"Annual Monster Christmas Sweep for 1850, two thousand subscribers, at 1s. each, and one hundred and fifty prizes, amongst which will be twenty sovereigns, five loads of best coals, five sacks of flour, a fat sheep, and three fat pigs. The above monster sweep (says the bill) will be drawn on Friday, December 20, 1850, at three o'clock in the afternoon, and the prizes distributed on the following Tuesday, at twelve o'clock, in the large Concert-hall, recently erected, and capable of holding one thousand persons. Open every evening, with first-rate talent, admission free.—N.B. The landlord takes the present opportunity of returning his sincere thanks to his friends and the public for the liberal support received upon each occasion of the monster sweeps, and refers his friends to the satisfactory results of last year's, the principal prizes of which were *fortunately won by very poor but deserving persons, and hopes to merit a continuance of their favours.*"

The list of the hundred and fifty prizes follows, and includes bottles of sherry, port, rum, gin, whisky, and brandy. Every fifth number includes the greater prize of a ton of coals or a sack of flour, a pig, a goose, a turkey, or a sheep. Number 150 entitles the holder to "a splendid fat show pig, a ton of large best coals, and a bottle of brandy." These "sweeps" are lotteries of the worst kind, and are clearly illegal. All that can be said in extenuation of the mischief they may cause is, that the risk is not great.

———

[With this Letter is concluded the series relating to the town of Birmingham. There are many important trades to be noticed, which have not been mentioned in the preceding Letters, especially the manufacture of articles in iron; but these trades and their various ramifications will more properly be described in the series to be devoted to the great manufacturing and mining districts, extending north-west from Birmingham to Wolverhampton, and including Smethwick, Oldbury, West Bromwich, Tipton, Wednesbury,

Bilston, Walsall, Willenhall, and Wolverhampton; and southwards from the last-mentioned town to Sedgley, Dudley, Halesowen, Stourbridge, and Kidderminster; and then again eastward to Redditch. The whole of this district abounds in manufactures, principally of iron and steel, and includes the production of machines of the most complicated and expensive kind—nails and screws of every description—locks for chests, doors, and guns—pots and pans—iron and tin plates—pins and needles—and an immense variety of other articles. It also includes the Staffordshire collieries, and the manufacture of iron itself.]

Index

Titles Available in the Series

LABOUR AND THE POOR

Volumes I to IV: **The Metropolitan Districts**
Henry Mayhew

ISBN 978-1-913515-11-9, 978-1-913515-12-6, 978-1-913515-13-3, 978-1-913515-14-0

Volume V: **The Manufacturing Districts**
Angus B. Reach

ISBN 978-1-913515-15-7

Volumes VI & VII: **The Rural Districts**
Alexander Mackay & Shirley Brooks

ISBN 978-1-913515-16-4, 978-1-913515-17-1

Volume VIII: **Wales**
Special Correspondent

ISBN 978-1-913515-18-8

Volume IX: **Birmingham**
Charles Mackay

ISBN 978-1-913515-19-5

Volume X: **Liverpool**
Charles Mackay

ISBN 978-1-913515-20-1

For information on these and other titles available please visit:

DittoBooks.co.uk

www.ingramcontent.com/pod-product-compliance
Lightning Source LLC
Chambersburg PA
CBHW060306030426
42336CB00011B/961

* 9 7 8 1 9 1 3 5 1 5 1 9 5 *